Family and Succession Law in Japan

Family and Succession Law in Japan

Fourth Edition

Satoshi Minamikata

This book was originally published as a monograph in the International Encyclopaedia of Laws/Family and Succession Law.

Founding Editor: Roger Blanpain
General Editor: Frank Hendrickx
Volume Editor: Walter Pintens

Wolters Kluwer

Published by:
Kluwer Law International B.V.
PO Box 316
2400 AH Alphen aan den Rijn
The Netherlands
E-mail: lrs-sales@wolterskluwer.com
Website: www.wolterskluwer.com/en/solutions/kluwerlawinternational

Sold and distributed by:
Wolters Kluwer Legal & Regulatory U.S.
7201 McKinney Circle
Frederick, MD 21704
United States of America
E-mail: customer.service@wolterskluwer.com

ISBN 978-94-035-4570-7

e-Book: ISBN 978-94-035-4580-6
web-PDF: ISBN 978-94-035-4590-5

The Author

Satoshi Minamikata (10 August 1948) (BA and MA, Tokyo University of Education (Japan); coursework for PhD, Kyushu University (Fukuoka)) retired as Professor of Law from Soka University (Tokyo) in 2019, having formerly held a research and teaching post at Kyushu University (Fukuoka), Ibaraki University (Ibaraki) and Niigata University (Niigata). His major research interests are in the areas of family and succession law and socio-legal studies. In particular, he has conducted research on adoption, divorce mediation, domestic violence, supporting schemes for families in trouble, the legal responsibility of counsellors and behaviours of the Japanese in legal disputes. He is a member of the International Society of Family Law.

The Author

Table of Contents

Table of Contents

Table of Contents

List of Abbreviations

A. Judgments of the courts

AD	Decree of the Appellate Court (Koto-Saibansho Hanketsu)
ATD	Decree of the Appellate Tribunal (Kosoin Hanketsu)
DD	Decree of the District Court (Chiho-Saibansho Hanketsu)
FO	Determination of the Family Court (Katei-Saibansho Shimpan)
FD	Decree of the Family Court (Katei-Saibansho Hanketsu)
HD	Decree of the High Court (Koto-Saibansho Hanketsu)
HK	Order of the High Court (Koto-Saibansho Kettei)
SD	Decree of the Supreme Court (Saiko-Saibansho Hanketsu)
SK	Order of the Supreme Court (Saiko-Saibansho Kettei)
STD	Decree of the Supreme Tribunal (Taishinin Hanketsu)
STK	Order of the Supreme Tribunal (Taishinin Kettei)

B. Law reports

CW	Court Website
FCJ	Katei-no-ho to Saiban (Family Court Journal)
Fuhokoi	Fuhokoi-ni-kansuru Kakyusaibansho Minji-Saibanreishu (Law Reports on the Torts Cases of the Lower Courts)
Hanji	Hanreijiho
Hanta	Hanreitaimuzu
Hyoron	Horitsu Hyoron
Kagetsu	Kateisaiban-geppo (Monthly Report on the Family Court Cases)
Kakei	Kakyusaibansho Keiji-Saibanreishu (Law Reports on the Criminal Cases of the Lower Courts)
Kamin	Kakyusaibansho Minji-Saibanreishu (Law Reports on the Civil Cases of the Lower Courts)
Keiroku	Daishinin Keiji-Hanketsuroku (Law Reports on the Criminal Cases of the Supreme Tribunal)
Keishu	Saikosaibansho Keiji-Saibanreishu (Law Reports on the Criminal Cases of the Supreme Court)

List of Abbreviations

Kokei	Kotosaibansho Keiji-Saibanreishu (Law Reports on the Criminal Cases of the High Courts)
Komin	Kotosaibansho Minji-Saibanreishu (Law Reports on the Civil Cases of the High Courts)
Minroku	Taishinin Minji-Hanketsuroku (Law Reports on the Civil Cases of the Supreme Tribunal)
Minshu	Saikosaibansho Minji-Saibanreishu (Law Reports on the Civil Cases of the Supreme Court) after 1947 and Taishinin Minji-Hanreishu (Law Reports on the Civil Cases of the Supreme Tribunal) before 1947
Shimbun	Horitsu-shimbun (Newsletter for Lawyers)

C. Statutes

Civ.	The Civil Code of 1898 and 1947
Cri.	The Criminal Code of 1907 and 2004
FAPA	The Family Affairs Proceedings Act 2011
PALA	The Personal Affairs Litigation Act 2007
FRA	The Family Registration Act 1947
RRA	The Residents Registration Act 1967
GRFRA	The Gender Recognition and Family Registration Act 2003
ARA	The Assisted Reproduction Act 2020
WCA	The Welfare of Children Act 1947

D. Others

Civ. Crim. Rep. No. of DGCCAB	Civil-Criminal Reply No. of Director-General of the Civil and Criminal Affairs Bureau (Kaito)
Civ. Ko. Rep. No. of DGCAB	Civil Ko Reply No. of Director-General of Civil Affairs Bureau (Kaito)

Preface

In the decade following the publication of the first edition of this volume in 1999, Japanese society has changed significantly. Rapid change has occurred not only in its political landscape and economy but also in people's perceptions and behavioural patterns in relation to the family and the family unit. Coupled with major medical advancements, such as in assisted reproduction technologies, these transformations have affected legal disputes involving families and the means by which they are resolved. This has led to revisions of family law and procedural laws for the resolution of legal disputes relating to the family, the passage of new laws to address unprecedented legal phenomena, and, further, the establishment of new case law. The purpose of this revised edition is to reflect the present reality of Japan's family law.

As in the first edition, the fundamental approach taken in this revision has been to present an overview of family law in Japan. While in practice, statute, case law and academic theories are applied in the interpretation of law for the purpose of resolving familial disputes, the focus of this encyclopaedia is to provide commentary on the statute and the interpretation of the courts, without touching upon academic theories. In light of the fact that most information concerning Japan's family law is only available in Japanese, it is intended that this general encyclopaedia will serve as a useful source of information to non-Japanese speakers. In the 2021 version, I have revised some incorrect information, added the recent news and statistics and made final adjustments. Finally, it would not have been possible to complete this revision without the continuous support of the editors, late Professor Roger Blanpain and Professor Walter Pintens. I am also indebted to Professor Shigeru Maruyama and Dr Hiroko Tanaka, co-authors of the first edition, whose earlier commentary I have drawn on to compile the present edition. Further, I would like to express my sincere apologies and heartfelt gratitude to the members of the General Editor's Office for their infinite patience in spite of the delay in the preparation of this revision. Moreover, I would like to thank Mrs Ruth Ikeda, Dr Teiko Tamaki, Dr Robin West, Ms Noe Minamikata and Dr Hiroko Tanaka for their kind assistance in the collection of data and information and their helpful advice.

General Introduction

§1. General Background of the Country

I. Geography, Climate and Natural Resources

1. Japan is situated on the eastern edge of Asia, covering a total area of approximately 378,000 square kilometres, roughly equivalent to one and a half times the size of the UK. The land mass consists of 5 main islands – Honshu, Kyushu, Hokkaido, Shikoku and Okinawa – and over 6,800 other smaller islands, including the 4 northern islands and the Senkaku Islands. A major characteristic of the terrain is that 66% of the land area is covered by forests, fields or mountains, including 108 active volcanoes. Located at the intersection of 3 massive tectonic plates, Japan experiences tremors from time to time and frequent earthquakes. Recently, Japan was hit by three big earthquakes; the 1995 Southern Hyogo Prefecture Earthquake (17 January 1995) (Magnitude 7.3) claimed 6,402 lives, Mid Niigata Prefecture Earthquake in 2004 (23 October 2004) (Magnitude 6.8), 61 lives and the Great East Japan Earthquake in 2011 (11 March 2011) (Magnitude 9.0), 15,899 dead and 2,525 missing. The 2011 earthquake brought about the destruction of the nuclear plant in Fukushima causing not only enormous financial loss but also catastrophic environmental pollution. According to Fukushima Local Government, the nuclear evacuation zone around the nuclear plant (non-residents zone) was 337 km^2 in 2020 and 37,814 people remain restricted from entering their hometowns.[1]

2. The Japanese archipelago stretches over an extensive arc of roughly 3,000 kilometres northeast to southwest, resulting in great climatic variation: ranging from subarctic in Hokkaido to subtropical in Okinawa, with the mid-region of Japan belonging to the temperate zone. Surrounded by seas on all sides, Japan, except Hokkaido, has high humidity throughout most of the year. The four seasons are clearly defined, and most areas with the exception of Hokkaido have a rainy season in early summer. Further, Japan lies in the path of typhoons, which sweep across the country in autumn. The accompanying high rainfalls cause floods and landslides, particularly in the hilly and mountainous regions.

3. Japan is impoverished in natural minerals and energy resources. As a result, it relies heavily on imports for its supply of petroleum and other sources of energy. To reduce this dependence, Japan has pursued an energy policy catering to the

1. https://www.pref.fukushima.lg.jp/uploaded/attachment/420325.pdf.

development of nuclear energy and alternative energy sources, stockpiling, as well as the relocation of energy-intensive industries overseas. However, the 2011 earthquake has dramatically changed the attitude of society towards the state's nuclear energy policy due to the extreme damages against society from indifference or positivity to concern and negativity. In contrast, the government decided to go ahead and push the restart of nuclear power plants throughout Japan.

II. Demographic Trends

4. The racial composition of the Japanese is largely Mongoloid, consisting of a mixture of the Northern line, Southern line and Western line groups originating in northern and southern China or Southeast Asia. The largest racial minority, the Ainu, are believed to have descended from the Northern group, resulting from intermarriage between Mongoloids and Caucasians, though there is some academic debate regarding their ancestry. Broadly speaking, Japanese society is not multiethnic in the sense that the United States (US) or China may be considered. From the 1980s, however, an increasing number of ethnically non-Japanese people – mainly from China (878,448), Korea (446,364), Vietnam (411,968), Philippines (282,798), and Brazil (211,677) – have taken up residence in Japan.[2]

5. The total population of Japan in 2019 was estimated provisionally as 126,167,000 of which 61,411,000 are male and 64,756,000 are female.[3]

6. The number of households totalled 53,403,226 in 2015 is broken down as follows: 18,418,000 single-person households and 29,754,000 nuclear households.[4] The average size of households has declined steadily from 4.14 persons in 1960 to 2.33 in 2015.[5]

7. The two main features of the current demographic trend are a decline in the number of children and an increasingly ageing population. First, the 'total fertility rate' (i.e., the total reproductive rate per woman in a lifetime) which was 4.54 in 1947 declined to 1.36 in 2019.[6]

---

2. The number of people registered as aliens stood at approximately 1 million in 1990 and 2.9 million in 2019 (Ministry of Internal Affairs and Communications, *Japan Statistical Year Book 2021*, (www.stat.go.jp/english/data/nenkan/70nenkan/zenbun/en70/book/html5.html#page=98), chart 2-10).
3. Ministry of Internal Affairs and Communications, *Japan Statistical Year Book 2021*, *supra*, chart 2-1.
4. Ministry of Internal Affairs and Communications, *Population Census (Basic Complete Tabulation on Population and Households) (2015)*, (http://www.stat.go.jp/english/data/kokusei/2015/Kekka.htm). The latest Population Census was conducted in 2020 but the final results were not available in July 2021.
5. *Ibid.*
6. Statistics and Information Department Minister's Secretariat, Ministry of Health, Labour and Welfare, *Vital Statistics 2019 (1)*, (https://www.e-stat.go.jp/stat-search/files?page=1&layout=datalist&toukei=00450011&tstat=000001028897&cycle=7&year=20190&month=0&tclass1=000001053058&tclass2=000001053061&tclass3=000001053069&result_back=1&tclass4val=0), table 4-1.

8. Second, in parallel with the overall trend towards a top-heavy age structure, there has been an increase in the number of elderly people living alone. The proportion of those over 65 within the entire population which was only 7.1% in 1970 increased to 26.6% in 2015.[7] In 2015, 11.4% of all households were those of married couples over 65 years of age, and 11.1% were households of a single person over 65. Contrasting these figures with corresponding percentages for 1980 (i.e., 2.8%, 2.5%), it is clear that the number of households which comprise exclusively of the elderly is on the increase.[8]

9. The increase in the elderly population has awakened public awareness on problems faced by the elderly, such as income security and management, the burden of care, and the relationships between the elderly and their careers (and especially women in the household). In addition, the elderly have been recognized to be socially vulnerable and likely to become victims of such crimes as a type of fraud involving phone calls feigning distressed family members seeking financial aid. The rise of elderly only families has highlighted legal issues relating to the provision of housing, medical care and day-to-day care for the elderly which has in turn become a political issue in the twenty-first century.

10. The pattern of marriage has undergone a rapid change since the 1980s. The average age of married couples continued to rise from 29.3 for bridegrooms and 26.4 for brides in 1985 to 33.6 and 31.4 respectively in 2019.[9] Meanwhile, the unmarried population at the age of 50 years increased from 12.4% for males and 5.1% for females in 2000 to 23.4% and 14.1% in 2015 respectively (estimated to 29.5% and 18.7% respectively in 2040).[10]

11. As indicated in paragraph 4, the number of registered foreign nationals residing in Japan has steadily increased since the 1980s and correspondingly the number of 'mixed marriages' between Japanese and non-Japanese increased from 12,181 in 1985 to 21,919 in 2019.[11] As a result, new legal issues surrounding 'mixed marriages', divorces and children by 'mixed marriages' and guardianship have arisen. (For family disputes between Japanese and non-Japanese, the General Rules for Application of Laws Act 2006 shall decide which country's jurisdiction should be applied).

III. The Language

12. The predominant language spoken throughout the country is Japanese, though there are numerous regional dialects. The Tokyo dialect, most of which has

7. Ministry of Internal Affairs and Communications, *Population Census 2015*, *supra*.
8. *Ibid.*
9. Statistics and Information Department Minister's Secretariat, Ministry of Health, Labour and Welfare, *Vital Statistics 2019*, *supra*, table 9-11.
10. Cabinet Office, (//www8.cao.go.jp/shoushi/shoushika/whitepaper/measures/w-2020/r02webhonpen/index.html.) chart 1-1-10.
11. Ministry of Health, Labour and Welfare, *Vital Statistics 2019 (1)*, *supra*, table 9-18.

been adopted as the 'standard' version, is preferred for use on official occasions and in educational settings. The use of standard Japanese has minimized potential problems of communication within the population. A notable feature of the Japanese language (especially spoken language) is the abundance of grammatical devices that may be employed to display relative social identity and infinitesimal differentiation of degrees of formality, politeness, social distance and intimacy.

13. As for other languages, the Ainu language is currently used by a very small minority of the population largely among those who are descendants of the Ainu race in the north of Japan. Chinese and Korean are spoken among certain immigrant populations in Japan. The Ainu language and Chinese have grammatical structures which diverge markedly from Japanese, while Korean grammar is convergent with Japanese. Due to the importation of the writing system of China into Japan, nearly 1,500 years ago, many Chinese characters are still found in common with Japanese. Nevertheless, the pronunciation of the characters differs, as do the prosodic properties of the languages.

IV. Religion

14. Article 20 of the Constitution enacted after the Second World War guarantees freedom of religion, creed and thought. There is no state religion, but a syncretic coexistence of diverse religions. The original belief systems of the Japanese have been subsumed under the rubric of 'indigenous Shinto', which was rich in regional variation and characterized by animism, awe of nature and primitive ancestor veneration. These ancient beliefs have been overlaid by and integrated with subsequent imports of 'foreign' religions such as Buddhism and have also undergone transformation through past governmental directives. After Buddhism was transmitted to Japan in the mid-sixth century, it maintained a major status until 1868, particularly through the implementation of the *Danka* or *Terauke* system as a 'state religion' by the Tokugawa Shogunate.[12] Christianity (Catholicism) was introduced in Japan in the sixteenth century but was banned between the seventeenth and nineteenth centuries. In the Meiji period, the Shinto shrines were unified and incorporated into the organization of State Shinto by the government, and played an integral role in gaining the allegiance of the people until the end of the Second World War. Currently, a plurality of religions is practised in Japan, including Buddhism, Shinto, Christianity, Islam (still a very small minority), as well as a large number of new religions. Thus, in contrast to Western industrialized countries and the Arab world, no single religion can be said to be the dominant national religion. The statistics show that the number of religious believers is reported to be 198 million out of the 126 million population in Japan in 2020.[13] It is also the case that the Japanese, in general, do not profess to be very religious. However, certain Shinto and Buddhist

12. The main purpose of this system was to rule and watch people with vigilance rather than to exercise religious activities.
13. Ministry of Education, Culture, Sports, Science & Technology, *Research on Statistics of Religion 2020*, (https://www.e-stat.go.jp/stat-search/files?page=1&layout=datalist&toukei=00401101&tstat=

sects have established links with political organizations and have had an impact on legal issues relating to the family that, in some cases, have obstructed the revision and implementation of the law.

15. Since the 1970s, new religious movements have begun to attract followers seeking to gain serenity in everyday life under the drastic diversification of personal, cultural and social values in the post-high-growth period of Japan. Meanwhile, some 'cults' are now regarded as harmful to society having caused a series of social problems such as religious conversion by forcible inducement, fraudulent trading of goods and other criminal acts (for instance, the Sarin gas attack on the Tokyo underground in 1995). In addition, strong preoccupation with religious activities has sometimes brought about conflicts between family members which have resulted in divorce and breakup of parent-child relationships.

V. Educational System

16. Governmental administration of compulsory education in Japan dates back to the establishment of the 'state educational system' in 1871. The educational system was radically transformed after the Second World War under the Allied occupation. At present, compulsory education covers six years of elementary school and three years of junior high school, after which pupils may attend either senior high schools (three years) or five-year technical high schools. Tertiary education consists of either four-year universities or two-year junior colleges. In addition, there are numerous miscellaneous schools for vocational training and obtaining qualifications in specific occupations such as cookery and hairdressing. Pre-school education is non-compulsory and includes kindergartens which are open to all 5 year olds and nursery schools that accept children between the ages of 0 and 5 whose family circumstances meet certain criteria.

17. Parents or guardians have a duty to ensure that their children receive six years of elementary education and three years of junior high school education. Should they neglect this duty, parents (or guardians) may face a loss of parental rights and duties (*see* Part II Chapter 6). In connection with this, an increasing number of non-Japanese residents have not assumed such parental role of sending their children under 15 years of age to school. Consequently, it is reported that the non-attendance of children is particularly evident in areas where newcomer parents reside. However, there are different interpretations on whether non-Japanese parents have a duty of ensuring that their children receive basic education, and no effective measures have been taken to provide proper education to these children.

18. Virtually, 95.6% of male pupils and 96% of female pupils completed compulsory education and continued to senior high schools or technical colleges in

---

000001018471&cycle=0&tclass1=000001148006&tclass2val=0), chart 3. This figure seems to be strange, but there are some who declare to believe more than two religions simultaneously.

2019.[14] The number of students who advanced to tertiary education has risen in the post-war period and amounted to approximately 58.6% out of the 18-year-old population in 2020.[15] Of special note is the dramatic rise in the matriculation rate of women in tertiary education (university/junior college) since the 1970s. In 2019, 50.7% of men and 56.6% of women attended some form of tertiary education.[16] Parents assume a heavy financial burden in providing fees and living expenses for their children in higher education. Furthermore, parents invest heavily in their children by funding additional tuition through *juku* (cram schools) and private tutors in order to maximize the chances of succeeding in the highly competitive educational system. As a consequence, disputes relating to children's maintenance tend to be viewed as a serious matter. In this connection, the Civil Execution Act was revised in order to ensure more effective enforcement procedure relating to matters on disclosure and acquisition of information of the obligator's property in disputes on maintenance in 2019 (*see* sections 197, 205 to 207 of the Civil Execution Act). As public support, a parent in financial difficulties can apply for welfare assistance for the education of his/her child if certain conditions are satisfied (section 19 of School Education Act 1947 and section 11(1)(ii) of Public Assistance Act 1950). In addition, in order to assist single-parent families financially, one local authority operated a temporary payment system on behalf of an obligor of maintenance from July 2020 to March 2021and it is reported that the amount paid can be up to Japanese Yen (JPY) 50,000 for each entitled minor in 18 out of 23 applications.[17]

VI. Industrial Structure and Patterns of Employment

19. The industrial structure of Japan has undergone a dramatic transformation since 1945. Of particular note are the major changes which have occurred since the period of rapid economic growth beginning in the 1960s. In 1953, 6.6% of the workforce was engaged in agriculture, but this figure had fallen to less than 1.1% by 2019.[18] Immediately after the war, it was common for couples and other family members to cooperate in running the family farm. Increasingly, however, many farming families are only partially engaged in agriculture, with one of the spouses (particularly husbands) finding work in large cities. Moreover, advances in farming technology have improved the efficiency of agriculture significantly, enabling wives to engage in part-time work outside of the farm. These employment patterns have had a significant impact on conjugal relations of farming households. The manufacturing industry has also experienced radical shifts. Automated production processes and the introduction of new product lines have made it possible to employ more

14. Cabinet Office (2020), *White Paper on Gender Equality 2020*, (https://www.gender.go.jp/about_danjo/whitepaper/r02/zentai/index.html), chart I-4-1.
15. Ministry of Education, Culture, Sports, Science & Technology (2020), *Press Release 25 dec. 2020: Gakko Kihonchosa (Survey on Basic Information of Education – confirmed value)*, (https://www.mext.go.jp/content/20200825-mxt_chousa01-1419591_8.pdf), chart 3.
16. Cabinet Office (2020), *ibid.*
17. The Mainichi 10 Apr. 2021 (https://mainichi.jp/articles/20210409/k00/00m/040/332000c).
18. The Japan Institute for Labour Policy and Training, *Visual Handbook of Long-Term Employment Statistics* (https://www.jil.go.jp/kokunai/statistics/timeseries/index.html), chart 5.

women in the secondary sector. Importantly, the dramatic expansion of the service sector has resulted in widening employment opportunities for women.

20. During the 1950s and 1960s, the majority of women in employment were young unmarried workers (63.6% in 1962).[19] The exception being those in the primary sector where married women also engaged in productive work. Since the 1970s, however, the number of younger working women has decreased due to more women going on to higher education. The vacuum created by the relative fall in the number of young women in the workforce has been filled by older married women whose rate of employment outside the home has been increasing steadily. Currently, approximately 56.0% of all married women are gainfully employed in 2019.[20] In the case of a household of an employed husband, 66.2% of wives were employed in 2019.[21] The overall employment pattern of Japanese women followed an M-curve, with many working women continuing to work once married, retiring temporarily for childbirth and childcare while retaining a strong will to return to work. They subsequently re-entered the labour market after some years. However, it has recently been observed that the M-curve gradually changed to a near Ayers Rock shape in 2019.[22]

21. As described above, many married women engage in work, but the primary purpose of this is to supplement the household budget. In many cases, wives work since their husband's income is insufficient to cover the mortgage and children's educational expenses.[23] Moreover, since the 1960s, Japan has increasingly become a consumer-oriented society where the husband's salary is insufficient in light of the seductive appeal of new products perceived to be necessary to maintain a modern lifestyle. 67.2% of temporary workers (part-timers) were women in 2019.[24] While part-time work allows for a degree of flexibility in working hours, it is nevertheless the case that wages and working conditions are relatively poor. In 2019, the average wage of women stood at approximately 76.6% of the average wage for men in the case of full-timers and 93.4% in the case of part-timers.[25]

22. In contrast, a vast majority of men engaged in full-time work, and the high average number of working hours by Japanese workers has earned them labels such as 'workaholics', 'busy bees' and 'corporate warriors'. Japan still has a relatively pronounced gender division of labour, and women are typically expected to take on

19. Economic Planning Agency (1997), *Annual Report on the National Life for Fiscal 1997,* Printing Bureau of Ministry of Finance, p. 300.
20. Ministry of Health, Welfare and Labour, *Working Women Today 2019,* (https://www.mhlw.go.jp/bunya/koyoukintou/josei-jitsujo/19.html),p. 4. In *Working Women Today*, the word of 'non-full-timers' is used for 'part-timers' or 'temporary workers'.
21. Ministry of Health, Welfare and Labour, *White Paper on Health, Labour and Welfare 2020* (https://www.mhlw.go.jp/stf/wp/hakusyo/kousei/19/index.html), chart 1-3-14.
22. Ministry of Health, Welfare and Labour, *White Paper on Health, Labour and Welfare 2020, supra,* chart 1-3-8.
23. Ehime Bank, *Survey on Working Women 2018*, (https://www.himegin.co.jp/research/report/pdf/anke_work_woman_2018.pdf), p. 1.
24. Ministry of Health, Welfare and Labour, *Working Women Today 2019, supra,* chart 1-5-2.
25. Ministry of Health, Welfare and Labour, *Working Women Today 2019, supra,* charts 1-4-4 and 1-5-3.

the main (if not sole) responsibility for running the home. The (male) work ethic of diligence and commitment to the company has been predicated on the presence of a wife at home to deal with domestic matters so that the husband can devote himself totally to his work. Indeed, husbands or fathers tend to have little time to spend with family members. As a result, the work ethic has been severely criticized by many as inimical to the establishment of strong bonds between the father and his family. Furthermore, the problem of *karoshi* or death from excessive fatigue, which has been attributed to overwork, has come to be regarded as a major social problem. However, the male working pattern changed during the period of low economic growth after a breakdown of the bubble economy around 1990. The national data revealed that the unemployment rate of males was 5.4% in 2010 but 3.0% in 2020 and that of females was 4.6% to 2.5% respectively,[26] while male part-timers increased from 21.2% in 2013 to 22.1% in 2020 but with female part-timers lowered from 55.8% to 54.4% respectively.[27] Accordingly, the work ethic of diligence and commitment to the company or institution has been shifting for nearly two decades and more workers now tend to give priority to their private life.

23. Moreover, Japanese employment practices (consisting of the three pillars of long-term employment, a partially seniority-based wage system and company unions) favour those who are diligent and loyal to the organization, while penalizing those who are seen to deviate from the ethic of hard work and dedication. For instance, there is an expectation for men to endeavour to remain with one employer until retirement. A worker who quits a job mid-career may encounter difficulties finding another job of equal standing. More recently, however, the number of men who change jobs is on the increase, particularly among younger workers.

24. New phenomena relating to the younger labour force have also been seen since the 1990s; NEET (Not in Education, Employment or Training) and *FREETER* – a person, particularly young person who engages in a succession of casual jobs in preference to steady full-time employment (from freelance and Albeiter). It is reported that the number of young-unemployed person (NEET) increased from around 710,000 in 2018 to 740,000 in 2019.[28] In the latter case, employment conditions such as wage levels are worse than the full-timers, and the longer they are 'FREETER', the less chance they have of being employed in the future (*see* paragraph 56).

25. The retirement age is set between 55 and 60 years in most companies, and 60 is the average for civil servants. Nevertheless, since full pension payments generally do not commence until the age of 60 or 65, making ends meet during this interim period can pose a grave problem. This situation has been aggravated by difficulties in finding re-employment among men of this age bracket. Meanwhile, the

26. Ministry of Health, Welfare and Labour, *Working Women Today 2019*, *supra*, chart 1-2-7.
27. Ministry of Internal Affairs and Information, *Labour Force Survey 2020*, (https://www.stat.go.jp/data/roudou/sokuhou/nen/ft/pdf/index1.pdf), chart 6-2.
28. NPO-SODATEAGE-NET, '740,000 NEET in 2019', (https://www.sodateage.net/researches/874/).

White Paper shows that 99.8% out of the companies with more than thirty employees adopted a scheme of assuring that their employees are offered employment after retirement, and 78.8% of them provide all applicants over 65 years of age with an opportunity to continue to be employed in 2019.[29] In relation to this, the Stabilization of Employment of Elderly Persons Act 1971 was revised in 2020 in order to secure stable employment for elderly people and revised section 9(1) of the act stipulates that an employer who fixes the mandatory retirement age (limited to under 65 years of age) must take measures for securing employment for elderly people; raising the mandatory retirement age (i), a continuous employment system after the mandatory retirement age (ii) or abolition of mandatory retirement age (iii).

26. Meanwhile, since the lives of the majority of men have centred heavily on their work, retirement can be a testing time for discovering a new raison d'être. Terms such as 'industrial waste' or 'oversized rubbish' are popularly used to parody a retired corporate warrior, who has lost his place within his own home after spending a lifetime alienated from his family. Such circumstances are also reflected in rising instances of marital disputes among older couples.

27. Since the end of 2019, the COVID-19 pandemic has resulted in drastic damage to the economy and employment of men and women. A survey in 2020[30] revealed that 18.7% of males and 26.3% of females responded that they had experienced changes such as loss of job, turnover, and layoff since April 2020. In the case of part-time workers, 32.8% of males and 33.1 of females experienced some change while in the case of full-time workers, 15.9% of males and 18.4% of females respectively. The survey points to the pandemic having affected females worse with respect to financial difficulties, mental health problems and heavy burden of household affairs. In particular, females often experience 'shesession' when deciding to return to work.

VII. The Political System

28. The central governmental organization is based on a separation of powers into three branches, consisting of parliament, which is the highest organ of the government, the executive and the judiciary, with a mechanism of mutual checks and balances. The legislature is composed of the upper house with 242 members and the lower house with 465 members. Under the normal election system, all citizens of 18 years and above have the right to vote, and those over 25 years of age are eligible to run for office. Lower house elections are held every four years, whereas half of the members of the upper house are re-elected every six years. The elections are conducted through a combination of the first-past-the-post (single-person voting system) with a system of proportional representation. The cabinet is selected from

29. Cabinet Office, *White Paper on Ageing Society 2020*, (https://www8.cao.go.jp/kourei/whitepaper/w-2020/html/zenbun/index.html), table 1-2-1-17.
30. Zhou Yenfei (2020), *NHK and JILPT Joint Survey on Employment and Life Affected by the COVID-19 Pandemic*, Japan Institute for Labour Policy and Training.

members of parliament, and the prime minister is elected by parliament. Meanwhile, gender imbalance is obviously observed in the current political system, and the Promotion of Gender Equality in the Political Field Act was implemented in 2018 (*see* paragraph 70).

29. In addition to the central government, local governments play a vital role in the daily lives of Japanese people. Local governments range from big metropolises such as Tokyo, prefectures and cities to towns and small villages. Some of the work of local government includes the provision of social welfare and administration of family matters such as the registration of births, deaths, marriages or divorces (Family Registration Office). Local governments also manage family registration and issue certificates relating to family members. The total number of local governments (city, town and village) changed from 4,768 in 1966 to 1,724 in 2021 after a couple of the consolidation of smaller municipalities to form larger ones.

§2. Families

I. Statistics

30. The number of households in Japan was 53,448,685 in 2015, where the term 'household' is used to refer to currently co-resident members of a family. The number of conjugal families (nuclear families) has slightly decreased from 58.3% in 2000 to 55.9% in 2015, while the number of one-person households increased from 27.6% to 34.6% in this period. The proportion of elderly households has been on the rise since 1960 and accounted for 40.7% of the total number of households in 2015.[31]

II. Marriage

31. The number of marriages stood at 599,007 in 2019.[32] There has been a gradual advancement in the age at which couples get married. In 1960, the average age at first marriage was 24.8 years for women and 28.1 years for men. This rose to 31.4 years for women and 33.6 years for men in 2019. The age difference between a wife and husband was 3.3 in 1960 and 2.2 in 2019.[33] Some factors cited for the postponement of marriage include the increasing proportion of people who proceed to higher education and the higher level of employment among young women. In addition, attitudes towards marriage among young people have begun to vary, such that some prefer to be single or to cohabit while others intend to marry.

31. Ministry of Internal Affairs and Communications, *Population Census (2015)*, (http://www.stat.go.jp/data/kokusei/2015/kekka/kihon1/pdf/gaiyou1.pdf), pp. 33ff. Elderly households mean a household of elderly people over 65 years of age. The latest version will be published in 2021.
32. Ministry of Health, Labour and Welfare, *Vital Statistics 2019 (1)*, *supra*, table 9-1.
33. *Ibid.*

Furthermore, young people are facing financial difficulties in marrying due to economic stagnation since the 1990s and often have limited means of meeting their future partners.[34]

32. Nevertheless, marriage is still the norm in Japan today, reflecting a relatively fixed notion of the course of life. In a survey conducted in 2009 by the Cabinet Office, only 16.7% of men and 14.0% of women replied that they had no intention of ever marrying, while 72.1% of men and 65.5% of women responded to a survey in 2014 that it is better to marry in life.[35] Meanwhile, according to the Cabinet Office survey of 2011, the number of respondents with the view that not all persons need to marry because marriage is a private individual matter has risen from 62.7% in 1992 to 70.0% in 2009.[36] The recent survey on 'Attitudes and Views of Japanese People 2018' shows that the number of respondents with the view that not all persons need to marry had increased from 51% in 1993 to 68% in 2018.[37] By way of contrast, it is believed that the instance of cohabitation or common-law marriage is relatively small in comparison to Western countries.

33. The relationship between the choice of a marriage partner and social class is not well known. This is partly due to the lack of clear class consciousness in Japan. However, it appears that couples of similar economic standing and educational level tend to get married. Survey results reveal a strong correlation between the educational levels of husbands and wives.[38]

34. 'Mixed marriages' between Japanese and non-Japanese have been increasing from 0.4% in 1965 of all marriages in Japan to 3.7% in 2019.[39] In particular, since the 1980s, marriages between a Japanese man and non-Japanese woman have risen significantly. According to the statistics,[40] the number of marriages consisting of Japanese husbands and non-Japanese wives was 1,067 in 1965, 5,697 in 1982, 19,423 in 1990, 14,911 in 2019 and those of non-Japanese husbands and Japanese wives were 3,089, 3,259, 5,620 and 7,008, respectively. From the mid-1980s, brides

34. The Cabinet Office, *A Survey on Marriage and Creation of Family,* http://www8.cao.go.jp/shoushi/shoushika/research/cyousa22/marriage_family/mokuji_pdf.html. The respondents are single and a couple of less than three years marriage between 20 and 30 years of age. In this survey, young persons of full-time employment tend to have future partners or have already married compared with part-timers.
35. The Cabinet Office, *supra* n. 34 and *the Cabinet Office Survey on Views of Marriage and Creating Families in 2014,* http://www8.cao.go.jp/shoushi/shoushika/research/h26/zentai-pdf/index.html, p. 35. The Survey on Decision-Making on Marriage conducted by the Cabinet Office in 2015 revealed that 53.1% of men and 61.8% women responded that it is natural to marry when a person reaches at certain age (Economic and Social Research Institute Discussion Paper No. 332 (September 2016), p. 15).
36. The Cabinet Office, *Public Opinion Poll on Gender Equality,* http://survey.gov-online.go.jp/h21/h21-danjo/index.html.
37. NHK news 16 Apr. 2021, (https://www3.nhk.or.jp/news/special/heisei/feature-articles/feature-articles_05.html).
38. M.C. Brinton, *Women and the Economic Miracle: Gender and Work in Postwar Japan,* at 119 (University of California Press 1993).
39. Ministry of Health, Labour and Welfare, *Vital Statistics 2019(1), supra,* table 9-19.
40. Ministry of Health, Labour and Welfare, *Vital Statistics 2019(1), supra,* table 9-18.

of Chinese nationality sharply increased from 1,766 in 1985, 5,174 in 1995, 11,644 in 2005 after the implementation of an open policy by the Chinese government but 4,723 in 2019. In connection, preferences in the choice of partners tend to differ between sexes. In 2019, 31.6% of Japanese men became married to Chinese women (4,723 out of 13,911 Japanese men married non-Japanese women), while 13.0% of Japanese women married Chinese men (917 out of 7,008 Japanese women married non-Japanese men). Meanwhile, marriages between Japanese and a partner of other nationalities comprise only 20.8% of Japanese married men and 33.6% of Japanese married women, so that it could be said that Japanese females are more open to choosing partners from a variety of nationalities whereas Japanese males tend to marry women from a particular country.

35. Marriages result either from natural meetings ('love matches') or through the aid of a go-between (*omiai*). The practice of *omiai* itself has undergone a radical change over the last fifty years. Before the war, courtship following an initial meeting was limited, and it was not rare that couples met for the second time at their wedding ceremony. In the post-war period, *omiai* came to be regarded primarily as an opportunity to meet a prospective marriage partner. After a formal introduction, a period of courtship might ensue, and it was normally left to the couple to decide whether to continue with the courtship and get married. However, given the strong desire of most people to eventually get married, *omiai* is considered a safety net for those who have not been able to meet a marriage partner by a certain age. A survey result indicates a clear trend towards love matches after the Second World War. Married couples reporting their marriage as 'omiai' and 'love marriage' were 69.0% and 13.4%, 14.6% and 69.1% in 1945, 21.4% and 59.8% in 1950, 41.1% and 49.8% in 1965, 48.7% and 44.9% in 1970, and 87.7% and 5.5% in 2015, respectively.[41]

36. Another conspicuous phenomenon is the growing trend towards the commercialization of *omiai* through professional matchmakers and computerized marriage agencies. The spread of urbanization after the war has led to the breakdown of rural community ties, which in turn has brought about the gradual disappearance of the traditional go-between. Not only are such services sought after in the cities but also in rural areas where there is a dire shortage of young women. From the 1980s, middle-aged farmers who are desperate to get married have been resorting to commercialized marriage services for arranging foreign brides (typically from Asian countries). Currently, this trend is not only observed in rural areas but also evident in urban areas.

37. There is a pronounced gender division of labour between husbands and wives. In response to women's growing participation in the labour market, especially after the breakdown of the bubble economy in the 1990s and in addition, to the implementation of the Gender Equality Act 1999 (GEA), there are some signs

41. The National Institute of Population and Social Security Research, *The Fifteenth Japanese National Fertility Survey in 2015: Marriage Process and Fertility of Married Couples Attitudes toward Marriage and Family among Japanese Singles Summary of the Survey Results on Married Couples/Singles*, p. 26 (Figure II-1-3).

that husbands are becoming more willing to assist with domestic chores. However, in the case of those with children under the age of 6, husbands spent only 84 minutes per day doing domestic chores and wives 370 minutes in the case of working couples in 2016. In the case of a housewife household, husbands spent 75 minutes and wives 565 minutes per day in 2016.[42] In this respect, women still shoulder the double burden of paid work and housework. Meanwhile, the Welfare of Workers Who Take Care of Children or Other Family Members Including Child Care and Family Care Leave Act was enacted in 1991 in order to support a working parent who cares for his/her child after the birth of the child. A parent is eligible to take paid childcare leave from his/her work until the child reaches around 1 year of age (section 5(1) of the act), but very few fathers take paternity leave. In 2021, the act was revised for the purpose of encouraging more working fathers (including part-time workers) to take paid childcare leave. According to section 21 of the act, for instance, employers shall take the action of providing a worker (father) with necessary information on childcare leave and interview him in order to ascertain his wishes and intentions relating to paternity leave when he notifies that his wife is expecting or has given birth to a child (section 21 of the act).

III. Divorce

38. The rate of divorce started to decline after 1945 but began increasing from 1960 as a turning point, reaching the highest post-war level in 1983. Thereafter, the divorce rate showed a decreasing trend until 1990 in contrast to the situation in other industrialized nations. However, the rate has been increasing annually since 1990, and the total number of divorces in 2019 was estimated to exceed 208,496 couples according to recent statistics. In addition to the overall increase in divorce, the average age of divorcing couples has been rising. Currently, the average number of years of marriage at the time of divorce is 11.9 years, and many of these couples have children (56.9% of all divorces in 2019). A noticeable trend over the past four decades has been an increase in the rate of marital years of divorcing couples over 35 years (0.3% in 1970 and 3.3% in 2019). The rate of remarriage is 19.7% for men and 16.9% for women in 2019.[43]

39. There is a dearth of data for the main reasons for divorce as some 90% of divorces are concluded through consent between the divorcing parties, who simply file a form with the Family Registration Office. As long as the couple agrees to the terms of divorce, they are not required to state the grounds for divorce. However, on the basis of the remaining 10%, which are contested cases dealt within the family court, the predominant grounds for divorce are listed as incompatibility (no-fault principle). Other grounds such as violence, lack of support by husband and conflict with the spouse's relatives are relatively rare. An indirect factor that may account

42. Cabinet Office, White Paper on Gender Equal Society (Summary), (https://www.gender.go.jp/about_danjo/whitepaper/r02/gaiyou/pdf/r02_gaiyou.pdf), chart I-S-2.
43. Ministry of Health, Labour and Welfare, *Vital Statistics 2019(1), supra,* tables 10-1, 10-5, 10-9 and 9-4.

for the rise in divorce is the growing economic independence of women, many of whom do not need to rely on marriage for financial support. In addition, people's view of divorce has gradually become more tolerant. Research has revealed that 31.2% of respondents (wives) regarded divorce as acceptable if the marital relationship has broken down irretrievably in 1992 compared to 43.8% in 2015.[44] Meanwhile, as a new view on marriage, it is reported that elderly people tend to sympathise with a view such as a 'let-alone policy' under which a marriage shall not be dissolved; however, each spouse should not intervene in other's life unless any act is necessary for conducting day-to-day life.[45]

40. Where children (minors) are involved in divorce, the mother and father acquired parental rights and duties after divorce in 84.5% and 11.9% of cases respectively in 2019.[46] Joint custody is not available under the Japanese Civil Code, and it may happen that one parent will hold parental rights and duties while the other obtains care and controls over the minor after divorce. It is presumed that a mother will be awarded custody of the minor as a parent with parental rights and duties in nearly 90% of divorce cases.

41. There are approximately 1.42 million (estimate) single-parent families in Japan, of which mother-headed families comprise 1.23 million and father-headed families 187,000 in 2016.[47] A majority of these families are said to have resulted from divorce, 79.5% in case of the former and 75.6% in the case of the latter in 2016.[48] The annual income of single-parent families is JPY 5.73 million for father-headed families and JPY 3.48 million for mother-headed families, in comparison to JPY 7.46 million for families with a minor child in 2015.[49] In such situations, the COVID-19 pandemic adversely affected the financial life of a single-parent family. A survey conducted by a single families support group revealed that the pandemic financially affected 52% of full-time workers, 75.2% of part-time workers and 95.5% of those self-employed and that the decrease in income of part-time workers was around JPY 4,000 on average and that of full-time workers about JPY 12,000,

44. National Institute of Population and Social Security Research, *Marriage and Childbirth in Japan Today: The Fifteenth Japanese National Fertility Survey, 2015 (Results of Singles and Married Couples Survey)*,(http://www.ipss.go.jp/ps-doukou/j/doukou15/NFS15_reportALL.pdf), table III-3-3 and *Report on the Fourteenth Japanese National Fertility Survey in 2010 Volume 1 – Marriage Process and Fertility of Japanese Married Couples*, (http://www.ipss.go.jp/syoushika/bunken/DATA/pdf/207616.pdf), chart 6-2.
45. Meiji Yasuda Institute of Life and Wellness, Inc. (2018), *Views and Facts of Marriage in the Era of 100-year-life* (25 Oct. 2018 https://www.myri.co.jp/research/report/pdf/myilw_report_2018_04.pdf).
46. Ministry of Health, Labour and Welfare, *Vital Statistics 2019(1)*, *supra*, table10-10.
47. Ministry of Health, Labour and Welfare, *Report on the Measures of Supporting the Parents of Mother-headed and Father-headed Families 2019*, (https://www.mhlw.go.jp/content/11920000/000753182.pdf), p. 6.
48. *Ibid.*
49. Ministry of Health, Labour and Welfare, *Report on the Measures of Supporting the Parents of Mother-headed and Father-headed Families* 2019, *supra*, p. 5.

respectively between February and May 2020. Under such circumstances the government decided that an emergency allowance of JPY 50,000 should be paid to each household headed by a single parent who is a current recipient of child benefit.[50]

42. The figures above indicate that single mothers clearly face severe financial hardships after divorce. Regarding maintenance payments for children of a mother-headed family in 2016, the proportion of divorce cases in which some agreement was reached between the husband and wife was 38.8%. In the case of divorces by consent and divorces by the family court, agreements were reached in 37.8% and 79.6% of cases, respectively.[51] As a general rule, parents are obliged to financially support their minors after divorce, and it is typically the father who makes the payments. Payment is made for 24.3% of divorced mothers and no payment for 56.0% in 2016.[52] Thus, single-parent families (and especially single-mother families) can face dire financial straits following divorce. Single fathers may fare well economically immediately after divorce, but they are also financially vulnerable. Indeed, fathers with dependent children are frequently unable to work overtime or accept job transfers – which are part and parcel of the male work ethic – and as a result, they may suffer a loss of income or in some cases be forced to change to less demanding jobs which would allow them to prioritize their family. In such circumstances, single parents have organized self-help groups in order to support each other and exchange useful information relating to family matters.[53]

IV. Children

43. The yearly decline in the birth rate in Japan has been highlighted as a grave problem in terms of demographic composition. Although the government has not adopted clear family policies to limit population growth since 1945, the net result of the legalization of abortions and advances in gynaecological techniques has shown a drastic reduction in the birth rate. The leniency of the eugenics law and the absence of religious taboos against abortion have meant that 164,621 abortions were performed legally in 2017.[54] This figure excludes a significant number of abortions that go unreported. The statistics indicate that a majority of women undergoing abortion are those between the age of 20 and 24 – 23.9% of all abortion cases, those between the age of 25 and 29 – 19.6%, and those between the age of 30 and 34 –

50. NPO Single-Mothers Forum conducted a survey in which about 1,800 single-parents responded (6 Sep. 2020 https://www.single-mama.com/topics/200906survey/).
51. Ministry of Health, Labour and Welfare, *The Results Report of National Survey on Single Parent Families in 2016*, (https://www.mhlw.go.jp/stf/seisakunitsuite/bunya/0000188147.html), p. 53. This survey will be conducted every five years.
52. Ministry of Health, Labour and Welfare, *The Results Report of National Survey on Single Parent Families in 2016*, *supra*, p. 54.
53. *See A father and child family*, http://www.singlemother.co.jp/father/ and *A mother and child family*, http://www.singlemother.co.jp/.
54. Ministry of Health, Labour and Welfare, *Outline of the Cases of the Public Health Administration 2017*, (https://www.mhlw.go.jp/toukei/saikin/hw/eisei_houkoku/17/dl/kekka6.pdf), chapter 9 table 4.

20.1% as reported in 2017.[55] The number of abortions has been gradually decreasing since 1955, in particular, the group of 30 to 39 years of age evidently declined for three decades.[56]

44. For reasons which will be made clear below, the number of adoptions involving children is relatively small in comparison to the adoption of adults in Japan. Even in instances where children are adopted, most cases result from marriages where the biological children of the spouse are adopted by the step-parent. Adoption of orphans and other children in need of care comprises a small percentage of the total number of adoptions (*see* Part II, Chapter 5 §8 Foster Child and Foster Parents).

45. The foster parent system is regarded as a system of the social care of children in need and that institutional care is available for those children concerned. In 2020, 5,382 children were cared for in foster homes and 47,841 by the eight types of childcare institutions.[57] The children cared for under the current social care system shall leave foster and institutional care when they reach the age of 18 and live independently. In 2021, the MHLW conducted a survey on the life of children after leaving the social care system for the first time. The survey revealed that one in five children lead isolated and solitary lives without assistance from society and some face serious difficulties such as instability of employment, health problems and the absence of close friends to seek advice from.[58] It could be said that the fact that only 35.7% of 25,000 questionnaires were delivered indicates the difficult situation facing such children once having left the social care system.

46. The examination system is a source of great anxiety for Japanese children and parents alike. Japan has often been described as an 'education credential society', where one's career prospects are largely seen to be dependent on success in the educational system. In order to proceed from one stage to the next (e.g., junior to senior high school, senior high school to university), pupils must normally pass a series of highly competitive exams. In anticipation of these exams, children in some cases begin preparation from as early as elementary school by attending supplementary cram schools or *juku* after school hours. As a result, opportunities for unstructured peer group socialization through interaction with other children tend to be restricted. Children also experience great psychological pressure to survive the 'examination hell'. On the one hand, the highly competitive, centralized and bureaucratized school regime has been acclaimed as an effective framework for producing competent workers for industry. It has also been pointed out, however, that the system stifles creativity, individuality and 'healthy' development of character.

---

55. Ministry of Health, Labour and Welfare, *Report of the Cases of the Public Health Administration 2017, supra,* chapter 9 table 6.
56. Ministry of Health, Labour and Welfare, *Outline of the Cases of the Public Health Administration 2017*, (https://www.mhlw.go.jp/toukei/saikin/hw/eisei_houkoku/17/dl/kekka6.pdf), chart 10.
57. Child and Family Policy Bureau (Jan. 2020), *Overview of Survey on Children Cared by Child Care Institutions at 1 February 2018* (https://www.mhlw.go.jp/content/11923000/000595122.pdf) p. 1.
58. NHK News 1 May 2021 (https://www3.nhk.or.jp/news/html/20210501/k10013008381000.html).

47. After the bubble economy burst in the 1990s, various problems relating to education appeared in families, schools and society due to the financial difficulties of most families and the turbulent education policy of the government. The Annual Survey[59] revealed that the number of non-attendants and reclusive adolescents at primary and junior high school was 112,589 in 2012 to 181,272 (1 per 53 students) in 2019 and at high school 85,883 to 76,775 (1 per 63 students), respectively, which places a heavy burden on family members. It also highlighted that the cases of violent behaviour in schools were reported to have risen from 55,836 in 2012 to 78,787 in 2019. In elementary schools, in particular, the number of cases sharply rose from 7,542 to 41,794, respectively. However, in junior high schools and high schools, these gradually declined from 38,218 to 28,518 and 9,322 to 6,655, respectively, while high school dropouts decreased from 51,781 in 2012 to 42,882 in 2019. In addition, schools and other educational institutions have faced difficulties such as 'class disruption' and 'helicopter parents' with Japanese society becoming more aware of the necessity to take action against such problems and improve the quality of education.

48. In a globalizing society, the number of non-Japanese children evidently increases and problems relating to their basic education in primary and junior high schools arise. The statistics show that non-Japanese children taking special classes in Japanese language increased from 18,142 to 26,316 in the case of elementary schools and 5,978 to 10,260 in the case of junior high schools between 2007 and 2018.[60] The top three native languages among non-Japanese children are Portuguese, Chinese and Filipino reflecting their parents' national origin and cultural background.[61] The Ministry of Education, Culture, Sports, Science and Technology acknowledges that these children face difficulties in communication, school life and at home and encourages local authorities that are responsible for primary and secondary education to create and operate support services aimed at improving the educational experience for non-Japanese children.[62] However, due to a lack of information, different attitudes and views of parents towards education[63] and the insufficient resources of educational institutions, non-attendance of pupils and students are estimated to reach up to 22,488.[64] Meanwhile, it is said that attending children also face various problems with respect to their learning and life at

59. Ministry of Education, Culture, Sports, Science and Technology, *Report on the Issues Relating to Education of the Students with Problem Behaviours 2019* (https://www.mext.go.jp/content/20201015-mext_jidou02-100002753_01.pdf), pp. 11, 74, 103 and 114.
60. Gender Equality, Cohesive Society Learning and Safety Division of Education Policy Bureau of Ministry of Education, Culture, Sports, Science and Technology (March 2020) *Current Situation and Future Tasks on Education of Non-Japanese Children*, p. 4.
61. *Ibid.*, p. 6.
62. *See ibid.*, p. 11.
63. The parents of non-Japanese children may bring their children to school but it is not their duty under the current law.
64. Gender Equality, Cohesive Society Learning and Safety Division of Education Policy Bureau of Ministry of Education, Culture, Sports, Science and Technology (Mar. 2020) *Survey on School Attendance of Non-Japanese Children*, p. 7.

school[65]and accordingly, for instance, enrolment rate for junior high school students is far lower than that of Japanese children.[66] For the purpose of observing the right to education stipulated in Article 13(1) and (2) of the International Covenant on Economic, Social and Cultural Rights 1976 (ratified in 1979) and in Article 28 of the Convention on the Rights of the Child 1989, the central government and local authorities have made further efforts to tackle the problems of not only non-attendance but also children in attendance.[67]

49. After the government adopted a neo-liberal financial policy in the 1990s and due to the influence of 'libertarianism', changes have appeared in the state education system. For instance, headmasters in some areas are appointed from business circles; the rule of competition has been introduced to the management of schools and teaching staff. Accordingly, schools are steadily incorporated into a solid hierarchy and polarized into 'good' and 'bad' institutions based mainly on the examination pass rate for 'prestigious' universities. Under such circumstances, it is not uncommon for parents to push their children to work hard in order to pass the examination of schools from primary (sometimes from kindergarten) to university level.

50. The examination system imposes heavy psychological and financial burdens on ordinary parents. Many parents (and especially mothers) consider it essential to provide a home environment conducive to educational achievement, as well as making large investments in their children's education. According to a recent survey,[68] the amount of money that parents spend on a child's whole process of transition from pre-school through to high school has been estimated at JPY 5.4 million (all state schools) and 18.3 million (all private schools), respectively. This is by no means a negligible sum in view of the fact that the national average family income is less than JPY 5.6 million. Moreover, since grants are far from sufficient to meet the costs of university education, parents feel a duty to provide economic support for their offspring until they graduate from university and gain financial independence. Consequently, it is often well into one's 50s that a couple can begin to prepare for old age, leaving only a few years in which to accumulate savings for retirement.

51. Not only in relation to education, but child poverty in general also became a political issue in the 2000s since the ratio of poverty among industrialized nations

65. *See* Kazuko Okuyama (2018), 'Need for Education about Foreign Students from the View Aiming the Career Formation: Analysis of TEM', Kobe Journal of Higher Education No. 26, 18.
66. *Ibid.*, p. 24.
67. It is pointed out that similar problems are observed with respect to an infant's life at nurseries because of cultural differences and communication difficulties (Mitsubishi UFJ Research & Consulting (March 2020), *Report of Survey on Responses of Nurseries to Non-Japanese Carers and Infants*, pp. 152–153). In this respect, it points to the importance of pre-school education for non-Japanese infants (Ako Koike (2020), 'Tasks Relating to EBPM for Policy on Education of Non-Japanese Children', Seijikenkyu No. 11, p. 52).
68. Press Release 18 Dec. 2019: *The Results of Survey on Expenditure for Education in 2018*, (https://www.mext.go.jp/content/20191212-mxt_chousa01-000003123_01.pdf), p. 4.

revealed Japan as an extremely poor performer (34th out of 41 countries),[69] similar to the performance of the US. As a result, the Reducing Poverty of Children Act was enacted in 2013. In order to support children in need, so-called Children Restaurants have been operating throughout Japan since 2010 run by non-profit organizations (NPO) or volunteers. These provide nutritional food to children who are in situations of financial difficulty or whose parents often fail to prepare meals or share sufficient time for meals due to various reasons. They also initiated a nationwide network to exchange relevant information and coordinate services in order to promote and develop their activities. In addition, Family Mart (one of the biggest convenience stores in Japan) opened its 'FamiMa Children's Restaurant' in 2019. Services provided by children's restaurants are similar to those run by the 'school breakfast club' in the UK. Under such circumstances, the ruling and opposition parties revealed their own proposals to establish a new ministry in 2021 to be mainly in charge of matters relating to family and children. In addition to the problems relating to children in poverty, the Ministry of Education, Culture, Sports Science and Technology assumed that the non-Japanese children of compulsory education age registered in the Resident Registration have serious problems in relation to their proper education. The survey revealed that somewhere in the region of 16,000 such children remain unknown throughout Japan, and local authorities were requested to take effective action to draw attention to the educational situation of such children.[70]

52. Assisted reproductive technology has been rapidly developed for more than twenty years and has caused difficult legal issues under the current Civil Code. The issues relating to assisted reproductive technology are on artificial insemination by a donor, surrogacy and posthumous conception by the frozen sperm of a deceased husband. In the case of artificial insemination, which started in the late 1940s, a legal problem arose as to how to acknowledge paternity of the husband, and it was settled by interpretation of a series of precedents and the Assisted Reproduction Act 2020 stipulates that a husband shall not be allowed to deny paternity of an AID baby when he had given full consent for the treatment (ARA section 10) (*see* paragraph 273).

53. As for the practice of surrogacy, the first case was reported in 2001 by a clinic doctor failing to obey the notice by the Japan Society of Obstetrics and Gynaecology 1983, and in 2008, the Assisted Reproductive Technologies Review Committee of Science Council of Japan submitted a report on 'Issues Related to the Assisted Reproductive Technologies Centred on Surrogate Pregnancy – Toward a Social Consensus –', in which the committee declared that surrogate pregnancy should be prohibited in principle by law and instead a new act should be implemented promptly.[71] Meanwhile, the courts stated that a surrogate mother should be

---

69. UNICEF (2016) Innocenti Report Card 13, *Fairness for Children: A League Table of Inequality in Child Well-Being in Rich Countries*, UNICEF, p. 4.

70. The Mainichi 18 Mar. 2019 (https://mainichi.jp/english/articles/20190318/p2a/00m/0na/005000c).

71. Science Council of Japan published the report 8 Apr. 2008 (http://www.scj.go.jp/ja/info/kohyo/pdf/kohyo-20-t56-1e.pdf). Japan Finance Corporation revealed that 43.7% of the household allocated

regarded as the mother, and no legal relationship should exist between a baby and a commissioning mother (father).[72] Finally, this rule is adopted in section 9 of the Assisted Reproduction Act 2020 and a surrogate mother (birth-mother) is now treated as the mother of a baby. It is, however, presumed that the practice of surrogacy is carried out clandestinely not only in Japan but also in foreign countries such as the US and consequently no public statistics are available.

54. It is a rare case of posthumous conception by frozen sperm where the wife gave birth by her deceased husband's frozen sperm three years after his death, the High Court accepted her appeal that a father-child relationship[73] existed, but the Supreme Court rejected it due to a lack of provision in the Civil Code.[74]

V. The Young Working Poor

55. The social and financial discrepancy has become evident among the well-educated and trained young people and those of a lower academic background. The financial insecurity of the latter has increased, especially after the breakdown of the bubble economy in the 1990s and the subprime mortgage crisis in 2008, leading to a drastic decrease in full-time employment.[75]

56. The young people in temporary employment are no longer guaranteed to retain their jobs and are more likely to lose their posts as their employer's decisions are affected by changes in economic conditions. As a result, it is not uncommon for some to become homeless and others to be forced to stay overnight in an internet café as a part of their daily lives. Under such circumstances, young people who either become unemployed or work in temporary jobs find it difficult to envisage a future due to poverty as well as coping with the mental stress and anxiety caused by their insecure financial situation. Consequently, a survey revealed that many young people show hesitation or postpone marriage for such financial reasons.[76] In this connection, academics point to a new phenomenon of SNEP (Solitary Non-Employed Person). One academic claims that people over 15 years and under 54 years of age who were unemployed, single and only with their family members were estimated at 1.45 million in 2017.[77] Some often express concern about their future

---

its10% and 19% of annual income to the expenditure for education (News Release 20 Mar.2019: *Expenditure for education of the household whose annual income is more than 2 million and less than 4 million (JPY) has dropped in successive four years,* (https://www.jfc.go.jp/n/findings/pdf/kyouikuhi_chousa_k_h30.pdf, p. 10)).

72. SK 23 Mar. 2007 Minshu 61-2-619.
73. Takamatsu HD 16 Jul. 2004 Kagetsu 56-11-41.
74. SD 4 Sep. 2006 Minshu 60-7-2563.
75. Cf. R. Kosugi & Y Hori, *Wakamono no Hokatsutekina Ikoni Kansuru Yobitekichosa (Preliminary Research on Change of Occupation among Young People)*, 4 Japanese Institute Labour Policy & Training (2006).
76. *Ibid.*, at 7.
77. Katsura Maruyama, *Nencho Freeter or Mugyosha no Seikatsu to Nenkin Nofu Jyokyo (Life of Aging Freeter or Unemployed and their Contribution to State Pension)*, (https://www.nensoken.or.jp/

when they reach the age of 60 and above are without family members and have poor financial resources. This is especially given the lack of social care and welfare support.[78]

VI. The Ageing Society

57. The population of Japan is becoming top-heavy at an alarming pace. While Western countries have taken roughly forty to hundred years to arrive at a population structure in which 14% consists of the elderly, it has taken only twenty-four years for Japan to reach the same level. Furthermore, the proportion of elderly aged 65 years and over (by definition of WHO) rose from approximately 5% in 1955 to 28.4% in 2019.[79] The annual budget for the ageing population such as pension and medical expenses up surged sharply JPY 120.2 trillion in 2017.[80] In this respect, the state is facing difficulties in maintaining the social security scheme for elderly people, and Japan is already witnessing grave social problems created by the heavy burden of support and care that families must bear to compensate for inadequate state welfare provisions for the elderly. Since care for the elderly person is seen as the responsibility of the family, it used to be normal for the spouse of a male child (the daughter-in-law) to become the carer. However, in 2016, 60% of those in care lived with his/her carer, 12.2% lived apart from their carer and 25.2% lived in an institution for elderly people. 25.2% of those in care living in the same household as his/her carer were looked after by his/her spouse, 21.8% by his/her child and 9.7% by his/her child-in-law. 70.1% of male carers and 69.9% of female carers were 60 years of age and over, which means an elderly carer was responsible for an elderly person.[81]

58. Meanwhile, the number of elderly households increased from 8.3 million in 1980 to 24.9 million in 2018, and in particular, single households increased from 0.9 million (10.7%) to 6.8 million (27.4%), respectively.[82] Under such population trends, mass media have continued to report that cases of unattended deaths or solitary deaths of elderly people have grown for decades. For instance, the number of solitary deaths of elderly people over 65 years of age examined by the Medical Examiner's Office of Tokyo Metropolitan Government increased from 5,061 (male 2,842 and female 2,219) in 2012 to 6,089 (male 2,534 and female 1,379) in 2019.[83] On the contrary, the number of suicides among the elderly decreased from 11,293

---

publication/nenkinkenkyu), pp. 3–4. Cf. Yuji Genda, *The Solitary No-Employed Person (SNEPs): A New Concept of Non-Employment*, (http://www.jil.go.jp/english/JLR/documents/2013/JLR40_genda.pdf), at 6.

78. Yuji Genda, *Koritsumugyou (SNEP)*, 2013, Nihonkeizaishimbunshuppansha, at 180–181.
79. Cabinet Office, *White Paper on Ageing Society 2020*, (https://www8.cao.go.jp/kourei/whitepaper/w-2020/html/zenbun/index.html), chart 1-1-1.
80. *Ibid.*, chart 1-1-13.
81. *Ibid.*, chart 1-2-2-13.
82. *Ibid.*, chart 1-1-8.
83. Medical Examiner Office of Tokyo Metropolitan Government, *Statistics of Solitary Death at Home in 23 Wards of Tokyo 2019*, (https://www.fukushihoken.metro.tokyo.lg.jp/kansatsu/kodokushitoukei

in 2008 to 7,953 in 2019.[84] This issue reflects the recent changes in family relationships, neighbourhood and living patterns of the family.

59. The problem of securing sufficient income in old age was seen as one of the most pressing issues facing Japanese society at the end of the millennium. Currently, every citizen is entitled to receive a basic pension in old age in accordance with the national pension scheme and the annual income of 51.4% of all pensioners in 2017 was derived solely from such the basic pension.[85] The average annual income of an elderly household is approximately JPY 3.3 million, while that of all households, JPY 5.5 million in 2017.[86] However, pension payments vary depending on whether individuals also subscribe to additional pension plans beyond the basic scheme. Therefore, the elderly population is likely to be polarized between those who will be able to enjoy economic stability and those who are likely to fall below the poverty line. In 2017, the ratio of welfare benefits recipients to the total population was 2.93% among elderly people and 1.65% for total recipients.[87] The MHWL survey revealed that the number of elderly households over 65 years of age which are supported by social security was 906,273 in April 2020 with 830,695 of these being a single household.[88] These figures suggest the highest number since statistics became available.

60. In many ways, the elderly can be said to be in a vulnerable position. Not only are they frequently victims of violence but they also are easy prey for swindlers and fraudulent businesses. As for violence by family members and staff of care institutions, surveys reveal that confirmed violence by family members and cases of reporting violence or seeking advice on violence were 2,267 and 34,057 respectively in 2019 and the confirmed violence by staff of care institutions and those of reporting or seeking advice on violence 644 and 16,927 respectively.[89] In such circumstances, the Prevention of Cruelty to Elderly and Support of Carers Act was implemented in 2005. In addition, elderly people are likely to become a victim of crime. A typical contactic is to attempt to take advantage of the financial anxieties and health concerns of the elderly. In particular, 97.4% of the victims of remittance scams in 2019 were elderly people of 65 years of age and over.[90] Meanwhile, the

/kodokushitoukei-1.html), chart 2-00-119. *See* Teiko Tamaki 'Live and Die in Solitude Away from the Family: Issues Relating to Unattended Death Kodokushi in Japan' Hoseiriron Vol. 46 No. 4, p. 203.

84. Cabinet Office, *supra*, chart 1-2-4-15.
85. *Ibid.*, chart 1-2-1-4.
86. *Ibid.*
87. *Ibid.*, chart 1-2-1-9.
88. Ministry of Health, Labour and Welfare, *Press Release 1 July 2020: Survey on Recipients of Social Security in April 2020* (https://www.mhlw.go.jp/toukei/saikin/hw/hihogosya/m2020/dl/04-01.pdf), p. 1.
89. Ministry of Health, Labour and Welfare, *Survey in 2019 on responses based on the Prevention of Cruelty to Elderly and Support of Carers Act 2005*, (https://www.mhlw.go.jp/content/12304250/000708459.pdf), table 1.
90. Cabinet Office, *supra*, table 1-2-4-6.

number of elderly people (65 years of age and over) arrested for committing crimes increased from 48,597 to 46.264 in 2007 and 2018 respectively, with the majority arrested for theft (71.1%).[91]

VII. The Social Activities of Married Women

61. As discussed above, the employment patterns of married women follow an M-curve, with many women opting to become full-time housewives while the children are young. This, however, does not imply that they become totally cut off from the outside world. Many women participate in the local PTA, co-operatives and volunteer activities. There are some who support activities such as feminist movements, anti-nuclear movements and nature conservation campaigns. In a society that places great value on motherhood, it is precisely through the status accorded by motherhood that women have been able to gain a voice in social and civil activities.

VIII. Violence in the Family

62. Wife beaten by husband was, in many cases, regarded as a not uncommon and blame-free act in a society based on the male dominance principle. In the mid-1980s, Japanese society began to consider violence against a wife to be unacceptable and to acknowledge the necessity of prevention and protection of victims. Furthermore, the understanding that domestic abuse was not innocent violence, but one that should be dealt with as a crime against a victim became prevalent in society after information on domestic violence and cases was revealed through media, action groups and government institutions.[92] In 2001, the Prevention and Protection of a Victim of Violence by Spouse Act 2001 (Domestic Violence Act) was implemented to provide legal remedies for the victims and make clear the responsibilities of the state and local governments. This was followed by the setting up of refugees throughout the country. The act was revised several times in order to make a cohabitee or an ex-cohabitee eligible to apply for legal remedies. The number of people seeking advice from the 'Support Centre on Domestic Violence' organized by local governments rose from 35,943 in 2002 to 119,276 in 2019[93] and those from the police, from 14,140 in 2002 to 77,482 in 2018 respectively.[94] Research shows that of spouses who experienced violence, 17.0% of wives and 12.1% of husbands suffered physical violence by her/his spouse, 14.6% of wives and 10.1% of husbands suffered emotional and verbal harassment and 8.5% of wives, 8.6% of wives and 2.8 of husbands suffered from financial violence and 1.3% of husbands suffered

91. *Ibid.*, table 1-2-4-7.
92. *See* Prime Minister's Office, *The Present Status of Gender Equality and Measures- Second Report on the Plan for Gender Equality 2000* – http://www.gender.go.jp/english_contents/about_danjo/whitepaper/plan2000/1998/index.html.
93. Cabinet Office, *Advice Cases of Support Centre on Domestic Violence 2019*, (https://www.gender.go.jp/policy/no_violence/e-vaw/data/pdf/2019soudan.pdf), p. 1.
94. Cabinet Office, *Report on Data of Domestic Violence*, (http://www.moj.go.jp/content/001335468.pdf), p. 18.

sexual violence in 2020.[95] In relation to the COVID-19 pandemic from 2019, the Cabinet Office revealed that the number of applications for seeking advice on domestic violence was 132,355 between January and November 2020, and it is assumed that the major reason for the increase in cases is the stressful life caused by the fact that people are confined to their homes longer than before and feel insecure about their life under COVID-19 pandemic conditions.[96]

63. The Domestic Violence Act provides preventative and remedial measures to the victims, but some claim that the act is not enough to protect victims and that it should be revised for more efficient protection of victims and educating perpetrators. In the Domestic Violence Act, 'spousal violence' means bodily harm caused by one spouse (illegal physical attacks that threaten the other spouse's body and life) or words and deeds by one spouse that cause the same level of psychological or physical harm to the other spouse, and the law applies to a spouse and an ex-spouse subject to continuing violence after divorce (DVA section 1(1)). On application by a victim (DVA section 12), a court can promptly issue a protection order, including non-molestation order and eviction order (DVA section 13); an order prohibiting the perpetrator from approaching and loitering around the victim for a six-month period from the day on which the order comes into effect (section 10(1)(i)), an order evicting the perpetrator from the family home and prohibiting him/her from loitering around the family home for a two-month period from the day on which the order comes into effect (section 10(1)(ii)). As with the above-mentioned orders, the court can ban the perpetrator from requesting a meeting (section 10(2) (i)), suggesting verbally to the victim that the perpetrator is monitoring the victim's behaviour or creating a situation where the victim could possibly become aware of the monitoring (section 10(ii)), using or carrying out extremely rude or violent words and deeds (section 10(2)(iii)), making a phone call without saying anything, or making phone calls, transmitting messages by fax, or sending e-mails incessantly, except in cases of urgent necessity (section 10(iv)), making phone calls, transmitting messages by fax, or sending e-mails between 10 p.m. and 6 a.m., except in cases of urgent necessity (section 10(v)), sending excrements, animal carcasses, or other extremely disgusting or repulsive materials, or creating a situation where the victim could possibly become aware of them (section 10(vi)), revealing matters that harm the victim's dignity, or creating a situation where the victim could possibly become aware of those matters (section 10(vii)) and revealing sexually insulting materials or creating a situation where the victim could possibly become aware of those materials, or sending documents, pictures or other sexually insulting materials or creating a situation where the victim could possibly become aware of those materials (section 10(viii)). In order to protect a minor living with a victim, a court can issue an order prohibiting the perpetrator from approaching the minor at the family home, the school the minor attends, or any other place, or from loitering around the family home, school, or any other locations normally frequented by the minor during a period from the day when the order is issued for the victim (DVA section 10(3)). In

95. Cabinet Office (2021), *Survey on Domestic Violence (Brief Version)*,(https://www.gender.go.jp/policy/no_violence/e-vaw/chousa/pdf/r02danjokan-gaiyo.pdf), p. 3.
96. Nikkei 12 Jan. 2021 (https://www.nikkei.com/article/DGXZQODG125JZ0S1A110C2000000/).

addition, a similar order shall apply to the victim's relative or other person with whom the victim has a close relationship in the person's social life (DVA section 10(4)).

64. When a police officer finds that there is a case of spousal violence, the officer must endeavour to take necessary measures for preventing the victim from suffering harm due to spousal violence (DVA section 8). If a perpetrator breaches the order, he/she shall be subject to imprisonment for not more than one year or a fine of not more than JPY 1 million (DVA section 29). For protecting the safety of the victim's family, the local authority can refuse disclosure of the address of the victim's family for preventing the perpetrator from tracing the residence of the family. Meanwhile, refugees managed by local authorities and voluntary organizations are available for the victim's family. In the case of abortion, consent of the husband required by section 14 of the Maternal Protection Act 1996 is not necessary in the case of domestic violence.[97]

65. Meanwhile, the Anti-Stalking Act was enacted in 2000 for controlling harassment and other unlawful activities by a person of close relationship who is not necessarily a family member. The White Paper on Crime 2020 shows that the case of warning notice and restraining order were 117 and 2 in 2000, and 2,052 and 1,375 in 2019, respectively (chart 4-5-3-1).

66. Baby farming and child labour were reported in past times, but child abuse, in general, was not acknowledged until the 1980s. At the same, it became more aware of domestic violence cases, and Japanese society also began to realize the existence of child abuse cases in ordinary families. Via a series of reports in the mass media, it was declared that effective legal measures of protection were necessary, and the Child Abuse Prevention Act was implemented in 2000. Accordingly, the number of applications for advice of the welfare section of local authorities rose from 1,100 in 1990, 17,725 in 2000, 56,384 in 2010 and 193,780 in 2019.[98] In addition, the number of applications to family courts to remove or suspend parental rights and duties on the grounds of child abuse rose from 139 in 2008 to 374 in 2019 (Civ. sections 834 and 834-2), and the number of determinations to place child victims in safety institutions (WCA section 28) rose from 329 to 596, respectively.[99] Child abuse does not occur only in family settings but also in childcare institutions. The 2019 annual report on child abuse cases in childcare institutions shows that 94 out of 290 cases notified to the authorities were confirmed as child abuse, such as physical abuse 62.8%, psychological abuse 20.2%, sexual abuse 13.8% and neglect

97. Reply of Head of Division of Child and Family Policy Bureau, Ministry of Health, Labour and Welfare dated 3 Mar. 2021.
98. Ministry of Health, Welfare and Labour, *Child Abuse Cases Dealt with at Child Guidance Center 2019*, (https://www.mhlw.go.jp/content/000696156.pdf), p. 1.
99. The Supreme Court, *Judicial Statistics 2019*, (https://www.courts.go.jp/app/sihotokei_jp/list?filter%5Btype%5D=1&filter%5ByYear%5D=2019&filter%5ByCategory%5D=3&filter%5BmYear%5D=&filter%5BmMonth%5D=&filter%5BmCategory%5D=), chart 2. The figures include applications for revocation of determination.

3.2%.[100] Recently, sexual abuse by schools teachers (obscene acts or sexual harassment) at schools and other private settings became acknowledged in society after revelations of a number of disciplinary actions against perpetuator teachers and criticism voiced by victims with respect to the absence of an efficient protection system for vulnerable school children. Finally, the Prevention of Sexual Abuse by School Teachers Act 2021 was implemented in 2021. In addition, abuse or ill-treatment of a child at a nursery of which details are not found since a child victim is too young to reveal his/her injuries led the MHLW to commence implementing a plan for a nationwide prevention and protection system for young victims.[101]

67. A further outcome for child victims was the introduction of compensation for emotional damage. In one case where a woman claimed compensation for emotional damages resulting from sexual abuse by her uncle around 6 years of age, the Supreme Court accepted her claim by stating that the limitation period started at the point that she was diagnosed to suffer from depression approximately thirty years after the wrongful act.[102] The community councils for protecting children in need constituted of various organizations such as the education, child welfare and health sections of local governments, police, schools, nurseries and local medical associations now operate to prevent and protect children involved in abuse from their carers. Throughout Japan, the community networks working towards the prevention of child abuse have been established in many areas for further prevention and protection of victims. Furthermore, section 179 (Indecent Assault and Sexual Assault by Custodian) of the Criminal Code was enacted in order to guard a minor against sexual abuse by family members. After the two cases of child abuse were reported in March 2018 and January 2019, the government decided to revise the Welfare of Children Act in order to provide further effective and professional protection for a victim minor.

68. Violence against and ill-treatment of elderly people recently captured public attention after the harmful consequences of domestic violence and child abuse in the family setting were recognized. In 2005, the Prevention of Cruelty to Elderly and Support of Carers Act was laid down in order to protect the vulnerable elderly victims of violence. In this respect, the home no longer appears to be a peaceful heaven.

---

100. Ministry of Health, Welfare and Labour (https://www.mhlw.go.jp/content/000763093.pdf), p. 1. In 1995, a head of a childcare institution and a son of the head were sentenced imprisonment for 8 months as injury (Cri. 204) and for four years as forcible indecency (Cri.176) respectively after MP referred to the case at the Parliament (Onchouen Case).
101. Tokyo Web 31 Aug. 2020 (https://www.tokyo-np.co.jp/article/52148).
102. SD 8 Jul. 2015 Katei-no-ho to Saiban (Family Court Journal) (FCJ) No. 4, at 66. A woman claimed compensation for emotional damages caused by sexual abuse from her uncle when she was around 6 years of age and the Supreme Court accepted her claim by stating that the limitation period started at the point that she was diagnosed to suffer from depression approximately thirty years after that wrongful act.

69. Research conducted jointly in 2021 by the Ministry of Health, Labour and Welfare and Ministry of Education, Culture, Sports, Science and Technology revealed that 1 in 17 junior high school students and 1 in 24 high school students regularly take care of their family members. In the former case, 23.5% of carers take care of parents and 14.7% of grandparents and for the latter, 29.6% of carers take care of parents and 22.5% of grandparents.[103] They look after their parents or grandparents on the basis of their physical disability. The students are referred to as 'young carers'. It is pointed out that they are likely to experience difficulties in school performance and to be isolated at school and that social problems such as poverty exist for many young carers.[104]

IX. Gender Issues

70. The World Economic Forum revealed that Japan ranked 120th among 156 counties in the gender gap rankings in 2021, the last place among the G-7 countries. Similarly, the Inter-Parliamentary Union revealed that female parliament members in Japan ranked 166th among 188 countries in the gender gap rankings and those in ministerial positions ranked 151th as of 1 January 2021.[105] In such situations, even some female parliament members of the Conservative Party claimed that they would participate in executive meetings, but the party decided in 2021 that they would be allowed to merely observe the meetings – to observe but not speak.[106] These cases indicate that Japanese women are still under-represented at the political level lagging far behind other countries in terms of current gender matters.[107]

71. While opportunities for same-sex marriage are not available in Japan (*see* paragraph 140), various opportunities of support and protection for same-sex couples are. An increasing number of private sector companies treat a same-sex couple as a married couple in the case of benefit programmes such as housing benefits.[108] In addition, a number of local authorities can issue a certificate of partnership for a same-sex couple, and one authority flexibly applies to a same-sex couple the provisions of the rules of employment for a married couple, such as special leave for caring family members to a same-sex couple.[109] However, discriminatory views

103. Tokyo Web 12 Apr. 2021 (https://www.tokyo-np.co.jp/article/97608).
104. Sawako Kitayama and Kenji Iwakura (2015), 'A Survey on 'Young Carer' – bearing heavy burden for family members-', the Journal of School Education 27, p. 28.
105. https://www.ipu.org/women-in-politics-2021.
106. https://www.bbc.com/japanese/56107717.
107. Table 1.1 the Global Gender Gap Index 2021 of Global Gender Gap Report 2021 – Insight Report Mar. 2021.
108. Panasonic, Sony, IBM and the Asahi Shimbun Company, etc. In April 2021, 157 private companies and organisations including Panasonic, Coca-Cola Japan, Facebook, Yahoo and Shiseido, etc. expressed their support for the 'Business for Marriage Equality' campaign which was commenced by three groups (Marriage For All Japan, Lawyers for LGBT & Allies Network and Nijiiro Diversity) aiming at implementing a same-sex marriage law (http://bformarriageequality.net/).
109. In 2015 Shibuya-ward in Tokyo enacted the Respecting Gender Equality and Social Diversity Regulation 2015 by which it can issue a certificate of partnership for a same-sex couple. Since then, the number of local authorities taking such action has increased to 100 in 2021 (Tokyo Web 1 Apr.

and attitudes in society still exist. For instance, in 2019, the Tokyo Metropolitan Government dismissed an application by a same-sex couple that they should be eligible to claim some benefit such as stipend holiday for caring for a minor or elderly parent, qualification for application of staff accommodation and special payment for marriage that are available for a marriage or de facto marriage of different-sex. Ironically, the 2018 Ordinance for Achieving the Principle of Respecting Human Rights Stated in Olympic Charter includes the ban of discrimination against a sexual minority.[110] Meanwhile, in some other local authorities, a same-sex couple can enjoy those services similar to a married and de facto married couple. The view that a same-sex couple shall not be a marital couple is still supported in the central government in a way that the Minister of Internal Affairs and Communications expressed her view that a household of same-sex couple shall not be aggregated in the Population Census 2020 as a household of marriage on the grounds that a marriage effects only between male and female in Japan and there is a need to distinguish between a marriage and a same-sex couple.[111] A prejudiced view against minority people is often seen in every sector of society and it is reported, for instance, that a flyer was distributed in mailboxes of residences in a local city that read, 'Beware of radical movements to legalize same-sex marriage!' and it included other messages of discrimination against sexual minorities.[112]

72. As for the protection of sexual minority groups, the local government ordinance ('Equality and LGBT Ordinance') was passed unanimously in the assembly of Mie prefecture in 2021 as the first prefecture in Japan to ban anyone from revealing an individual's sexual orientation or gender identity without consent or legitimate reason and prohibiting anyone from forcing the 'coming out' of an individual. The ordinance aimed at encouraging a society where people recognize sexual diversity and eliminate discrimination against an individual belonging to a sexual minority.[113] Meanwhile, Akashi city, a local authority, decided that it will start the 'Akashi Partnership and Familyship Scheme' in 2021. Under this scheme, an LGBT couple and their child shall be recognized as a family and enjoy the services operated by the city such as qualification of applying for a council house, requesting the issuing of a certificate of family and obtaining permission for attending medical operations as a family member. Though those services are available only in the city, this scheme reflects recent changes in society on LGBT issues.[114] Meanwhile, the LGBT Bill (the Promotion of Understandings of the People on Gender Orientation and Identity Bill 2021) was planned to be discussed in the parliament but finally failed

---

2021 (https://www.tokyo-np.co.jp/article/95171)). In 2016, Chiba City also made this decision as a means of enforcing the policy of supporting minority groups such as LGBT (SOGI).

110. Tokyo Web 30 Sep. 2020 (https://www.tokyo-np.co.jp/article/58671).
111. Kyodo 25 Aug. 2020 (https://www.kanaloco.jp/news/government/entry-451912.html).
112. The Mainichi 5 Dec. 2020 (https://mainichi.jp/english/articles/20201205/p2a/00m/0na/008000c).
113. Japan Times 5 Apr. 2021 (https://www.japantimes.co.jp/news/2021/04/05/national/mie-lgbt-same-sex-marriage-takatora-kobayashi-ldp/).
114. Kobe Newspaper Next 10 Dec. 2020 (https://www.kobe-np.co.jp/news/sougou/202012/0013928971.shtml).

before being placed on the agenda before the parliament due to a strong objection from the conservative members of the Liberal Democratic Party claiming that such a bill would harm Japanese society.

73. Awareness of sexual harassment and other discriminatory phenomena has developed in society. As a case of sexual harassment and sexual assault, the case of Ms Shiori Ito is a recent landmark case that became to be a trigger for victims (women) voicing their difficulties and plights caused by sexual assault. She bravely held a press conference in her own name and revealed that she filed a case of physical and emotional damages by torts against a journalist of a prominent TV company alleging that she was intoxicated and raped by him. After revealing her case, she faced a huge amount of libellous comments from anonymous people through the internet that, she said, harmed her mental state and reputation. He seemed to be nearly indicted but escaped arrest and prosecution for unknown reasons. However, she kept her original stance towards the case and a court decided that he had to pay compensation for her damages in 2019. Now she has come to be regarded as the face of the Me Too movement in Japan.[115] Verbal harassment and inappropriate remarks are often observed in day-to-day life. For instance, in 2021, Mr Mori, former Prime Minister, had no choice but to step down from his position in the Tokyo Olympics organizing committee after coming under criticism for his derogatory remarks, such as 'meetings with women tend to "drag on" because they talk too much' and even following his resignation, he spoke in public that a female political staffer colleague of his was 'too old to call a woman'.[116]

§3. The Judicial System: The System of Courts

74. The court system consists of: (1) 438 summary courts which deal with civil cases involving small sums of money, minor criminal cases and traffic violations; (2) 50 district courts (1 for each prefecture) and 203 branches which are normally the Courts of First Instance; (3) 8 high courts (8 districts) and 6 branches which are appellate courts; and (4) the Supreme Court with 15 judges (located in Tokyo), which is the highest Court of Appeal. Furthermore, 50 family courts (1 for each prefecture) with 203 branches and 77 sub-branches have jurisdiction mainly over family and succession cases. In addition, the Intellectual Property High Court was established in 2005 as a special branch of the Tokyo High Court in order to meet the increasing demands of intellectual property disputes. In addition, two family courts of Tokyo and Osaka have the authority to deal with a cross-border child abduction case after the Hague Convention on the Civil Aspects of International Child Abduction took effect in 2012. As it is generally the case that judges begin their legal careers as judges and remain a part of the bench until retirement, they are

115. CNN (https://edition.cnn.com/2019/12/18/media/japan-shiori-ito-legal-intl-hnk/index.htm). *See* Shiori Ito (2017), ***Black Box***, Bungeishunju (English version available https://www.tiltedaxispress.com/books#/black-box/).
116. Okinawa Times 26 Mar. 2021 (https://www.okinawatimes.co.jp/articles/-/728059).

referred to as 'career judges'. Judges have the authority to adjudicate cases and have wide discretionary powers to decide on sentences and damages.

75. Family disputes are dealt with either in the family court or in a district court depending on the nature of the case.[117] In principle, family court hearings are conducted in closed chambers, and the adversarial system, which is the norm for ordinary civil cases, does not apply to family cases. The family court employs family court probation officers who may be ordered by the judge to investigate cases or assist in resolving family conflicts. Attached to each family court is a medical officer who may provide counselling and other medical treatment where necessary. In addition, a part-time family court judge who is appointed from attorneys for a two-year term has been engaged in family court mediation since 2002 (FAPA section 250). The family court also offers services to the community by providing procedural advice.

76. The Law Reform Committee started to examine the existing judicial system in 1999 and submitted a report on reform in 2001, emphasizing more participation of citizens in the judiciary system. Accordingly, the lay judge system was introduced in 2004 for serious criminal trials such as abduction, arson and homicide, and the first case was heard in 2009. The court is composed of three qualified judges and six lay judges and has the power to jointly examine facts, find a defendant guilty or not guilty and decide the final sentence. In this respect, the lay judge system is different from the jury system. The courts select and appoint lay judges from a panel of candidates who are over 20 years of age and registered in the electoral roll. The service of a lay judge is basically compulsory so that a candidate is not allowed to refuse unless he/she has a legitimate reason. Finally, the bar consists of lawyers, and there is no occupational distinction such as the British system of barristers and solicitors.

§4. The Family Law

I. Pre-war Family Law

77. A legal system in line with those of Western countries was created in Japan towards the end of the nineteenth century. As an integral part of the modernization policies put forward by the Meiji Imperial government, a special effort was directed towards the establishment of a modern judiciary system. The drafting of the Family Law (Family and Succession) was spearheaded by a group of Japanese legal specialists under the supervision of Gustave Emile Boisonard de Foutarabie (1825–1910). The fruits of their labour – a draft Civil Code (now called the 'Old

117. Since the family courts decided to suspend hearings and sessions of in-court mediation from 7 to 29 May due to the COVID-19 pandemic, the parties faced problems such as no contact between a minor and a non-resident parent. From 1 Jun. 2020, a judge can proceed a case at his/her discretion under special arrangements for preventing the parties from infection (*see* Notice of Family Court dated 12 Apr. 2021).

Civil Code') based on the French Civil Code and Japanese legal customs – are submitted to the Imperial Parliament in 1889, but its implementation was delayed due to opposition from conservative quarters claiming that it contravened the ethical and cultural climate of the country. It was only a decade later in 1898 that a Civil Code mainly based on the German Civil Code (Pandecten system) was enacted, of which Part 4 (Family) and Part 5 (Succession) comprise the Family Law (called the 'Meiji Civil Code').

78. The content of the Meiji Civil Code was essentially convergent with the Old Civil Code. A distinctive feature of this Code was the introduction of the *Ie* (household) system, founded on the concepts of *koshuken* (the rights or authority of the household head) and *katokusō-zoku* (succession of family assets).

79. The *Ie* was defined as a familial group under the control of a powerful head. While the household head was empowered to expel members of the household from the *Ie*, he also had a duty to protect its members. Thus, even though the head had vast powers over its membership, he was obligated to exercise this power for the benefit of the collectivity. For instance, although the head was in a position to inherit the whole of the family assets, he was, in principle, not permitted to spend the assets for his individual gain. However, in the event that a household head was deemed unsuitable (e.g., a prodigal son who might wile away the household assets), a committee of relatives (*Shinzokukai*) could force him to take early retirement, thereby abdicating the headship to another member of the *Ie*. In this sense, even the household head was constrained by the *Ie*.

80. As a rule, a system of male primogeniture governed the selection of the household head. Thus, the eldest son was the first candidate for headship, and this position was normally passed down to the eldest male of the next generation.

81. Sexual inequality was also instituted by law. For instance, a woman became legally incompetent through marriage.[118] In the case of married couples, the father had sole parental rights and duties over children, and the mother had little legal leverage vis-à-vis her children. Moreover, while unfaithfulness on the part of the husband did not constitute grounds for divorce (unless prosecuted under the Criminal Code), adultery by a wife was regarded as immediate grounds for divorce. Other socially acceptable grounds for divorce included barrenness of the wife and a perceived inability of the new bride to blend into the tacit 'ways' of the *Ie* that she marries into. Sexual inequality also applied to children. If a man had only daughters but had an illegitimate son, the latter could inherit the family assets so long as parenthood was acknowledged.

82. The *Ie* system was buttressed not only by the Civil Code but also by the *Koseki* Act 1898 (Family Registration Act).[119] The registration of citizens was not

118. Paradoxically, this meant that a common-law wife could remain legally competent.
119. The first Family Registration Act was enacted in 1872.

based on the individual, but on the unit of the *Ie* as members of the *Ie* under a household head. Taking marriage as an example, marriage meant that a woman left the family registry of her father (although in some cases, her grandfather maybe the household head) and was entered into her husband's family registry: a process involving her transfer from one *Ie* to another.

83. However, it should be noted that the family registry did not necessarily reflect the actual living arrangements. For instance, it was often the case that parents and children listed under the same *Ie* lived apart from each other geographically. The so-called *Ie* ideology predicated on the idea that members appearing on the registry constitute a family unit regardless of their real circumstances has deep roots in Japanese society.

II. Characteristics of Post-war Reforms

84. The new Constitution of Japan promulgated in 1946 guaranteed the respect of the individual and sexual equality in the family as fundamental human rights. Sections in the Meiji Civil Code pertaining to the family were completely rewritten in accordance with the spirit of the Constitution. Most importantly, the *Ie* system was abolished. It was also during the immediate post-war years that family courts specializing in family matters were established throughout the country.

85. The Family Law was redrafted based on a completely different set of principles. The main features included: (1) a move away from collectivism founded on the *Ie* and towards individualism (e.g., epitomized by the new concept of marriage not as a union of two *Ie*, but as the union of two individuals); (2) a realization of sexual equality between men/women and father/mother (e.g., sharing of parental rights and duties over their child(ren) by both parents); (3) equality of family members (e.g., equal inheritance by all siblings); (4) family registration no longer based on the unit of the *Ie*, but on the conjugal family as a unit. Although some compromises with the Meiji Civil Code were made as in the treatment of estates for ancestor veneration, the new Civil Code represented a radical departure from the principles of the Meiji Civil Code.

86. In particular, the new Civil Code has been acclaimed as promoting the protection of wives embroiled in family disputes. From its implementation in 1946 until the 2010s, some major revisions have been partly undertaken. For instance, the following revisions were implemented in the intervening years: (1) the 1962 partial revisions pertaining to adoptions, guardianship, representation, forfeiture of inheritance, and persons with special relations with a deceased; (2) the 1976 revisions relating to divorce and changes to surnames; (3) the 1980 revisions increasing the spouse's entitlement to succession from one-third to one-half; (4) contact and maintenance of minors in separation and divorce clearly stated in section 766 and suspension measures of parental rights and duties enacted (The Civil Code of 1898 and 1947 (Civ). section 834-2) in 2011; (5) an illegitimate child has the equal portion as an heir in 2013; (6) the six months waiting period for remarriage on only women reduced to one hundred days (revised Civ. section 730) in 2015. These revisions aimed to achieve substantive sexual equality and the promotion of the welfare of children. Furthermore, some provisions of the Civil Code and the Family Affairs Proceedings Act relating to the making of last will, the right of a surviving spouse to division of the deceased person's property, liquidation procedure of legitim, the right to claim payments by a relative person who took care of a deceased person, the age of marriage for male and female and the age of majority (sections 731 and 4) were revised in 2018 and shall be implemented by 2022.

87. During 1996 and 1997, in the light of the discussions generated by the International Year of Women and the International Year of the Child, new revisions of the Civil Code were under deliberation. Such moves included the revision of the minimum age of marriage (18 years for both men and women), the abolition of the provision prohibiting remarriage for six months for women, separate surnames for husbands and wives, revision of the system of dividing the matrimonial property, the assurance of visitation rights after divorce, revision of grounds for divorce, revision of discrimination against illegitimate children relating to succession, etc. Among these revisions, the bill to permit spouses to register different surnames was quashed by right-wing members of parliament in 1996 on the ground that it would subvert the unity of the family. As for discrimination against illegitimate children relating to succession, the Supreme Court declared such discrimination was against the equality principle of the Constitution, and section 900 was revised in 2013.[120] In 2018, the major part of the succession law was revised in order to reflect recent changes in Japanese society and economy and to meet the necessity of protecting the interests of those involved in succession disputes in an ageing society. For these purposes, some provisions of the Civil Code were revised, and the Revision of a Part of the Civil Code and the Family Affairs Proceedings Act 2018 and the Lodging Last Will in Legal Affairs Bureau Act 2018 were enacted. The revision and enactments aim at mainly the following items: first, protection of the surviving spouse's right to residence (short-term and long-term right to residence) (*see* paragraphs 794ff); second, providing the more effective measures of distributing the estate of a deceased (*see* paragraphs 827ff); third, the user-friendly procedure relating to a will (*see* paragraph 742); fourth, the whole revision of the legitim scheme (*see* paragraphs 749ff); fifth, revision relating to the effects of succession (*see* paragraphs 581, 745 and 832); finally, enactment of the right of a relative as special contributor who makes great contribution for the interests of a deceased (*see* paragraph 652).

88. On 9 February 2021, the Civil Code (Part of Parent and Child) Subcommittee of the Deliberative Council on the Legal System published the Interim Report on Revision of the Civil Code (Part of Parent and Child) in which it invited the public to express their comments and views relating to the provisions of a waiting period for remarriage (section 733), presumption of legitimacy (section 722), parental rights and duties (820), discipline of a child (section 822), challenging paternity (sections 774 and 777) and acknowledgement of paternity (sections 799ff).

120. SK 4 Sep. 2013 Minshu 67-6-1320.

III. Current Family Law

89. The principal source of family law is the Constitution of Japan. Article 24 of the Constitution holds that a marriage can only be concluded through the joint agreement of the parties as well as based on the fundamental equality of the sexes. Indeed, the Constitution clearly spells out the legal equality of spouses as well as other members of the family as a fundamental human right. Further, Article 13 of the Constitution declares that an individual's pursuit of happiness should be respected, including the guarantee of an individual's right to pursue happiness within family life. Article 13 of the Constitution stipulates equality under the law, not only with respect to civil liberties but also in the context of the family.[121] Article 20 which concerns freedom of religion and belief is pertinent to disputes relating to rights to perform ancestor veneration and the religious education of the children. Furthermore, Article 25 stipulating the right of survival impacts problems concerning the maintenance of family members. However, Article 26 provides for rights and obligations to receive an education, which in turn spells out parental duties towards children. In addition, Article 31 on guaranteeing due process of law, Article 33 pertaining to the right to a fair trial and Article 82 on the right to a public hearing, which are mainly applied to criminal cases, may also be relevant to the resolution of family disputes.

90. The following is a summary of the main statutes concerning the support and protection of family members and minority groups in society:

(i) Fundamental laws relating to the family:
  - Part 4 (Family) and Part 5 (Succession) of the 1947 Civil Code (Civ.).
  - Guardianship by Contract Act 1999 (GCA).
  - Registration of Guardianship Act 1999 (RGA)
  - Gender Recognition and Family Registration Act 2003 (GRFRA).

(ii) Laws relating to sexual equality:
  - Equal Employment Opportunity Act 1972 (revised 1986) (EEOA).
  - Promotion of Gender Equality in the Political Field Act 2018 (GEA).

(iii) Laws relating to violence in the family:
  - The Prevention and Protection of a Victim of Violence by Spouse Act 2001 (Domestic Violence Act: DVA).
  - Child Abuse Prevention Act 2000 (CAPA).
  - Anti-Stalking Act 2000.
  - Prevention of Cruelty to Elderly People Act 2004.

(iv) Laws relating to children:
  - Mother and Child Health Act 1965 and Welfare of Workers Who Take Care of Children or Other Family Members Including Child Care and Family Care Leave Act 1991.

---

121. Sendai District Court of 28 May 2019 referred to the reproductive right in the case of forced abortion by the Eugenics Act 1948 and stated that the reproductive right is the right to decide whether to have a child and bring it up based on the principle of Art. 13 of the Constitution (CW).

- Welfare of Children Act 1947 (for foster and institutional care, child abuse and supporting children in need).
- Education Fundamental Act 1947 (education of children).
- Child Maintenance Allowance Act 1961, Mother-Child and Widows Welfare Act 1964, Child Benefit Act 1971, Child Benefit Special Measures Act 2010, Reducing Poverty of Children Act 2013 (for the financial support of children).
- Regulation and Punishment of Acts Relating to Child Prostitution and Child Pornography, and the Protection of Children Act 1999
- Implementation of the Convention on the Civil Aspects of International Child Abduction Act 2013 (ICAA).
- Adoption Agency (Regulation) Act 2016.
  Assisted Reproduction Act 2020 (ARA).

(v) Laws concerning the elderly:
- Welfare of Elderly People Act 1963 (relating to welfare in general).
- Employment Security for the Elderly Act 1971 (with respect to employment).
- Care of the Elderly People Act 1997 (concerning care of bedridden elderly).
- Prevention of Cruelty to Elderly People and Support of Carers Act 2004 (protection of elderly victims of violence and support of carers for elderly people).
- Stabilization of Employment of Elderly Persons Act 1971 (revised in 2020)

(vi) Laws relating to family health:
- Health Insurance Act 1922, National Health Insurance Act 1958, and Old Age Health Act 1982 (medical care).
- Mental Health and Welfare of the Mentally Disabled Act 1995 (Mental Health Act 1950).
- Maternal Protection Act 1996 (Eugenics Act 1948) (protection of life and health of mother).

(vii) Laws relating to the family and economic security:
- Social Welfare Act 1950 (relating to economic hardship).
- Employment Pension Act 1954 and National Pension Act 1985 (economic security after retirement).

(viii) Laws relating to criminal cases:
- Juvenile Act 1947 (pertaining to juvenile crimes).
- Compensation for Juvenile Case Act 1992.

(ix) Laws pertaining to registration of individuals and place of residence:
- Family Registration Act 1947.
- Residents Registration Act 1967.
- Calculation of Age Act 1902.
- Declaration of Age Act 1949.

(x) Laws relating to dispute resolution procedures:
- Family Affairs Proceedings Act 2011 (FAPA).
- Civil Litigation Proceedings Act 1996.
- Civil Execution Act 1979.

- Personal Affairs Litigation Act 2003 (The Personal Affairs Litigation Act 2007 (PALA)).
- Habeas Corpus Act 1948 (relating to child abduction).
- Registration of Foreign Juristic Person and Ante-Nuptial Settlement Act 2011.
- Non-Litigious Proceedings Act 2011.

(xi) Laws relating to foreign residents:
- Citizenship Act 1950 (pertaining to naturalization).
- Immigration and Refugee Act 1951
- Foreign Registration Act 1952 (for leave to stay in the country).
- General Rules for Application of Laws Act 2006.
- Standard Testament Form Act 1964.
- Standard Maintenance Duty Act 1986.

(xii) Others:
- Facilitation of Succession of Management of Small and Medium-Sized Enterprises Act 2008.
- Inheritance Tax Act 1950 (pertaining to taxes).
- Lodging Last Will in Legal Affairs Bureau Act 2018.
- Lease of Land and House Act 1991 (for protection of de facto relationships)
- Special Cases in Handling Gender Status for Persons with Gender Identity Disorder (GID) Act 2003.

91. Treaties pertaining to family matters include the Treaty to Eliminate All Forms of Discrimination Towards Women (ratified in 1985), Treaty Concerning Children's Rights (ratified in 1994) and the Hague Convention on the Civil Aspects of International Child Abduction (ratified in 2013). From April 2014, the Ministry of Foreign Affairs acts as the Central Authority and Tokyo and Osaka Family Courts have jurisdiction over the international abduction cases.

92. Since the revision of acts is an elaborate and time-consuming process, judicial precedents have played a significant role in assuring the appropriateness of procedures and outcomes of dispute resolution. As will be dealt with in detail below, judicial precedents, in some cases, have yielded results, which are practically equivalent to a statutory revision. For instance, common-law relationships have largely been protected through judicial precedents, and the system of conjugal assets (Civ. section 762) and the right of Revocation of Conjugal Contracts (Civ. section 754) have been radically transformed through precedents. The major impact of judge-made laws can also be seen in the practice of resolving divorce claims by the offending party through the interpretation of the court.

93. Under the current system of courts, all cases, whether they are ordinary civil cases, criminal cases or administrative cases, are handled in district courts (the Court of First Instance), high courts (having jurisdiction over appeals) and the Supreme Court (highest Court of Appeal). Thus, no specialized courts such as administrative courts exist in Japan. However, summary courts deal with civil cases involving small sums and minor criminal cases. As stated earlier, the family court, which was founded in 1949, is the Court of First Instance for family disputes and juvenile cases.

94. The family court has special procedures to deal with family problems. For instance, deliberations are not open to the public in order to protect the privacy of the parties. As mentioned previously, adversarial procedures are only sparingly applied, with a majority of disputes dealt with ex officio. The court initially encourages the parties to take the initiative to resolve their own disputes, under the rule of mandatory in-court mediation *Chotei* prior to litigation. Furthermore, family court probation officers are at hand to assist in collecting and submitting vital information for the resolution of disputes, and medical officers may provide supporting services for parties if deemed necessary.

95. There is the same debate regarding the constitutionality of the special procedures of the family court, in that they impose an undue restriction on the right to a public hearing and the right to a fair trial through adversarial procedures. Those who hold the view that the special procedures are unconstitutional argue that it should be possible to deal with issues relating to rights and duties through civil procedures. With respect to the allocation of marital expenses, for example, they claim that even though the special procedures of the family court may be employed to decide on the amount which should be borne (i.e., a matter of quantum) by either party, it is inappropriate for the family court to adjudicate whether either party has the duty to bear the expenses (i.e., a matter of responsibility) in the first place.

96. Family disputes are dealt with through the Family Affairs Proceedings Act and the Personal Litigation Proceedings Act. Due to the application of the rule of mandatory in-court mediation before litigation, many disputes are first subject to mediation, after which they may undergo determination proceedings (*shimpan*), and finally, litigation. Depending on the case, the actual processing of a case may by no means be straightforward. Take, for instance, divorce cases. First, matters relating to whether the divorce will go ahead, the settlement of the matrimonial property and custody of the child(ren) will be handled through mediation. In the event that mediation proves unsuccessful, the decision concerning divorce itself can be transferred to the family court for litigation, while matters relating to the matrimonial property and custody of children will be dealt with by the family court. However, once divorce litigation has been initiated, then the settlement of the matrimonial property may be handled in the family court as part of the process of litigation (PALA section 32).

97. The cases dealt with in the family court through determination can be roughly divided into two groups shown in the annexed list (FAPA section 39). Group One includes those cases relating to guardianship, curatorship, tutorship, missing and absent persons, legal parenthood, financial support among relatives, succession, family registration, gender recognition, child abuse, social benefit, mental impairment, bankruptcy (with respect to family assets) and succession of small and medium enterprises. Group Two includes cases involving marriage, divorce, adoption, parental rights and duties, financial support among relatives, succession, division of a deceased person's property, disposition of employees' pension and social benefits. Most of the Group Two cases are initially dealt with through in-court mediation, excluding those which have a negligible chance of a successful outcome. If mediation fails, then the next step is determination. Even if the mediation is successful, however, the agreement reached through mediation is not accepted automatically, and instead, the family court, where appropriate, reserves the power to overturn the result of mediation (FAPA sections 272 and 284). Furthermore, those who are dissatisfied with the determination can gain redress by commencing litigation or by appealing to the high court.

98. Family court mediation *Chotei* is a process by which a family court mediation committee consisting of a judge and two commissioners are chosen from the public (at least one woman and one man) aids disputing parties to reach an amicable settlement through conciliation. In principle, both parties are expected to attend, but the committee may proceed with *Chotei* by holding separate meetings with each of the parties if it is deemed inappropriate for both parties to come face-to-face. There are circumstances where the committee may suggest a settlement even where the parties themselves have not reached an agreement.

99. Even though family court determination is based on the judgment of the judge, the judge may, where deemed necessary, request the opinion of an expert commissioner chosen from the public. As mentioned earlier, determination is conducted in closed chambers and follows procedures that diverge from ordinary civil procedures. Moreover, family court determinations have a binding power, and there is a system for assuring that parties conform to the substance of the determination.

100. Two systems exist for ensuring that a family court determination is adhered to: the system for the request of performance (FAPA section 289) and the system for ordering performance (FAPA section 290). A failure to follow a decision of the family court is sanctionable by fines (FAPA section 291). In order to obtain effective sanctions against a person to fail to perform, the detailed description should be necessary to be made in a determination, and otherwise indirect compulsory execution such as penalty payment would not be approved by a court (*see* paragraph 423). If a disagreement is so intense that it is deemed improper for the parties to exchange any monies in person, bank transfers can be made to obviate the necessity for a face-to-face exchange of monies.

101. To repeat, the family court is a specialized court dealing with numerous cases relating to family disputes. The family court has been acclaimed for aiding many people with vexing family disputes since its founding in 1949. Access is easy as family courts are located throughout the country, and it dispenses services of a uniform standard at a low cost. Taking in-court mediation, for example, parties have no duty to retain a lawyer, and the current cost is set at about JPY 2,000. The family court also engages in the dissemination of information through its advisory service.

IV. Family Dispute Resolution Outside Court

102. There is no uniform system of dispute resolution outside court. As for services related to legal matters, the Japanese Legal Support Centre which was established in 2006 with the sponsorship and assistance of central and local government and the Japan Bar Association provides civil legal aid, information relating to legal disputes and advisory services (The Comprehensive Legal Support Act 2004). This centre operates throughout the country so that a citizen in trouble has good access to seeking practical and legal help and advice. In addition, the local authorities and local bar associations provide free legal advice services. In some cases, advisory services are also provided by welfare commissioners and by the police (especially regarding disputes involving delinquent children).

103. After the implementation of the Alternative Disputes Resolution Act 2004, private institutions approved by the government have started to provide their services in various fields, but few organizations exist for family disputes. One of the institutions specializing in family matters, the Family Problems Information Center in Tokyo, Osaka and some other cities provides out-of-court mediation services for disputes relating to marriage, divorce and minors involved in marital disputes by mediators who are experienced in dealing with family problems.[122]

104. With respect to instances of conjugal domestic violence and child abuse, local governments have telephone helplines as well as providing refuges in conjunction with voluntary organizations.

105. Voluntary groups have begun to support themselves and educate people on social issues such as poverty among single-parent families and isolation of sexual minority groups hidden from society since the 1990s. A couple of NPO or voluntary organization have begun providing support and advice to single-parent families,[123] transgender people[124] and sexual minority groups.

---

122. Each party is required to pay JPY 3,000 upon application and JPY 10,000 for each session. In this respect, availability of this service may be limited to parties belonging to a particular social class. It is reported that approximately fifty organizations provide support with respect to contact (The Mainichi 5 May 2021: https://mainichi.jp/articles/20210505/k00/00m/040/054000c).
123. One example, Wink was approved as NPO in 2002 for mother-child and father-child families, http: //www.npo-wink.org/.
124. The GID support organization sends messages and practical information and offers a space for exchanging views on GID matters (http://www.npogid.or.jp/).

Part I. Persons

Chapter 1. The Status of a Person

§1. Definition of a Person

106. A person includes both a natural person and a legal person such as a corporation. For the purpose of civil cases, a human being is regarded as becoming a person at the time of his/her birth when his/her body has completely appeared. Under current medical and legal practices, a person is not considered dead and will not lose the capacity to hold rights and duties until such vital signs as cardiac arrest, respiratory arrest and mydriasis are observed.[125]

§2. Capacity

I. The Capacity to Hold Rights and Duties (*Rechtsfähigkeit*)

107. The Civil Code of 1898 stipulates two types of legal capacity: the capacity to hold rights and duties (*Rechtsfähigkeit*) and the capacity to enter into legal acts (*Handlungsfähigkeit*). Any natural person obtains the former capacity at the time of his/her birth without any condition and loses it at the time of his/her death. An unborn child – who is not a person under Japanese law – is presumed irrebuttably to have been born in cases of inheritance (Civ. section 886(1)), a testamentary gift (Civ. section 965) and damages in tort (Civ. section 721).[126] However, his/her parent (mother) is not entitled to act as a representative for him/her since he/she is not regarded as a natural person. Accordingly, the parent must wait to act as a representative for the unborn child until its time of birth.[127] Non-Japanese citizens are entitled to hold this legal capacity under certain restrictions (Civ. section 3(2) and the State Redress Act section 6, etc.). In 2013, a ward of adult guardianship was entitled to have the active and passive right to vote after revision of section 11 of the Election Act 1950.

125. The Organ Transplantation Act 1997 introduced the concept of brain death under strict conditions, but it is still uncertain that the concept of brain death could be applied to an ordinary civil case.
126. There is no decisive interpretation on whether a fertilized egg should be regarded as an unborn child in the case of in vitro fertilization under the current law.
127. Decree of the Supreme Tribunal (Taishinin Hanketsu) (STD) 6 Oct. 1932 Minshu 11-2023.

II. The Capacity to Enter into Legal Acts (*Handlungsfähigkeit*)

108. A natural person is entitled to hold this capacity when he/she attains the age of majority – 20 years (Civ. section 4). The age of majority shall be decreased from 20 to 18 years of age by 2022 following the revision of section 4 of the Civil Code in 2018. With this capacity, he/she can act independently, obtain rights and assume responsibilities. For protecting the interests of a person with insufficient capacity and any person with whom he/she undertakes transaction, the statutory scheme of persons with limited capacity has been implemented: a minor (Civ. section 5), a person under guardianship on an adult who is equivalent to an incompetent (Civ. sections 7 and 838(2)) and a person under curatorship who is equivalent to a quasi-incompetent (Civ. sections 11 and 876), are restricted in most cases from entering into legal acts, and a ward under tutorship must obtain consent from the tutor in order to enter into legal acts (Civ. sections 15(1) and 876-6). In addition to the statutory guardianship, guardianship of adult by contract is also available (the Guardianship by Contract Act 1999). In the case of legal acts concerning the forging of family relationships such as marriage and adoption, a person is eligible to enter into legal acts unless he/she loses the capacity to make reasonable decisions.

109. A minor is a person who is under the age of 20 (18 years of age from 2022). A minor is, in general, regarded as unable to enter into legal transactions by himself/herself. In order to engage in legal acts, he/she is required to obtain approval from his/her statutory agent(s) – usually his/her parents(s) with parental rights and duties (Civ. section 5(1)). Otherwise, the statutory agent(s) acts on behalf of the minor. In the case where a minor acts independently without the agents' approval, that act will be voidable, while the agent(s) can subsequently ratify the minor's act (Civ. section 5(2)).

110. A minor is entitled to act independently when he/she either obtains rights or is exempt from duties where his/her interests are unlikely to be infringed upon. In addition, a minor is treated as competent in the following situations: where he/she disposes of property such as pocket money where he/she appears to have been given the general approval of the statutory agent(s) to so dispose (Civ. section 5(3)), where he/she has been given the approval of the statutory agent(s) to engage in business (Civ. section 6(1)) and where he/she is claiming his/her wage from an employer (Labour Standard Act 1947 sections 58 and 59). Furthermore, a minor is eligible to act independently in certain cases of family affairs (*see* marriage, adoption and will). When a minor is married, he/she is regarded as a person of full age (Civ. section 753), but this shall not be applied by 2022 due to revision of section 4 and abolition of section 753. However, it is not clear whether or not a minor is eligible to give valid consent to undergo a medical operation.

111. When a person continuously has an impairment of, or a disturbance in the functioning of, the mind or brain and is lacking in sufficient capacity to make reasonable decisions, the family court can issue a determination declaring the person as a ward of guardianship on application by the person himself/herself (hereinafter cited as a person with a mental health condition),[128] relatives within the fourth degree, the guardian of a minor, the supervisor of the guardian of a minor, the curator, the supervisor of the curator, the tutor, the supervisor of the tutor or the prosecutor (Civ. section 7 and FAPA section 39). When the family court determination is made and registered in the Guardianship Registration Book, a guardian should be appointed to look after the ward and administer his/her property. In addition to a spouse of the ward, relatives within the fourth degree, the guardian and the supervisor of the guardian or prosecutor, a ward can apply for discharge of the family court determination when he/she regains a normal state of mental health (Civ. section 10). All acts conducted by a ward are voidable except for minor acts such as the payment of electricity, purchasing foods and daily necessities independently (Civ. section 9).

112. The curatorship system, which was modified in 1999, is equivalent to the quasi-incompetent scheme in the previous Civil Code (Civ. section 11). Curatorship commences by a family court determination when a person *extremely* lacks sufficient capacity to understand the nature and quality of his/her acts due to mental problems (Civ. sections 11 and 876). The procedure for application is similar to guardianship. The new scheme is different from the old one in that a curator holds the authority to invalidate the effects of actions taken by a ward (a person under curatorship), he/she is given the authority by a determination of a family court to represent the ward in some legal matters, he/she can consent to a legal action by the ward with respect to 'important assets' and he/she may act as a legal representative like a guardian (Civ. section 13(1)(vii) (such as transactions of the ward's real estate) (*see* curatorship).

113. Tutorship is a new scheme introduced by the revision of the Civil Code in 1999. The aims of this scheme are to protect and promote the interests of a person who is intellectually disabled or mentally impaired by utilizing his/her surviving capacity to the maximum. When a person is lacking sufficient capacity to understand the nature and quality of his/her acts due to mental problems, either the same category to persons in the case of an application for guardianship or the head of a local authority can make an application to a family court (Civ. section 15). A family court will assign a tutor (Civ. section 876-7(1)), and the tutor must administer the tutorship by considering the physical and mental state of the ward.

114. When a person is involved in transactions with a minor, a ward of guardianship, a ward of curatorship or a ward of tutorship, the Civil Code provides two types of measures for the purpose of protecting the parties. First, if person A discovers that person B was a ward, A can remind B about B's right to set aside or ratify the transaction within a suspension period of one month or more after A has discovered that B was a ward. Failure to respond by B will be regarded as ratification (Civ. section 20(1)). In the case where B is still ward, this rule shall apply to

128. He/she can apply only during the period when he/she temporarily regains a normal state of mental health.

his/her statutory agent(s) (Civ. section 20(2)). However, in the case of acts requiring special formalities or the consent of a ward's agent, failure to respond by the ward will be regarded as revoking the act (Civ. section 20(3) and (4)). Second, a ward is not allowed to discharge his/her act if he/she pretends to be a competent person during the process of communicating with a counter-party to a transaction (Civ. section 21).

III. The Capacity to Understand the Meaning and Effects of One's Acts (*Willensfähigkeit*)

115. A person with the sufficient capacity to enter into legal acts is usually considered to have the capacity to understand the meaning and effects of such acts. Meanwhile, a person without the capacity to understand the meaning and effects of one's acts cannot make any valid act (all acts shall be regarded void).[129] For instance, an infant, a drunken person or a person suffering from grave mental illness are treated as lacking this capacity of understanding. However, a minor who is 15 or over is eligible to enter into valid legal acts relating to marriage, adoption, acknowledgement of paternity and making a will.

IV. The Capacity to Assume Liability

116. A person must be held accountable for his/her conduct causing damage against a third person if he/she has the capacity to assume liability. Although there is no provision defining the capacity to assume liability in the Civil Code, a person of approximately 12 years of age is deemed to have such capacity (*see* Civ. sections 712 and 713). When a person lacks this capacity and has caused damage by his/her conduct, his/her supervisor such as a parent(s) must take liability for the result (Civ. section 714).

§3. Absentees

I. Definition of Absentee

117. An absentee is a person who is unlikely to return to his/her residence for reasons such as long-term stays overseas. For the purpose of administering his/her property and protecting the interests of any interested person, the absentee can appoint an administrator of his/her estate before giving up residence. Where the absentee does not appoint an administrator and is missing, any interested person or a prosecutor can apply to the family court for the appointment of an administrator

129. STD 11 May 1905 Taishinin Minji-Hanketsuroku (Report on the Civil Cases of the Supreme Tribunal) (Minroku) 11-706. The level of such understanding to be is in general considered that capacity of a child between the age of 7 and 10.

(Civ. section 25(1)). Moreover, any interested person or a prosecutor can apply to the family court to make a decision necessary for the administration of the property (Civ. section 25(1)).

II. Procedure of Applying for a Determination in the Case of a Missing Person

118. When a person has remained incommunicado for a certain period, a family court can issue a family court determination declaring him/her as a missing person on an application by any interested person. There are two types of family court determinations. First, a family court can issue an ordinary determination declaring the person to be missing provided that the person has not been heard from for seven years (Civ. section 30(1)). Second, a family court can make a special determination declaring a person missing who has been involved in a war, shipwreck or other peril and missing for one year since the moment of a ceasefire in the case of war or the time of the incident (Civ. section 30(2)). In unusual circumstances, the following procedures shall be taken:

- When several people die either in one place or in various places and the order of each death is not clear, those people are presumed to have died simultaneously (Civ. section 32-2). For instance, a parent and a child are presumed to have died concurrently if they are involved in an aeroplane accident together. Accordingly, no inheritance can then pass between the deceased parties.
- Where the death of a person involved in an accident is almost certain based on all the circumstances despite the fact that the body is not recovered or recognized. In such a case, a person or institution investigating the incident usually notifies the mayor of the local city in which such death occurs.[130] A mayor shall confirm the death officially, and thus, the person is treated as deceased (The Family Registration Act 1947 (FRA) section 89).

119. Once a family court determination has been declared, the person is presumed to be dead after a period of seven years in the former case, and in the latter case at the time of the ceasefire, the shipwreck or the termination of the peril (Civ. section 31). From the time of the family court determination, the death of the person shall become legally effective: a marriage will terminate and succession of the missing person's estate ensues.

120. Either the person declared to be dead or any other interested person can make an application to the family court to revoke the determination on the following grounds: the person was alive at the time and date of his/her presumed death as stated in the determination or the person died at a different time and date from that which was declared in the determination (Civ. section 32(1)). If the missing person appears some years after the determination has been made, his/her appearance will bring about some legal issues. For instance, if a spouse of the missing person and

130. A mayor of a local city indicates a mayor of any city, town or village.

his/her new partner have remarried in good faith, it is understood that the new marriage shall survive as a valid one. However, if either party to the new marriage entered into it in bad faith, it is deemed that such marriage gives rise to grounds for divorce (i.e., adultery) during the previous marriage and also indicates grounds for revocation of the new marriage (i.e., bigamy). In regard to succession, since succession is deemed not to have taken place once the family court determination has been revoked, anyone who has gained any interests from the succession in good faith must return the remaining part of those interests to the living benefactor (Civ. section 32(2)).

Chapter 2. Registration of Civil Status

§1. Registration

I. Family Registration in the Family Registration Book

121. Under the family registration system (*Koseki* system), a Japanese national[131] shall be registered in the Family Registration Book according to the principle that members of a conjugal family holding the same family name shall be registered as a unit.[132] In this respect, non-Japanese citizens are not registered in the Family Registration Book. For instance, only a note of the name of a non-Japanese spouse is made on the page of his/her Japanese spouse in the family registration book when they get married. Theoretically, all Japanese people shall be registered in the family registration book. However, it may happen that some are not registered for some reasons and a non-registered person shall face various difficulties in day-to-day life because he/she cannot confirm his/her identity via an official document such as a family registration certificate. In September 2020, a senior woman who was presumed to be 78 years of age was found to have died of starvation and her son of a presumed 49 years of age was in debilitation. The son stated that they hesitated in seeking advice, asking help from the local authority and calling an ambulance when they had no food and survived only by salt and water for a month. She was thought to be a war-orphan and had no family registration since she was born in the chaos of war and then did not submit a birth notice for her son. It was reported that the Ministry of Justice acknowledged 881 non-registered people at the time of 10 February 2021 and it invites such people to take the action of proceeding for family registration. A husband and wife and their child(ren) are registered at their principal address (*Honseki*), which is similar to a domicile.[133] In the Family Registration Book, the names and the birth dates of the married couple and their child(ren), the cause of registration such as birth, marriage or adoption, the parents' name(s) of any spouses and the name(s) of the birth parent(s) of any adopted child(ren) are entered.[134] For the purpose of protecting the privacy of individuals, only a family member is eligible to apply to the local government for the issuing of either a long-form (*Koseki Tohon*) or a short-form (*Koseki Shohon*) certificate of family registration upon the payment of a fee, and a third party is required to satisfy the conditions for obtaining a certificate (FRA sections 10(1)(2) and 10-2(1)). The certificate can, for instance, be used as identification for the purpose of applying for a driving license or a passport.

131. A member of the royal family shall be registered in the registration book exclusive of their family members through birth or marriage. When Ms Masako Owada married Prince Naruhito (Emperor from 2019), her entry was transferred from her father's principal address in the family registration book to the Royal Family Registration Book. After the time of marriage, Ms Owada is to be recognized only by her first name, Masako, since a member of the royal family is known by their forename alone in contrast to ordinary Japanese citizens.
132. Kansai TV 26 Feb. 2021 (https://www.ktv.jp/news/feature/20210226/).
133. The principal address differs from domicile in that domicile requires 'physical fact of residence and the intention of remaining' but the principal address does not require such factors.
134. The names of natural parent(s) shall not be entered in the case of special adoption.

122. The mayor of a local city is responsible for keeping the Family Registration Book. The individual information entered in the Book is available to the public on a limited basis, and an applicant must declare in writing the purpose of usage of the certificate if he/she is applying for a certificate of another person (FRA sections 10(1), (2) and 10-2(1)).

123. When a baby is born to a married couple, one of the parents is required to notify the fact of the birth to the local city and present a birth certificate issued by a medical doctor (FRA section 52(1)). Accordingly, the baby must be registered at the parents' principal address. If the baby is born after the divorce of the parents, the mother is responsible for submitting the notice (FRA section 52(1)). Similarly, in the case of an illegitimate baby, its mother should notify the birth of the child to the local city (FRA section 52(2)).

124. On the occasion of marriage, individual descriptions of both parties are, in most cases, transferred from their parents' principal addresses to their own personal principal address created by reason of the application. In the case of marriages between Japanese and non-Japanese nationals, only the Japanese partner shall be registered in the new principal address with a note referring to his/her marriage with the non-Japanese partner (*see* FRA sections 6 and 16(3)).

II. Resident Registration

125. A person who is a resident in Japan is required by law to notify the details of their residence to their local city (RRA 1967 sections 21ff). On such notice, the following items shall be registered in the Residents Registration Book: the name(s) and the birth date(s) of the resident(s), their principal address, their sex and information regarding their status of the National Health Service and Pension Scheme, etc. (RRA 1967 section 7). A person is entitled to make an application to read the Resident Registration Book and/or to have a resident certificate (*Jyuminhyo*) issued upon satisfying similar requirements as in the case of family registration certificates (RRA sections 11-2 and 12). Similar to a certificate of family registration, a resident certificate shall be effective as an official document proving the fact of residence.

III. Alien Registration

126. Non-Japanese persons are obliged to register as an alien at an office of the local city within ninety days after their entry into the country (Alien Registration Act 1952 section 3). At the time of registration, an alien registration card is issued. Under the current law, a non-Japanese person who is aged 16 and over should always carry the card and must show it at any time to an official (usually police) on request (Alien Registration Act section 13(1) and (2)). Non-Japanese persons are required to renew such registration every five years, and they must also obtain entry permission from the immigration bureau. Meanwhile, any non-Japanese persons who are 16 years of age or over must register their fingerprints at the time of entry to Japan, except in the case of special permanent residents (Immigration Control and Refugee Recognition Act section 6(3)).[135]

IV. Issues Relating to Family Registration: Freedom of Information Versus Privacy

127. No opposition has been voiced against the principle that either the Family Registration Book or the Resident Registration Book should be, in general, open to the public, since most people believe that these registration systems are a convenient and reliable source of information on individuals. For instance, in the case of marriage, one party can make sure that the other party is not already married by obtaining a certificate of the other party's family registration. In this sense, it was widely accepted that the Registration Book should be open to the public.[136] It is claimed by some lawyers, however, that for the purpose of protecting the privacy of individuals, special measures should be established to restrict the public from having free access to the registered information and allowing only certain people with legitimate reasons to read or obtain the information registered in the books. Consequently, by the revision of the acts, in order to keep a balance between freedom of information and privacy, the registrar of a local city is entitled to dismiss an application by a person to read the Residents Registration Book or have a certificate issued if he/she finds no justifiable purpose for the application (*see* FRA sections 10(2), 11-2 and 12(6)).

V. The Gender Recognition and Family Registration Act 2003

A. A History of the Enactment

128. In the early 1990s, some people started to publicly claim that a sex affirmation procedure should be implemented in order to respect their fundamental right (gender identity) and realize their welfare in everyday life so that they can choose and spend their lives according to their preferred gender identity. Until that time, gender minority groups were perhaps not strongly suppressed historically because, unlike a society with strict social and religious sanctions against minority groups, few religious sanctions existed in Japanese society. However, discriminatory views and attitudes against the minority prevailed explicitly and implicitly in every corner of society. In this respect, it could be said that the gender minority groups were treated as unseen or invisible in Japanese society. On a very few occasions, a legal case relating to the gender minority was reported, such as the '*Blue Boy* Case'[137] in 1965 in which a medical doctor conducting sex affirmation surgery was found guilty

135. This rule was implemented in 2006 merely following US-VISIT scheme.
136. In the Residents Registration Book, a child has been entered as just 'child' and not as 'natural child', 'adopted child', 'legitimate child' or 'illegitimate child' since 1994 (*see* Tokyo HD 22 Mar. 1995 Hanreijiho (Hanji) 1529-29).
137. Tokyo DD 15 Feb. 1969 Hanji 551-26.

of violating the Eugenic Protection Act 1948 (now the Maternal Protection Act 1996).In 1998, the first transsexual surgery was carried out in Japan following several cases where transgender people 'came out' in the mid-1990s.[138] Under the law at that time, such people whose sex had changed were not entitled to alter the description of the sex registered in the Family Registration Book.[139] In 2003, the act was enacted for the purpose of meeting the needs of such people in changing their 'sex' legally as well as medically. As one of the legal effects of changing one's sex, an FTM person is entitled to register him as a father of the child who is born by Artificial Insemination by a Donor (AID) to his wife in the Family Registration Book (*see* paragraphs 274ff).

B. Procedure and Requirements for Application

129. A family court can make a determination of change of registered sex in the Family Registration Book when the court is satisfied with the following conditions (GRFRA sections 3 and 5, and FAPA section 39):

(1) an applicant must be 20 years old and over;
(2) he/she must be unmarried at the time of application;
(3) he/she must have no minor child;
(4) he/she must lack generative functions;
(5) he/she must maintain the physical characteristics similar to those of the opposite sex to which he/she seeks to change;[140]
(6) he/she must have a medical examination.

When the application is granted, the applicant is deemed to have changed his/her sex (GRFRA section 4).

By this act, a person intending to change his/her sex can now make an application to a court, but some difficulties still exist due to the rigid condition in the act. For instance, a person argued in litigation at the Supreme Court that section 3(1)(iv) of the act violates the Constitution (the right to liberty of Article 13 and equal treatment under the law of Article 14) since for achieving a change of his/her sex, he/she shall be forced to take medical surgery against his/her will in order to satisfy the requirement of section 3(4). The Supreme Court dismissed the case stating that the above-mentioned requirement is so far acceptable in the current society in order to avoid sharp and rapid changes relating to gender issues, but that this may possibly be revised according to changing views and attitudes towards gender and family life in the future.[141]

138. More details in Teiko Tamaki, 'Can One Choose One's Own Sex?', in Peter Lodrup, & Eva Modvar, eds., (2004), *Family Life and Human Rights,* Gyldendal, p. 889.
139. Hachioji Branch of Tokyo FD 9 Aug. 1999 Hanji 1718-86.
140. Gender reassignment surgery is mandatory for meeting this requirement (Tsuyama Branch of Okayama FO 6 Feb. 2017 unreported (http://lex.lawlibrary.jp/commentary/pdf/z18817009-00-040891484_tkc.pdf)).
141. SK 23 Jan. 2019 Hanji 2421-4.

Chapter 3. Names

§1. Family Names and Forenames

130. The name of a person consists of his/her family name and his/her forename – the family name comes first and the forename follows.[142] Currently, there is no custom of giving a middle name in Japan. In addition, the usage of compound or joint family names is not available under the law.[143] Although some insist that a person's family name and forename represent his/her individuality, section 750 of the Civil Code states that from the time of marriage a couple must share the same family name, either that of the man's or woman's family name before marriage. The courts have stated up to now that this rule does not violate the principles of Article 13 of the Constitution[144] while the Supreme Court has declared that to keep one's own name should be protected as the right of personality (*Persönlichkeitsrecht*) under the Constitution.[145] In this sense, a family name is currently regarded as the icon of a unit – a conjugal family – but not as the icon of a person's individuality.[146]

I. Family Name (Uji)

131. A legitimate child takes the family name of his/her parents from the moment of its birth, whereas an illegitimate child takes that of his/her mother. A child born to Japanese and non-Japanese parents is given the family name of his/her Japanese parent. In the case of a deserted child, the mayor of a local city will name him/her (FRA section 57). A family name is changed in the following instances: marriage, divorce, adoption, dissolution of adoption, acknowledgement of paternity, legitimation and marriage to a non-Japanese person and on application of alteration.

---

142. For instance, in the case of Mr Kurosawa Akira, Kurosawa is his family name, Akira is his forename. Unlike ordinary Japanese citizens, members of the royal family are registered in the Royal Family Registration Book and have no family name due to historical reasons. When Princess Masako married Prince Naruhito (Emperor from 2019), she lost her maiden name – Owada (*see* note 132 and the Imperial House Act 1947 s. 26).
143. In the case of a marriage between Japanese and non-Japanese persons, the courts sometimes approve of the couple creating a compound or joint family name if there is absolute necessity for using such name in the case in question (Akashi Branch of Kobe FO 26 Jan. 1994 Kagetsu 47-6-78 and Tokyo FO 25 Oct. 1994 Kagetsu 47-10-75).
144. Tokyo DD 19 Nov. 1993 Hanji 1486-21. Art. 13 stipulates, 'All of the people shall be respected as individuals. Their rights to life, liberty, and the pursuit of happiness shall, to the extent that it does not interfere with the public welfare, be the supreme consideration in legislation and in other governmental affairs.' In 2021, the Supreme Court decided to review this matter not at a petit but a grand bench, which indicates a possibility of alteration of the precedent.
145. SD 16 Feb. 1988 Minshu 42-2-27. This was not stated in a marriage case.
146. Since the 1960s, a number of people –particularly women – have been calling for the revision of the current law in order to allow one to keep his/her original family name even after marriage. In 1996, the Ministry of Justice nearly submitted a proposal to revise s. 750 to Parliament but failed due to concerns about the political reaction from the conservatives.

II. Forename (Na)

132. Usually, parents give their child a forename after its birthday selecting some characters of their preference. It is interpreted that the right to give the child a forename is a part of their parental rights and duties so that the parents should exercise this right in accordance with the best interests of the child. If the forename chosen by the parents clearly infringes upon the best interests of the child, the parents are held responsible for such an abuse of their parental rights and duties. Indeed, on submission of the form of birth notice by the parents, a mayor can refuse to register the chosen forename of the child in the Family Registration Book if he/she thinks that the forename is contrary to the best interests of the child.[147]

§2. Changing of Names

133. A person can apply to a family court to issue a determination changing either his/her family name or forename. An applicant should present to the court such proof indicating that the change of the name is absolutely essential for the well-being of the applicant. For instance, the fact that the applicant faces much inconvenience in everyday life because his/her neighbour in a small community holds the same name – which consists of the same Chinese characters and is pronounced in the same way – would be a good cause for the application. In practice, a family court seems to be reluctant to accept an application to change a family name but relatively lenient in relation to one concerning the change of a forename.

147. Hachioji Branch of Tokyo Family Court declared that the parents should hold and exercise the right to give their child a forename as part of their parental rights and duties by taking account of three factors: whether the forename (1) would be in the best interests of the child, (2) be socially acceptable and (3) functions appropriately as a tool for identifying the individual child. Furthermore, the court stated that the mayor of a local city would be entitled to refuse to register the child's name into the Family Registration Book on the grounds that the parents had abused their parental rights and duties in naming their child 'Akuma (demon)' (31 Jan. 1994 Hanji 1486-56).

Chapter 4. Nationality

§1. Acquiring Nationality

134. A child is considered a Japanese National in the following situations: (1) either parent holds Japanese nationality; (2) his/her deceased father had Japanese nationality; or (3) the child is born within Japanese territory and his/her parents are unknown[148] (Nationality Act 1950 section 2). A minor legitimatized by his/her parents' subsequent marriage can also be given Japanese nationality on the ground that: (1) either parent was a Japanese national at the time of his/her birth or (2) either parent (whether now deceased or still living) is considered as a Japanese national (Nationality Act section 3(1)). In addition, a non-Japanese person can obtain Japanese nationality by naturalization by fulfilling the requirements laid down in sections 4 and 5 of the Nationality Act.

135. Under the current law, an illegitimate child used to face difficulties in obtaining Japanese nationality. Where the child's father acknowledged paternity before the time of birth, he/she was regarded as a Japanese national at the time of birth. However, he/she could not be considered as a Japanese national if the father acknowledged paternity only after birth.[149] The only remedy available for a child in such a situation was the procedure of legitimation by the parents' subsequent marriage. However, the Supreme Court decided in 2008 that an illegitimate child acknowledged by his/her father even after birth should be given Japanese nationality.[150]

136. A Japanese national loses his/her Japanese nationality when he/she acquires a foreign nationality either on the basis of his/her intention to do so or by operation of law (Nationality Act section 11). In the case of a child of Japanese nationals who is born in a foreign country adopting the territorial principle, he/she can hold dual nationality. As a result, he/she will lose his/her Japanese nationality unless he/she manifests to the Japanese authorities his/her intention to retain Japanese nationality. In the case of a person holding dual nationality, he/she is required to choose one or the other nationality either before reaching the age of 22 or within two years from the time of acquiring a non-Japanese nationality (Nationality Act section 14).

148. The Supreme Court adopted a wider interpretation of this term in a case where the parents were unknown but Japanese nationality was granted to an infant whose mother was presumed to be a Filipino (27 Jan. 1995 Hanji 1520-32).

149. In an exceptional case where acknowledgement of paternity before the child's birth is regarded extremely difficult, this rule does not apply (Tokyo FO 29 Nov. 1995 Hanji 1564-14).

150. SD 4 Jun. 2008 Kagetsu 60-9-49.

Chapter 5. Residence and Temporary Residence

137. For the purpose of legal acts, the parties are required to confirm their residence. In general, residence is interpreted to be the place where a person mainly resides on a daily basis. Unlike the concept of domicile in the Western legal system or a principal address of the family registration system in Japan, residence can be confirmed by taking account of the nature or aims of an individual legal act. Where a person has no residence or his/her residence is unknown, their current address can be used for the purpose of engaging in legal actions.

Chapter 6. Persons with Mental Impairment

138. In order to protect a person, the Civil Code provides the ways in which a court can make a determination (*see* Chapter 1 §2. Capacity and Part II and Chapter 7 Guardianship). In addition, Mental Health and Welfare of the Mentally Disabled Act 1995 (Mental Health Act 1950) sets out that any person who has known a person with mental disorders or a person suspected of having mental disorders may apply to the prefectural governor for an examination by a designated physician and protection of the said person, such as receiving medical treatment or hospitalization (section 22(1)). Furthermore, the new scheme for protecting a person with mental problems was implemented in the Civil Code and the Guardianship by Contract Act 1999 (*see* Guardianship).

Part II. Family Law

Chapter 1. Marriage

§1. The Nature of Marriage

I. Definition of Marriage

139. Neither the provisions of family law nor precedents of the courts have defined marriage. It is generally interpreted that marriage is the unit of a man and a woman which continues until the time of dissolution of the relationship by either divorce or the death of one party to the marriage.[151] Accordingly, a couple of the same sex or a couple agreeing to enter marriage with a time limit shall not be regarded under Japanese law as able to enter into a marriage.[152]

140. Recently an issue relating to same-sex marriage has come to attract social attention. In one case where a Japanese man married a Filipino female but later discovered that she was not a female but male, he commenced a litigation by claiming their marriage was void because same-sex marriage was not legal under Article 24 of the Constitution stipulating that marriage shall be based only on the mutual consent of *both sexes* and it shall be maintained through mutual cooperation with the equal rights of *husband and wife* as a basis.[153] In 2019, however, the Mooka Branch of Utsunomiya District Court ordered a partner of same-sex partnership who had committed infidelity to pay compensation for damages in tort to the other partner by interpreting such relationship as 'de facto marriage',[154] which was confirmed by the Supreme Court in 2021 (*see* paragraph 243). Coincidentally, Sapporo District Court declared on 17 March 2021 that the state policy that same-sex marriage is not allowed is against the equality principle of Article 14 of the Constitution since a

151. Article 24 of the Constitution: marriage shall be based only on the mutual consent of *both sexes* and it shall be maintained through mutual cooperation with the equal rights of husband and wife as a basis. With regard to choice of spouse, property rights, inheritance, choice of domicile, divorce and other matters pertaining to marriage and the family, laws shall be enacted from the standpoint of individual dignity and the essential equality of the sexes.
152. Since a marriage only takes effect between human beings, an intelligent ape or a friendly computer is not eligible to be a party to a marriage.
153. Saga FO 7 Nov. 1999 Kagetsu 51-6-71.
154. SK 17 Mar. 2021 CW

same-sex couple has no legal measure of enjoying any legal effects of marriage, though it stated that marriage shall be on the basis of male and female union.[155]

II. Marriage and Ceremony

141. From a historical point of view, it can be said that, unlike most Christian and Islamic countries, the strong influence of religious doctrine upon marriage custom has rarely been observed in Japan. During the period of the Shogun regime (from the early seventeenth century to the late nineteenth century), for instance, parties to a marriage not belonging to certain social classes were required to notify their union to the parish temple of their denomination for the purpose of marriage registration, after having held their wedding ceremony under secular circumstances. This procedure did not necessarily reflect religious conviction amongst citizens but rather indicated that the temple in those days functioned moreover as an office of registering civil statuses such as marriage, birth and death.

142. However, social control over marriage has been widely observed in many sections of society in past times. A couple who resided in rural areas, where most of the population lived before the time of industrialization, was strongly expected to abide by the unwritten rules of their peer group before entering into marriage. While young people could enjoy the freedom of having relationships in their community during adolescence, a couple were expected to remain faithful to each other under the rules of the peer group once the couple's relationship developed into a 'steady' one. In other words, their relationship as a couple would be protected by social rules if it was first accepted by the members of their peer group and violation of the rules would be severely sanctioned by the group, such as '*sharivari* or rough music' as it was known in the Western culture.

143. It is not easy to draw a clear picture of whether the marriage system in the past was one of monogamy or polygamy. Generally speaking, monogamy was the prevailing marriage institution in Japanese society, and polygamous relationships were observed only in a particular social class and period before the nineteenth century. Indeed, it can be said that the social attitude towards a man's extramarital relationship was quite relaxed so that a man could keep a mistress without facing strong social disapproval so long as he had the financial means to do so.

144. A marriage will take effect under the current family law if the parties fully consent to the marriage and submit a notice of marriage to the family registration section of the local authority. A wedding ceremony whether secular or religious is not required in order to establish a valid marriage. In modern Japanese society, it is common for a couple to have a wedding ceremony at either a church or shrine (though the couple may belong to neither church nor shrine) and then to hold a wedding reception at a banquet hall. From a legal point of view, such rituals have no legal effect but may be considered as evidence for proving the start of a marriage.

155. BBC News Japan (https://www.bbc.com/japanese/56424717).

III. Registration of Marriage

145. A marriage shall be effective from the time a couple brings a form of marriage notice to either the family registration office of the local authority where they have a residence or that office in which their principal address is registered. In the marriage notice form, they are required to fulfil the relevant requirements, sign their names and apply their seals in the presence of two witnesses of full age who must also sign their names.[156] The parties can either appear at the registration office with two witnesses of full age for the registration or send by post the completed notice form to the office. Theoretically, in order to produce a valid notice, the parties should write their signatures by themselves on the notice form, although in practice they can ask a third party to write their signatures for them. The registration office has no authority to confirm the authenticity of the signatures.

146. The registrar of the family registration office must register the marriage in the Family Registration Book unless the marriage notice fails to meet the requirements laid down by the law (*see* Civ. sections from 731 to 737 and 740). A couple residing abroad can notify their marriage to an Embassy or the Consulate of the Japanese Government in the country where they reside (FRA section 40). A registrar must refuse to accept the marriage notice if he/she finds any defects in the notice or violations of legal requirements (for instance, one party has already married). If a defective marriage notice has been mistakenly accepted, the marriage can be later revoked (Civ. sections 743 and 744). In terms of the power of a registrar, he/she is only empowered to inspect formalities of a marriage notice and has no power to examine substantial factors in the notice. Accordingly, he/she can refuse, for instance, to accept the marriage notice if he/she discovers that both the signatures written on the form are evidently identical. However, even if he/she suspects that each signature has not been written by each respective party, he/she must accept the notice because he/she has no power to examine the authenticity of those signatures.

IV. Engagement

147. The law regarding engagements has developed by case law since there is no such provision in statute law. An engagement – which is considered as a type of contract – takes effect when a man and a woman make an agreement to marry sometime in the future. It is interpreted that a contract of engagement can be formed with a genuine intention to marry in the future as evidenced, for example, by the following incidents: (1) a couple has decided on the date of their wedding ceremony; (2) a couple has exchanged betrothal gifts;[157] (3) a couple has dispatched a letter of

156. It is possible to ask random strangers to be witnesses since there are no legal requirements for the eligibility of witnesses except the capacity to understand the meaning and effect of his/her act.

157. SD 20 Dec. 1963 Minshu 17-12-1708 stated that the party who was guilty of breaking off an engagement should be liable for emotional damages where no betrothal gifts were exchanged but the couple were engaged for some time.

invitation to their wedding ceremony to their acquaintances; (4) a couple has a continual sexual relationship with the expectation of both parties to marry in the future; or (5) a couple introduce themselves as engaged to their parents and friends.[158]

148. An engagement contract shall not be effective if either the parties are related within a prohibited degree of consanguinity, or if either party lacks the capacity to understand the meaning and effect of his/her act.

149. One party to engagement is not permitted to force the other into marriage (in other words, to force submission of the marriage notice to the registrar's office). This is because marriage is regarded as valid only if it is the result of two fully consenting parties participating of their own free will (*see* Article 24 of the Constitution). Once an engagement has been formed, it is not uncommon that the parties will expend a sum of money in preparation for their future life. In the case that one party breaches the engagement contract without any reasonable cause, the other shall be entitled to claim compensation for any expenditure and/or an allowance for injured feelings by reason of breach of contract.[159] In interpreting 'any reasonable cause', the courts apply the rigid criteria,[160] but in one case, it was found that neither the disapproval of either party's parents of the proposed marriage nor simply personality differences between the parties were acceptable as a 'reasonable cause' for dissolving the contract.[161] Once reasonable cause has been established – i.e., one party's behaviour is considered inappropriate for a party to an engagement contract according to common-sense – his/her behaviour constitutes grounds for damages to be awarded to the other party. In the case that engagement results in dissolution due to one party having had an affair with a third party, the other party is entitled to claim damages in tort from the third party.[162]

150. Damages cover financial loss and emotional suffering caused by the consequences of dissolving the engagement. For example, if one party retires in expectation of the future proposed marriage, he/she will be awarded the amount of compensation that would have been gained if he/she had not retired. Remuneration of a go-between is regarded as a financial loss, but neither the expenses for the meeting arranged by the go-between nor any expenses incurred in the preparation of trousseaux are regarded as losses arising from the dissolution.

151. It is common practice for couples to exchange betrothal gifts at the time of their engagement. In the event of dissolution of the engagement, the following procedures will usually ensue under the 'fair and equitable' principle; if the engagement is dissolved under mutual agreement, both parties are liable to return the gifts to each other; if the giver mainly caused the dissolution, he/she is not entitled to

158. Kobe DD 22 Oct. 2002 the Supreme Court database.
159. STD 26 Jan. 1915 Minroku 21-49 and SD 21 Oct. 1952 Minshu 6-9-849.
160. Osaka DD 28 Mar. 1963 Hanta 492-187.
161. Tokyo DD 31 Mar. 1993 Hanta 857-248.
162. Osaka HD 5 Oct. 1978 Kagetsu 32-10-48.

claim back the gifts,[163] whereas if the receiver is mostly responsible for the dissolution, the giver is entitled to claim a return of the gifts.

152. The responsibilities of go-betweens have decreased in recent years as the matchmaking industry has grown and now increasingly serves to introduce people to their future bride/bridegroom as a business (a go-between used to undertake such in the past). A matchmaking business may be liable to pay tortious damages if it intentionally gave a customer inaccurate information on a person to be introduced and/or misled him/her to get married,[164] while a go-between rarely takes such responsibilities.[165]

§2. The Capacity to Enter into Marriage

153. A marriage takes effect only on the agreement of both parties and through the submission of a marriage notice to the family registration office (Civ. section 739). In order for a marriage to be valid, three requirements must be fulfilled: (1) both parties must have the intention to be married; (2) one or both parties are not a party to another valid marriage; and (3) the marriage notice form must be valid, i.e., not defective.

154. A marriage is voidable if the parties are under 18 (Civ. section 731).[166] There were no special formalities required in submitting a notification of parental consent. The parties must simply submit the marriage notice form to a family registration office. If the parties were minor, they must attach to that notice form a document stating that parental consent has been given (FRA section 38(1)). If the marriage notice form, without such a document attached, was mistakenly accepted by the registrar, the marriage would still be valid if parental consent had, in fact, been given. As for proof of the fact that parental consent had been given, this could be shown by the parents' signatures as witnesses to the marriage (on the marriage notice form), or simply by the parents' attendance at the wedding ceremony, or their presenting a gift to the couple. The law had been interpreted such that once parent(s) had given their consent, they did not then have the right to later withdraw it.

155. Some criticism was voiced against the provisions concerning parental consent to the marriage of minors. It was understood that the main objective in requiring parental consent was to protect the welfare of minors. However, such an objective could not be achieved in some cases due to the fact that parental consent could be dispensed with in certain circumstances and the fact that a parent still retained the power to give or withdraw consent even after his/her parental rights and duties had been suspended or removed by reason of his/her unsuitability to look

163. Tokyo HD 27 Apr. 1982 Hanji 1047-84.
164. Osaka DD 25 Feb. 1994 Hanta 861-266.
165. Tokyo DD 11 Mar. 1972 Hanta 277-224.
166. A proposal for the minimum age for marriage to be 18 years for both parties was being considered by the Deliberative Council on the Legal System and the minimum age shall be 18 years of age in 2022.

after the minor. Finally, after the revision of section 731 of the Civil Code in 2018, a man and woman attaining 18 years of age are eligible to marry, and they do not need to obtain consent from their parents due to the abolishment of section 737 of the Civil Code.

§3. Effects of Marriage (*See* Part III. Matrimonial Property Law)

156. Both parties to a marriage assume the duty of living together once they enter into the institution of marriage (Civ. section 752). In the case that one spouse refuses to cohabit with the other, the latter cannot force the unwilling spouse into cohabitation even if there is no reasonable cause for the refusal. In such a case, the latter is eligible to make an application to the family court for issuing a determination to cohabit against the former. The court stated in one case that a determination to cohabit should be issued if there is a possibility for the parties to reconcile[167] and in another case that a determination should not be issued if a relationship could not be restored.[168] In practice, it is interpreted that a determination cannot force any party to a marriage to cohabit with the other.[169] Accordingly, the latter is usually eligible to claim either maintenance or damages for failure of marital duty from the former. In addition, such a refusal (without reasonable cause) can also form a ground for divorce (Civ. section 770(1) (ii)). However, the following facts will constitute a reasonable cause for refusal to cohabit: if one party is imprisoned or stays abroad for a prolonged period for business, if a marriage has broken down irretrievably, if a claimant is responsible for separation, or if the parties have reached an agreement to live apart through family court mediation. As for separation, although there is no provision on separation in the Civil Code, the parties can live apart legally through their own private agreement or by an agreement through family court mediation or by a separation determination issued by a family court (FAPA sections 39 and 150(1)).

157. If a third party intentionally jeopardizes the couple's ability to cohabit, he/she shall be responsible for damages to the couple in tort (*see* Part III Chapter 2 §4. Compensation for Distress Caused by Divorce). For instance, if an employer maliciously transfers the husband to another city so that the parties must live apart, that employer may be sued for unfair labour practice.[170]

158. A married couple has a duty to cooperate with each other in everyday life (Civ. section 752). Though a conclusive definition of this duty is not obvious, it is interpreted that the duty to cooperate with each other comprises various activities which are necessary for maintaining a stable family life. For example, under this

167. Osaka HK 14 Jan. 2005 Kagetsu 57-6-154.
168. Osaka HK 13 Aug. 2009 Kagetsu 62-1-97.
169. Sapporo FO 18 Oct. 1998 Kagetsu 51-5-57.
170. Kobe District Court granted a remedy for a couple in 12 Sep. 1986 (Hanji 1210-131), while the Supreme Court dismissed a similar case in 14 Jul. 1986 (Hanji 1198-149). In this respect, the court seems to stand in favour of the employer (Fukuoka HD 21 Aug. 2001 Hanta 1126-198 and SD 20 Oct. 1992 Rodohanrei 618-6).

interpretation, if a wife neglects most of her domestic chores due to excessive indulgence in missionary activity, such neglect shall constitute good grounds for divorce by reason of violation of this duty to cooperate with the spouse in everyday life.[171]

159. A couple is also responsible for supporting each other (Civ. section 752); in practice, this means mainly financial support. The necessary degree of such support is construed as that between parent(s) and dependent child(ren)[172] (*see* Part II Chapter 8). In light of this duty, a spouse has to provide the other with financial support sufficient to allow the receiver to maintain a standard of living similar to that of the provider. Questions have been raised regarding the relationship between this duty to support and the duty to bear matrimonial expenses laid down in section 760. Where one spouse wishes to claim his/her living expenses from the other during a period of separation, he/she can invoke either section 752 or 760 in order to recover such expenses.

160. The duty of maintenance will only terminate at the time of dissolution of the marriage. As a result, a separated couple are still liable to provide maintenance to each other. In dealing with a dispute regarding financial support between a separated couple, the court may alleviate one party's burden of support having considered all the circumstances of the case. In addition, the court may make a preservative resolution or a revising resolution due to change in circumstances of the parties in order to secure the financial situation of the parties (FAPA section 105).

161. As mentioned earlier (*see* Part I Chapter 3), one party to a marriage must change his/her family name to the other's at the time of marriage (Civ. section 750). In fact, more than 90% of women change their family name to that of their husbands' on marriage. In the event of the death of a spouse, the surviving spouse may revert to his/her previous family name if it was changed at the time of marriage (Civ. section 751(1)). The compulsory rule of changing one's family name at the time of marriage is now criticized by some. It has been pointed out that this rule brings about many inconveniences to wives who are actually required to renew family names stated in all official documents such as a driving licence. It is asserted that this rule is an infringement upon human rights as wives are forced to abandon their maiden names which represent their individuality or identity. The Supreme Court decided that section 750 of the Civil Code does not violate the principles of Articles 13, 14 and 24.[173] In 2020, however, the Supreme Court was reported to have transferred three cases to the grand bench (fifteen justices) from the petit bench to examine whether section 750 of the Civil Code violates the Constitution in those cases. It is usually thought that the Supreme Court may change the rule taken by its precedents if a case is transferred from a petit bench to the grand bench. The Supreme

171. Osaka HD 14 Dec. 1990 Kagetsu 43-11-73.
172. In practice, it is interpreted that there are two categories of maintenance responsibility to family members. The first applies between parent(s) and dependent child(ren) and the second applies within a circle of relatives within a certain degree (*see* Civ. s. 877).
173. SD 16 Dec. 2015 Minshu 69-8-2586.

Court, however, did not overturn the precedent and just mentioned that the issue relating to section 750 should be discussed in the parliament.[174] Meanwhile, Tokyo District Court decided in 2021 that section 750 of the Civil Code does not violate the Constitution but a marriage is valid since the couple got married using his and her own family name according to the procedure of the State of New York in 1997.[175]

162. It has been interpreted that spouses have a duty of chastity to each other under the currently recognized institution of monogamy. In the case that one spouse commits adultery, the innocent party can present a divorce petition on the grounds of adultery (Civ. section 770(1)(a)). In addition, he/she is eligible to sue his/her unfaithful spouse and/or the person with whom the spouse commits adultery for compensation for injured feelings (Civ. section 709).[176] However, no party is liable for adultery if the marriage had already broken down before the adulterous affair took place[177] or if the marriage is deemed not to have broken down even though the affair took place.[178]

163. A minor was treated as a person of full age (*see* paragraphs 108–110) from the time of marriage (Previous Civ. section 753). Through marriage, a minor acquires the capacity to enter into legal acts and shall be considered as a parent with parental rights and duties if he/she has a child. Once the marriage has taken effect, the legal status acquired by the minor continues even after any dissolution of the marriage, unless the marriage is revoked by reason of violation of section 731. This rule of presumption of full age only applies in civil cases.[179] As mentioned in paragraphs 108 and 109, section 753 shall not be effective from the time of implementation of revised section 731.

164. There are some instances where one spouse may be liable to the other in tort. For example, there have been cases where a husband has caused his wife's injuries due to careless driving. In such a case, the question arises as to whether the wife can make a claim against his motor insurance company asserting that she should be regarded as a 'third party' for the purpose of being awarded compensation under section 3 of the Motor Vehicle Accident Compensation Act 1955. A court in such a case will generally grant the injured spouse the right to claim from the company

---

174. Asahi Digital 9 Dec. 2020 (https://www.asahi.com/articles/ASND96WCBND9UTIL049.html) and SK 23 June 2021 Court Website.
175. Asahi Digital 21 Apr. 2021 (https://www.asahi.com/articles/ASP4P4QVXP4PUTIL02B.html).
176. SD 30 Mar. 1979 Minshu 33-2-303.
177. SD 26 Mar. 1996 Minshu 50-4-993.
178. It is interpreted among lawyers that the duty of chastity in matrimonial life reflects the doctrine that each spouse should only participate in exclusive sexual relationships. Currently, some assert that chastity is rather interpreted as a matter of self-determination or as a right to control one's sexual life. In this sense, a husband shall be guilty of raping his wife should he force her to engage in a sexual affair against her free will (Matsue Branch of Hiroshima HD 18 Jun. 1987 Hanji 1234-154).
179. A person of 18 years and over has the right to vote after 2016 (s. 9(1) of the Public Office Election Act 1950).

insurance.[180] However, the court is unlikely to allow such a claim for compensation if it foresees that to do so would cause conflict between the married couple.

§4. VOID AND VOIDABLE MARRIAGES

I. Validity of Marriage

165. A valid marriage shall take place provided that two conditions are met: first that the genuine consent of both parties to the marriage exists, and second, that the legal formalities for a valid marriage are satisfied. Failure to meet these conditions results in either a void or voidable marriage. In the case of a void marriage, any interested person is eligible to commence proceedings for the marriage to be declared void. This can be done without obtaining a court judgment, and it will then be construed that no marriage had ever existed. In the case of a voidable marriage, only a limited number of persons are eligible to challenge the validity of the marriage, and it is considered that the marriage will remain in force unless and until it is stated voidable by the court.

II. Void Marriages

166. A marriage is void if one or both of the parties had no real intention to marry – due to a mistake regarding the identity of the person or through any other reason[181] – at the moment that the marriage notice was drawn up or at the time of submission of the notice to the family registration office (Civ. section 742(1)). As a rule, the real and true intention of both parties should exist at both the time of drawing up the notice and its submission. When a marriage is declared void, it is regarded as though no marriage ever existed. Accordingly, any child(ren) produced between the parties shall be regarded as illegitimate.

167. When a third party submits a marriage notice to the registration office without the knowledge of the parties concerned, the marriage shall be absolutely void by reason of the lack of any real and true intention of the parties to be married. In 1996, the Supreme Court declared that a marriage should be declared void on the grounds of a lack of any real and true intention of one party to be married even after 40 years had passed since the submission of the marriage notice.[182] In the case that one party to a marriage submits a marriage notice to the registration office without the knowledge of the other, the marriage shall also be void. However, the marriage can be regarded as valid from the time of submission of the marriage notice should the partner(s) lacking in any real intention subsequently ratify the marriage. In one case,[183] the court stated that such a marriage should be considered valid owing to

180. SD 30 May 1972 Minshu 26-4-898.
181. If X marries Y by believing that Y is Z, X is entitled to claim the marriage void.
182. SD 8 Mar. 1996 Kagetsu 48-10-145.
183. SD 25 Jul. 1972 Minshu 26-6-1263.

the fact that the couple continued to live together even after the man's discovery that a marriage notice had been submitted to the registration office against his will.

168. A marriage shall be void in circumstances where either party loses his/her real and true intention to marry during the time that elapses between completion of the marriage notice form and submission of it. In order for the marriage to be declared void, the unwilling party should notify the other or the registrar that he/she no longer has the intention to marry. Otherwise, the marriage shall be considered valid and thus registered in the Family Registration Book. Meanwhile, in a case where one party becomes unconscious at the moment of the submission of the marriage notice after having expressed his/her intention to marry, the marriage shall be valid if either party can prove that there is no special circumstance indicating the unconscious party's withdrawal of intention to marry.[184]

169. In some cases, the parties may submit a marriage notice to the family registration office for the purpose of achieving particular ends, this is known as a sham marriage. Such ends may be, for example, in order to obtain Japanese nationality or to give their child the status of a legitimate child. Such a marriage shall be ineffective due to the lack of any real and true intention to marry.[185]

170. Both parties or any other interested third parties can claim that a marriage is void. On an application by such a person, the family court shall issue 'a determination corresponding to agreement'[186] after an investigation of the case (FAPA section 277). If any person objects to that determination, he/she can commence litigation in the family court (cf. PALA section 2(1)). When the parties to a marriage die, any interested person can take proceedings for void marriage against a public prosecutor (PALA section 12(3)).

III. Voidable Marriages

171. A marriage shall be voidable if, for instance, the marriage notice contains the name of a party who is below the minimum age for marriage but is nonetheless mistakenly accepted and registered in the Family Registration Book.[187] The parties,

184. SD 3 Apr. 1969 Minshu 23-4-709.
185. SD 31 Oct. 1969 Minshu 23-10-1894. In Fukuoka DD 7 Oct. 1993 Hanta 831-258, a district court declared the marriage to be void under the circumstances that, due to strict religious directions, the parties had to suspend cohabitation for six years after the time of submission of the marriage notice. They were uncertain as to whether they would start cohabitation even after the expiry of six years. They had submitted the notice for the convenience of their missionary activities.
186. This applies to the case where the parties reach an agreement that the marriage is void through *Chotei* proceedings at a family court.
187. Minors leave compulsory education at the age of 15 and some of them live independently. In this respect, some assert that the minimum age for marriage should be reduced to 15 for both parties. However, it is proposed that the age of majority including the minimum age for marriage should be changed to 18 years equally for men and women in accordance with revised s. 4 of the Civil Code.

their relatives or a public prosecutor can then apply for a revocation of the marriage. The public prosecutor will not be eligible to take such proceedings in the case where either party has died (Civ. sections 744(1) and 731).

172. A marriage shall also be voidable in the case of bigamy if either party is already married to a third party (Civ. sections 744(1) and 732). Bigamy not only provides grounds for declaring a marriage voidable but also constitutes a crime under the Criminal Code (Cri. section 184). Although very few cases of bigamy are ever reported, it may occur in the following situations: first, if one party marries a third party after a court has issued a determination declaring the previous spouse missing but the determination is subsequently revoked, or second, if one party remarries a third party after the dissolution by mutual consent of a previous marriage, but the dissolution is later declared void.

173. For the purpose of creating a valid remarriage, a woman was first required to wait six months after the dissolution of her previous marriage but is now required to wait for a hundred days after the Supreme Court decision in 2015. If she violates this requirement, the remarriage shall be voidable (Civ. sections 746 and 733).[188] However, this requirement does not apply if the woman is pregnant during the new marriage, or if her former husband has not been heard from for more than three years prior to the new marriage. In addition, a registrar can accept a marriage notice regardless of this requirement if a woman remarries her ex-husband, or if a divorce decree was issued either on the ground of one party being registered as a missing person, or on the ground of wilful desertion for six months, or if a woman is presumed to be too old to become pregnant.

174. A marriage shall be pronounced voidable if the parties are within the prohibited degrees of relationship, i.e., the prohibited degrees of consanguinity and affinity (Civ. sections 734 and 735).[189] For instance, a man shall not marry his direct blood relatives such as his mother, daughter, grandmother, granddaughter, sister, aunt or niece. Furthermore, he is also prohibited from marrying his relatives by affinities such as his wife's mother, grandmother, his stepdaughter or step-granddaughter. This rule applies even after the relationship by affinity has been terminated through either divorce or death. In the case of adoption, an adoptive parent (or the ascendant of the adoptive parent) is prohibited from marrying the adopted child (or the descendant of the adopted child) or the spouse of the adopted child (or

188. It is generally explained that this requirement aims to clarify whether the paternity of the baby belongs to the previous husband or the new husband. Some criticize that this requirement infringes upon the right to equality between the sexes by putting women in an unfair situation. Usually, a woman is unlikely to conceive a baby with her former husband around the time of divorce because divorce generally follows a period of separation. Furthermore, scientifically reliable measures such as DNA testing are now available for determining paternity. Consequently, it has been claimed that a woman should not need to wait for six months before entering into a new marriage. In the past, the courts have dismissed such a claim (SD 5 Dec. 1995 Hanji 1563-81) but the Supreme Court modified the rule in 2015 (SD 16 Dec. 2015 Minshu 69-8-2427).

189. Levirate and sororate marriage is valid under Japanese law.

the spouse of the descendant of the adopted child) during the period of adoption or even after dissolution of the adoption (Civ. sections 735 and 736).

175. Furthermore, marriage will be voidable if fraud or duress were employed in bringing it about (Civ. section 747(1)). If one party can prove that inaccurate or false information concerning the nature and personality of the other or any other relevant matters substantially influenced their decision to marry, that party can then revoke the marriage by reason of fraud. For instance, a marriage shall be voidable if a woman of 52 years disguises herself as a 24 year old in order to marry a man.[190] A marriage will also be declared voidable if it can be established that duress was used to bring about the marriage; that is to say that one party was forced to express their intention to marry due to grave fear caused by either the use of physical force or such measures as malicious threat or words.

176. The parties, their relatives (*see* Civ. section 725), or a prosecutor is eligible to apply to have the marriage declared voidable on the above-mentioned grounds except in the case of fraud or duress, where only the parties to the marriage can apply for such a declaration (Civ. section 747(1)). Meanwhile, in the case of bigamy or violation of the six-month waiting period, the current spouse or the ex-spouse of either party to the marriage is also eligible for making an application to have the marriage declared voidable.

177. Where a marriage has taken place between minors (*see* section 731), no interested party can contest the validity of the marriage once the minors reach the age of majority. However, minors themselves can revoke the marriage within three months of their attaining the age of majority unless they have already ratified the marriage since their attainment (Civ. section 745(2)).

178. A Marriage in which a woman violates the waiting period cannot be voided if this period has already passed since the date of either the dissolution, or the revocation of the former marriage, or if it is proved that a wife has become pregnant only after the new marriage was registered (Civ. section 746).

179. In the case of fraud or duress, neither party can claim the marriage to be voidable after a period of three months has expired from the date when he/she has discovered the fraud or escaped from the duress, or if the parties subsequently ratified the marriage (Civ. section 747(2)).

180. As stated earlier, the effects of marriage being declared voidable do not operate retrospectively, and the marriage is considered as having validly existed until the date of revocation (Civ. section 748(1)). In this respect, the effects of marriage being declared voidable are similar to those of divorce (*see* Civ. section 749):

(1) Concerning the child(ren) of the parties, he/she will be given the status of a legitimate child of the parties. He/she shall be rebuttably presumed to be the

190. Tokyo FD 26 Jul. 2006 TKC (LEX/DB28131218).

legitimate child of the husband if the wife became pregnant before the date of the revocation. Similar to divorce cases, the parties can make an agreement regarding the care and control of the child(ren) and/or their parental rights and duties.[191]

(2) The party who took his/her partner's family name at the time of marriage can change back to his/her original family name.

(3) Both parties are entitled to their division of the 'matrimonial' property. In terms of the arrangements as to which party will hold the genealogy and the estate for the purposes of ancestor worship, the same rule as for divorce cases shall apply.

(4) In the case of any transaction of property between the parties, each party is liable to return such property if there is found to be unjust enrichment (Civ. sections 748(2) and 703). If the party acted in bad faith at the time of the submission of the marriage notice, thus providing a ground for revocation, and acquired property from the other party, he/she is responsible for returning the whole benefit obtained from the marriage (Civ. section 748(3)). In addition, in such a case, the party who acted in bad faith shall be liable to pay damages to the other who was acting in good faith (Civ. section 748(3)).

---

191. The marriage of an uncle and niece was revoked because they were within the prohibited degrees of consanguinity, but their offspring was given the status of a legitimate child. After the dissolution of the marriage, the uncle and the other niece started to cohabite and had a child who was an illegitimate child by recognition of the paternity. In the case of succession by his death, the latter child was entitled to claim only half portion of the former child because of its illegitimacy (Tokyo DD 31 Oct. 1997 Hanta 1008-230).

Chapter 2. Termination of Marriage and Divorce

§1. Termination of Marriage

181. Marriage shall terminate on the death of either party or by divorce. In the event that either party to a marriage dies before the marriage notice is delivered to the family registration office, but such notice has already been posted by the parties, it is deemed that the marriage shall take effect momentarily and then immediately dissolved on the ground of the death of one of the parties (FRA section 47). On the dissolution of a marriage by either party's death or other grounds (*see* Part I Chapter 1 §3 Absentees), a surviving spouse is free to remarry, and the succession opens.

§2. Outline of Divorce

I. A Brief History of Divorce

182. Historically, the principle against the dissolution of marriage has not been enshrined in Japanese law. Although the details are unclear before the eighth century, it seems that a husband could declare that he would divorce his wife at any time during the marriage. After the eighth century, divorce by mutual consent was available and in addition the law laid down seven grounds for and three bars to divorce. Later, when the custom that a wife was absorbed into her husband's family through marriage became prevalent among ordinary citizens, it was commonly observed that a letter declaring the divorce was issued by a husband to his wife at the time of divorce as evidence to indicate that he was divorcing her and approved her remarrying. In this situation, a husband was required neither to prove any ground for divorce nor state anything in respect to any cause for the divorce. In the letter, all he was required to do was simply to state the fact that he was divorcing his wife. It has been pointed out that this custom illustrated the principle of male dominance over family life at the expense of the woman's interests, but recently some have claimed that this rule sometimes operated to save the woman because it did not necessarily result in the disclosure of any misconduct on the woman's part or of any other matrimonial disputes that might have occurred. For example, if a woman was divorced as a result of her adulterous behaviour, she could start her new life after the divorce relatively easily as the letter of divorce stated nothing about the real cause of the marital breakdown.

183. After the seventeenth century, this custom became much more widely used among ordinary people. However, there were some bars restricting the husband from freely exercising his right to divorce and also some grounds authorizing the wife to divorce her husband. For example, a husband who had spent all his wife's dowry would not be allowed to divorce his wife unless he could return it in full. In addition, if he disposed of his wife's trousseau without her consent, he was not then able to divorce her. However, a wife could obtain a divorce under certain conditions, for example, if she sheltered herself at a refuge, such as a temple.

184. For the samurai class, divorce was available if the mutual consent of the heads of the husband's family and the wife's family was obtained and also the permission of their lord. In this respect, a more rigid procedure for divorce applied to the samurai class.

185. In 1873 after the Meiji Restoration, a law was enacted to allow either party to a marriage to claim divorce through legal process. Subsequently, the Civil Code of 1898 stipulated the procedure of divorce by mutual consent and divorce by litigation on a fault basis. Unlike Christian countries, divorce by mutual consent was accepted in Japanese society without strong opposition; this was due to the fact that divorce was considered a private matter between two family groups. Strong religious influences restricting divorce were rarely observed in Japanese society, although the prevailing view was that divorce litigation in a courtroom was akin to 'washing one's dirty linen in public' and brought shame upon the family, thus the whole procedure should be kept closed and private.[192] In this respect, while in principle divorce by mutual consent characterized modern divorce law – i.e., the parties could dissolve their marriage by their own free will – divorce by mutual consent under the Civil Code reflected in practice the conservative views of society. Indeed, under the divorce law set out in the Civil Code of 1898, equality of the sexes, one of the fundamental principles of modern divorce law, was unlikely to ever be achieved. For instance, a wife's adulterous behaviour constituted unconditionally a ground for divorce while that of the husband was treated as such a ground only if he was declared guilty of adultery in a criminal court of law. However, the courts, in later years, delivered some decisions regarding this matter, which brought the same justice to wives and improved their legal status.[193] As a result, equality of the sexes was gradually achieved under the Civil Code of 1898.

186. In 1947, the parts of the Civil Code relating to family and succession were completely revised in accordance with the principle of Article 24 of the Constitution,[194] leading to the introduction of new divorce procedures; divorce by mutual consent, divorce through family court mediation, divorce by a family court determination and divorce by a decree of an ordinary court (family court since 2003). With respect to judicial separation, no provision was enacted. The revised family law laid down grounds for divorce on the basis of the no-fault principle and provisions on securing the financial status of the parties after divorce.

192. This applied to certain social classes such as samurai families, upper merchants and wealthy farmers but not to the lowest social classes who had no family name to be shamed.
193. In STD 19 Dec. 1918 Minroku 24-2364, the court granted a divorce to the wife on the ground of behaviour constituting a serious insult to the spouse in the case of her husband's adultery.
194. It stipulates '(1) Marriage shall be based only on the mutual consent of both sexes and it shall be maintained through mutual cooperation with the equal rights of husband and wife as a basis. (2) With regard to the choice of spouse, property rights, inheritance, choice of domicile, divorce and other matters pertaining to marriage and the family, laws shall be enacted from the standpoint of individual dignity and the essential equality of the sexes.'

II. Current Divorce Law and the Voice for Reform

187. Since the 1960s, social and economic changes have had a significant effect on families. Accordingly, calls for reform of family law were voiced among some quarters since several provisions in the family law were far removed from the reality of ordinary family life. The Deliberative Council on the Legal System began to revise several provisions of family law in order to meet the current needs of the people. In 1994, the Committee publicized their recommendations among which they suggested that a new five-year separation clause should be inserted into section 770(1) for advancing the no-fault principle of divorce. Also, a new provision on allocation and distribution of matrimonial property at the time of divorce was recommended to be implemented for the purpose of achieving equality of both parties, and the addition of a new provision on visitation was also suggested. However, these recommendations have not been realized due to the strong opposition from conservative groups claiming that the new idea on divorce matters would be harmful to maintaining stable family life.

§3. Divorce by Mutual Consent

I. Procedure of Divorce by Mutual Consent

188. Divorce shall take effect when the parties submit a notice of divorce by mutual consent to the family registration office after having privately reached an agreement on the divorce, financial matters and arrangements regarding child(ren), if any (Civ. section 763).[195] Under this procedure, the parties are simply required to fill in a divorce notice form stating that they hold a real intention to divorce and that one party will retain the parental rights and duties after divorce and then sign in person on the notice form. The parties can notify their divorce to a family registrar orally if they appear at the family registration office with two competent witnesses and fulfil the aforementioned requirements. In the case that a third party writes the name of each party on the divorce notice form on their behalf, such a notice can be accepted as valid as long as the parties have a real and free intention to divorce.[196] In this respect, the simplicity, speed and economy of divorce by mutual consent can meet the needs of busy parties.

II. Special Notice to Veto One Party's Submission of a 'Mutual Consent' Divorce Notice

189. Due to the simplicity of procedure of divorce by mutual consent, a party may submit a divorce notice completed by himself/herself to the family registration office without the knowledge of the other party to the marriage. In addition, one

195. In the case of divorce involving a Japanese and a non-Japanese party, the Japanese divorce law – the law of habitual residence – usually applies.
196. SD 31 Jan. 1969 Kagetsu 21-7-67.

party may submit a divorce notice to the family registration office where the other party has given their consent to the divorce but has subsequently withdrawn it and has notified such withdrawal to the party submitting the notice. In these cases, the registrar will accept and register such a divorce notice because he/she has no power to investigate whether both parties continue to have a real intention to divorce but only the authority to examine any defects in the formalities of the divorce notice. To avoid such one-sided submission of a divorce notice, a party is eligible to notify the relevant family registration office of his/her principal address that any notice of divorce submitted on his/her behalf should not be accepted and registered. Once this notice has been made, the registrar must not accept any divorce notice unless he/she has confirmed that the divorce notice has been genuinely submitted (FRA sections 27-2(3)–(5)).[197] This special notice shall be valid until withdrawal by the applicant. In the case of divorce between a Japanese and non-Japanese, the latter is eligible to submit this notice to the relevant family registration office of the respondent's principal address.

190. If the family registration office discovers that it has mistakenly accepted a notice of divorce by consent of a spouse while a special notice against divorce has already been submitted by the other spouse, the family registration office must correct the description of divorce by consent on its motion.[198]

III. Divorce by Mutual Consent Deemed as Void or Voidable

191. Divorce shall only be effective on the basis of the parties' real intention to divorce and submission of a divorce notice to the family registration office. Accordingly, divorce by mutual consent shall not take place if either party lacks a real intention to divorce[199] or a valid notice is not submitted.

192. As mentioned earlier, the simplicity of the procedure of divorce by mutual consent may cause some problematic circumstances:

(1) A third party can submit a divorce notice to the registrar without any knowledge of the parties to the marriage; one partner can also submit a divorce notice without the knowledge of the other partner.[200]

---

197. A party can submit a notice to the family registration office of his/her residence which would then be transferred to the office of his/her principal address.
198. Kobe FO 16 Apr. 1974 Kagetsu 27-4-78.
199. Sapporo HD in 29 May 1980 (Hanta 419-116) held that there was no real intention to divorce if one party unwillingly signed in person under the threat of violence from the other. It was pronounced in Tokyo DH 21 Dec. 1965 (Hanji 460-53) that the party had a true intention to divorce if he/she had accepted through agreement an offer of solatium by the other party.
200. In a very rare case, Z submitted a divorce notice against his wife's (X's) will. Z then submitted a notice to register his marriage to Y, without Y's knowledge. Y later ratified this marriage, but then Z submitted a divorce notice terminating his marriage to Y, without Y's knowledge or permission. Z then submitted another notice of his marriage to X, without X's knowledge. Under such circumstances, X claimed that the first divorce should be void because of the lack of a real intention to divorce (Fukuoka HD 16 Mar. 1994 Hanta 860-247).

(2) A couple may submit a divorce notice, despite having no real intention to divorce in order to achieve particular legal consequences: e.g., a sham divorce.[201]
(3) A divorce notice may be completed under duress or fraud.

193. Under the current legal practice, in the case of (1), such divorce will be void due to a lack of intention to divorce on the part of the parties. As for case (2), such divorce will be valid because the parties are considered to have a real intention to submit the divorce notice to the registrar on the basis that such notice was presented to the office,[202] notwithstanding their lack of 'intention' to terminate their de facto marital life. In case (3), duress or fraud will render the divorce voidable (Civ. sections 764 and 747). If one party is, for instance, forced to sign the notice in person, he/she is subsequently eligible to rescind the divorce on the ground of a lack of real intention. An individual can revoke divorce by reason of fraud if he/she mistakenly agreed to the divorce upon believing the promise of the other party that they would surely be remarried sometime in the future after first dissolving their marriage.[203]

194. Similar to the case of marriage, a question may arise as to the forming of the divorce process when a real intention to divorce should be necessary. As a rule, the law requires that such an intention should exist at the time that the divorce notice is drawn up and at the time of the submission of the notice to the family registration office. A party is entitled to withdraw their intention to divorce before the time the notice is accepted and registered. For the purpose of validating the withdrawal, the party should inform their change of mind either to the other party or to the registrar.[204]

195. A party to the divorce is eligible to contend that the divorce should be void. In the case that a petitioner is a person with limited capacity, he/she can dispute the validity of the divorce unless he/she loses the capacity to understand the meaning and effects of his/her act (PALA section 13(1)). However, a judge can appoint a lawyer as a guardian *ad litem* either on application or at its own motion for the purpose of legal proceedings (PALA section 13(2)). Where one party intends to render the divorce void after the death of the other party, he/she must bring litigation against a prosecutor (PALA section 12(3)). In such a case, litigation shall terminate if the petitioner dies. If one party to a marriage submits to the registrar a notice of divorce by mutual consent without obtaining the consent of the other and subsequently claims nullity of the divorce by reason of a defective notice (lack of mutual consent of both parties), a court must accept such a petition even if the petition is made after

---

201. For instance, in order to avoid the seizure of a husband's property by a third party, a couple may divorce and transfer his assets to her name under the guise of 'allocation of the matrimonial property' as effect of divorce (*see* Civ. s. 768).
202. SD 28 Nov. 1963 Minshu 17-11-1469 where the wife agreed to divorce in order to give her husband the status of the head of their family.
203. Nagano DD 26 Feb. 1971 Kagetsu 24-11-76.
204. SD 7 Aug. 1959 Minshu 13-10-1251.

the death of the other party.[205] Any petition relating to the invalidity of divorce shall be dealt with first at the family court (by family court mediation or a family court determination and then a family court decree) (PALA sections 2 and 4).

196. Only the parties to a marriage are entitled to seek a declaration that the divorce is voidable on the grounds of fraud or duress (Civ. section 747(1)). The petition should be brought to a family court within three months of the date when he/she discovers the fraud or has been released from duress (Civ. section 747(2)). This petition shall follow a similar procedure as that applied to a petition for a divorce to be declared void (*see* FALA section 2(1)).

197. When a divorce is declared either void or voidable, the marriage will continue. For instance, it may happen that a divorce is void due to the lack of mutual consent of both parties where the divorce was registered mistakenly on the false submission of a divorce notice by one party without the consent of the other. If one party is remarried to someone after the registration of divorce which could potentially be void afterwards, the other party may petition for the subsequent marriage to be declared voidable on the ground of bigamy even before he/she obtains either a family court decision (determination or decree) pronouncing that the divorce was void.[206] In the case of a voidable divorce, the divorce shall be regarded valid until the court declares it is voidable. Once a divorce is declared voidable, the valid marriage will continue.

198. If a divorce is pronounced void due to the lack of real consent of one or both of the parties, subsequent ratification by one or both of the parties can render the divorce valid. Ratification should be made in the form of oral or written declaration or some other behaviour by the parties. The following are regarded as acts of ratification of a divorce: an agreement in which one party accepts solatium during a mediation session at a family court,[207] submission of a marriage notice by a husband to another woman while the previous submission of a divorce notice by his 'ex-wife' is in his knowledge,[208] and taking no action against submission of a divorce notice by the other party.[209] However, the fact that one party submits a notice of divorce by mutual consent during any period of separation shall not be regarded as ratification of an invalid divorce.[210]

IV. De Facto Divorce

199. Since judicial separation is not available under current family law in Japan, all effects of marriage generally continue to take place even after a couple has separated. Accordingly, a question may arise as to whether the effects of divorce should

205. Nagoya HD 27 Feb. 1985 Hanta 552-263.
206. SD 9 Mar. 1978 Kagetsu 31-3-79.
207. SD 8 Dec. 1967 Kagetsu 20-3-55.
208. Tokyo HD 13 Nov. 1969 Kamin 20-11/12-815.
209. Tokyo DD 30 Jan. 1981 Hanta 443-132.
210. Tokyo HD 23 Dec. 1971 Hanta 275-318.

be applied to a separated couple whose relationship has irretrievably broken down. In many cases, it has been decided that the consequences of divorce shall take place for such a couple. For instance, a court held that a wife who had lived apart from her husband for a prolonged period of time should not have any entitlement to the pension awarded on the death of one's husband considering that she was not regarded as his 'wife' as stated in the Friendly Society Act (Kyosai Kumiai Ho).[211] In respect of the birth of a child, a court pronounced that a child should not be presumed to be fully legitimate if he/she was born to a de facto divorced couple.[212] Moreover, a court made a decision on the care and control of children involved in their parents' separation by applying the provision usually applied to a divorced couple.[213]

§4. Procedure and Grounds for Divorce

I. Divorce at Family Court

A. Divorce Through Family Court Mediation

200. When a couple fails to reach an agreement on their divorce and related matters, they are required to apply to a family court for divorce mediation under the rule of mandatory mediation prior to litigation (FAPA section 257). Despite this rule, a party to a marriage can bring a case to a family court seeking a divorce decree under the following circumstances: the whereabouts of the other party is unknown (both parties are required to attend mediation sessions), the other party has no capacity to understand the meaning and effects of an act (a valid agreement shall not take place if he/she is not of sound mind), or a court considers that family court mediation is inappropriate for resolving this particular case.

201. A party is eligible to apply for in-court mediation at any time either to the family court whose jurisdiction covers the residence of the respondent party or to that family court that the parties choose by agreement (FAPA section 66). While a representative of a party to a marriage is entitled to make an application for mediation, it is the rule that both parties should appear in person at each session of the family court mediation. No agreement on divorce through mediation shall take place through any representatives of the parties. However, when either party cannot attend mediation sessions for some reason, the representatives of both parties can make an agreement at a mediation session that the parties will submit a notice of 'divorce by mutual consent', not 'divorce through family court mediation'. Furthermore, when

211. SD 14 Apr. 1983 Minshu 37-3-270. In SD 21 Apr. 2005 Hanta 1180-171, a cohabitee was entitled to claim the payment as 'spouse' of a deceased due to the fact that the marriage had already broken down and the period of cohabitation was long.
212. SD 29 May 1969 Minshu 23-6-1064.
213. SD 10 Apr. 1997 Minshu 51-4-1972 (maintenance case) and SD 1 May 2000 Minshu 54-5-1607 (contact case).

either party fails to appear at the mediation sessions, a family court can issue a family court determination as an alternative to family court mediation if it thinks fit to do so (FAPA section 284).

202. On an application for divorce through family court mediation, a family court mediation committee will commence mediation sessions privately. The committee comprises one family court judge,[214] and at least two lay family affairs mediators[215] (one man and one woman) who will encourage and help the parties to reach an agreement over the divorce and other relevant issues. A family court mediation committee can order a family court investigation officer to submit a report on the details of a case in order to assist effective mediation if it thinks it necessary. Sometimes, the committee may refer a party to the medical section of a family court in the hope of alleviating the hostility between the parties through counselling or other medical treatment.

203. In general, the parties are required to attend mediation sessions, but both parties need not appear in the same mediation room during a mediation session. If a family court mediation committee thinks it necessary, it can interview either party separately and assist them to exchange information indirectly. For the mediation procedure, it not necessary for the parties to employ their own lawyers since the committee, of which one member is a family court judge, can protect the interests of both parties from a legal perspective. In this respect, family court mediation is regarded as a 'simple, safe and economical way of divorce that is easily accessible'.[216] Meanwhile, safety of the parties has become a critical issue in relation to family court mediation following the killing of a wife on family court premises by her husband when she appeared at a session of the family court mediation in 2019.[217]

204. When the parties reach an agreement on divorce through in-court mediation, a record of the mediation, the effects of which are equivalent to those of a court decree, shall be issued (FAPA section 268). If a family court mediation committee thinks it necessary, the committee can order a provisional resolution in order to protect the interests of the parties.[218] If the parties succeed in agreeing on their divorce

---

214. A lawyer who has experienced more than five years in practice can be appointed as a part-time family mediation judge by the Supreme Court (FAPA s. 250). He/she has authority over issues arising from mediation (FAPA s. 251).
215. A family court affairs mediator is a part-time civil servant appointed by the Supreme Court from the general public. No special qualifications are required for the appointment except that the person must be a good citizen. In practice, lawyers are likely to be allocated to particular cases such as the adjustment of estates of a deceased person for which mediators do need some legal knowledge.
216. Currently, parties are required to pay approximately JPY 2,000 as a fee for mediation to a court (this excludes the payments for any lawyers employed by either party).
217. Asahi Digital 20 Mar. 2019 (https://www.asahi.com/articles/ASM3N56RKM3NUTIL03T.html).
218. In Sapporo FO 5 Nov. 1962 Kagetsu 15-20-160 an application for divorce mediation was made by a wife on the ground of her husband's serious drinking habit. The family court pronounced a provisional resolution ordering him to stop his drinking habit and accept medical treatment under the guidance of the family court investigation officer.

but fail to reach an agreement regarding their children, only a record of the mediation on divorce shall be issued, and then a family court will grant one of the parents the parental rights and duties through a family court determination. Within ten days after the date of agreement of divorce through a family court mediation, either party must submit to a registration office the notice of divorce attached with a full form of the record of divorce (FRA sections 77(1) and 63), while the family court must notify the divorce to the relevant registration office of the parties' principal address.

205. A party can withdraw from mediation at any time. Furthermore, if the parties fail to reach an agreement on divorce through in-court mediation, mediation will terminate. If a family court mediation committee finds that there is little prospect of the parties reaching an agreement through mediation and the family court will not issue a determination, the committee can conclude the mediation (FAPA section 272). In addition, the committee can end the mediation if it considers that any agreement made by the parties is inappropriate.

B. Divorce by Family Court Determination

206. In cases where the parties fail to reach any agreement on divorce through family court mediation, a family court, if it deems it necessary, can issue 'a determination as an alternative to family court mediation' by hearing the views of the mediators and having in mind an equitable outcome for both parties and considering all the circumstances, to the extent that the determination is not inconsistent with the aim of the application of the parties (FAPA section 284). In some cases, either party may find it difficult to attend in-court mediation sessions due to the reason stated in the next paragraph; in these cases, the family court can determine an alternative to family court mediation (FAPA section 277).[219] A determination can be issued under such reasoning in cases of divorce, solatium for a divorced party, adjustment and allocation of the matrimonial property and appointment of a parent with parental rights and duties.

207. The circumstances in which the family court can issue a determination as an alternative to family court mediation are as follows: both parties have a real intention to divorce, but either or both parties find it difficult to attend mediation sessions because they are living abroad,[220] or due to the nature of their work,[221] imprisonment[222] or sickness.[223] Furthermore, a family court can make a determination if it finds that an applicant has a clear intention to divorce, but a respondent

219. In Yamaga Branch of Kumamoto FO 20 Aug. 1964 Kagetsu 16-12-55, the family court held that such a determination could be made in a case where the parties reached an agreement on all matters of a divorce except that relating to their children.
220. In Hachioji Branch of Tokyo FO 10 Sep. 1986 Kagetsu 39-3-60, a husband was living in Germany and the wife in Japan.
221. A husband was employed as a sailor on an international route (Fukuoka FO 18 Sep. 1958 Kagetsu 10-10-69).
222. Kobe FO 9 Aug. 1957 Kagetsu 9-9-32.
223. Kokura Branch of Fukuoka FO 18 Oct. 1988 Kagetsu 41-1-162.

wilfully refuses to attend mediation sessions in spite of his/her availability to attend.[224] In the case of an absent party, a family court is generally not allowed to issue a determination for divorce because of the need to protect the right of that party to challenge the determination. However, in such a case, the family court can issue a determination if it is satisfied under all circumstances that both parties have a real intention to divorce. In addition, the family court can make such a determination in a case where the absent party mistakenly believes that he/she does not need to appear at the final session of the mediation because an agreement has been achieved during previous sessions.[225]

208. A family court can make a determination as an alternative to family court mediation on the basis of the grounds for divorce stipulated in section 770 of the Civil Code (cf. Part II Chapter 2). A family court is authorized to exercise its discretionary power over the following issues 'in so far as it is not inconsistent with the intent of the application of the parties': divorce, appointment of a parent with s and duties, solatium for divorce, resolution over care and control of children, maintenance of children after divorce and visitation arrangements. A family court cannot, however, make a decision on any matters to which the parties do not refer in the application. If either party objects to the determination, he/she can take the case to a high court within fourteen days from the date of the determination being issued, and seek to invalidate the determination (FAPA section 286).

209. In addition to a determination as an alternative to family court mediation, a family court can also issue a determination in lieu of an agreement (FAPA section 277).[226] For example, cases where the validity of a divorce or the dissolution of adoption are in contest should be heard in accordance with the Personal Affairs Litigation Act. However, the parties are entitled to apply for mediation to the family court under the rule of mandatory mediation prior to litigation and can reach an agreement on matters which should have been decided under the Personal Affairs Litigation Act. In such case, the family court can make a determination as an alternative to an agreement on its motion after having investigated the case and examined all the circumstances.

C. Divorce by Court Decree

210. When a couple fails to reach an agreement on divorce by mutual consent, one party can institute divorce litigation at a family court whose jurisdiction covers their current address (PALA sections 2 and 4). The procedure of divorce litigation is based mainly on an inquisitorial rather than an adversarial approach.

224. Tokyo FO 28 Jul. 1967 Kagetsu 20-2-60.
225. Fukuoka FO 25 Apr. 1957 Kagetsu 9-4-75.
226. For non-Japanese parties from jurisdictions which only accept divorces pronounced by a court, this type of determination shall be applied (Tokyo FO 25 Apr. 1983 Hanji 1123-105).

211. Where a defendant is missing, a court will commence divorce litigation after it has issued service by publication (the Civil Litigation Proceedings Act section 110)[227] and will seek the views of the defendant's relatives in lieu of listening to a statement of the missing defendant himself/herself.

212. A spouse with limited capacity is eligible to be a party to divorce litigation only if he/she has the capacity to understand the meaning and effects of his/her acts. Where a defendant spouse is continuously mentally unstable but is not declared to be a ward of adult guardianship, the plaintiff spouse is first required to make an application to a family court to issue a determination declaring the defendant spouse to be a ward of adult guardianship, whereby a guardian or a supervisor to a guardian will be appointed for him/her. The plaintiff can then bring divorce litigation against either the guardian or the supervisor (PALA section 14).

II. Grounds for Divorce

213. Section 770(1) stipulates five grounds for divorce on the basis of a no-fault divorce principle. These grounds are as follows:

(i) the defendant has committed unchaste conduct;
(ii) the defendant has maliciously deserted the plaintiff;
(iii) the defendant has not been heard from for three years or more;
(iv) the defendant has had an incurable impairment of, or a disturbance in the functioning of, the mind or brain
(v) other serious circumstances under which the parties cannot reasonably be expected to continue the marriage.

A. *Unchaste Conduct*

214. 'Unchaste conduct' covers adultery and other conducts of infidelity. This ground is established where a spouse commits an unchaste act voluntarily, whether or not the other party to the misconduct is involved on a voluntary basis. Accordingly, if a husband raped a third party, his conduct shall be regarded as adultery,[228] or if a wife is artificially inseminated with a donor's sperm without her husband's consent, this will constitute unchaste conduct and thus provide a ground for divorce. Any purpose behind engaging in the unchaste conduct will in no way legitimatize that conduct in the eyes of the law, and it remains a ground for divorce regardless

227. For instance, an appellee (respondent) used a service by publication for divorce litigation in a case where the appellant resided in Germany (SD 24 Jun. 1996 Minshu 50-7-1451). However, if a plaintiff obtains a divorce decree through service by publication either knowing a defendant's whereabouts or failing to know it at serious fault, the defendant can seek a re-trial of the case by claiming the service to be void or voidable (Cf. the Civil Litigation Proceedings Act s. 338 and Yokohama DD 6 Sep. 1978 Hanji 938-93).
228. SD 15 Nov. 1973 Minshu 27-10-1323.

of motive[229] If either spouse has a homosexual relationship with another person, it is deemed not to be unchaste conduct but rather to fall under the fifth ground of other serious circumstances.

B. Malicious Desertion

215. 'Malicious desertion' constitutes a violation of one's matrimonial obligation as laid down in section 752: cohabitation, cooperation and support during marriage. As well as instances in which one spouse leaves the family home,[230] if a spouse expels the other from the family home and refuses without good reason to allow him/her to return, that will also constitute malicious desertion. A court will find grounds for malicious desertion if a plaintiff can prove that the defendant has deserted him/her either maliciously or without reasonable cause. While there is no clear definition of desertion under the law, in one case the court granted a divorce of nine months of separation.[231]

216. A plaintiff will lose his/her case for divorce if the defendant can satisfy the court that there was a reasonable ground for living apart such as the existence of a mutual agreement to separate, the defendant being hospitalized, or the defendant being required to travel on business or the defendant being forced to leave the matrimonial home on the ground that the defendant could not reasonably be expected to live together with the plaintiff.

C. The Whereabouts of the Defendant Is Unknown

217. The fact that a defendant has not been heard from for three years or more constitutes a ground for divorce. A court will pronounce a divorce decree on this ground by considering all the circumstances including the period of absence, the age of the defendant and his/her health. Unlike dissolution of marriage by a family court determination declaring a partner is missing, divorce shall not be revoked if the absent defendant appears after the divorce.

D. Mental Health Condition of a Defendant

218. The court will issue a divorce decree if the parties cannot reasonably be expected to cohabit due to a lack of emotional communication caused by the incurable insanity of the defendant. In granting the divorce, the court will focus mainly on whether the parties can live together, rather than assessing the actual degree of

229. It was held in SD 4 Jun. 1963 Kagetsu 15-9-179 that a wife was responsible for unchaste conduct when she was engaged in prostitution in order to financially support her family after her husband had deserted them.
230. SD 17 Sep. 1964 Minshu 18-7-1461.
231. Iiyama Branch of Nagano DD 15 Nov. 1965 Hanji 457-53.

insanity. In this respect, when it is declared that the defendant becomes a ward of adult guardianship by reason of insanity, a divorce decree will not be made unless the court has judged the insanity to be intolerable for the purpose of continuing married life.[232]

219. A court shall not regard a defendant as a person with a mental health condition if he/she can manage to look after himself/herself, perform simple tasks or cope with social life with the assistance and protection of either his/her family or medical doctors. Whereas, in the case where the defendant has temporarily recovered from insanity, he/she is 'still considered to have an incurable impairment of, or a disturbance in the functioning of, the mind or brain unless the court can find any implication that the parties should be reasonably expected to live together'.[233]

220. When one spouse claims divorce by reason of having an incurable impairment of, or a disturbance in the functioning of, the mind or brain, a court will generally apply rigid criteria and thus pronounce divorce by invoking section 770(2) unless a plaintiff can satisfy the court that he/she can provide sufficient and practical measures for securing the well-being of the defendant after divorce.[234] Thus the court is likely to consider who will financially support the defendant, whether appropriate medical care will be provided for him/her, and what proportion of the matrimonial property will be allocated to the defendant. In considering all the circumstances, if the court finds that the defendant will at least be financially secure after a divorce it will in practice normally grant the divorce.[235]

221. As for the procedure for divorce on this ground, a plaintiff will make an application for appointing a guardian of an adult for the defendant spouse and he/she will file for divorce litigation against the guardian of an adult (PALA section 14(1)). When a plaintiff has already been appointed as a guardian of an adult for the defendant spouse, he/she will apply for the appointment of a supervisor of the guardian of an adult (PALA section 14(2)).

E. Irretrievable Breakdown of Marriage

222. Other serious circumstances under which parties cannot reasonably be expected to continue the marriage and thus constitute grounds for divorce reflect the principle of divorce without allocating fault. Under this ground, a judge can grant a divorce if he/she is satisfied that the marriage has irretrievably broken down. In coming to a decision, the judge should take into account all the circumstances, such as the respective behaviour of the parties during the marriage, the length of the marriage and the separation, any sincere intention to continue the marriage, the circumstances regarding any children, the age of the parties and any children, the status of

232. For cases of Alzheimer's dementia or comatose patient, *see* para. 224.
233. SD 24 Nov. 1970 Minshu 24-12-1943.
234. SD 25 Jul. 1958 Minshu 12-12-1823.
235. SD 24 Nov. 1970 Minshu 24-12-1943.

employment of the parties and their financial situations, and any other matters relating to the marriage. If the court finds any prospect of reconciliation after considering these matters, it shall not, as a rule, grant a divorce. An example case is where a plaintiff husband was not granted a divorce even after a thirty-year period of separation as the court considered that there remained a possibility of reconciliation of the parties.[236]

223. It is not uncommon for a plaintiff to invoke ground (v) in addition to one other (grounds (i)–(iv)) in his/her application for a divorce when he/she considers that one ground alone will not be strong enough to establish sufficient grounds for divorce. For example, a court granted a divorce to a plaintiff wife not by reason of ground (i) but of ground (v) when it dismissed her claim that her husband's frequent visits to a woman during their marriage constituted 'adultery' as laid down underground(i).[237] While the fact that a husband is often away from home on business or for other reasons will not constitute sufficient ground under (ii) 'malicious desertion', it will be sufficient underground (v).[238] Where the defendant has not been heard from for just two years, ground (v) instead of ground (iii) can be employed.[239] In a case where the defendant had completely recovered from manic-depressive psychosis, the court declared a divorce not on the basis of ground (iv) but on that of ground (v), having judged that the marital relationship had already irretrievably broken down after ten years of separation caused by the defendant's hospitalization.[240]

224. A court may confirm that a marriage has irretrievably broken down by reason of ground (v) when it finds one or more of the following facts:

– Cruelty or violence on the part of the defendant so that the plaintiff cannot reasonably be expected to continue to live with the defendant. If such cruelty or violence occurs only one time but is nevertheless regarded as sufficiently serious, it shall be considered as sufficient proof of the breakdown. Issues of domestic violence – particularly violence between spouses – are increasingly recognized by society. Indeed, it has been reported that the number of cases reported domestic violence has increased significantly since 1990s. In 2001 the so-called Domestic Violence Act[241] was enacted in order to provide protection and prevention of violence by a partner through a court order.[242] Where emergency protection is needed, local governments and voluntary organizations do now arrange refuges for victims throughout the county.

236. SD 7 Jun. 1963 Hanji 338-3.
237. Tokyo HD 30 Nov. 1972 Hanji 688-60.
238. Osaka DD 27 Jun 1968 Hanji 533-56.
239. Tokyo DD 13 May 1963 Hanji 339-32.
240. Tokyo HD 22 Dec. 1988 Hanji 1301-97.
241. The Prevention and Protection of a Victim of Violence by Spouse and Partners Act 2001 (latest revision 2006). In this Act 'violence' includes physical and verbal violence injuring one's mind and body (DVA s. 2).
242. A court can issue a protection order such as non-molestation order and occupation order (DVA s. 10).

- Serious insult to the plaintiff by the defendant. If the defendant regularly reviles the plaintiff or ignores him/her as a result of which conduct the latter gives up continuing the marriage, the defendant's behaviour is construed as a serious insult to the plaintiff.
- Wasteful habits, unwillingness to work, or running into debt without good cause. The fact that the defendant is unwilling to work without good reason shall constitute a serious circumstance under which the parties cannot reasonably be expected to continue the marriage. For example, if the defendant frequently changes his/her job without serious consideration of his/her life plan, or he/she repeatedly gets into debt or wastes money without good cause, such behaviour will be judged as a sign of marital breakdown. However, in the case where the defendant runs into debt in trying to financially support the family, such a case for the debt will be considered reasonable and thus not an indication of marital breakdown.
- The defendant's involvement in criminal offences.[243]
- Serious discord between the defendant and the relatives of the plaintiff. A court usually grants a divorce by taking into account facts such as the defendant's discord with the plaintiff's relatives and failing to make sincere efforts to resolve such conflicts.
- Problems relating to the parties' sexual relationship. The fact that the defendant lacks the capacity to engage in sexual intercourse due to a physical defect,[244] or is inclined to demand abnormal sexual practice,[245] or is homosexual[246] shall be accepted as proof of marital breakdown.
- Sickness or physical defects on the part of the defendant shall not alone constitute proof of a marital breakdown. Only when the defendant's sickness or physical defect leads to a situation where the plaintiff cannot reasonably be expected to live with the defendant, will the court grant a divorce decree. In one particular case,[247] the wife had suffered from senile dementia for some time and the court issued a divorce decree in favour of the husband stating that the wife's senile dementia had brought about their marital breakdown. In another case, a court granted a divorce to a husband because there was no prospect of his wife to recovering from a coma due to a brain tumour.[248]
- Breach of the undertakings of the matrimonial obligation. The fact that the defendant fails to undertake domestic tasks due to his/her frequent participation in a particular hobby, or spends little time caring for family members due to excessive involvement in religious activities shall be deemed as a proof of marital breakdown.[249]

---

243. Niigata DD 30 Aug. 1967 Hanji 519-84.
244. *See* SD 6 Feb 1962 Minshu 16-2-206.
245. Osaka DD 23 Jun. 1960 Hanji 237-27.
246. In Nagoya DD 29 Feb. 1972 Hanji 670-77 the court held that the defendant's homosexual relationship did not constitute 'adultery' but instead an 'irretrievable breakdown of the marriage'.
247. Nagano DD 17 Sep. 1990 Kagetsu 43-6-34.
248. Yokosuka Branch of Yokohama DD 21 Dec. 1993 Hanji 1501-129.
249. Osaka HD 14 Dec. 1990 Hanji 1384-55.

- Lack of emotional communication leading to the plaintiff not being reasonably expected to live with the defendant.[250] Since a judge will sometimes evaluate the degree of lack of emotional communication by his/her own subjective standards, this factor may give rise to some difficulty for a plaintiff.[251]
- Long period of separation. In considering all the surrounding circumstances, a court may consider a long-term separation as a sign of irretrievable marital breakdown.
- A court is likely to find that there has been an irretrievable breakdown of marriage if the defendant has brought about a counter-claim for divorce to the plaintiff's claim.

III. Divorce Application by a Guilty Party

225. There is no legal bar prohibiting the party responsible for the marital breakdown from petitioning divorce on the basis of section 770(1)(v) of the Civil Code. Consequently, the courts have produced a considerable body of case law on whether or not to grant a divorce to a guilty party. Until 1987, the Supreme Court generally dismissed petition by guilty parties for the purpose of protecting the innocent parties. The Supreme Court stated as a rule that such claims by guilty parties should be seen as an abuse of rights or contravening the principle of fairness and equity.[252] However, since 1987,[253] the Supreme Court has granted divorces to guilty parties under certain conditions: (1) the marital relationship has become merely nominal after a long-term separation; (2) the couple has no children to be cared for and supported;[254] and (3) the guilty party has provided or can afford to provide sufficient measures to secure the innocent party's financial, social and emotional stability after the divorce.

226. When a court is assessing whether the term of separation is sufficient proof of a breakdown of marriage, it will compare the term of separation with the term of marriage. As a result, in a particular case the court did not grant a divorce to a couple who had been separated for eleven years during eighteen years of marriage,[255] but in another case it gave a divorce decree to a couple who had been separated for ten years out of the twelve years that they had been married.[256] In addition, a court will take account of the behaviour of the guilty party, such as to what extent

250. Osaka HD 26 May 2009 Kagetsu 62-4-85.
251. Okazaki Branch of Nagoya DD 20 Sep. 1991 Hanji 1409-97 rejected a divorce petition by a wife whose husband dominated the family life for over thirty years and stated that she should continue her marriage and make efforts for finding 'a blue bird' in somewhere close to her in the future.
252. SD 19 Feb. 1952 Minshu 6-2-110.
253. SD 2 Sep. 1987 Minshu 41-6-1243.
254. In SD 8 Feb. 1994 Kagetsu 46-9-59, the Supreme Court granted a divorce to the guilty party for the reason that the minor involved, who was 17 years old, would be independent in the very near future. In addition, the Supreme Court found that the innocent party and child had been supported financially by the guilty party but that the innocent party had no sincere intention of maintaining their marriage.
255. Tokyo HD 23 Aug. 1988 Hanji 1288-86.
256. SD 8 Dec. 1988 Kagetsu 41-3-145.

he/she has financially supported the innocent party during the separation, as well as the behaviour of an innocent party during the marriage.[257] A court is likely to grant a divorce to a guilty party where it finds that he/she has provided sufficient maintenance for the innocent party. However, a court will not issue a divorce decree if it predicts that the innocent party will face financial difficulties in the foreseeable future.[258]

IV. Bar to Divorce

227. Even if a court finds that one of the grounds (i)–(iv) exists, it may not grant a divorce if it thinks it is not the right decision to make after considering all the circumstances of the case (Civ. section 770(2)). This clause, which allows the judge a certain amount of discretion, is often criticized by lawyers who claim that judges sometimes dismiss a petition for divorce without sufficient examination of the case, and at times makes an 'arbitrary judgment', that is likely to cause the plaintiff to suffer extreme hardship (*see* Part II Chapter 2 §4, II Grounds for Divorce – the defendant has been considered as a person with mental health condition.

§5. Divorce and Relevant Matters

228. When a couple dissolves their marriage, they are required to resolve several issues regarding any children they have and the matrimonial property (*see* Part III Chapter 2). Such matters will be dealt with through negotiation between the parties in cases of divorce by mutual consent, through the proceedings of a family court in cases of family court mediation, a family court determination and a divorce decree if the parties bring divorce litigation.

I. Divorce and Family Name

229. A spouse who has changed his/her family name to the other's at the time of marriage must make a decision as to whether he/she will continue to hold his/her current family name or to revert to his/her maiden name (Civ. section 767 and FRA section 77). If a spouse intends to retain the current family name, he/she is required to notify his/her intention to the family registration office within three months of the divorce. If he/she is reverting to his/her maiden name after divorce, he/she can apply to a family court to make this change (FRA section 107). A family court will approve such an application if it considers changing the family name to be an absolute necessity. In the case where a spouse seeks to change his/her family name after

257. SD 8 Nov. 1990 Kagetsu 43-3-72.
258. SD 18 Nov. 2004 Kagetsu 57-5-40. In particular, divorce is unlikely to be granted if the couple has a minor with disability (Takamatsu HD 26 Nov. 2010 Hanta 1370-199).

having decided to keep the family name of the previous marriage, the same procedure shall apply. It is generally understood that a court is more likely to grant the change of the family name in the latter case than the former.[259]

230. The legal mechanism behind the complex practice of registering family names is as follows: if Mrs Biden whose maiden name is Trump intends to keep the name of Biden after the divorce, she can retain the name of Biden upon giving notice to the family registration office. Legally, however, the name 'Biden' will be regarded as different from her ex-husband's family name, although the pronunciation and letters are exactly the same.

231. As for official documents such as a passport and driving license, a spouse changing his/her family name at the time of divorce must report a new family name to the office as soon as possible.

II. Divorce and Disposition of Estate for Ancestor Veneration

232. Where one party takes his/her partner's family name at the time of marriage and is thereby authorized to exclusively possess the estate of ancestor veneration of the partner, such as a grave[260] or family altar (cf. Civ. section 897(1)), a couple must decide, either through private arrangement or through a family court procedure as to who should administer these materials after divorce (Civ. section 769). For instance, if a husband takes his wife's family name on marriage and subsequently is invested with the materials of her family, the couple should make a decision as to which party should retain the materials after divorce.

III. Divorce and Minor Children

233. On divorce, a couple must decide various issues on their minor children (*see* Part II Chapter 5 and Chapter 6).

259. Osaka HK 4 Sep. 1991 Hanji 1409-75. In Nagoya HK 31 Jan. 1995 Kagetsu 47-12-41, the court held that there was no reason to dismiss an application to change the family name if the application was issued shortly after divorce and would be unlikely to infringe upon the interests of any third party.

260. It is still commonly observed in Japanese society that a family owns one grave for all its members; therefore, for instance, the grave is known as that of the Kurosawa family not as that of Mrs Kurosawa or of Mr Kurosawa.

Chapter 3. Cohabitation of Unmarried Couples

§1. Historical Background

I. Cohabitation under the Old Household System ('Ie' Household System)

234. Before the revision of the Civil Code in 1946, the old family law, as set out in the fourth and fifth part of the Code, had no special provisions for cohabitation. In fact, it was not uncommon that a couple held a marriage ceremony and wedding reception but they would not register their marriage at a later stage in life; such as at the birth of their first child (who was expected to inherit *'Ie'* household) or at the time when a wife was recognized by her husband's relatives as a full member of his family. In this respect, a marriage indicated that a woman would leave her family and be absorbed into her husband's family. This custom illustrated the prevailing attitude that a marriage should be formally approved by the relatives of the husband and the community in general, which would happen only if the marriage proposed visible benefits to the husband's family under the *'Ie'* household system.

235. Furthermore, the '*Ie*' household system and the old family law sometimes contributed to the emergence of cohabitation. Under the '*Ie*' household rule, the eldest child, who was expected to inherit the family name and any other household assets, was generally not allowed to remove his/her name from his/her own entry in the Family Registration Book. Under this rule, if an only son and an only daughter intended to get married, one or the other had to leave his/her family to join the other's. If neither wanted to leave his/her own family, it would be impossible for them to submit a marriage notice to the family registration office. As a result, they were forced to choose cohabitation if they strongly wished to live together. In general, such couples held a marriage ceremony and reception and were recognized by the community as a legitimate couple. As a consequence, the court tended towards providing protection for cohabitees.

II. Cohabitation under the Current Law after 1947

236. Under the current family law, based on the principles of individualism and equality of both sexes, there are no statutory obstacles against a couple to marry. However, a new type of cohabitation has emerged while the number of couples cohabiting for traditional reasons has declined. Some couples do not submit a marriage notice for the reason that they are reluctant to allow the state to intervene in their private lives, or that they intend to avoid the necessity of one partner having to change his/her family name (*see* Civ. section 750).

§2. History of Legal Protection for Cohabiting Couples

237. Traditionally, a couple could not expect any of the legal protection accorded to a husband and wife unless their marriage was registered in the Family

Registration Book. Accordingly, no court offered protection to a couple unless they had submitted a marriage notice to the family registration office of their own free will.[261] The courts, however, did declare that a man should be liable for damages in tort for infringing upon his cohabitee's chastity if he deceived a woman into cohabitation by leading her to believe that he would marry her in the future.[262]

238. In the landmark case of 1915, a court held that cohabitation could be protected as a valid promise of marriage (as a matter of contract) and that a party to this relationship would be responsible, in damages, if he/she breached that promise without reasonable grounds (Civ. section 415).[263] Following this case, the courts repeatedly protected the interests of cohabitees in this sense, and eventually the Supreme Court acknowledged that cohabitation could be treated as a quasi-marriage[264] and be protected through invoking the provision of tort (Civ. section 709).

§3. COMMENCEMENT OF COHABITATION AND ITS LEGAL CONSEQUENCES

239. Cohabitation will take effect if the parties consider their relationship to be that of husband and wife (the subjective element) and if they live together as husband and wife and are recognized by their relatives and community as such a couple (the objective elements). In this respect, if the court regards the parties not to have an intention of maintaining a regular and continuous relationship (not a mere visiting relationship), it will not protect such relationship as cohabitation.[265]

240. During cohabitation, a couple can enjoy similar protection as that afforded to a married couple in terms of marital obligation, property and child maintenance (as a quasi-marriage). In addition, if one party is killed in a traffic accident, the surviving party is generally entitled to bring an action for damages against the driver (Civ. section 709 for financial damages or section 711 for emotional damages) and he/she can also claim for compensation as 'the victim' of the accident under the Motor Vehicle Accident Compensation Act 1955.[266] Moreover, surviving cohabitees have been entitled to occupy their homes in the following cases: (1) a successor of a deceased cohabitee brought a claim to expel a surviving cohabitee from their 'matrimonial' home and the Supreme Court interpreted that such a claim was an abuse of right while the surviving cohabitee did not have the right to occupy the

261. STD 25 Mar. 1911 Minroku 17-169.
262. STD 26 Jan. 1911 Minroku 17-16.
263. STD 26 Jan. 1915 Minroku 21-49. In this case, a plaintiff lost her case since she claimed damages in tort not breach of contract.
264. SD 11 Apr. 1958 Minshu 12-5-789.
265. SD 18 Nov. 2004 Saibanshojiho 1376-3.
266. Utsunomiya DD 30 Nov. 1971 Kotsujiko Minji-Saibanreishu 4-6-1750. A surviving cohabitee is entitled to claim damages against the government under s. 72(1) of the Motor Vehicle Accident Compensation Act if a perpetrator is not known (SD 6 Apr. 1993 Minshu 47-6-4505).

home; (2) a surviving cohabitee was eligible to occupy their family home by invoking the successors' tenancy against a third party.[267] In respect of entitlement to a lump sum payment for a deceased employee, a surviving cohabitee will come under the definition of 'a member of the family'.[268] A cohabitee may be appointed as a statutory carer under section 20(1) of the Mental Health and the Welfare of the Mentally Disabled Act 1995 when the other is declared to be a person suffering from a mental impairment. Some statutes actually stipulate that a cohabitee should be treated as a quasi-spouse for the purpose of the protection of the interests of the cohabiting couple.[269]

241. If a child is born to cohabitees, no father-child relationship will take effect under law until the father acknowledges paternity. In cases where cohabitees and their child live together as a family, however, the courts take the view that the child is entitled to claim for damages in the event of the 'father' being killed in a traffic accident (*see* Civ. section 711),[270] or that the child has a right to financial support from the 'father'.[271]

242. The legal effects of cohabitation differ from those of marriage in the following matters. Neither party is allowed to change and register his/her family name to that of the other (*see* Civ. section 750). Neither party has a right to succession of the other[272] (cf. Civ. section 890). The provisions relating to marriage settlement will not apply to cohabitees (cf. Civ. section 755). Where a minor starts cohabitation, he/she will not be treated as a person of majority (cf. Previous Civ. section 753). No relationship of a relative will be established between one cohabitee and the relatives of the other (cf. Civ. section 725). Concerning children of the cohabitees, provisions on legitimation (Civ. section 789) and presumption of legitimacy (Civ. section 772) will not be available for such offspring. Furthermore, cohabitees cannot invoke some privileges laid down in taxation law.

§4. Dissolution of Cohabitation

243. Legal provisions concerning divorce will generally apply to a case of dissolution of cohabitation. For instance, a cohabitee is eligible to claim division of their property as in the division of matrimonial property by applying section 768 *mutatis mutandis*. If one party dissolves the relationship of cohabitation without reasonable grounds, he/she will be liable to pay damages either because of breach of

267. SD 13 Oct. 1964 Minshu 18-8-1578 and SD 21 Feb. 1967 Minshu 21-1-155. *See* s, 36(1) of the Lease of Land and House Act 1991.
268. SD 31, 1985 Kagetsu 37-8-39.
269. *See* s. 16-2(1) of the Workman's Compensation Act 1973, s. 3(7) of the Health Insurance Act 2002 and s. 5(8) of the State Pension Act 2004.
270. Tokyo HD 5 Jul. 1961 Kagetsu 14-2-123.
271. Tokyo FO 15 Jul. 1975 Kagetsu 28-8-62.
272. In a case where a cohabitee dies with no heirs, the surviving cohabitee can claim to be 'a special related person' for the purpose of succession (Civ. s. 958-2).

promise or in tort. Similar to divorce, a third party shall be responsible for damages in tort to the injured party if he/she contributes towards the breakdown of cohabitation.

244. In the case of dissolution of cohabitation by the death of one party, the provisions on succession will not apply. When a deceased cohabitee has stated in their insurance policy that their 'heirs' shall be the beneficiaries, a surviving cohabitee is not entitled to the insurance money. However, for the purpose of the protection of a surviving cohabitee, in practice, the courts grant payment to a surviving cohabitee as a reward for his/her contribution to the deceased cohabitee acquiring the assets.[273] Moreover, on invoking the analogy of adjustment of the matrimonial property (Civ. section 768), a court can hold that a surviving cohabitee is entitled to claim a certain portion of the deceased's assets.[274]

§5. Legal Effects of Plural Relationships of Cohabitees

245. It sometimes happens that one party to cohabitation is already married to a third party or lives with another cohabitee simultaneously. Such relationships are labelled as 'quasi-bigamy' cohabitation. It is generally interpreted that such plural relationships will not be legally protected on the basis that it is against public policy and contrary to the principle of monogamy (Civ. section 90). In practice, however, particular circumstances and other reasons result in such relationships. For example, a husband may start to live with a woman for a long period of time after he has left his wife as a result of marital conflict. He may have thought that to commence divorce proceedings would be troublesome and so did nothing in order to dissolve the marriage. As a result, he has become involved in 'quasi-bigamy' cohabitation. In this sense, a court will deal with such cases according to the individual circumstances.

246. A court will protect cohabitees if it is satisfied that the relationship has completely broken down, that both partners have a real intention to dissolve the relationship, and there has been a prolonged period of separation (for instance, ten years), and that the cohabitees are socially recognized as husband and wife. 'Quasi-bigamy' cohabitees will enjoy similar protection as ordinary cohabitees with some limitations. In the following cases, the court pronounced that a cohabitee wife should be entitled to claim damages or adjustment of the 'matrimonial' property if the cohabitee husband terminated cohabitation without any sufficient reasons even in the case where the former started to cohabit with the latter who was already married at the time.[275]

273. Osaka HD 31 Nov. 1982 Kagetsu 36-1-139.
274. Osaka FO 23 Mar. 1983 Kagetsu 36-3-51 which was rejected by the Supreme Court (SK 10 Mar. 2000 Minshu 54-3-1040).
275. Tokyo DD 25 Dec. 1959 Kagetsu 12-6-146 and Matsue Branch of Hiroshima HK 15 Nov. 1965 Kagetsu 18-7-33.

247. Unlike in a case of ordinary cohabitation, if a surviving party of 'quasi-bigamy' cohabitation seeks damages from a driver who killed the deceased cohabitee in a motor vehicle accident, the court may calculate the amount of damages to the surviving cohabitee by taking account of a share which should be paid to a surviving spouse.[276]

248. Statutory provisions on cohabitation generally apply to quasi-bigamous cohabitation. In a case where the marriage of one cohabitee has already broken down irretrievably and the chances of any reconciliation are minimal,[277] it is very likely that the court will protect the cohabitees. For instance, the court is likely to make a favourable decision to benefit the family members of the deceased[278] as well as in cases involving workman's compensation,[279] by considering the facts of the case and the purpose of the law.

§6. Cohabitees Within Prohibited Degrees of Consanguinity

249. What are the legal effects for cohabitees who are within the prohibited degrees of consanguinity? In the case of an uncle and a niece who lived as a husband and wife for more than forty-two years with recognition by community, the surviving wife (the niece) claimed her husband's pension as his surviving spouse. The Supreme Court declared that she was entitled to make such claim for the purpose of protecting the deceased's family life rather than the public interest.[280] Whereas, in the case of cohabitation of a widow and her son-in-law whose relationship started seven years after the death of the deceased husband (the father of the son-in-law) and lasted for twenty-three years, the court denied such claim because such relationship should be strongly against the public policy (cf. Civ. section 90).[281]

276. Tokyo DD 10 Dec. 1968 Kagetsu 21-6-88.
277. *See* SD 14 Apr. 1983 Minshu 37-3-270 where the entitlement for benefit of deceased family members was at issue.
278. Tokyo HD 11 Jul. 2007 Hanji 1991-67.
279. Tokyo DD 27 Mar. 1998 Rodohanrei 739-20.
280. SD 8 Mar. 2007 Minshu 61-2-518. In one case, the period of cohabitation is 57 years (Saitama DD 23 Mar. 2011 CW).
281. SD 14 Feb. 1985 Shomugeppo 31-9-2204.

Chapter 4. Filiation

§1. Outline of the Law Relating to Parent and Child

I. Principles of the Law on Parent and Child

250. The primary purpose of the law relating to children is to protect and promote their welfare. It is commonly interpreted that this purpose is too obvious to be actually stated in the provisions of the Civil Code. The law on children may be classified into two groups: first the law regarding the establishment of the status of parent and child, and second the law protecting the interests of children involved in various disputes. In addition to the Civil Code, several statutes, such as the Fundamental Principles of Education Act 1947, the Juvenile Act 1948, the Welfare of Children Act 1947 and the Child Abuse Prevention Act 2000 apply to cases connected with children.

II. Legal Relationship of Parent and Child

251. Concerning paternity, there are two views under the existing law on how to recognize the father-child relationship; some focus on the blood relationship (the objective approach) whereas others emphasize the real intention of the parties (the subjective approach) for the purpose of finding and confirming a legal relationship. It is generally interpreted that the current family law adopts both views in dealing with disputes regarding paternity. On the one hand, the objective approach can apply in such a way that a court finds and confirms paternity based on the evidence of a blood relationship between a man and 'his child' notwithstanding the fact that the former rejects a claim by the child to acknowledge his paternity. On the other hand, in a case where a child has been fathered by a third party due to the wife's adultery, only the husband is entitled to make a decision as to whether to confirm or refuse paternity between him and the child (Civ. section 774). In such a case, paternity is determined subjectively.

252. With respect to the mother-child relationship, it is considered to be effective from the moment of birth.[282] However, statutory provisions concerning the acknowledgement of maternity may apply in very exceptional cases.

253. Recent developments in human reproductive technology have brought about many difficulties in dealing with disputes regarding parent-child relationships: (1) In the case of a child engendered by artificial insemination by the husband, no legal problems arise. If a child is born of artificial insemination by a donor and the husband has given his full consent to the procedure, the child will be considered a legitimate child of the husband. Where full consent has not been given, the husband is eligible to dispute paternity of that child. (2) Surrogate motherhood

282. SD 27 Apr. 1962 Minshu 16-7-1247.

is not approved either by law or in medical practice in Japan. However, the first case was reported in 2001 in Japan and a number of Japanese couples have had children through American surrogate mothers in the US since 1991. Although there is no effective way to prohibit such activities, lawyers warn that this may come under the definition of the trafficking of human beings and thus violate section 90 of the Civil Code. In 2007, the Supreme Court denied the existence of a mother-child relationship in the case where a Japanese married couple obtained a baby with the husband's sperm and the wife's egg through a surrogate mother in the US.[283] (3) The number of children in Japan born through the in vitro fertilization method now exceeds ten thousand. This method of reproduction is only available to a married couple and only during the period of reproductive capability of the couple. As for issues concerning frozen eggs and sperm, the current law has no effective and sufficient provisions to deal with such matters. For instance, the Supreme Court has decided that acknowledgement of paternity shall not be allowed in a case in which a surviving wife becomes pregnant by her deceased husband's frozen sperm about one year after his death and then gives birth.[284]

254. The various legal statuses of a child in relation to its parents can be classified into the following:

Natural child – a child born to a married couple

(1) Legitimate child (marital child)
   - Category A legitimate child who is under the presumption of paternity stated in section 772 of the Civil Code.
   - Category B legitimate child who lacks the presumption of paternity stated in section 772 of the Civil Code.
   - Category C legitimate child who appears to be a category A legitimate child but is mostly considered as an illegitimate child.

(2) Illegitimate child (non-marital child)
   - A child born to unmarried parents.

Adopted child

(1) Ordinary adopted child whose adoptive relationship generally takes effect by contract between the parties.
(2) Special adopted child whose adopting relationship can be created only by a family court determination.

Foster child

If a child needs to be looked after by a person other than the birth parents for some reason, he/she will be placed with a non-relative family under special arrangement by a local government on the basis of the Welfare of Children Act. Under such an

283. SK 23 Mar. 2007 Minshu 61-2-619.
284. SD 4 Sep. 2006 Minshu 60-7-2563.

arrangement, foster parents will be vested with some rights and duties concerning the care of the child but no legal parent-child relationship is created.

Deserted child

A child whose parents are unknown since the time of birth and regarding whom no one submits to the authority a notice of birth.[285] When a deserted child is found, the mayor of the local city must register the child in the Family Registration Book after giving the child a family- and forename, deciding the principal address and the presumed birth date of the child (FRA section 57(2)).

§2. Children Born in Wedlock

I. The Legal Status of a Legitimate Child

255. Section 772 stipulates that: (1) a child conceived by a wife during marriage shall be presumed to be the child of the husband and (2) a child, born two hundred days or more after the day on which the marriage was formed or born within three hundred days from the day on which the marriage was dissolved or annulled, shall be presumed to have been conceived during the marriage.[286]

256. Section 772 indicates that the law does not lay down any clear definition of a legitimate child except that a legitimate child is a child born to married parents. A mother-child relationship, whether legitimate or not, can be usually confirmed without difficulties by the fact of birth. However, a father-child relationship is not always obvious even if the child is born to a married couple. Accordingly, a father-child relationship can be established in law if some conditions stated in section 772 can be satisfied and such relationship is classified into three categories. In the case of a transgender couple, the lower court has refused to acknowledge a legitimate father-child relationship between a 'Female to Male' husband and the child of his wife who conceived the child by artificial insemination by a donor on the basis that there was no biological relationship between them but the Supreme Court dismissed the lower court decision and approved the legitimate relationship between them in 2013.[287]

285. In the case where a mother, whose identity is not clear, deserts her child immediately after the birth, the medical doctor in charge of the birth is responsible for submitting a notice of birth (FRA s. 52(3)). In this sense, this child is not a 'deserted child'.

286. In the case that a baby is born within 300 days after the date of divorce or annulment of the previous marriage, he/she can be registered as either an illegitimate child of the mother or a category B legitimate child of the current marriage if a medical certificate stating that the mother conceived the child after the divorce or annulment of the previous marriage is submitted to the authority (7 May 2007 Notice of the Director-General of Civil Affairs Bureau (DGCAB) Min 1 No1007).

287. Tokyo 31 Oct. 2012 Minshu 67-9-1897 and SK 10 Dec. 2013 Minshu 67-9-1847.

257. In general, a legitimate child is entitled to receive care and financial support from its parents, the right to succession and the right to take the family name, while the parents obtain parental rights and duties and the right to succession on the death of their child.

II. Category A Legitimate Child

258. A child shall be presumed to be fathered by a husband if a wife conceives the child during their marriage. A wife is presumed to conceive a child by her husband either: (1) if a child is born after two hundred days of the parents' marriage or (2) if the child is born within three hundred days of the dissolution of the marriage by reason of divorce or a voidable ground (Civ. section 772(1) (2)).

259. In the case of marriage, it is interpreted that the two hundred days includes the day of submission of the marriage notice to the family registration office and that the three hundred days starts from the day after the dissolution. The day of dissolution is interpreted as the day on which the divorce notice is accepted by the family registration office in the case of divorce by mutual consent, the day on which the divorce mediation is completed in the case of family court mediation, or the day on which a family court determination or a decree is finalized at a family court, respectively.

260. A category A child shall be registered as the legitimate child of the husband and wife (FRA sections 49ff). As long as the presumption of legitimacy takes effect, the child must be first registered as a legitimate child even if he/she is in fact fathered by a third party.

261. Where a husband intends to challenge the paternity of a category A child by reason of his wife's adultery, he can bring proceedings to a family court against either the child or the wife (Civ. sections 774 and 775). Otherwise, no other party is entitled to contest the paternity if the husband has accepted the child as his own legitimate child voluntarily (Civ. section 776). The Supreme Court held this rule even when the court acknowledged the fact that no biological father-child relationship was evident by DNA test while the child lives with and is cared for by the biological father.[288] A husband is not entitled to challenge the paternity of a category A child merely on the basis that their marriage has broken down.[289]

262. In a case where the husband is registered as a ward of guardianship, his guardian or a supervisor to his guardian, if his wife is appointed as his guardian, is

288. SD 17 Jul. 2014 Minshu 68-6-547.
289. SD 14 Mar. 2000 Kagetsu 52-9-85.

qualified to act as a petitioner in proceedings contesting paternity[290] (PALA section 14). If the husband dies either before the birth of the child or within one year of the birth of the child, an interested relative of consanguinity within the third degree[291] can present a petition denying paternity (PALA section 41(1)). The respondent in these proceedings shall be either the child or the mother with parental rights and duties (Civ. section 775). In the event that the child is left with no person holding parental rights and duties, the mother loses parental rights and duties, or she resigns from her role with parental rights and duties, a family court must appoint a special representative for the proceedings (FAPA sections 39 and 159). No one is eligible to dispute the legitimacy of an unborn child.[292]

263. An application by a husband denying the legitimacy of a child shall be dealt with through in-court mediation and by a family court determination tantamount to an agreement (FAPA sections 244, 257 and 277). Unlike litigation concerning the denial of legitimacy under the strict proceedings of the Personal Affairs Litigation Act, it is interpreted that the wife of the husband (the natural mother of the child) or the child qualifies as a petitioner under the proceedings of family court mediation or family court determination.[293]

264. As regards restrictions in proceedings for which paternity is in dispute, a husband shall lose the right to deny legitimacy once he has accepted the child as his legitimate child (Civ. section 776). While no particular measures for conveying acceptance are laid down, express, implied, written or oral forms of acceptance shall be valid. However, under circumstances where a husband mistakenly believes that he is required by law to submit a notice of birth of the child to the family registration office, despite knowing that the child is not his own, the mere fact that the husband submits the notice will not constitute valid acceptance of paternity.[294] Once a husband approves the legitimacy of the child for any reason, he loses the right to withdraw his acceptance except in cases of fraud or duress.

265. Moreover, a husband shall lose the right to deny legitimacy of the child if he does not present a petition for denial to a court within one year after he has discovered the birth of the child (Civ. section 777). However, since the strict rule of one year may cause hardship to a husband, a court can interpret section 777 in a more flexible way in order to bring justice to the parties. While section 777 literally spells out that a husband should present the petition denying legitimacy of the child

290. If a husband is a ward of guardianship, his wife is usually appointed as a statutory guardian. In cases relating to s. 774 of the Civil Code, the wife shall not be an appropriate person for representing the husband because her position as a mother of the child in question may cause a conflict of interest in the case.
291. In the case that a husband with no children dies intestate, his parents – blood relatives within the first degree – will be entitled to succession. In this sense, certain groups of relatives can be regarded as interested persons.
292. 25 Nov. 1899 Civ.-Crim.Rep. No. 2064 of DGCCAB.
293. Sapporo FO 30 Aug. 1966 Kagetsu 19-3-80.
294. 10 Jan. 1899 Civ-Crim.Rep. No. 2289 of DGCCAB and cf. Nagoya Decree of the Appellate Tribunal (Kosoin Hanketsu) (ATD) 15 Sep. 1941 Shimbun 4740-9.

within one year after he has discovered the birth of the child, it is now interpreted that he should bring about proceedings if he so wishes within one year of discovering that the child is not his legitimate child. For instance, in a case where a wife confessed to her husband two years after the birth of the child that the child was in fact fathered by a third party, the court held that the term of one year should start at the time of this confession unless there was any malicious intention or serious negligence on the part of the husband.[295] Meanwhile, this rule may cause great hardship to the parties. A child registered as a category A legitimate child brought a case against his legitimate father asserting that DNA test proved no blood relationship between them, but he lost the case since only the husband is eligible to challenge paternity in the case of a category A legitimate child.[296]

266. When a court grants a petition by a husband, the child will lose the status of a legitimate child of the husband and it will be retrospectively interpreted that no father-child relationship in law existed from the time of birth (this interpretation shall be applied to category B and category C legitimate child).

III. Category B Legitimate Child

267. A category B legitimate child is a child whose parents are married at the time of its birth but who does not fulfil the requirements for the presumption of paternity as laid down in section 772(2).[297] For instance, a child may be born within two hundred days after the submission of a marriage notice by the parents because they had cohabited for a certain period of time prior to the marriage registration.[298] In very rare cases it may happen that a child is born after two hundred days of the parents' marriage but was evidently conceived before the time of the marriage by reason of a combination of factors such as that the parents rushed to marry after discovering the wife's pregnancy and the child was born overdue. The presumption of paternity in section 772 will also not apply to rare instances in which a child is conceived during the parents' marriage but born after three hundred days of the dissolution of the marriage.

268. Disputes concerning the legitimacy of a category B child are subject to section 2(2) of the Personal Affairs Litigation Act. A case must be dealt with first through in-court mediation followed by a section 277 determination at a family court and then through personal litigation at a family court if the mediation fails. A person who has any interest in disputing the child's legitimacy is entitled to be a party to these proceedings. If the father or child is dead, a public prosecutor will act

295. Tokyo FO 18 Feb. 1967 Kagetsu 19-9-76.
296. SD 17 Jul. 2014 Minshu 68-6-547.
297. Section 772(2) of the Civil Code stipulates that a child, born two hundred days or more after the day on which the marriage was legally formed or born within three hundred days from the day on which the marriage was dissolved or annulled, shall be presumed to have been conceived during the marriage.
298. STD 23 Jan. 1940 Minshu 19-54. Before this decision, a category B legitimate child was treated as an illegitimate child.

as a defendant.[299] A third party can file a petition after the death of the parents and child as long as he/she has an interest in disputing the legitimacy of the child. A minor is eligible to present a petition to the court independently if he/she has the capacity to understand the meaning and effects of his/her act. In the case where a plaintiff dies during the proceedings, the petition will terminate. However, should the defendant die a prosecutor will act as the defendant.

IV. Category C Legitimate Child

269. It may happen that a child has not evidently been fathered by the husband of the mother despite meeting the conditions of a category A legitimate child. For instance, there may be cases where a wife gives birth during a long period of imprisonment of the husband. It would be inappropriate for such a child to be regarded as a category A legitimate child of the husband. Accordingly, such a child is treated as a category C legitimate child.

270. Since it is interpreted that anyone is entitled to dispute the paternity of a category C legitimate child, the privacy of the parties involved is likely to be infringed upon. In order to protect the interests of the parties, a petition can only be filed in the following limited circumstances:[300] the parents are de facto divorced but have delayed the submission of a divorce notice for some reason,[301] the husband is missing, imprisoned or is overseas for a long period,[302] the husband is proved to be infertile,[303] racial dissimilarity[304] or incompatibility in blood types[305] between the child and the husband. In addition, the court may refuse a petition to dispute the paternity if it thinks the petition to be an abuse of the right to dispute the paternity due to the existence of special circumstances in the case.[306]

V. Presumption of Paternity for a Child of Cohabitees

271. It is claimed by some lawyers that a presumption of paternity can apply to a child of cohabitees if the child satisfies the requirements of paternity as laid down in section 772, since cohabitation is now regarded as a quasi-marital institution in terms of protecting the parties concerned. Such an interpretation can be beneficial to the child since the child is not required to prove paternity but instead the burden is on the cohabitee husband to provide evidence for the absence of paternity in any

299. SD 15 Jul. 1970 Minshu 24-7-861. In the case where a defendant dies, it is not clear whether a prosecutor is qualified to act as the defendant where the case is dealt with at a family court through mediation or a court determination.
300. Tokyo HD 28 Mar. 1994 Kagetsu 47-2-165.
301. SD 29 May 1969 Minshu 23-6-1064.
302. Tokyo FO 8 Oct. 1987 Kagetsu 40-10-49 and SD 31 Aug. 1998 Kagetsu 51-4-75.
303. Niigata DD 30 Oct. 1957 Kamin 8-10-2002.
304. Fukuoka FO 11 Dec. 1969 Kagetsu 22-6-93.
305. Tokyo FO 5 Mar. 1977 Kagetsu 29-10-154.
306. SD 31 Aug. 1998 Kagetsu 51-4-75.

proceedings of acknowledgement.[307] However, a presumption of paternity does not apply to a child of cohabitees under the current family law.

VI. Child Born by Artificial Insemination

272. Artificial Insemination by the Husband will not give rise to any problems regarding paternity and the child will be considered as a legitimate child of the husband. In the case of AID, a child will be regarded as a legitimate child of the husband as long as the husband has given his full consent to such treatment.[308] Once the husband has given his full consent to AID treatment, not only he but also any other person will lose the right to dispute his paternity.[309] In the event that the husband has not given his full consent to AID treatment, he can bring proceedings to either challenge legitimacy or confirm the father-child relationship.

273. A child born by AID treatment with full consent by a husband is regarded as a legitimate child of the husband, but two interpretations exist for the categorization of the child. One asserts that the child is a category A legitimate child whereby the husband loses his right to argue paternity and, as a consequence, the child is not eligible to claim acknowledgement of paternity against his/her birth father. The other interpretation places the child in the bracket of a category B legitimate child who is able to dispute the father and child relationship since no presumption of legitimacy between the husband and the child exists. Under the current legal system, there is no statute or other laws directly regulating the treatment of artificial insemination, but the Assisted Reproduction Act was enacted in 2020 by which a husband is not allowed to deny paternity if he had given full consent for AID treatment (ARA section 10). If a child is born by AID to a married couple of FTM husband and wife, it can be regarded as a category A child.[310]

VII. Issues on Surrogacy and Frozen Fertilized Eggs and Sperm

274. While there is neither any clear rule nor specific statute concerning surrogacy, frozen fertilized eggs and sperm, the following measures may be taken. In 2020, the Assisted Reproduction Act was implemented in which the mother-child relationship shall be established between surrogate mother and child (ARA section 9) and a husband shall not be allowed to deny paternity of an AID baby when he gave full consent for the treatment (ARA Section 10). The Assisted Reproduction Act 2020 is based on the previous measures taken by the court and interpretation of lawyers.

307. SD 21 Jan. 1954 Minshu 8-1-87.
308. Oosaka DD 18 Dec. 1998 Kagetsu 51-9-71.
309. Tokyo HK 16 Sep. 1998 Kagetsu 51-3-165.
310. SK 10 Dec. 2013 Hanji 2210-27.

275. Where a child is born to a third-party woman and the husband acknowledges his paternity, that child will be an extramarital child of the husband (an illegitimate child) and will have no mother-child relationship with the wife of the husband even if the wife has given her consent to the production of such a child.

276. If a surrogate mother (a third party woman) gives birth having been implanted with the wife's egg that has been fertilized by her husband, the child will be considered as an extramarital child of the surrogate mother.[311] In addition, this rule may be applied to a case where a surrogate mother (Ms A) gives birth with an egg of a third party woman (Ms B) fertilized by the husband.[312] Since there is no mother-child relationship between the child and the wife, adoption is the only means to establish a legitimate relationship between the couple and the child.

277. There may be extremely rare cases where a surrogate mother gives birth having been implanted with the wife's egg that has been fertilized by a man other than the husband, in which case the child will be an extramarital child of the surrogate mother.

278. A child whose mother has become pregnant by the frozen sperm of her deceased husband after his death is not eligible to apply for a court decision of acknowledgement of paternity even though a biological father-child relationship exists.[313]

§3. Children Born Out of Wedlock

I. Non-marital Child (Illegitimate Child)

279. A non-marital child is defined as a child born to a father and mother who are not legally married.[314] As mentioned earlier, the mother-child relationship is usually confirmed by the fact of birth, while the father-child relationship takes effect only through a certain procedure for acknowledging paternity in the case of a non-marital child.

280. A non-marital child has several disadvantages under the current family law compared with a legitimate child. A non-marital child is required to be registered as an illegitimate child in the Family Registration Book even if his/her parents live as de facto husband and wife.[315] A non-marital child was entitled to claim only half of

311. SK 23 Mar. 2007 Minshu 61-2-619.
312. Osaka HK 20 May 2005 Hanji 1919-107.
313. SD 4 Sep. 2006 Minshu 60-7-2563.
314. It was reported that the number of illegitimate children born in one year in Japan was at most 102,580 (3.8% of all births) in 1947, at least 12,548 (0.8%) in 1980, 23,032 (2.3% of all birth) in 2015 and 20,171 (2.3%) in 2017 (Ministry of Health, Labour and Welfare, *Vital Statistics 2019 (1), supra*, table 4-29. A non-marital child includes a legitimate child whose paternity is refused by the husband of the mother (*see* paras 263ff).
315. SD 26 Sep. 2013 Minshu 67-6-1384.

the entitlement of a legitimate child in the case of succession from his/her parents. Although such discrimination was challenged and declared to be a violation of Article 14 of the Constitution by a court in 1993,[316] this interpretation was overturned by a decision of the Supreme Court in 1995.[317] However, this discrimination was finally declared to be a violation of Article 14 of the Constitution in terms of succession and section 900 was revised in 2013.[318] A non-marital child will automatically take his/her mother's family name at the time of birth and must make an application to the family court in order to change his/her family name to that of the father. Recently an increasing number of people have voiced criticism of such discrimination towards non-marital children, which has resulted in a publication by the Law Reform Committee which considers revising the family law relating to the status of non-marital children. However, the law has not yet been revised.

281. In order to establish a father-child relationship, a non-marital child must take certain measures to have the paternity acknowledged, or a non-marital father can also undertake similar procedures for the same purpose. Two such measures or procedures exist: (1) voluntary acknowledgement of paternity by a non-marital father, whereby paternity can be confirmed by the intention of the father to be considered as the father (a subjective factor) or (2) acknowledgement of paternity by family court proceedings in the event that the non-marital father is unwilling to acknowledge paternity of the child.

282. Acknowledgement of paternity is available not only during the lifetime of the parties concerned but also after their death. It can also be made by the father's will (Civ. section 781(2)).

II. Voluntary Acknowledgement of Paternity

283. The acknowledgement of paternity will take effect on the basis of a voluntary submission by a non-marital father of a notice of acknowledgement to the family registration office (Civ. section 781(1)). Accordingly, whether a biological father-child relationship actually exists between the parties may be irrelevant for the acknowledgement of paternity since only the true intention of the father to be considered as the father is essential. As a result, acknowledgement of paternity may be invalid if the father lacks a true intention to acknowledge the paternity for some reason, despite the fact that a father-child relationship can be observed objectively.[319]

284. A man, including minors and a ward of adult guardianship, is eligible to acknowledge paternity independently as long as he has the capacity to understand the meaning and effects of such an acknowledgement (Civ. section 780). In the case

316. Tokyo HK 23 Jun. 1993 Kagetsu 45-6-104.
317. SK 5 Jul. 1995 Minshu 49-7-1789.
318. SK 4 Sep. 2013 Minshu 67-6-1320.
319. SD 14 Feb. 1977 Kagetsu 29-9-78.

of a minor over 15 years of age, he is usually considered to have such capacity.[320] Where a father has requested a third party to submit a notice of acknowledgement of paternity on his behalf, but he is unconscious at the time of submission, the notice will nevertheless be valid.[321] In addition, a father is eligible to acknowledge paternity by his last will (Civ. section 781(2)).

285. Only a non-marital child who has not already had his/her paternity acknowledged is eligible to have his/her paternity acknowledged. Thus, no one can acknowledge paternity of a child who has already been acknowledged by another, unless that previous acknowledgement of paternity is declared either void or voidable.

286. In a case where a man attempts to submit a notice of acknowledgement of paternity for a child who is registered as a category A legitimate child of someone else, such notice will not be accepted by a family registration office.[322] The former can make a valid submission of acknowledgement of the paternity of such child only after the person who has been registered as the legitimate father has successfully challenged the paternity of the category A child (Civ. sections 774 and 775).[323]

287. On submission of acknowledgement of paternity, the consent of the child will be necessary if he/she has reached the age of majority (Civ. section 782). This requirement aims to protect the interests of the adult child under such circumstances, for instance, in cases where the father, having deserted the child for a long period of time, intends to acknowledge paternity of the adult child only in order to seek financial assistance from that child (*see* Civ. section 877). In cases where the adult child lacks the capacity to enter into legal acts, a legal representative of the child is eligible to give consent on his/her behalf. However, the adult child can also give consent if he/she has the capacity to understand the meaning and effects of his/her acts. Where a guardian of an adult child wishes to acknowledge paternity of the child, the guardian must obtain consent from his/her supervisor (i.e., the supervisor to the guardian) or from a special representative of that child.[324] There are no special requirement formalities for an adult child to give his/her consent except that consent must be in written form. With respect to a minor, no requirements for giving consent to an application acknowledging paternity is laid down in the law. Accordingly, a father can have his paternity of a child acknowledged without the consent of either the child or its representative even in instances where he is in fact only seeking such acknowledgement to further his own interests.

320. 15 Oct. 1948 Civ.Ko.Rep. No. 660 of DGCAB.
321. SD 30 Mar. 1979 Kagetsu 31-7-54.
322. 7 Oct. 1949 Civ.Ko.Rep. No. 2286 and 436 of DGCAB and 2 Mar. 1963 Civ.Ko.Rep. No. 582 of DGCAB.
323. Fukuoka HD 29 Nov. 1951 Kamin 2-11-1367.
324. 31 Jan. 1979 Civ.Ko.Rep. No. 464 of DGCAB. For example, a non-marital father intends to acknowledge paternity of the child after he has been appointed as guardian of the child, following the death of the mother who had parental rights and duties over the child. In such case, a supervisor of the guardian or a special representative will usually be appointed.

288. In the case of an unborn child, the consent of the mother is necessary for a man to successfully confirm paternity (Civ. section 783(1)). Any form of consent is valid for this purpose. The father usually submits a notice acknowledging paternity of the unborn child to the family registration office where the mother's principal address is registered (he is required to state the name and the principal address of the mother in such notice (FRA section 61)).

289. After the death of a child, a man can acknowledge paternity of his deceased child only if such child him/herself had direct issues. When the issues of the deceased child are of full age, their consent will also become necessary (Civ. section 783(2)).

290. A child who is born to a couple within the prohibited degrees of consanguinity can still be acknowledged by the father as his own. For instance, despite the fact that a man is prohibited from marrying his stepdaughter, he can still acknowledge paternity of a child born by her.[325]

291. Voluntary acknowledgement of paternity will take effect subject to the procedures laid down in the Family Registration Act (Civ. section 781 and FRA section 60). In the case of a child born out of wedlock, unless a notice of acknowledgement of paternity is submitted, acknowledgement will not be effective even if a man names the child and looks after him/her for a certain period of time. However, if a last will that includes an acknowledgement of paternity is declared void because it fails to confirm to the necessary formalities, the part regarding the acknowledgement will not necessarily be void.[326]

292. Once the illegitimate father-child relationship has been established by a valid acknowledgement of paternity, the father will assume parental responsibilities and rights over the child such as care, maintenance, contact and succession. Unless a valid acknowledgement exists, no legal effects emanating from the father-child relationship take effect. However, in terms of financial support, a court has held that prior to acknowledgement of paternity, a father should be responsible for financially maintaining the child if the father-child relationship was evident.[327] Concerning the family name of a child born out of wedlock, such child must retain his/her mother's family name even after the acknowledgement of paternity until a petition to alter his/her family name to the father's is approved by a family court. The effects of acknowledgement of paternity will operate retrospectively to the time of the child's birth, but any rights acquired by a third party prior to the acknowledgement will not be prejudiced by the acknowledgement (Civ. section 784).

325. STD 23 Jan. 1931 Shimbun 3227-14.
326. Sendai HD 25 Jan. 1980 Kagetsu 33-2-169.
327. Osaka DD 15 May 1951 Kamin 2-5-657 and Tokyo FD 15 Jul. 1975 Kagetsu 28-8-62.

III. Void and Voidable Acknowledgement of Paternity

293. Interested parties can apply to have an acknowledgement of paternity rejected as void or voidable, by stating that it was not made with the true intention of the father. It is not possible to dispute the validity of an acknowledgement of paternity declared by a court, but an interested party may file a petition for a re-trial of the case.[328]

294. If a notice of acknowledgement of paternity is submitted by a third party to the family registration office without the knowledge of the man concerned, the man can claim the acknowledgement of paternity to be void by reason of his lack of true intention to so acknowledge in spite of the fact that a father-child relationship is objectively recognized between the man and the child.[329] However, what happens in the following circumstances may be open to debate: where a man truly intending to acknowledge paternity requests a third party to make and submit the notice;[330] or where a man has completed a form acknowledging paternity and intends for a third party to submit the form to the family registration office, but is unconscious at the time of submission of the notice.[331] It is interpreted by the courts that unless special circumstances exist, the intention to acknowledge paternity will exist.

295. In addition to a lack of intention rendering an acknowledgement void, the following persons are eligible to claim an acknowledgement of paternity to be void by proving that the acknowledgement is not based on actual fact. Such eligible persons include the man acknowledging paternity, the child acknowledged, the mother of the child,[332] relatives of the man (his spouse, child, parents and siblings), and a third person who intends to acknowledge paternity of the child. The courts hold conflicting views on the issue of whether the man can dispute the validity of his acknowledgement of paternity by asserting that he made an acknowledgement which was not based on actual fact. One court has stated that such a claim should not be accepted if the man voluntarily recognized the father-child relationship,[333] but another court has declared that the man may annul the acknowledgement if no biological relationship between him and the child is proved.[334] The Supreme Court decided that a man may annul the acknowledgement of paternity even though he knew of no biological relationship between the child and him at the time of acknowledgement.[335]

296. The following are potential defendants in proceedings to annul an acknowledgement of paternity: a man acknowledging a child where the child is a petitioner, a child where a man who previously acknowledged paternity is a petitioner (PALA

328. *See* SD 26 Jun. 1953 Minshu 7-6-787 and Nagoya DD 21 Feb. 1950 Kamin 1-2-255.
329. Cf. SD 14 Feb. 1977 Kagetsu 29-9-78.
330. Hachioji Branch of Tokyo DD 31 Aug. 1961 Kamin 12-8-2144.
331. SD 30 Mar. 1979 Kagetsu 31-7-54.
332. SD 14 Apr. 1978 Kagetsu 30-10-26.
333. Tokyo HD 31 Aug. 1988 Hanta 694-161.
334. Osaka DD 18 Jul. 1988 Hanta 683-178.
335. SD 14 Jan. 2014 Minshu 68-1-1.

section 12(1)) (albeit in such event litigation will be terminated if the man dies),[336] a prosecutor where the child is a petitioner and the man in question has died,[337] a man and child jointly (or the survivor in the case of the death of either party) where a third party is a petitioner (PALA section 12(2)), and a prosecutor if neither the man nor the child is alive where a third party is a petitioner (PALA section 12(3)).

297. Since there is no time limit for a petition to annul an acknowledgement of paternity, a court has held that it is not an abuse of the relevant man's right if a wife and child dispute the validity of an acknowledgement of paternity by their husband/father even fifty years after the acknowledgement had been made.[338] The proceedings to annul the acknowledgement of paternity will end in the death of a petitioner as the right to annul only rests in the petitioner personally and it is not passed to heirs through inheritance.[339] When a court declares the acknowledgement of paternity to be void, the father-child relationship will be considered not to have ever existed.

298. Despite section 785 stipulating that neither father nor mother can set aside an acknowledgement of paternity/maternity already made, some assert that a petition to rend the acknowledgement voidable should be available to the parties; for instance, in a case where fraud or duress has been employed to secure the acknowledgement. Meanwhile, others interpret that only a person in a position of giving consent to an acknowledgement of paternity can set aside that acknowledgement if they do not fully consent. Accordingly, a petitioner asserting the existence of fraud or duress in a case should challenge the acknowledgement as being void, and not voidable, on the ground that the acknowledgement was made contrary to actual facts. Once acknowledgement of paternity has been declared voidable or void, no father-child relationship will take effect retrospectively from the time of the acknowledgement. However, the rights acquired by third parties prior to a declaration that an acknowledgement is voidable will not be prejudiced.

IV. Acknowledgement of Paternity by a Family Court Determination

299. When a man refuses to acknowledge paternity of a child voluntarily, on an application by the child, a court, under consideration of promoting the welfare of the child, can issue a determination to confirm the father-child relationship against the will of the man. Conversely, acknowledgement of maternity is unlikely to be disputed since the mother-child relationship can be evidently confirmed by the fact of the birth, except in the case of a deserted child.

300. Section 787 of the Civil Code provides that a child, his/her direct descendants or a legal representative of those persons (the mother of the minor child in

336. SD 17 Dec. 1982 Kagetsu 35-12-61.
337. SD 6 Apr. 1989 Minshu 43-4-193.
338. SD 14 Apr. 1978 Kagetsu 30-10-26.
339. SD 17 Dec. 1982 Kagetsu 35-12-61.

many cases)[340] are eligible to apply to a court to have a decision of acknowledgement of paternity issued. A person who is not a real child of the parent but registered as the child in the Family Register Book is also entitled to apply to the court for such a determination against his/her birth parent.[341] An unborn child or the mother of the unborn child has no right to apply for a decision but can make an application for a decision after the birth of the child even if the alleged father has already died.

301. Procedures for an application of acknowledgement of paternity vary according to the category of the child concerned. First, if a child is registered as a category A legitimate child, he/she cannot apply to be acknowledged by the biological father unless the person registered as his/her father denies the child's legitimacy.[342] Second, a category B legitimate child is eligible to make an application to be acknowledged by his/her biological father directly, in spite of the fact that a person registered as the father does not deny the legitimacy of their father-child relationship.[343] Third, a category C legitimate child can commence litigation for acknowledgement of his/her paternity.[344] Fourth, where a child has been registered as a category A legitimate child by reason of a false notice of birth, he/she can bring proceedings to be acknowledged by his/her biological father.[345] Fifth, a child who has already been acknowledged by a third party is not allowed to make an application to be acknowledged by his/her biological father unless the previous acknowledgement of paternity is declared void.[346] However, such a child can apply for his/her entry on paternity in the Family Registration Book to be changed if the previous acknowledgement is obviously void.[347]

302. A minor with the capacity to understand the meaning and effects of his/her acts is entitled to apply independently for the acknowledgement of his/her paternity (PALA section 13(1)). Whether or not an application by a minor is accepted depends on the nature of the individual case, but common practice dictates that a minor of 15 years of age or more will be regarded as having such capacity. Where a ward of adult guardianship makes an application for acknowledgement of paternity, a court can appoint a representative for him/her *ex mero motu* (PALA section 13(3)). A representative of a child can make an application to have paternity acknowledged on behalf of either the child or its direct descendants[348] unless the application is against the intention of the child or that of its descendants (PALA section 13(2)) (this rule will also apply to a case of a ward of adult guardianship (PALA section 14)).

340. It is interpreted that a minor child can make an application if he/she has the capacity to understand the meaning and effects of such acts (PALA s. 13).
341. SD 11 Oct. 1974 Kagetsu 27-7-46.
342. STD 29 Apr. 1916 Minroku 22-824.
343. SD 15 Feb. 1966 Minshu 20-2-202.
344. SD 29 May 1969 Minshu 23-6-1064.
345. STD 14 Dec. 1932 Minshu 11-2323.
346. Tokyo DD 12 Sep. 1964 Hanji 396-45.
347. Sapporo FO 27 Feb. 1971 Kagetsu 23-11/12-118.
348. SD 27 Aug. 1968 Minshu 22-8-1733.

303. Either a direct descendant of the child or a representative of the descendant can take over the proceedings for acknowledgement of paternity within three years of the death of the defendant and within six months after the death of the child who has already brought the proceedings (PALA section 42(3)).

304. The defendant in proceedings of acknowledgement of paternity is the alleged 'biological' parent or a prosecutor in the case of the death of the father (PALA section 42(1)). Where acknowledgement of paternity is sought after the death of an alleged 'biological' father, any interested parties such as a child of the deceased 'biological' father may participate in the proceedings in order to protect the interests of those parties and enable the court to reach an appropriate judgment (*see* PALA section 28 and PALR rule 16).

305. An application can be made at any time during the lifetime of an alleged 'biological' father or it must be commenced within three years after his death. For instance, in one case, a person of 60 years of age was entitled to make an application.[349] As to the starting point of the three-year limitation period, the courts have held that it will commence from the time at which the death is evident and not necessarily the actual time of death.[350]

306. One question may arise as to whether a petition confirming the father-child relationship (not an application for acknowledgement of paternity) may be accepted after the expiration of three years. It is generally interpreted that such a petition should not be allowed because it aims to circumvent that three-year limitation period. Even if the father-child relationship is confirmed by such a petition for some reason after more than three years has elapsed, acknowledgement of paternity will not take effect.[351]

307. A case regarding the acknowledgement of paternity will first be dealt with through family court mediation under the rule of mandatory mediation prior to litigation (PALA section 2(1)(ii) and FAPA section 257). In the case of litigation, a court can investigate the facts of the case *ex mero motu* and make a decision regarding the existence of a father-child relationship by examining both biological and sociological factors.[352] Results of a DNA test in particular will be considered for the purpose of proving the existence of the relationship.[353]

---

349. Fukuoka HD 1 Jun. 1972 Hanji 688-70.
350. SD 19 Mar. 1982 Minshu 36-3-432. In the case of a child who was deserted in China during the post-war chaos in 1945, a court held that time should run from the point at which the child was admitted into Japan after the restoration of diplomatic relations between Japan and China rather than the time at which the child had been notified of the death of father. In this case, twenty-six years had passed after the death of the father (Fukuoka HD 2 Jul. 1985 Kagetsu 37-10-67).
351. SD 19 Jul. 1990 Kagetsu 43-4-33.
352. SD 13 Sep. 1956 Minshu 10-9-1135.
353. One limitation is that a court has no authority to force the parties to provide blood samples for the test.

308. A court, by reference to section 772, is likely to issue a decision of acknowledgement of paternity of a child whose parents are cohabitees. In other cases, a court will declare the existence of a father-child relationship by examining the following facts: (1) the fact that the mother of the child had a sexual relationship with the man in question around the time she became pregnant;[354] (2) the fact that there is corresponding DNA[355] and blood type between the man and the child; (3) the fact that biological characteristics such as skeletal structure, fingerprints, palm prints and cerumen of the father and child do not negate the existence of a biological relationship;[356] (4) the fact that the man has admitted that the child is his own in his social circle such as the fact that he treated the child as his own and supported him/her financially.[357]

309. A child is not allowed to waive the right to apply for acknowledgement of paternity.[358] This restriction is justified by the fact that the right has not only a private but also a public nature for deciding a crucial status in family relationships. In addition, it may prevent a child from giving up the right of establishing a father-child relationship in exchange for a paltry amount of consolation money. Accordingly, an application for the acknowledgement of paternity will not be regarded as an abuse of right where a child has already made an agreement waiving his/her right in exchange for accepting payment of a large amount of money from the man concerned. However, the court can take account of the amount of money paid by the man when it is assessing a maintenance contribution towards the child or the child's portion of a deceased father's estate.

V. Others

310. Voluntary acknowledgement of paternity will usually only take effect by satisfying the prescribed formalities. However, in some cases, an acknowledgement of paternity, despite lacking in formality, may still be valid. For instance, if a man submits a false notice of birth to register his illegitimate child as legitimate,[359] or if he submits a notice of birth of his illegitimate child to the family registration office,[360] his conduct will be considered as a valid indication of his voluntary acknowledgement of paternity.

354. In order to defeat an allegation by a man that the mother was promiscuous around the time she became pregnant, women were formerly required to prove that they had no sexual relationship with any other men during that time. Now, the burden of proof is on the man to provide evidence indicating that the mother did have promiscuous relationships with other men during the period before and during the pregnancy (SD 26 Sep. 1961 Kagetsu 14-1-99).
355. Hiroshima HD 29 Jun. 1995 Hanta 893-251.
356. SD 13 Sep. 1956 Minshu 10-9-1135.
357. SD 26 Sep. 1961 Kagetsu 14-1-99.
358. SD 10 Apr. 1962 Minshu 16-4-693.
359. STD 11 Oct. 1926 Minshu 5-703.
360. SD 24 Feb. 1978 Minshu 32-1-110.

VI. Acknowledgement of Maternity

311. Section 779 of the Civil Code stipulates that an illegitimate child may be acknowledged by its father or its mother, although it is usually interpreted that the mother-child relationship will be established by the fact of the birth.[361] This section may however apply to exceptional cases; such as where a mother cannot be identified because she has deserted her child immediately after the time of birth or where an illegitimate child was registered by a false notice of birth as the legitimate child of a third party couple.[362] An interested party is eligible to argue the existence of maternity by way of a petition to confirm the mother-child relationship rather than making an application of acknowledgement of maternity.[363]

VII. Effects of Acknowledgement of Paternity

312. Either by voluntary acknowledgement of paternity by a father or by acknowledgement of paternity by either a family court determination or a decree, an illegitimate father-child relationship can take effect retrospectively from the time of the child's birth, although any rights acquired by third parties prior to the acknowledgement will not be prejudiced by such acknowledgement, determination or decree (Civ. section 784). On the basis of the father-child relationship, a child is eligible to claim maintenance from the father, the right to inherit from him (Civ. section 900(1)(iv)), to apply to have the parental rights and duties transferred from the mother to the father (Civ. section 819(4)) or to change his/her family name to that of the father (Civ. section 791).

313. The mother of an illegitimate child assumes the rights and duties of her child from the time of birth, but the father can take over such rights and duties by mutual agreement after acknowledging paternity. Similar to divorce cases, sections 788 and 766 may apply in the event that there is any change to the child's custodian, for the purpose of protecting the interests of the child. Thus, a family court is able to appoint the mother as the parent with rights and duties over the child while the father acts as the custodian.

314. An illegitimate child will take his/her mother's family name at the time of birth (Civ. section 790(2)). However, after paternity has been acknowledged, the child is entitled to change his/her family name to that of his/her father (Civ. section 791(1)). Two measures are available to effect a change to the family name. If there is no prospect that a claim to change the family name will cause any conflict between the interested parties, all the child is required to do is to submit a notice declaring the change of family name to the family registration office subject to the

361. SD 27 Apr. 1962 Minshu 16-7-27.
362. STD 14 Dec. 1932 Minshu 11-2323.
363. Tokyo DD 18 Oct. 1971 Hanji 659-79 and SD 29 Mar. 1974 Kagetsu 26-8-47.

Family Registration Act;[364] this simply involves an administrative measure. However, if the claim is likely to bring about a dispute between the interested parties, a family court can make a determination on whether an application for the change should be approved by taking account of all the circumstances of the case, such as the welfare of the child and the interests of all the parties concerned.

315. On an application for a change of the family name, a family court will consider the motive of the application, the living standards of the child and parents, and the wishes of the parties concerned. For instance, a family court may take account of any emotional bitterness on the part of the child in not sharing the same family name as his/her father. The court may also pay attention to the wishes of the other members of the father's family such as his wife or any legitimate children, and the social consequences which may be caused to them by the change of family name.[365]

§4. LEGITIMATION

I. Definition of Legitimation

316. If the birth of an illegitimate child is followed by the marriage of his/her mother and father, the child, even though acknowledged by the father, will be treated differently at law from his/her siblings who are born after the marriage in terms of the right of succession, taking the father's family name, other protection provided by the father and the manner in which entries are made in the Family Registration Book, despite any acknowledgement by the father. In order to avoid such discriminatory treatment, the child can apply to have his/her status changed from that of an illegitimate child to a legitimate child through the procedure of legitimation in the event of the subsequent marriage of the parents (Civ. section 789). There

364. Such scenarios may involve the following: an illegitimate child takes the mother's family name at birth and is later acknowledged by the father as his own. Then, the mother takes the father's family name by reason of marriage. The child still holds the mother's family name and wishes to change his/her family name to that of the father so that the family can all share the same family name. The child therefore only needs to take the administrative measure (Civ. s. 791(2)). A scenario 2 is the case of cohabiting parents in which a father has acknowledged paternity (Sapporo HK 11 Jan. 2008 Kagetsu 60-12-42).

365. The fact that a father acknowledges paternity of his illegitimate child will be included in the father's entry in the Family Registration Book. The Family Registration Book is in principle open to the public but requires some conditions for the purpose of protecting the privacy of the family (FRA ss 10(2), 10-2 and 133). It is still regarded as a social stigma in Japan if a married man has an illegitimate child. Even now, marriage is considered not only as a matter for the couple involved but also as an important event for the relatives (for instance, siblings of an acknowledged child). Accordingly, the social reputation of the relatives of the couple may affect the marriage. Therefore, when the legitimate child of such a man wishes to get married, for instance, the fact of his parent's adultery may cause discord among the relatives resulting in some being reluctant to support the marriage. One (Takamatsu HK 10 Nov. 1993 Kagetsu Hanta 863–268) denied an application and the other (Osaka HK 25 Apr. 1997 Kagetsu 49-9-116) granted by considering all the circumstances.

are two procedures for legitimation; legitimation by subsequent marriage of the parents and legitimation by acknowledgement of paternity after the parents' marriage.

A. *Legitimation by Subsequent Marriage of Parents*

317. Legitimation by the marriage of the parents subsequent to acknowledgement of paternity of the child will take effect if the following requirements are satisfied: (1) the child has been acknowledged by his/her father before the time of the parents' marriage; (2) the marriage is valid; and (3) the parents have the capacity to understand the meaning and effects of their acts. A voidable marriage will not affect the consequences of legitimation since it is regarded as valid until the time of revocation (Civ. section 748(1)).

318. Where a child's legitimation by the subsequent marriage of his/her parents is valid, the child will be treated as a legitimate child retrospectively from the time of the marriage (Civ. section 789(1)). A child can change his/her family name to that of either of his/her parents simply on submission of a notice to change his/her family name to the family registration office, without any approval by a family court (Civ. section 791(2)).

B. *Legitimation by Acknowledgement of Paternity*

319. An illegitimate child can be legitimatized by his/her father through the latter's acknowledgement of paternity during the period of his/her parents' marriage. Despite section 789(2) which states that a child acknowledged by its father and mother during their marriage shall acquire the status of a legitimate child as from the time of such acknowledgement, it is interpreted in practice that all effects of legitimation will operate retrospectively from the time of the marriage. A question may arise as to whether legitimation should be valid if the acknowledgement of paternity is pronounced after the dissolution of the parents' marriage. According to section 789(2), in order for such legitimation to be valid, acknowledgement of paternity must be made during the period of the parents' marriage. In practice, however, it is construed that valid legitimation will be effective if the parents are married and acknowledgement of paternity was made subsequent to that marriage.[366]

320. With respect to Japanese nationality, a child who is born to a non-Japanese mother and acknowledged by a Japanese father either before or after its birth may acquire Japanese nationality (Nationality Act section 3(1)).[367]

366. 28 Dec. 1950 Civ.Ko.Rep. No. 3358 of DGCAB.
367. SD 17 Oct. 1997 Minshu 51-9-3925 and 12 Jun. 2003 Kagetsu 56-1-107.

Chapter 5. Adoption

§1. Outline of Adoption

I. History of Adoption

321. Traditionally, adoption often functioned as a means of enabling the smooth succession of '*Ie*' household from one generation to another. Under the primogeniture scheme of the old family law, the head of an '*Ie*' household generally had to adopt a man as heir apparent if he had no son. Nowadays, unlike the Western adoption system which mainly aims to protect and promote the welfare of children, most adoption cases in Japan consist of cases such as inter-family adoption and adoption between adult persons.[368]

322. Under the current family law, adoption is divided into two types: adoption by contract between adults or between adults and a minor, or special adoption only between adults and minor parties. Under the former type, the relationship of the adoptive parents and the adoptee can be established by agreement of the parties. As mentioned later, different procedures will apply to this type according to the status of the parties. Whereas special adoption, which was introduced in 1987, can only take place by a family court determination and is subject to strict requirements.

§2. Adoption by Contract

I. Procedure for Adoption by Contract

323. In the case of adoption between adults, adoption by consent will take effect on the basis of the mutual agreement of the parties and by the submission of a valid notice of adoption by contract to the family registration office (Civ. sections 799 and 739). When adopting a minor, the approval of a family court is necessary but this additional requirement does not apply to inter-family adoption cases such as an adoptive parent and a minor of his/her spouse (Civ. section 798).

368. In 2019, cases involving the adoption of non-relative minors numbered 1,004 and special adoption cases comprised 816 out of 72,739 all adoption cases (The Supreme Court, *Judicial Statistics 2019*, *supra,* chart 2 and the Ministry of Justice, *Family Registration Statistics 2019*, (https://www.e-stat.go.jp/stat-search/files?page=1&layout=datalist&toukei=00250008&tstat=000001012466&cycle=8&year=20191&month=0&tclass1val=0), chart 19-41-2). It is understood that the number of adoptions between adults and the minor children at law is increasing but the current data on family matters does not show the details of such adoptions. The number of adoptions between Japanese people and non-Japanese is presumed to be small but precise data is not available.

II. Requirements for Adoption by Contract

324. A prospective adopter(s) must be a person (1) who is 20 years of age and over[369] and (2) who has the capacity to understand the meaning and effects of his/her acts. A court can decide whether prospective adoptive parents have such a capacity by either taking account of or disregarding any evidence provided by experts.[370] Wards under adult guardianship are eligible to become adoptive parents (*see* Civ. section 799).

325. An adult couple is expected to adopt a minor jointly unless one spouse intends to adopt the legitimate child of the other spouse or the other spouse is unable to express his/her intention regarding adoption (Civ. section 795). In the case of adoption between adult parties, a spouse may adopt or be adopted with the consent of the other except where the couple adopts or is adopted jointly, or where the other is unable to express his/her intention regarding adoption (Civ. section 796).

326. A guardian is required to obtain the approval of a family court in order to adopt his/her ward (a minor or adult) during and after his/her office (Civ. section 794).

327. Adoption will be effective as long as the adopter(s) is older than the adoptee[371] and unless he/she is a descendent of the adoptee (Civ. section 793).[372] Although such cases are rare, adoption can also take effect between a biological parent(s) and his/her illegitimate child. Such adoption may occur where the biological parent wishes to vest the child with the status of legitimacy.[373] Additionally, in the case of an adoption in which an elderly person adopts a married couple, a question may arise concerning the status of any child of the adopted couple. If the child is born after the time of adoption, he/she will be considered a blood relative of the adopting person (e.g., 'an adoptive grandparent'). Meanwhile, if the child is born before the time of adoption, no blood relationship will be considered to exist between the child of the adopted couple and the adopting person. Consequently, it may happen that an elder sibling has no blood relationship with the adopting party whereas a younger sibling does.

328. In the event of adoption of a minor under the age of 15, a statutory agent (legal representative) must give consent to the adoption on behalf of the minor (Civ. section 797(1)). In the case where one parent of the adopted child has sole parental rights and duties over that child, that parent is the statutory representative, but where

369. When a notice of adoption by contract which does not comply with this requirement is mistakenly registered in the Family Registration Book, the adoption will be voidable (Civ. ss 803 and 805).
370. Tokyo HD 31 May 1985 Hanji 1160-91 and Urawa DD 29 May 1992 Hanta 823-283.
371. As a very rare example, it may be possible for a husband to adopt his divorced wife if she was born on the same day as him, as she is technically not older than him.
372. Due to the interpretation that ascendants exclude relatives by affinity, a person can potentially adopt his/her deceased spouse's aunt/uncle, if he/she is older than her/him.
373. 23 Apr. 1914 Civ. Ko Rep. No. 154 of DGCCAB.

the other parent is appointed as custodian after their divorce, the statutory representative must obtain the consent of the custodian to proceed with any adoption in order to avoid a claim being brought by the custodian concerning the subsequent legitimacy of the adoption (Civ. section 797(2)).

III. Intention of Adoption by Contract

329. Adoption by contract will be effective where the parties involved truly intend to enter into the contract. Accordingly, adoption will be void if this requirement is not met, for example, where a notice of adoption is submitted without the knowledge of all the parties concerned,[374] or where one party mistakes the other for someone else, or the essential consent of the representative of a minor is not obtained (Civ. section 802).[375]

330. It is interpreted that an intention for adoption is the will to establish a substantial relationship of an adoptive parent(s) and an adopted child. Similarly to marriage, a court may find that an intention exists even if either party is unconscious at the time of submission of the notice unless there are special circumstances indicating that either party wished to withdraw their intention.[376] Meanwhile, in cases where the prospective adopter seems so old that his capacity to make a reasonable decision is suspected (e.g., due to senile dementia)[377] or adoption is kept secret from the interested party without justifiable reason, the court will declare that no true intention exists between the parties to effect adoption.[378]

331. A sham adoption is void. The courts have held that an adoption is void for lack of a principal intention to adopt in the following cases; adoption for the purpose of evading conscription,[379] adoption to raise the family rank,[380] adoption to change a family name which was considered as an obstacle to marriage,[381] or adoption to gain admission into a school within a different catchment area.[382] However, under similar circumstances, the court may nevertheless interpret that adoption will

374. STD 6 Nov. 1907 Minroku 13-1093.
375. STD 13 Feb. 1924 Shimbun 2243-19.
376. SD 24 Nov. 1970 Minshu 24-12-1931.
377. Tokyo HD 6 Aug. 2009 Hanta 1311-241.
378. Tokyo HK 31 May 1990 Hanji 1352-72.
379. STD 27 Nov. 1906 Daishinin Keiji-Hanketsuroku (Report on the Criminal Cases of the Supreme Tribunal) 12-1288. Under the '*Ie*' household system, the eldest son was exempt from conscription in the early Meiji-era. In some cases, a man was adopted by a couple with no son for the purpose of evading conscription.
380. Tokyo HD 8 May 1980 Hanji 967-69.
381. Takamatsu HD 5 Apr. 1955 Kamin 6-4-640. In this case, the adoptee wished to take on the family name of the adoptive parents because the adoptee was afraid that keeping his biological father's family name might prejudice any future of marriage upon the revelation of his father's bankruptcy.
382. Okayama DD 7 Mar. 1960 Hanji 223-24.

take effect if it is satisfied that the parties lived together as a family or they demonstrated an emotional relationship such as between a parent and child,[383] and it was decided that tax avoidance does not necessarily indicate the absence of intention for adoption.[384]

332. Where the intention behind an adoption is contrary to public policy, such adoption will be void. Adoption will not take place for this reason where the adoptive parents intend to adopt a girl in order to employ her as a prostitute. However, adoption will not necessarily be void by reason of the fact that the adopting party and adoptee have had previous sexual relationships.[385]

333. Any person whose interests may be directly affected by the adoption (not simply the adopter and adoptee) is eligible to bring proceedings as a petitioner to claim that the adoption should be void because of a lack of true intention of the parties with respect to the adoption. For instance, the mother of an adoptive parent is eligible to bring such a petition,[386] but not a person who has provided special care and devotion to either the adopting party or adoptee (*see* Civ. section 958-2(1)).[387] Any person who can prove to have a valid interest in the adoption is entitled to bring proceedings to annul the adoption even after the death of the adoptive parents and the adopted child. A petition for annulling adoption will terminate on the death of the petitioner (PALA section 27(1)).

334. When a petition for annulling an adoption is presented, either the adoptive parents or the adoptee will act as the defendant. Where a third party challenges the validity of an adoption, the adopting party and adoptee will act as joint defendants. When either the adoptive parents or the adoptee dies, any surviving parties will act as defendants in any petition presented. In the event of the death of all the parties involved, a prosecutor will act as the defendant (PALA section 26(2)).

335. In the case of a joint adoption by a husband and a wife, the adoptive parent-child relationship will be established individually between the parent and the child (for instance, the adoptive father-child relationship and the adoptive mother-child relationship).[388] Accordingly, if one of the spouses lacks a true intention to adopt in the case of a joint adoption, only that spouse will act as a party to any proceeding for annulling the adoption, while the other spouse can maintain a valid adoptive

383. SD 20 Dec. 1963 Kagetsu 16-4-117 and Osaka HD 30 Mar. 1984 Hanta 528-287.
384. SD 31 Jan. 2017 Minshu 71-1-48.
385. SD 22 Oct. 1971 Minshu 25-7-985.
386. STD 5 Jul. 1918 Shimbun 1474-18.
387. SD 1 Mar. 1988 Minshu 42-3-157. The Supreme Court held that a beneficiary given a universal gift by will of a deceased adoptive parent is not entitled to argue validity of adoption without any condition since his/her interests are not directly affected by adoption (SD 5 Mar. 2019 CW). Section 958-3 becomes s. 958-2 after deletion of s. 958 in 2021.
388. SD 17 Jul. 1978 Minshu 32-5-980.

relationship with the child.[389] If a third party disputes the validity of a joint adoption, the adoptive parent and adoptee who purportedly lack a true intention for adoption will act as joint defendants.[390] If a spouse adopts a minor without the consenting of the other spouse (Civ. sections 795 and 806-2), adoption between the consent spouse and the adopted child will be valid only if special circumstances exist.

336. An adoption will not take effect if it is declared void by reason of a lack of intention for adoption on the part of the persons involved. However, there is an exception in which adoption may be subsequently ratified where it was previously annulled due to the lack of consent by a representative (*see* Civ. section 797(1)). For instance, although the adoption of a minor is void if it is based on the consent of someone other than the statutory representative, it may be subsequently ratified by the adoptee when he/she reaches 15 years of age.[391] For the purpose of this procedure, either the adopted child or his/her representative, who is entitled to subsequently ratify the adoption, should notify their intention to ratify to the adoptive parent(s). Since no special measures for ratification are required, it is interpreted that ratification can be made in either oral or written form and can be either expressed or implied. Subsequent ratification will cause the adoption to operate retrospectively as from the time of the submission of the adoption notice (Proviso of Civ. section 116[392] does not apply to such case).

337. Where a notice of adoption is mistakenly accepted and registered in the Family Registration Book, the ensuing adoption will be voidable under the following circumstances:

- The adoptive parent is under 20 years of age (Civ. section 792). However, the adoption will be validated either if the adoptive parent(s) does not set aside the adoption within six months after his/her reaching 20 years of age, or if he/she ratifies it subsequently (Civ. section 804).
- A person(s) attempts to adopt either his/her ascendant or any other person who is older than him/her (Civ. sections 793 and 805). However, where one adopting spouse to a joint adoption is younger than the adopted child, only the adoption between the younger adoptive parent and the adopted child will be voidable.[393]
- A guardian adopts his/her ward without the approval of a family court (Civ. section 794). However, the adoption will be validated either if six months pass after completion of the guardianship, or if the adopted child ratifies it after completion of the guardianship (Civ. section 806(1)). The adoption will remain valid until the adopted child reaches majority age or recovers his/her legal capacity (Civ. section 806(2)).

389. *See* SD 12 Apr. 1973 Minshu 27-3-500.
390. Cf. Tokyo HD 10 Apr. 2008 Kagetsu 60-12-46.
391. SD 3 Oct. 1952 Minshu 6-9-753 and SD 8 Sep. 1964 Minshu 18-7-1423.
392. The proviso states that the rights of third parties may not be prejudiced thereby.
393. SD 17 Jul. 1978 Minshu 32-5-980.

- A spouse adopts or is adopted without the consent of the other spouse (Civ. section 796). In this case, the adoption will be validated either if six months pass after the non-consenting spouse discovers the existence of the adoption or if he/she ratifies it (Civ. section 806-2(1)).
- A legal representative of an adopted minor fails to obtain the consent of a custodian parent of the minor (Civ. section 797(2)). However, the adoption will be validated in the following cases: a non-consenting custodian ratifies the adoption subsequently, six months pass after the adopted minor reaches 15 years of age or the adopted minor ratifies the adoption (Civ. section 806-3).
- A minor is adopted without the approval of a family court (Civ. section 798). However, the adoption will be validated either if six months pass after the adopted child reaches the age of majority or if the adopted child ratifies the adoption (Civ. section 807).
- The adoption is achieved through fraud or duress, in which case the parties must revoke the adoption within six months of discovering the existence of any fraud or duress (Civ. sections 808, 806-3(2) and 747).

338. An adoption will be void in the following instances:

- If a minor is adopted without the consent of a legal representative (usually the parents) (Civ. section 797(1)). However, the adopted minor can ratify the adoption when he/she reaches 15 years of age and thereafter.[394]
- If a spouse adopts a minor without the consent of the other spouse (Civ. sections 795 and 806-2). In this case, only the adoption between the non-consenting spouse and the adopted child will be void for lack of intention for adoption.[395]

IV. Notice of Adoption by Contract

339. The parties to an adoption must complete and sign the prescribed form of notice of adoption (Civ. section 799). If a third party copies the signatures of the parties on behalf of them, the adoption will still take effect if the notice is accepted and registered in the Family Registration Book.[396] Although a notice of adoption should be submitted to the family registration office during the lifetime of the parties, adoption will still be valid if the notice is delivered to the office after the death of a party as long as the notice was posted before the death of the relevant party (FRA section 47).

340. There have been some cases where a couple or an individual has submitted a false birth notice of a legitimate child for a new born baby who is in fact not their legitimate child. In such a case, some argue that the false notice should be converted to a valid notice of adoption, on the basis of an interpretation that the submission of a notice, despite being false, implies that the parties have expressed an

394. SD 3 Oct. 1952 Minshu 6-9-753.
395. SD 12 Apr. 1973 Minshu 27-3-500.
396. SD 19 Jul. 1956 Minshu 10-7-908.

intention to become caring parents of that child as either biological or adoptive parents. The Supreme Court, however, has refused to apply such an interpretation in a series of cases, notwithstanding the fact that the parties lived together as parent and child.[397] According to the Supreme Court, first, adoption of a minor should take place with the approval of a family court in order to protect the interests of the adoptee. Second, the parties are required to comply strictly with the formalities laid down in the Civil Code.[398] Indeed, the Supreme Court has refused to apply such interpretation even in a case where a de facto adoptive relationship existed for more than fifty years.[399] However, more recently, the court has sought to protect a de facto adoptee in one case stating that the claim by the parent to dispute the validity of a false birth notice of a legitimate child should be considered to be an abuse of right as long as the parent himself/herself submitted the notice and a long time had passed since the time of submission.[400]

341. Although a de facto adoption may arise where a party to cohabitation and the child of the other cohabitee live together, or a biological father and his child, who is not acknowledged by him, live as a family or the parties live together with the intention of future adoption, such adoption will not be effective if no notice of adoption has been submitted to the family registration office. However, if one of the parties to such a de facto adoption has dissolved their relationship without any good reason, he/she may be liable for damages caused by the dissolution.[401]

V. Adoption of a Minor by Contract and Special Requirements

342. For the purpose of adopting a minor, the approval of a family court is essential and, moreover, for a minor under 15 years of age, consent by the child's statutory representative is required. No approval of a family court is required where a prospective adopter intends to adopt his/her direct descendant (for instance, a grandparent adopts his/her grandchild) or stepchild. However, approval must be obtained where the adoptive parent wishes to adopt a child of his/her deceased spouse (Civ. section 798).[402]

343. As for the identity of an applicant seeking the approval of a family court, it is interpreted that a prospective adopter, an adoptee or the parent of an adoptee

397. In a similar case, the Supreme Court pronounced that the false notice could be regarded as a valid notice of acknowledgement of paternity in terms of protecting the welfare of the child (SD 24 Feb. 1978 Minshu 32-1-110).

398. SD 28 Dec. 1950 Minshu 4-12-701. Some district courts have held that adoption could take effect on the basis that the parties truly intended to establish the adoptive relationship and that they actually lived together as a family (Osaka DD 15 Jun. 1970 Kagetsu 23-8-60 and Takasaki Branch of Maebashi DD 17 Jun. 1974 Kagetsu 27-2-104).

399. SD 11 Mar. 1979 Kagetsu 49-10-55.

400. SD 7 Jul. 2006 Kagetsu 59-1-98.

401. Nagoya DD 20 Mar. 1985 Kagetsu 38-3-83.

402. 15 Aug. 1948 Civ.Rep.Ko. No. 2413 of DGCAB and 4 Feb. 1949 Civ.Rep.Ko. No. 3876 of DGCAB.

are entitled to apply. On an application, a family court must examine whether the parties truly intend to adopt and if the adoption by contract will be of benefit to the child.

344. A family court may dismiss an application for approval by reason of a lack of a true intention for adoption in cases where the court discovers that the adoption does not aim to establish a family life but instead to enable the child to enrol in a school in the adoptive parents' catchment area or where it recognizes that the main purpose of adoption is to change the family name of the child.[403]

345. A family court will not approve an application for adoption if it finds that adoption will not be in the best interests of the child. For instance, approval will not be given where an adopted child is likely to be forced into taking a particular job,[404] the adoption aims at only achieving succession of the family name,[405] the adoptive parent intends to secure care in later life which would be provided by the adoptee,[406] adoption is applied for simply with the aim of maintaining an extended family relationship and protecting the family assets[407] or adoption is only being sought to change an entry in the Family Registration Book.[408]

346. In the case of a child who is under 15 years of age, the consent of his/her statutory representative is essential for establishing a valid adoption (Civ. section 797(1)). Parents of the child (or sometimes a guardian of the child) are usually eligible to act as the statutory representative. When one parent retains parental rights and duties and the other obtains the status of custodian after divorce, consent by the custodian will also be necessary for a valid adoption (Civ. section 797(2)).

347. Adoption made on the basis of consent by an unauthorized representative will be void. In a case where third parties are registered in the Family Registration Book as the biological parents of the child by a false notice of birth of a legitimate child, they will be formally vested with rights and duties over the child but will not be able to exercise such rights or duties at law. In such a case, a family court will dismiss an application for issuing a determination for approval of adoption by reason of the absence of consent by an authorized representative. However, once such 'defective' application is mistakenly accepted and as a result the 'defective' adoption is mistakenly registered, it may be ratified subsequently by either an authorized

403. Sapporo FO 2 Dec. 1963 Kagetsu 16-5-163 and Sasebo Branch of Nagasaki FO 2 Feb. 1966 Kagetsu 18-9-57.
404. A Buddhist nun in Niigata FO 10 Aug. 1982 Kagetsu 35-10-79 and a Shinto priest in Saga FO 14 Aug. 2009 Kagetsu 62-2-142.
405. Osaka FO 1 Apr. 1969 Kagetsu 22-1-116 and Tokyo HK 12 Apr. 1976 Hanji 817-71 in which a 95-year-old applicant intended to adopt a 9-year-old girl. It was decided that approval could be granted for this type of case as long as the parent-child relationship substantially existed and the adoption was in the interests of the child.
406. Mifune Branch of Kumamoto FO 30 Oct. 1959 Kagetsu 11-12-140.
407. Tokyo FO 26 Jul. 1967 Kagetsu 20-2-42.
408. Tokyo FO 29 Jul. 1966 Kagetsu 19-2-96.

representative or by the adopted child when he/she reaches 15 years of age, by notifying the adoptive parents of their intention to ratify the adoption.[409] The effects of ratification will apply retrospectively as from the time of the 'defective' adoption and the proviso of section 116 of the Civil Code will not apply.[410]

VI. Adoption and a Married Couple

348. When a married couple intends to adopt an adult person, the law creates a parent-child relationship between each spouse and the adoptee independently. Consequently, one spouse in a marriage can adopt a person independently if he/she obtains consent from the other spouse, who will have no adoptive relationship with the adoptee (Civ. section 796). This rule similarly applies to adoptees. Thus, for instance, a wife is not required to be adopted by the adoptive parent(s) of her husband.

349. Whereas, when a married couple intends to adopt a minor, they must adopt him/her jointly (Civ. section 795). Although, in such mandatory joint adoption, the adoptive relationship is interpreted as existing independently between each parent and the adopted minor.[411] If one spouse intends to adopt the legitimate child of the other spouse, the rule of mandatory joint adoption will not apply. In addition, where one spouse is missing or is unable to express his/her true intention as to the adoption, this rule will not apply and adoption will not take effect between that spouse and the child. However, the joint adoption rule will apply to a case where one spouse intends to adopt an illegitimate child of the other;[412] this is to avoid a result where a legitimate parent-child relationship is created between the adoptive parent and the minor, while an illegitimate parent-child relationship still remains between the birth parent and the minor (Civ. section 795).

350. If one spouse submits a notice of joint adoption without the knowledge of the other spouse, it is construed that adoption will only be effective between the spouse who submitted the notice and the child under certain circumstances; that there is no prospect of a joint adoption taking place because of a long period of separation of the spouses or the sole adoption is unlikely to infringe upon the interest of the other spouse.[413] In line with this approach, a joint adoption, where two independent adoptive relationships are established, will be void if the adoption is likely to bring about disadvantages to one spouse or any natural children in such a way as to infringe upon any rights to succession.[414]

409. SD 3 Oct. 1952 Minshu 6-9-753.
410. SD 8 Sep. 1964 Minshu 18-7-1423. Section 116 of the Civil Code stipulates that in the absence of any declaration of intention to the contrary, ratification shall be effective retrospectively as from the time the contract was made; however, the rights of third persons may not be prejudiced thereby.
411. SD 12 Apr. 1973 Minshu 27-3-500.
412. 17 Sep. 1988 Notification (Tsutatsu) No. Civ-2-5165 of DGCAB.
413. SD 12 Apr. 1973 Minshu 27-3-500.
414. Tokyo HD 26 Jun. 1975 Kagetsu 28-7-29.

351. Where one spouse fails to obtain consent from the other spouse, the joint adoption will be voidable (Civ. sections 806-2(1) and 796). However, the joint adoption will be effective if the latter subsequently gives his/her consent to the adoption or six months pass after the non-consenting spouse discovers the existence of the adoption. Otherwise only a single party adoption between one spouse and the adoptee will be created.

§3. Effects of Adoption by Contract

352. Adoption will take effect on the day that the notice of adoption is accepted by the registrar of the family registration office. Through adoption, an adopted child will have the status of a legitimate child of the adoptive parent(s); he/she will have rights to care, maintenance and succession (Civ. section 809). In the case of the adoption of a minor, the adoptive parent(s) will be vested with parental rights and duties and will become primarily responsible for the support and care of the minor. Although the adoptee must take the family name of the adoptive parent(s) (Civ. section 810), the adoption will not sever the legal relationship between the adoptee and his/her biological parents. The adoptee is still treated as a child of its biological parents in terms of rights to succession and maintenance.

§4. Dissolution of Adoption by Contract

I. Dissolution of Adoption by Mutual Consent

353. Similar to divorce proceedings, adoption may be dissolved either by mutual consent or through court procedure. If a surviving party wants to dissolve the relationship created by adoption after the death of the other party, he/she is entitled to terminate the adoptive relationship by obtaining the approval of a family court (Civ. section 811(6)).

354. Otherwise, adoption will terminate if the parties intend to dissolve the adoption and a notice of dissolution of adoption is submitted (Civ. sections 812 and 813). The parties to the dissolution must be the adoptive parent(s) and the adoptee. Where the adopted child is under 15 years of age, his/her statutory representative will be responsible for making any agreements regarding the dissolution on behalf of the minor (Civ. section 811(2)). If the biological parents are divorced before the dissolution of the adoption, they must make an agreement as to which parent should hold parental rights and duties after the dissolution of adoption (Civ. section 811(3)). For adopted children under 15 years of age, the following persons can take office as a statutory representative (Civ. section 811(2) to (5)):

- The biological parents, if they are alive. A single biological parent can act as a representative if the other is unable to act due to certain circumstances, such as that his/her whereabouts are unknown.

- The biological parent of the adoptee in the case of an adoption between the spouse of the biological parent and the child. If the adoptive parent is entitled to retain parental rights and duties over the adoptee in the event of his/her divorce from the biological parent, a special representative will be appointed for the adoptee.
- When the biological parents of the adoptee are divorced after the adoption has taken place, either biological parent can be appointed as a parent with parental rights and duties (a statutory representative) by mutual agreement or a family court determination.
- If the biological parents have died, a family court will appoint a guardian on an application by any interested parties; such as biological relatives or relatives from the adoption.

355. While adoptive parents of an adopted minor must jointly dissolve the adoption (Civ. section 811-2), the following measures must be taken where the adopted child intends to dissolve the relationship with just one of the divorced adoptive parents or to terminate the relationship with only one of the adoptive parents after that parent's death:

- After the time of divorce of the adoptive parents, the adoptive parent with parental rights and duties over the adopted minor will be a representative for the adoptee if the adoptee intends to dissolve his/her relationship with the other adoptive parent.
- After the divorce of the adoptive parents, a guardian will be appointed for the adopted minor if the adoptee intends to dissolve his/her relationship with the adoptive parent holding parental rights and duties over him/her.
- A surviving adoptive parent will be a representative for the adopted minor who intends to terminate the adoptive relationship with the deceased adoptive parent.
- A guardian will be appointed if the adopted minor intends to terminate the relationship with the surviving adoptive parent after the death of the other adoptive parent. When the adoptee intends to dissolve the relationships with both the deceased adoptive parent and the surviving adoptive parent, it is interpreted that his/her biological parent(s) will act as representatives if a guardian has not been appointed.[415]

356. Adoption will be dissolved by consent on the basis of the true intention of the parties. For the purpose of this procedure, some claim that the intention of dissolution must relate to the substantial will of the parties to terminate the adoption, and others assert that the intention must relate to the submission of a notice of dissolution of adoption by consent. Since dissolution of adoption by consent is valid if the parties so intend, a ward of guardianship is entitled to make an agreement on dissolution without obtaining consent from his/her guardian as long as he/she can produce evidence to show that he/she has the capacity to understand the meaning and effects of dissolution of the adoption (*see* Civ. section 812 and FRA section 32). If a party intends to withdraw the dissolution of the adoption, he/she must notify

415. Kanoya Branch of Kagoshima FO 12 Dec. 1974 Kagetsu 28-1-75.

the withdrawal to the other parties involved, return the special payment for dissolution to them or submit an application vetoing the notice of dissolution of adoption by consent to the family registration office.[416]

357. The use of fraud or duress to gain consent to dissolution of adoption by consent will constitute grounds for setting aside that dissolution (Civ. section 808). To revoke dissolution of adoption by consent, the same provisions as those governing the revocation of a voidable marriage will apply by analogy with the only difference that the period of three months is amended to six months. A person who claims the dissolution of adoption by consent to be voidable must make a petition to a family court for mediation prior to litigation. When the dissolution of adoption by consent is pronounced voidable, adoption will continue to be effective.

358. Although there is no provision concerning a void dissolution of adoption by consent, dissolution may be declared void in some cases through a similar procedure applied to marriage and divorce. When a notice of dissolution of adoption by consent is submitted by one party without the knowledge of the others, the adoption will be void by reason of the lack of the parties' full intention for dissolution. However, a void dissolution of adoption due to a lack of full intention can be ratified under the circumstances similar to those to void marriage.[417] If one party is dead at the time of submission of the notice, dissolution will not take place. Whereas, dissolution will be valid as long as a notice was posted before the time of death of one party and is only delivered to the family registration office after the time of the death. In the event that a party is unconscious at the time of submission of a notice of dissolution of adoption by consent, the notice will be regarded as valid unless there are any particular circumstances indicating that that party has withdrawn their consent to the dissolution. Similar to divorce, even sham dissolutions of adoption will be valid.

359. In addition to adoptive parents and adopted children, any interested parties are entitled to dispute the validity of dissolution of adoption by consent. Disputes relating to validity of adoption must be brought under the Personal Affairs Litigation Act (PALA section 2(1)(c)).

360. A notice of dissolution of adoption by consent must be submitted with the signatures of two witnesses as well as the parties (Civ. sections 812 and 739(2)). Where a representative is required to give his/her consent on behalf of an adoptee under 15 years of age, he/she should attach to the notice a document certifying that he/she is entitled to represent the adopted child. When a notice of dissolution of adoption by consent is submitted to the family registration office and the requirements laid down in the Civil Code are fully satisfied, the notice will be accepted (Civ. section 813). Even if the notice fails to fulfil the requirements and is mistakenly accepted by a family registration office, it will still take effect (Civ. section 813(2)).

416. Tokyo DD 5 Mar. 1951 Kamin 2-3-339.
417. Osaka HD 28 Jun. 1990 Hanta 738-154.

361. Similar to divorce, either party to dissolution by consent is eligible to notify the family registration office of his/her principal address that a notice of dissolution of adoption by consent should not be accepted and registered. On receipt of this caveat notice, the registrar must not accept any notice of dissolution of adoption by consent which has been submitted in the name of the unwilling party.

II. Dissolution of Adoption by a Family Court

362. When the relevant parties fail to reach an agreement on the dissolution of an adoption, they are required to make an application of mediation to a family court prior to litigation (FALA section 2(3) and FAPA section 257). If the parties agree on the dissolution of adoption through family court mediation, the adoption will be dissolved. There are two types of agreements that can be made through a family court: (1) an agreement to dissolve the adoption through family court mediation and (2) an agreement to submit a notice of dissolution of adoption by consent to the family registration office.

363. If the parties do not reach an agreement through family court mediation, a family court, by considering the views of the court mediation committee, may issue a determination to dissolve adoption in a way that is consistent with the original purpose of an application by the parties (FAPA section 277). The determination will be invalidated on an appeal by party within two weeks of the day when the determination is issued (FAPA sections 85 and 86).

364. If the parties are not satisfied with the result reached by the family court, they may file a claim to a family court on the basis of one of the grounds laid down in section 814. Either the adoptive parent(s) or the adopted child is eligible to be a party (plaintiff or defendant) in such proceedings; a representative will be appointed for an adopted minor under 15 years of age (Civ. section 811).

365. The grounds for dissolution of an adoption are based on a no-fault principle (Civ. section 814). Section 814 stipulates that one party to an adoption can bring an action for dissolution in the following circumstances:

(1) if the defendant has maliciously deserted the plaintiff;
(2) if the defendant has not been heard from for three years or more; or
(3) if there exists some other grave reason by which the parties cannot be reasonably expected to continue the adoption.

366. Malicious desertion stated as ground (1) refers to such acts as an intentional failure to provide maintenance, care or to fulfil other responsibilities. For instance, if the adoptive parents ordered the adopted child's absence, during which time they sold all their property for their own profit, this act would come under the category of malicious desertion and constitute a ground for dissolution.[418] In another case the court has stated that the acts by an adopted child will constitute desertion on the ground that he left his elderly adoptive mother and did not provide any financial support or other caring assistance.[419]

367. Where a case is brought under on the basis that the defendant is missing (Civ. section 814(1)(ii)), similar court procedures are to be followed as those in a divorce case where the defendant is missing.

368. For the purpose of constituting ground (3), an irretrievable breakdown of the adoptive relationship has been demonstrated in the following process: an act of insult and cruelty against the adoptive parent(s) by an adoptee such as that the latter plotted to take away the property of the adoptive parents;[420] when an adopted child declines to take over the family business of the adoptive parents,[421] an adoptive father petitions for dissolution of the adoption by reason that he discovers the existence of a sexual relationship between his wife and the adopted child;[422] divorce of the adoptive parents where a wife adopted an illegitimate child of her husband and she subsequently sought the dissolution of that adoption after divorcing the husband,[423] sexual abuse against an adopted by an adoptive parent[424] and a lack of intention to maintain a caring relationship.[425]

369. As a rule, a 'guilty' party under these grounds has not been entitled to bring proceedings for dissolution of the adoption.[426] However, similar to divorce litigation brought by a guilty party, a court has granted the dissolution of an adoption to a 'guilty' party in one case where the relationship of the parties had broken down since more than ten years ago and the 'innocent' party was unlikely to face financial difficulties after the dissolution of the adoption.[427]

§5. Effects of Dissolution of Adoption

370. Any relationship created by an adoption will terminate on its dissolution, but any relationships of affinity prohibiting marriage will remain effective. Accordingly, an ex-adoptive parent and an ex-adopted child are not permitted to marry (Civ. section 736).

418. Fukushima DD 18 Jan. 1957 Fuhokoikakyuminshu-Showa32nendo (jo) 407.
419. Fukushima FO 12 Sep. 1967 Kagetsu 20-4-52.
420. SD 18 Dec. 1952 Minshu 6-11-1190.
421. Yokohama DD 16 Apr. 1965 Hanta 180-132.
422. Osaka DD 26 Sep. 1954 Kagetsu 7-3-21.
423. Nagano DD 5 Jul. 1963 Kagetsu 16-4-138.
424. Fukushima FO 11 Aug. 1966 Kagetsu 19-3-84.
425. Tokyo DD 23 Aug. 2004 Hanta 1177-262.
426. SD 4 Aug. 1964 Minshu 18-7-1309.
427. Takada Branch of Niigata DD 21 May 1992 Kagetsu 45-2-175 and Tokyo HD 25 Aug. 1993 Kagetsu 48-6-51.

371. On the dissolution of an adoption, an adopted child will change his/her current family name to the surname that he/she took before the adoption. If the adoption had continued for more than seven years, the adoptee is entitled to retain the current family name even after the dissolution of adoption (Civ. section 816(2)). When an adoptee dissolves the adoptive relationship with only one of the adoptive parents, he/she will keep the current family name even after the dissolution of adoption. In other words, the adoptee does not need to change his/her current family while an adoptive relationship with either adoptive parent still exists. This rule applies to cases where the adoptive parents are married, divorced or either or both are dead at the time of dissolution of adoption.

372. Concerning the disposition of special assets such as the family tree, utensils of religious rites, tombs and burial grounds (Civ. section 897(1)), section 769 will apply to cases of dissolution of adoption (Civ. section 817). Meanwhile, unlike divorce cases, the court is reluctant to grant any division of property of an adoptive family on the dissolution of adoption for the reason that it is rare for the adoptive parents and adopted child to have made substantial contributions together to establish the family property.[428] However, a court may grant to either party an award for any pain and suffering caused by the dissolution of adoption (Civ. section 709).

§6. Special Adoption

I. Outline of Special Adoption

373. The procedures for special adoption were enacted in 1987 following a high-profile case which triggered a movement for a new adoption law. In 1973, a gynaecologist admitted to the public that he had suggested to an unmarried mother that she give up her new-born baby and hand it over to a childless couple, and the baby was registered as the legitimate child of the couple through a false certification of birth issued by him. He stated that he had been following this practice for nearly ten years and asserted that his aim was only to save the life of a baby who might otherwise have been aborted and to protect the mother, who might otherwise have faced a social and financial difficulties in the future as an unmarried mother and so registered in the Family Registration Book.

374. He strongly blamed the adoption law and practices of that time by pointing to the fact that the relationship between an adoptee and his/her biological parents would not be severed by adoption and he also criticized the fact that the names of the parties concerned are entered in the Family Registration Book which is generally open to the public, who widely believe the principle that 'blood is thicker than water'. Accordingly, it sometimes happened that a childless couple adopting a minor concealed the fact of adoption from not only the adoptee but also from the community in order to prevent someone from intervening in family matters, and to stabilize the adoptive relationship. For this purpose, a false notice of the birth of a

428. Tokyo DD 24 Dec. 1993 Kagetsu 47-11-86.

legitimate child would be submitted to the family registration office by a childless couple who were handed a baby through informal arrangements by a private go-between (albeit in a small number of cases).

375. However, this practice raised several questions: such adoption of a minor might infringe upon the welfare of the child because of the lack of checks and controls from public intervention, the family registration system might lose its accuracy by reason of falsely entered information, and such a practice could render vulnerable the status of the parties involved because the adoptive relationship could be pronounced void at any time on an application by any interested person.

376. Accordingly, in order to balance the requirement of protecting the interests of the parties involved and the demand to prohibit public disclosures of the adoption of a minor, the special adoption procedures were introduced in the Civil Code (revised in 1987) for providing a more secure status to the parties to adoption. Unlike adoption by contract, a special adoption requires the parties to fulfil rigid conditions.

377. In general, special adoption can be summarized as follows: it only applies to a minor with particular requirements, it will be effected by a family court determination, any dissolution of the adoptive relationship(s) will be under certain restrictions, the special adoption terminates the legal relationship between an adoptee and his/her biological parents, and it will be stated in a prescribed way in the Family Registration Book. In addition, any privately arranged placement was prohibited for protecting the interests of an adopted child but it is now available after the implementation of the Adoption Agency (Regulation) Act 2016. Under the strict rule and procedure of the regulations of the Ministry of Health, Labour and Welfare (section 9 of the Adoption Agency (Regulation) Act), an agency should be approved and registered by a local government, and it is only eligible to claim the fee but no other commission. Special adoption is a beneficial measure for protecting a child in need of special protection but there are very few special adoption cases applied for to a family court. In order to encourage more people to apply for a special adoption and to promote the welfare of a child in need of special protection, the Subcommittee on Special Adoption of the Deliberative Council on the Legal System published 'The Outline of the Draft on Revision of Special Adoption' in 2019. It proposes revision of the special adoption procedures stating that the determination process shall be divided into two stages; in the first stage, a family court shall investigate whether an application meets the requirements stipulated in section 817-6 (consent by birth parents) and 817-7 (special necessity of protecting a child) and in the second stage, it shall examine if the application shall be appropriate for achieving protection of the child and to promote the interests of the child. After this process, the special adoption shall take effect by a family court determination. The Subcommittee also proposes that a minor, a person with insufficient capacity and a director of a child guidance centre shall be eligible to make an application and a family court should hear the view of a child over 15 years of age. In 2019, the relevant provisions were revised on the proposal of the Council.

II. Procedures for Special Adoption

378. A married couple must jointly apply to a family court to be granted a special adoption. A single person is not eligible to be an adoptive parent except where he/she intends to adopt a legitimate child of his/her spouse (Civ. section 817-3). Prospective adopters must be 25 years of age or over, although one applicant of 20 years of age or above is eligible to be an adopter as long as his/her partner is 25 years of age or above (Civ. section 817-4). There is no condition regarding the disparity of age between the adoptive parents and an adoptee.

379. A prospective adoptee should be under 15 years of age at the time of application or under 18 years of age at the time of adoption determination being completed (Civ. section 817-5(1)). However, this rule shall not apply to a case where the prospective adoptee has been taken care of by the applicants prior to 15 years of age and there are unavoidable circumstances for failure of making an application on reaching the age of 15 years (Civ. section 817-5(2)). If a prospective adoptee is 15 years of age or over, his/her consent must be obtained for valid adoption in order that the prospective adoptee can choose either ordinary adoption or special adoption (Civ. section 817-5(3).

380. Prospective adopters shall make application to a family court for seeking determination to confirm suitability of adoptee for special adoption and shall make a simultaneous application for seeking the determination of a finalizing valid special adoption (Civ. section 817-2 and FAPA sections 164(1) and 164-2(1)). In some cases, the head of a child guidance centre can also be eligible to make application for the former determination and to participate in the court hearing as an 'Interested Party Intervenor' (CWA sections 33-6-2 and 33-6-3 and FAPA section 42(7)). Unlike the previous procedure, the new process of special adoption is divided into two stages. In the first stage, a family court shall confirm if consent by the parents of a prospective adoptee is obtained and examine if the parents of a prospective adoptee are incapable or unfit to care for the child or if there are any other special circumstances, and it shall make sure that the special adoption is especially necessary in the interests of the child (Civ. section 817-7). As a procedural requirement, the family court must hear statements from the prospective adoptee, the parents of a prospective adoptee, the person exercising the parental right and duties over a prospective adoptee, and a guardian of a prospective adoptee (FAPA section 164-2(6)).

381. Consent by the parents of the prospective adoptee is necessary (Civ. section 817-6) and for this purpose it is construed that a parent may include biological parents of the adoptee and the current adoptive parent(s) if the child has already been adopted. A family court may require the consent of a biological father who has not in fact made any acknowledgement of paternity of the adoptee.[429] Consent for

429. Cf. SD 14 Jul. 1995 Kagetsu 47-10-50.

special adoption will be dispensed with when those parents of the prospective adoptee are missing,[430] having an incurable impairment of, or a disturbance in the functioning of, the mind or brain, unknown, abusive to the adoptee,[431] or unreasonably refuse or withdraw consent (*see* Civ. section 817-6).[432] If consent has been given, the biological or previous adoptive parent(s) may withdraw it at any time without showing any particular reason for withdrawal before a determination of special adoption is finalized.[433] However, consent shall not be withdrawn if the consent given two weeks after the date of birth of the prospective adoptee is made by document submitted to a family court which was created by family court investigation officer or consent was made at the time of court hearing (FAPA section 164-2(5)). While the court seems to regard the consent by the biological parent(s) important for approval of special adoption,[434] a court may dismiss the withdrawal of consent by those parents if it considers the withdrawal to be against the welfare of the adoptee.[435]

382. Once the family court makes the former determination, the biological parents of the adoptee and the current adoptive parent(s) shall lose the right to withdrawal of consent and the case goes to the second stage where it will set up a six-month probationary period for the applicants during which it examines how the applicants have been taking care of the minor before and during the period (Civ. section 817-8(1)). At the same time, the family court will examine the statements issued by the parties concerned. If the family court finds that the child has been brought up at the applicants' home for a certain period of time under proper arrangements made by a welfare organization or biological parents, it may include that period in the six-month period (Civ. section 817-8(1)).[436] The family court must hear statement from the prospective adoptee of 15 years of age and over, the person(s) who is entitled to exercise the parental rights and duties over the prospective adoptee, and a guardian of the prospective adoptee (FAPA section 164(6)). If the family court finds that the requirements of special adoption are met and special adoption shall promote the welfare of minor, it shall make a determination of finalizing valid special adoption (Civ. section 817-2(1)). For the interests of the parties, a family court may not notify a prospective adoptee of the result of determination for confirming suitability to special adoption (FAPA section 164-2(10)) and it may not notify a prospective adoptee under the age of 15 years or the parents of a prospective adoptee of the result of determination for finalizing valid special adoption (FAPA section 164(10)).

430. Sapporo FO 18 Mar. 1988 Kagetsu 40-7-185.
431. Goshogawara branch of Aomori FO 21 May 2009 Kagetsu 62-2-137.
432. Cf. Fukuoka HK 27 Dec. 1991 Kagetsu 45-6-62.
433. Tokyo HK 27 Mar. 1989 Kagetsu 41-9-110.
434. Tokyo HK 16 Dec. 2002 Kagetsu 55-6-112.
435. Fukuoka HK 27 Dec. 1991 Kagetsu 45-6-62.
436. Yokohama FO 11 Mar. 1988 Kagetsu 40-7-181.

III. Criteria for Approving Special Adoption

383. On an application, a family court will issue a determination for special adoption if it considers that: (1) the biological parents or any other carer face great difficulties in looking after the child, or they have failed to provide appropriate care for the child; (2) the child has special circumstances, such as a need for special protection; and (3) a determination is essential for protecting the welfare of the child (Civ. section 817-7).

384. On considering whether the child has special circumstances and thus in need of special protection, the family court will examine the situation of the biological parents and the child; for example, whether the parents are missing, lacking either intention or capacity to look after the child, facing severe financial difficulties, abusing the child or are imprisoned, as well as whether the child is illegitimate or fathered by rape and whether the biological relationship needs to be severed in the interests of the child.[437] In addition, the family court will consider the age of the prospective adoptive parents, their social and financial situations and their emotional stability.

385. Where a child has already been adopted under the procedure of adoption by contract, the current adoptive parents are eligible to apply for special adoption of their adopted child as long as they fulfil the requirements (Civ. sections 817-3 to 817-7).[438] In a case where one party to a marriage intends to make an application of special adoption of his/her stepchild, he/she is usually required to show strong evidence that special adoption is essential for the welfare of the child and that it is highly likely to contribute to the promotion of the best interests of the child. In practice, the courts seem to be cautious about issuing a determination of special adoption in such a case.[439]

386. On a determination of special adoption being issued, the adoptee will be registered in a family registration page that has been newly prepared for this very purpose under the name of the adoptive parents, and he/she shall be transferred from this page to that of the adoptive parents (FRA sections 20-3(1) and 18(3)). Only the fact of special adoption will be added to the entry of the adoptive parents in the Family Registration Book.

IV. Effects of Special Adoption

387. When a special adoption takes effect, the adopted minor will hold the status of a legitimate child of the adoptive parents, take the family name of the adoptive parents, and all relationships with the biological parents and other relatives by blood will be terminated except for the purpose of the restrictions on marriage. In

437. Tokyo HK 20 Nov. 1996 Kagetsu 49-5-78 and Nagoya HK 14 Nov. 2003 Kagetsu 56-5-143.
438. Nagoya HK 17 Oct. 1989 Kagetsu 42-2-181.
439. Nagoya HK 23 Mar. 1989 Kagetsu 41-12-112 and Naha FO 7 Sep. 1992 Kagetsu 45-9-55.

this respect, a biological father will lose the right to assert his paternity of the adopted child.[440] A child adopted by his/her step-parent will not lose the relationship with his/her biological parent (and the relatives by blood through this parent) who is married to the step-parent (Civ. sections 817-3 and 817-9). Furthermore, the parties will hold a special status in relation to the Criminal Code, the Criminal or Civil Litigation Proceedings Acts (*see* Part II Chapter 8).

V. Dissolution of Special Adoption

388. A family court may issue a determination dissolving special adoption on an application by the adoptee, biological parents, or a public prosecutor if it discovers that the adoption has proved harmful to the welfare of the adoptee (Civ. section 817-10(1)). For the purpose of dissolution, the biological parents must show that they are capable of looking after the child. Accordingly, only a new special adoption will be available to the child if the biological parents are dead, missing or lacking in capability. Upon the dissolution of a special adoption, the adoptee's relationship with his/her adoptive parents will terminate, while his/her relationship with the biological parents and other relatives by blood will be restored (Civ. section 817-11). However, the restriction on marriage between an ex-adoptive parent and ex-adoptee will remain after the dissolution of the special adoption (*see* section 736).

§7. Foster Child and Foster Parents

I. Outline of Foster Child and Parents

389. A foster child and its foster parents are not regulated by the Civil Code but instead by the Welfare of Children Act 1948. Section 6-3 of the act stipulates that a foster parent is the person approved by a governor of local government as a proper person who wants to look after a child who has no carer or whose carer is considered to be unsuitable for taking care of them (Cf. paragraph 516). Any person is required to notify their local government if he/she intends to have a child under 18 years of age stay at his/her home for more than three months, the child is not his/her relative within the fourth degree, and the child is being kept biologically away from his/her parent(s) with parental rights and duties or his/her guardian (WCA section 30(1)). In addition to foster care, 'Family Home' shall be available when bringing up a child by foster parents is likely to be difficult (WCA section 6-2(8)). 'Family Home' provides caring services similar to foster care but the number of children living at a family home (between 5 and 6 children) is larger than in the case of foster care (up to four children).[441]

---

440. Cf. SD 14 Jul. 1995 Minshu 49-7-2674.
441. In 2019, 1,660 children lived at family homes (Ministry of Health, Labour and Welfare, Annual Report on Administration of Social Welfare 2019, (https://www.e-stat.go.jp/stat-search/files?page=1&layout=datalist&toukei=00450046&tstat=000001034573&cycle=8&tclass1=000001149061&tclass2=000001149069&tclass3val=0), table 50.

390. Fostering relationships can be classified into the following four types:[442]

(1) Ordinary foster parents looking after children who need day-to-day care because they have no carer or their carer is unsuitable to take care of the children (this includes a couple who intends to make an application for adoption). The parents can take care of a maximum of six children until the age of 18 (in some cases 20).
(2) Foster parents who intend to adopt children.
(3) Special foster parents looking after children for two years who need special care due to abuse by their carer (CAPA section 2). The number of children under such foster care should be below three for each fostering case.
(4) Relative foster parents looking after children who are relatives within three degrees of the foster parents and who have lost proper care by their parents or another carer who are dead, missing or imprisoned.

391. The requirements for a foster parent are as follows:[443]

- For ordinary foster parents, they must be in good health and sound mind,[444] understanding and caring towards children, not in any financial difficulties, and have no records of child abuse or crimes violating the Welfare of Children Act and the Regulation and Punishment of Acts Relating to Child Prostitution and Child Pornography Act, and the Protection of Children Act 1999 and the Child Abuse Prevention Act. Similar conditions will be applied to a resident cohabiting with the foster parent (WCA section 34-20). A person with physical disabilities or disease is eligible to be a foster parent unless such disabilities and disease will affect their care.
- For special foster parents, in addition to the same requirements for ordinary foster parents, the parents must satisfy one of the following conditions: (a) they need to have experience as registered ordinary foster parents for more than three years; (b) they have been engaged in welfare activities for children for more than three years with qualifications such as being a nanny, child tutor, child welfare officer, medical doctor, nurse, health nurse, school teacher or person with professional qualification for child welfare, health and medical activities, school education or correctional task and they must obtain approval by a local governor as being an appropriate person for foster care; (c) they must be persons who are accredited by a local governor to have capacity similar to or more than that of persons in (a) or (b). Moreover, special foster parents must have completed a special course for foster care and must be able to devote themselves to take care of the child.
- For relative foster parents, the same requirements for ordinary parents will apply except for the financial requirements.

---

442. In 2019, the number of registered foster parents was 11,047 for ordinary fostering, 716 for special fostering, 618 for relative fostering and 5,053 for adoption, while ordinary foster children numbered 4,456, special foster children 215, relative foster children 817 and 344 for adoption (Ministry of Health, Labour and Welfare, *supra*, table 49.
443. Cf. Osaka City approved a same-sex couple as a foster parent in 2017.
444. This means a candidate must not be a ward of guardianship (Welfare of Child Act ss 34-20(1)(i)).

II. Procedure of Establishing Foster Parent-Child Relationship

392. Applicants wishing to become foster parents must apply for registration at their local authority. On application, a committee associated with a child guidance centre in the area will investigate whether the applicants are a married couple,[445] capable of looking after the child and whether their home environment is suitable to bring up a child. Now a same-sex couple is considered eligible to apply for foster parent registration in many places in Japan after a same-sex couple's registration was accepted in 2017 in Osaka. Applicants must take an introductory course in foster care. If the governor of the local government is satisfied with the circumstances of the applicants, he/she will register the applicants as prospective foster parents (*see* WCA section 34-19). A child guidance centre will place the child with the family that it considers most appropriate for looking after that child. After placement of the child, the child guidance centre may provide various assistance to the foster family for the purpose of helping the parties to maintain a good relationship.

III. Legal Status of Foster Parents and Child

393. No legal parent-child relationship will be created between the parties of foster care. Indeed, foster parents have some authority to take care of the child and take necessary actions for the purpose of the care, education or discipline of the child notwithstanding the existence of any parent(s) with the case parental authority or guardian(s) (WCA section 47(2)).

394. Everyday expenses such as food, medication or school fees will be paid to the foster parents by the relevant local government.[446] In addition, foster parents are eligible to claim favourable treatment in terms of taxation.

395. Foster parents will be supervised by the relevant local government and required to submit a report concerning the care of each foster child (WCA sections 30-2 and 46(1)). If the local government considers that foster parents are unsuitable for taking care of the child or finds that the relationship between the foster parents and the child has broken down, it will terminate the foster care.

---

445. Although a single person has been considered as eligible to be a foster parent since 1987, he/she is unlikely to be registered in practice due to his/her lack of sufficient experience in caring for children.

446. As of 2020, 90,000 yen as foster care and about 50,000 yen plus necessary expenditure per child shall be paid monthly to foster parents (MHLW, Foster Care System (data), (https://www.mhlw.go.jp/content/000676361.pdf), p. 1.

Chapter 6. Parental Rights and Duties (Parental Power)

§1. Outline of Parental Rights and Duties (Parental Power)

I. Principles of Parental Rights and Duties

396. Parents are usually vested with parental rights and duties with respect to the care and property management of their minor children. Although these rights and duties are literally described as 'parental rights' in the Civil Code, it is commonly interpreted that 'parental rights' outline the legal status of the parents in protecting and promoting the interests of their children, rather than any authoritative power over the children. In this respect, 'parental rights' may be synonymous with parental responsibilities for the welfare of minors. Under current Japanese family law, one's parental rights and duties consist of, first, the rights and duties to look after one's children and, second, those for administering any property of the children.

397. Parents (including adoptive parents) must exercise their parental rights and duties jointly over their legitimate minor child during the period of their marriage in the interests of that child (Civ. sections 818 and 820). A mother will hold such rights and duties over her illegitimate child who has not been acknowledged by its father, or either the mother or the father in the case of an illegitimate child who has had its paternity acknowledged by the father.

398. A minor or a person without legal capacity is generally not eligible to hold the status of a parent with parental rights and duties except where a court finds that the appointment of such a person as a parent with parental rights and duties is necessary to uphold the best interests of the child.[447] Where the parent is an unmarried minor, the parent(s) of such minor (the grandparent(s) of the child) will exercise parental rights and duties over the child on behalf of the minor parent (Civ. section 833).[448] If the minor parent dies, a guardian will be appointed for the child, and if the parent(s) of the minor parent dies, a guardian will be appointed for the minor parent and will exercise parental rights and duties over the child on behalf of the minor parent.

II. The Parental Rights and Duties of Parents to a Legitimate Child

399. During the period of their marriage, the parents of a legitimate child will be vested jointly with parental rights and duties in relation to such child. In the case of a child legitimatized by the subsequent marriage of his/her parents (Civ. section 789), he/she will be under the control of both parents from the time the child acquires the status of a legitimate child. While parents are, as a rule, required to exercise their parental rights and duties jointly during their marriage, one parent

447. Osaka DD 18 Dec. 1958 Kamin 9-12-2505 (a case of incompetent) and 13 Jul. 1950 Civ.Ko.Rep. No. 1920 of DGCAB (a case of quasi-incompetent).
448. 20 Feb. 1948 Civ.Ko.Rep. No. 87 of DGCAB.

may exercise those rights and duties independently except where one parent wishes to independently bring legal proceedings.[449] Furthermore, a parent may independently exercise those rights and duties if the other parent dies, is pronounced to be under guardianship, is deprived of his/her parental rights and duties, or is unable to exercise those rights and duties because he/she is missing or is overseas for a prolonged period (Civ. section 818(3)).

400. In the event of divorce, either parent shall thereafter be singly vested with parental rights and duties on the agreement of both parents (Civ. section 819(1)). The parents must complete a notice of divorce by mutual consent stating who is to be the parent to assume parental rights and duties after the divorce and, if necessary, who will be the custodian. If the parents fail to reach an agreement on the issue of who is to assume parental rights and duties, they must then apply for family court mediation and the issuing of a family court determination.

401. In the case of divorce by mutual consent, the divorce itself will still be effective even if a notice of divorce by mutual consent which fails to state the name of the parent to assume parental rights and duties after divorce is mistakenly accepted by the family registration office.[450] In such a case, the parents would retain parental rights and duties jointly even after the divorce; however, they are required to decide promptly which parent should be the parent to assume those rights and duties.

402. Where one parent has subsequently ratified a notice to the divorce but not the part relating to the assignment of parental rights and duties of a void divorce notice, both parents must then decide which parent should be the parent to hold parental rights and duties.[451] Naturally, this rule does not apply to a case where one parent has ratified all parts of a void divorce notice.[452] If the parents agree to divorce but do not reach an agreement relating to the parental rights and duties at a family court mediation, the family court will make a determination with respect to the parental rights and duties (*see* FAPA section 272(4)).[453]

403. In a case of divorce litigation at a family court, the court is entitled to grant a divorce decree and to decide which parent should be vested with the parental rights and duties after divorce. In the case of a voidable marriage, the issue of the assignment of parental rights and duties will be dealt with under similar rules and procedures as those governing divorce litigations.[454]

404. Where a child is born after his/her parents' divorce, the mother will be regarded as the parent with parental rights and duties. The father may afterwards

449. Cf. SD 26 Nov. 1982 Minshu 36-11-2296.
450. Nagoya HD 29 Nov. 1971 Kotosaibansho Minji-Saibanreishu (Report on the Civil Cases of the High Courts) 24-4-438.
451. Fukuoka FO 22 Oct. 1974 Kagetsu 27-9-102.
452. Takamatsu FO 4 Sep. 1980 Kagetsu 33-11-118.
453. Osaka FO 9 Feb. 1996 Kagetsu 49-3-66.
454. Tokyo HD 27 Apr. 1977 Hanji 857-84.

assume that status through agreement with the mother, or if they fail to reach an agreement, a family court will decide which parent should hold parental rights and duties by way of a determination (Civ. section 819(1), (2), (3) and (5)).

405. In the event of the death of a parent who has been solely vested with parental rights and duties after a divorce, there are two courses of action. First, a guardian may be appointed for the child(ren) from the time of death or second, the surviving parent may have his/her parental rights and duties restored. The former course of action is taken when the court considers, by taking account of all the circumstances, that the appointment of a guardian is more appropriate for protecting the interests of the child than restoring the rights and duties to a surviving parent.[455] However, advocates of the second course of action claim that the restoration of a surviving parent's rights and duties accords more with common sentiment than the appointment of a guardian.[456]

406. In response to criticism against the appointment of a guardian after the death of the parent with parental rights and duties, the courts have modified their approach by vesting the surviving parent with parental rights and duties by applying section 819(1) with necessary modification, or appointing a guardian in accordance with section 838(1) of the Civil Code and the attached list of section 39 of the Family Affairs Proceedings Act.[457]

407. The notion that the surviving parent should be reinvested with his/her rights and duties is based on the view that in most cases a parent loses their parental rights and duties after divorce not because they lack sufficient capacity to care for the child but simply because no post-divorce joint-custody system is incorporated into the current family law (Civ. section 819(1) and (2)). Therefore, since it is usually observed that the surviving parent shows sufficient capacity to look after the child and is an appropriate person for protecting the welfare of that child, he/she can be regarded thenceforth as the parent with parental rights and duties even if a guardian has already been appointed.[458] This transfer of parental rights and duties is achieved under the procedure set out in section 819(6) of the Civil Code. However, if a family court finds that the transfer of the rights and duties from the deceased to the surviving parent is likely to be against the best interests of the child, it may dismiss an application for such a transfer and appoint an appropriate person as a guardian.[459] This rule may also cover a case where the parent currently vested with parental rights and duties is alive but unable to exercise those rights and duties due to sickness or for some other reasons (cf. Civ. section 838(1)).[460]

455. Sapporo HK 10 Aug. 2007 Kagetsu 54-6-97.
456. Yamagata FO 14 Oct. 1988 Hanji 1298-123.
457. Tokyo FO 25 Mar. 1975 Kagetsu 28-3-51.
458. Karatsu Branch of Saga FO 16 Jul. 2010 Kagetsu 63-60103.
459. Sapporo HK 10 Aug. 2001 Kagetsu 54-6-97.
460. Kojima Branch of Okayama FO 28 Jun. 1991 Kagetsu 44-6-76.

III. The Parental Rights and Duties of Parents to an Illegitimate Child

408. A mother will be vested with all parental rights and duties over her illegitimate child. However, if the father acknowledges paternity, those rights and duties can be transferred to him by an agreement between the parents (Civ. section 819(4)). If the parents fail to reach an agreement, a family court may issue a determination tantamount to an agreement as to which party should be vested with the parental rights and duties over the child (Civ. section 819(5)).

409. After the death of the child's mother, the father who has acknowledged the child can be appointed by a family court determination as the parent with parental rights and duties over the child.[461] This rule will also apply to a mother where a father dies having previously assumed parental rights and duties over the child under agreement with the mother. In order to protect the best interests of the child, a family court must examine whether the surviving parent is capable of caring for the child at the time of issuing the determination.

IV. The Parental Rights and Duties of Parents to an Adopted Child

410. Adoptive parents, or an adoptive parent and a biological parent if they are married, must exercise parental rights and duties jointly. In the event of divorce, such parents will be considered equally when allocating parental rights and duties to one of them. Accordingly, in some cases, an adoptive parent rather than a biological parent may be vested with parental rights and duties after the divorce.[462]

411. Where both adoptive parents die there are two interpretations of the law governing the subsequent allocation of parental rights and duties. The first interpretation asserts that the adoptive relationship continues until steps are taken for its dissolution,[463] and thus the biological parent-child relationship cannot be legally restored until this time, resulting in the need for guardianship of the children involved during the interim period. The second interpretation asserts that parental rights and duties will be restored to the biological parents from the moment of the death of the adoptive parents regardless of the dissolution of the adoptive relationship.[464] In practice, family courts tend to hold that guardianship will start immediately after a determination of transferal of parental rights and duties is issued to the surviving biological parent(s).[465]

---

461. Numazu Branch of Shizuoka FO 5 Mar. 1990 Kagetsu 42-8-81 and Osaka FO 8 Nov. 1962 Kagetsu 15-3-153.
462. Iizuka Branch of Fukuoka DD 19 Jan. 1962 Kamin 13-1-36.
463. Tokyo HK 2 Sep. 1981 Kagetsu 34-11-24.
464. Ootawara Branch of Utsunomiya FO 21 May 1982 Kagetsu 34-11-49.
465. Osaka FO 13 Mar. 1981 Kagetsu 33-12-64.

412. In the case of dissolution of an adoption, the biological parent(s) will be reinvested with the parental rights and duties. Where an adoptive parent and biological parent are married, the latter will retain sole rights and duties after the dissolution of the adoption. These situations are relatively clear-cut but there are cases where the allocation of parental rights and duties is not defined. For example, there may be a case where an adoptive parent dissolves the adoptive relationship having been granted sole parental rights and duties after he/she divorced the other adoptive parent or, in the same situations, dies. In these cases, there are differing views as to what course of action should be followed: the first dictates that guardianship of the child should commence, the second that the biological parent should be reinvested with those rights and duties, and the third asserts that the other adoptive parent should be appointed as the parent with parental rights and duties.

V. Jointly and Solely Held Parental Rights and Duties

413. While both parents must exercise jointly the parental rights and duties during their marriage, one may exercise those rights and duties independently under the implied or expressed consent of the other. If one parent fails to obtain consent from the other, his/her act of solely assuming these rights and duties will be void by reason of unauthorized agency, although this invalid act may be subsequently ratified by the other. Meanwhile, if one parent performs an act on behalf of a child in the name of both parents or he/she gives consent for the child to perform an act, the act will take effect even if it is contrary to the intention of the other parent (Civ. section 825). However, the act will not take effect if the other party to the act conducts him/herself in bad faith. If a dispute arises concerning the exercising of parental rights and duties between the parents, then a family court may issue a determination to settle the dispute.

414. Despite the rule that parental rights and duties should be exercised jointly, one parent is eligible to exercise solely these rights and duties if the other parent (Civ. section 818(3)):

(1) is declared a ward of adult guardianship (Civ. section 7);
(2) is declared a ward of curatorship (Civ. section 11);[466]
(3) is declared a ward of tutorship (Civ. section 15);[467]
(4) is under provisional suspension from exercising rights and duties (the Civil Provisional Remedies Act 1989 sections 23 and 24);
(5) is disqualified from exercising rights and duties (Civ. sections 834 and 835);
(6) gives up his/her position as a parent with parental rights and duties, or as a parent with the right to administer property belonging to his/her minor child (Civ. section 837(1));

466. Some assert that a parent under curatorship is entitled to exercise parental rights and duties only for the purpose of caring for the minor.

467. Similar to curatorship, some interpret that a parent under tutorship will not lose their parental rights and duties.

(7) is actually unable to exercise these rights and duties in the circumstances, for example, where the parent is missing or hospitalized because of serious illness; or
(8) has lived separately for a long period of time.[468]

VI. Custodianship

415. In the event of divorce or de facto separation,[469] parents may make an agreement to assign parental rights and duties to one parent and to appoint the other parent, or if necessary a third party who satisfies the conditions, as the custodian to care for the child on a day-to-day basis (Civ. section 766).[470] If they do not reach such an agreement, a family court will issue a determination appointing a custodian; case law suggests that the courts are in favour of appointing one of the parents as the person invested with parental rights and duties as well as with care and control over the child.[471] If the child in question is a minor over 15 years of age, he/she will be given the opportunity of expressing his/her wishes regarding a custodian to the family court (PALA section 32(4) and FAPA sections 65 and 152(2)). In divorce litigation, a family court may appoint a custodian and state its opinion on custodianship in the divorce decree (PALA section 32(1)). This procedure can be applied to parents in separation.[472]

416. A custodian may be vested with certain powers to enable him/her to provide sufficient care to the child, but not with rights for administering the assets of a minor or making an application to a family court to have significant changes made to the legal status of a minor such as an application for changing the family name of a minor.[473] For that purpose, even a parent with parental rights and duties may be prevented from intervening in the exercise of the custodian's authority. Once a person is appointed as a custodian, he/she may resign from his/her office by an agreement between the parties through family court mediation or family court determination.

417. A third party may be appointed as a custodian under a contract between the child's parents and the third party. Such a contract will terminate on the death of the custodian. If disputes occur over this issue, a family court can appoint a suitable person as a custodian.[474] As for an application for the appointment of a custodian by a

468. Cf. A case of mutual agreement of parents (Takamatsu HK 26 Jun. 1974 Kagetsu 27-5-121) and of no agreement (Tokyo HK 28 Jun. 1983 Hanta 510-191).
469. Osaka HK 22 Jun. 2005 Kagetsu 58-4-93.
470. Tokyo HK 9 Dec. 1976 Kagetsu 30-8-42 and Fukuoka HK 13 Sep. 2002 Kagetsu 55-2-163 appointed a grandmother as a custodian.
471. Tokyo HK 6 Sep. 1993 Kagetsu 46-12-45.
472. Tokyo HK 28 Jun. 2005 Kagetsu 58-4-105 and SK 15 Sep. 2005 Kagetsu 58-4-90 but Takamatsu HK 7 Aug. 1992 Hanta 807-235.
473. Tokyo HK 11 Sep. 2006 Kagetsu 59-4-122.
474. A grandmother was appointed as a custodian (Nanao Branch of Kanazawa FO 11 Mar. 2005 Kagetsu 57-9-47).

third party,[475] some courts may refuse such application on the basis of an interpretation of the law that only parents are eligible to apply under section 766,[476] while other courts may accept an application by a third party.[477] Eventually, in 2021 the Supreme Court declared that a grandmother is not eligible to make an application for family court determination on custody by literally interpreting section 766 where she took care of her grandchild for more than nine years.[478]

§2. Care and Control over a Child

I. Definition of Caring for a Child

418. Parental rights and duties include the right to look after one's child (Civ. section 820). Parents with this right to care and control are expected to take measures to meet the physical, emotional and financial needs of their child.

419. In exercising their right of care and control, parents must look after their child, ensure that he/she is provided with an adequate education (Principles of Education Act 1947 section 4), give their consent to medical treatment[479] and protect him/her from any unlawful intervention by third parties which are likely to cause harm to the child. On the basis of exercising this right, parents may apply to a court for an injunction against a third party's intervention if they consider such intervention to be against the best interests of the child. The parents may also claim damages for the wilful intervention of a third party. Meanwhile, a parent shall be legally responsible for compensation for damages when a minor injured someone due to failure of the parent's proper care and control over the minor (*see* Civ. section 714).[480]

475. FAPA does not mention the status of a third party in the determination procedure in a family court on custodian disputes (Cf. FAPA ss. 150(4) and 151).
476. Sendai HK 22 Jun. 2000 Kagetsu 54-5-125 and Tokyo HK 30 Jan. 2008 Kagetsu 60-8-59. In the former case, the high court rejected an application by foster parents to appoint themselves as custodians, where they had taken care of an abused minor for a few years, stating that s. 766 of the Civil Code stipulates that only parents are eligible to make an application to appoint a custodian.
477. Nanao Branch of Kanazawa FO 11 Mar. 2005 Kagetsu 57-9-47.
478. SK 29 Mar. 2021 CW (case no. 2020-14). The grandmother took care of her grandchild by herself for nearly two out of about nine years after the mother left their home and was remarried (*see* n. 499).
479. No case has so far been reported in Japan of parents who are Jehovah's Witnesses refusing to give their consent to a blood transfusion for their child, a minor.
480. *See* SD 22 Mar. 1974 Minshu 28-2-347 and SD 9 Apr. 2015 Hanji 2261-145 (The Supreme Court declared that the parents shall not be liable for compensation in a case where a motorcyclist fell and later died after avoiding a rolling soccer ball kicked by a boy playing in his school grounds).

II. Expenses Incurred in Caring for a Child

420. Parents must support their child financially irrespective of whether they hold the parental rights and duties. The courts generally hold the view that divorcing parents have an obligation to pay the expenses necessary for the everyday care of their child according to their own individual financial resources. This strong parental obligation for the child's maintenance (maintenance in the first degree) derives not from the parental rights and duties but from the fact of parenthood.[481] However, a parent without sufficient financial resources will be released from this responsibility. In addition, a father of a category A legitimate child can refuse a maintenance claim from his child if no blood relationship exists between them and there are reasonable grounds for refusal.[482]

421. Parents must agree between themselves as to their respective financial contributions to the child's maintenance after their divorce by giving priority to the interests of minors (Civ. section 766(1)). This agreement may be altered in terms of the sums concerned or the date of termination[483] to be extended to a later date to take account of any change in their financial circumstances. For example, after an agreement has been made between the divorcing parents that the father will thenceforth make a periodical financial contribution to the child's maintenance, he may then apply to the family court to have the contribution reduced should the mother's financial situation be improved by her remarrying.[484] The court will alter the previous agreement made by the parties or by way of *Chotei,* or a determination if it finds reasonable grounds to make an amendment, such as an increase or reduction of income, unemployment or remarriage[485] which have altered the financial circumstances of the parties.

III. Contact with a Child after Divorce

422. It is widely acknowledged that regular contact between a parent and a child separated by the parents' divorce or separation is essential to promote the welfare of the child. The Supreme Court stated in 2000[486] that a family court is empowered to issue a determination on contact by use of analogy to section 766 after a series of decisions by lower courts.[487] In granting the right of contact, the courts have accepted various means for contact ranging from not only direct[488] but also indirect

481. Fukuoka HK 20 Dec. 1977 Kagetsu 30-9-75.
482. SD 18 Mar. 2011 Kagetsu 63-9-58.
483. Cf. Osaka HK 9 Nov. 2007 Kagetsu 60-6-55.
484. Tokyo FO 6 Mar. 1990 Kagetsu 42-9-31.
485. Aizuwakamatsu Branch of Fukushima FO 9 Nov. 2007 Kagetsu 60-6-62.
486. SK 1 May 2000 Minshu 54-5-1607.
487. Osaka HK 24 Dec. 1968 Kagetsu 21-6-38 held that a case regarding the right to contact should be dealt with only through family court mediation because this right was not considered as a statutory right.
488. Tokyo FO 31 Jul. 2006 Kagetsu 59-3-73 decided that a third party should be present at the time of direct contact for protecting the interest of a minor.

modes of contacts, such as letters and e-mail[489] if they have found that it would be in the interests of the minor.[490] Concerning the nature of such right to contact, some claim that only the child is vested with that right to contact his/her parents, but others assert that a parent retains that right despite not living with his/her child. Promoters of both views, however, agree that the right to contact should be exercised in order to promote the welfare of the child.[491] Meanwhile, the Supreme Court only stated that contact between non-resident parent and child is included in a matter relating to custody of child without referring to whether contact is right or not.[492]

423. Due to the lack of specially stipulated provisions on the right to contact in the Civil Code, the family court, as mentioned above, has historically dealt with an application for contact as a case of care and control over the child by use of analogy to section 766. However, section 766 was revised in 2011 so that a family court can now issue a determination granting contact between the non-resident parent and child if it is satisfied, having considered all relevant matters to the case such as the age, sex, and wishes of the child, other human relationships around the child, and the circumstances of the parents, that contact would promote the child's welfare (Civ. section 766(1)). When a family court finds that contact might cause harm to the child, it may either restrict or suspend the non-resident parent's exercise of the right to contact.[493] Meanwhile, a family court may start to examine the suitability of the parent living with the child as the parent with parental rights and duties if he/she prevents a non-resident parent from making contact with the child.[494] On 28 March 2013, the Supreme Court made a decision on enforcement of contact activities that the court could not enforce an obligor parent to realize contact unless the details of contact activities were not stated in the contact agreement (or determination).[495]

IV. Residence and a Child

424. For the purpose of achieving effective care and control, parents have the right to designate where a child should reside (Civ. section 821). If parents cannot reach an agreement on this issue, a family court will make the decision on their behalf (FAPA sections 150(1)(i) or (iv)). Should a custodian be appointed for the child, his/her views as to the child's residence will be interpreted to take priority over the views of the parents with parental rights and duties.

489. Hachioji Branch of Tokyo FO 31 Jan. 2006 Kagetsu 58-11-79 (by letter or telephone), Oogaki Branch of Gifu FO 18 Mar. 1996 Kagetsu 48-9-57 (by photo and video recording) and Tokyo HK 12 Jun. 2015 Hanji 2266-54 (only letter and photo).
490. Osaka HK 16 Jan. 2009 Kagetsu 61-11-70 granted the right to contact for a non-Japanese father who might be deported in the future.
491. Tokyo HK 8 Dec. 1965 Kagetsu 18-7-31.
492. SK 1 May 2000 Minshu 54-5-1607.
493. *See* SD 6 Jul. 1984 Kagetsu 37-5-35.
494. Nagoya FO 31 May 1990 Kagetsu 42-12-51.
495. SK 28 Mar. 2013 Hanji 1391-126 and 1391-128. The Supreme Court ordered a resident parent to perform her obligation since the details of contact were specified in the family court determination (SK 28 Mar. 2015 Minshu 67-3-864).

425. Where a third party assumes the control of a child against his/her parents' (or custodian's) wishes, the parents with parental rights and duties (or the custodian) can make a claim to the family court to have the child released from the third party's control on the basis of their right to designate the child's residence. However, if a child who has the capacity to understand the meaning and effects of his/her actions does not obey the parents' wishes, no procedure is available under the current family law to force the child to comply with those wishes.

V. Discipline of a Child (*See* §5. Removal and Suspension of Parental Rights and Duties)

426. The parents with parental rights and duties are also entitled to discipline their child and administer reasonable punishment if they consider it necessary in the interests of the child (Civ. section 822). A guardian or the director of a child welfare agency who lawfully acts for and on behalf of the parents has the same authority over the child (WCA section 47(1)). In addition, parents can delegate these rights and duties to the teachers of an educational institution.[496]

427. The measure and degree of discipline should be reasonable according to contemporary social standards and within the limits of necessity to bring up the child (Civ. section 822). If those administering disciplines are interpreted as having deviated from the social standards or as having acted against the interests of a child, the parents will have their parental rights and duties removed or suspended by reason of their abusing the right to discipline the child (Civ. sections 834 and 834-2). Alternatively, they may be prosecuted for bodily injury (Cri. section 204), intimidation (Cri. section 222), or false imprisonment (Cri. section 220). A court will decide whether the act of discipline was reasonable in consideration of the social class of the parties, the age, physical constitution and personality of the child, and the nature of behaviour of the child.[497] After a 2019 case in which a girl of 10 years of age was killed by her father who then asserted that his intent was to disciple her as her parent, the Revision of Part of the Welfare of Children Act, the Child Abuse Prevention Act, Prevention and Protection of a Victim of Violence by Spouse Act and the Improvement of Child Abuse Prevention Act were implemented in 2019 and the government decided that section 822 of the Civil Code shall be revised or abolished for improving protection of a minor from parental abuse within two years.

428. The family court will make a determination to suspend parental rights and duties for up to two years until the causes of abuse cease to exist and by considering all the circumstances including the physical and emotional condition of the minor (Civ. section 834-2(2)).

496. Fukuoka HD 26 May 1976 Kotosaibansho Keiji-Saibanreishu (Report on the Criminal Cases of the High Courts) 29-2-284.

497. Tokyo HD 13 Feb. 1960 Kakyusaibansho Keiji-Saibanreishu (Report on the Criminal Cases of the Lower Courts) (Kakei) 2-2-113. Concerning a teacher who excessively disciplines a child, the School Act 1947 s. 11 and/or one or other of the sections of the Criminal Code mentioned above may apply.

VI. Consent to Employment of a Child

429. In order to protect the welfare of children, a minor is required to obtain the consent of his/her parents with parental rights and duties when he/she is either to be employed or intends to set up in business (Civ. section 823 and *see* Civ. section 6). No particular requirements are laid down for the form that this parental consent must take.

430. Parents with those rights and duties are prohibited from making an employment contract between their child and an employer on behalf of the child as well as from receiving the wages in the name of the child (Fundamental Labour Act sections 58(1) and 59).

VII. Others

431. Parents holding parental rights and duties are only entitled to represent their child in the following situations:

- Where the child is the defendant in a petition to deny legitimacy (Civ. section 775).
- Where the child applies to have his/her paternity acknowledged (Civ. section 787).
- Where the child, who is under 15 years of age, applies to have his/her family name changed (Civ. section 791(3)).
- Where the child, who is under 15 years of age, intends to dissolve adoption through consent (Civ. section 811(2)).
- Where the child, who is under 15 years of age, presents a petition to dissolve adoption (Civ. section 815).
- Where the child surrenders his/her right to succession (*see* Civ. section 917).

VIII. Disputes Concerning the Care and Control of a Child

432. A child's care is viewed as the exercise of necessary control over the child in order to provide him/her with sufficient care. Thus, the child should not be wrongfully removed, against his/her will, from the carer's control.

433. If one parent, during the period of separation from the other parent, abducts their child, the other parent can apply to a family court for a determination that the child should be returned to him/her on the basis of the following provisions. First, the family court, if it thinks necessary, may make a determination placing the child back in the hands of the applicant parent by applying section 752 of the Civil Code which operates in the case of a husband and wife failing to fulfil their obligation of cooperation. Or second, the family court may issue a determination granting the applicant parent care and control of the child by using an analogy of section 766 of the Civil Code, which relates to divorce cases but can be equated to the consequences of separation.[498] Third, one parent can file a petition to a district court for abatement of obstruction by asserting that the other parent is wrongly preventing the petitioner from exercising his/her parental right to look after the child. In order to achieve a prompt and effective resolution, a provisional disposition to have the child returned (similar to an interlocutory injunction) is available (FAPA sections 105 and 106).

434. When a non-resident parent abducts a child under the care of the resident parent who has been assigned parental rights and duties after divorce, the family court, on the application of the abducting parent, may make a determination appointing him/her as the new parent with those rights and duties, revising the previous decision or agreement (Civ. section 819). Naturally, on the child's abduction, the parent vested with parental rights and duties is entitled to file a petition to the district court for the abatement of the abducting parent's obstruction (as mentioned in the paragraph above) or may make an application to the family court to have the child returned to their care and control.

435. With respect to disputes over childcare and control between a parent with parental rights and duties and a third party, the parent can bring a petition to a district court under a similar procedure. For example, if a parent holding parental rights and duties over a child previously agreed to place that child under the care of a third party. That third party intended to become the child's adoptive parent, but the parent with parental rights and duties later reneged on the agreement and the third party refused to return the child. In such a situation, the parent may bring a petition to the district court for the child's return. In this connection, some raise the question of whether this rule should be applied to a dispute between a parent with parental rights and duties and a grandparent who is caring for the minor because the grandparent may be interpreted as different from a non-relative third party. In one case, the grandmother has occasionally looked after her grandchild with her son since he and his ex-wife took care in rotation. In this case, the Supreme Court overturned the decisions of the lower courts stating that section 766 of the Civil Code shall exclusively apply to the parents of a child but not a third person such as grandparent.[499] In addition, this procedure will apply to a dispute between non-parents; for instance, the director of a children's home who is authorized to exercise care and control over a child and a third party detaining that child unlawfully. In this instance, the director may bring a petition to the district court for the return of the child to his/her care and control. However, taking such steps for resolving a dispute would be unusual.

436. Moreover, a writ of habeas corpus can be available for resolving disputes concerning a child who is allegedly wrongfully detained.[500] The characteristics of

498. SK 1 May 2000 Minshu 54-5-1607.
499. SK 29 Mar. 2021 CW.
500. SD 28 May 1958 Minshu 12-8-1224.

this measure are sure that it can apply to a case involving parents, a custodian, or a third party and it can also provide a prompt remedy to the parties compared with other measures of resolution.

437. A writ of habeas corpus will be issued if the petitioner is able to fulfil the following conditions:

– The child is detained, against his/her will, by an unauthorized person.
– The nature of the detention is obviously illegal.[501]
– No other effective remedies are available except for a writ of habeas corpus.[502]

438. In practice, the court usually decides whether to issue a writ of habeas corpus by considering all the circumstances emerging from the commencement of detention. In particular, the court will focus on whether the detention has been obviously harmful to the child's welfare and who is the person most suitable for taking care of the child.

439. Before issuing a writ of habeas corpus, it is commonly observed that the court first examines whether the child has stayed with the detainer of his/her own will. Accordingly, in the case of a detained minor, particularly an infant, the court is likely to declare any detention as illegal since the minor is not considered as having the capacity to understand the meaning and effects of his/her conduct. Even if the minor has that capacity, the detention will be illegal if the detainer has intentionally prevented the minor from voluntarily making a decision as to the detention.[503] In one case, the Supreme Court held that the detention of a minor of 13 years of age was obviously wrong and he should be freed since the mother did not obey the court decision ordering her to return him to his habitual residence and she continued to keep him under her control.[504]

440. The court will question whether the unauthorized detention would be substantially detrimental to the welfare of the child.[505] In this respect, the court will not issue a writ of habeas corpus if it finds that the child's best interests are not jeopardized by the unauthorized detention. In general, the court is likely to pronounce that the detention is illegal if one parent abducts the child from the other by

501. The Supreme Court held that it must be proved that the detention of the child is obviously not in his/her best interests in a dispute over care and control between the parents (19 Oct. 1993 Minshu 47-8-5099), while it seemed to maintain the view that the illegality of detention might be pronounced easily in the dispute between the parent and a third person (SD 8 Nov. 1994 Minshu 48-7-1337).
502. SD 29 Mar. 1984 Kagetsu 37-2-141.
503. SD 6 Dec. 1990 Kagetsu 43-6-18 declared that there was no evidence to show that a child of 12 years and 8 months was being detained under her own free will simply because she had been brought up by the detainer for a prolonged period without sufficient information to make her own reasonable decision regarding the detention.
504. SD 15 Mar. 2018 Minshu 72-1-17.
505. Kobe DD 21 Mar. 1991 Kagetsu 44-10-48.

force,[506] or if one parent continues to detain the child contrary to a previous agreement with the other.[507] While habeas corpus is useful for achieving a quick resolution, the Supreme Court seems to prefer resolution by a family court determination rather by habeas corpus.

441. Three measures are available for the enforcement of a decision to return the child to the applicant.[508] The first is the indirect enforcement of the writ (a decree) by which the court can order the detainer to make a certain payment per day until he/she complies fully with the decree.[509] The second is direct enforcement, which enables the court bailiff to take the child from the detainer and return him/her to the applicant.[510] The third is a combination of indirect and direct enforcement, depending on the nature of the case.[511] For instance, the indirect measure is employed where the detention can be seen as in some way reasonable and direct intervention is employed where the detention of the child is considered highly unreasonable, such as forcible kidnapping of the child. In 2019 the Civil Execution Act was revised in order to ensure more effective enforcement procedure relating to abduction disputes (*see* sections 174 and 175 of the Civil Execution Act for domestic cases and sections 136 and 140 of the Implementation of the Hague Convention on the Civil Aspects of International Child Abduction Act 2013).

442. The Implementation of the Convention on the Civil Aspects of International Child Abduction Act (ICAA) was implemented in 2013 for resolving disputes relating to abduction of minors across the border. The central authority is the Ministry of Foreign Affairs (ICAA section 3) and the family courts of Tokyo and Osaka have jurisdiction on this matter (ICAA section 32(1)(i)). The hearing shall not be open to the public provided the court permits observation by a person whom it considers to be appropriate (ICAA section 60). The central authority shall provide assistance in facilitating the child's return to Japan (ICAA section 11(1)) and child's return to a foreign state (ICAA section 26) and also assistance contact (visitation or other contact with a child in Japan or foreign state) ICAA (section 16(1) and 21(1)). According to the statistics,[512] applications for return of a child to Japan (outgoing return cases) is 20, that for return of child to foreign states (incoming return cases) 23, and application for contact with child staying in Japan (incoming access cases) 13, that for contact with child staying in foreign states (outgoing access cases) 3 in

506. Tokyo HD 25 Jan. 1989 Hanji 1305-82.
507. SD 8 Jul. 1994 Hanji 1507-124.
508. *See* SD 19 Jan. 1993 Kagetsu 45-10-33 and Sapporo DD 8 Jul. 1994 Kagetsu 47-4-71.
509. Osaka HK 14 Dec. 1955 Hanji 71-16.
510. Tachikawa Branch of Tokyo DK 28 Apr. 2009 Kagetsu 61-11-80.
511. Cf. Osaka HK 24 Sep. 2010 Kagetsu 63-3-124.
512. Hague Convention Division, Ministry of Foreign Affairs of Japan, 'Status of Implementation of the Hague Convention' (Convention on the Civil Aspects of International Child Abduction dated 1 Apr. 2021) https://www.mofa.go.jp/files/100012160.pdf.

2020. Out of 100 finalized incoming return cases, a return case amounts to 58 and non-return 42, and out of 78 finalized outgoing return cases, return is 49 and non-return 29 in 2020.[513]

443. Upon an application, the court shall hear the case and shall conduct an examination of the facts either ex officio or upon petition (ICAA section 77(1)). If necessary, it may order a family court investigation officer to examine details of the case (ICAA section 79(1)). The court shall hear statements from the parties except where the petition for the return of a child is unlawful or it is obvious that the petition is groundless (ICAA section 85(1)). During hearing sessions, the child may intervene in the proceedings of the case (ICAA section 48(1)) and if necessary, the court may allow ex officio the child to intervene in the proceedings (ICAA section 48(2)). In relation, if necessary, the court may appoint an attorney at law as a representative of the child (ICAA section 51). The court shall decide on the rule that a child in wrongful removal or retention should be returned promptly to the state where the child held his/her habitual residence for promoting the interests of children (*see* ICAA section 4). As mentioned above, the court shall endeavour to understand the will of the child through appropriate means such as hearing of his/her statements and examination by a family court investigating officer, and shall take into account his/her will according to his/her age and degree of development in making a final order (ICAA section 88).

444. When either party challenges the court decision, he/she is eligible to file an immediate appeal or a special appeal to the higher court (ICAA sections 101(1) and 108(1)). In addition, for the interests of the parties, the party can file a petition of retrial (ICAA section 119(1)) and of modification of the decision (ICAA section 117(1)). In a recent case, the Supreme Court decided that the court could modify the agreements made by the parties if it finds that enforcement of the agreement is likely to harm the interest of the child before the return of the child.[514] In addition to resolution by petition to the court, the central authority can take necessary measures such as facilitating the discussion between the parties in order to reach agreements on return of child, contact with child and other relevant matters (ICAA section 9). When the obligor party fails to perform his/her obligation, the court may recommend the obligor to perform such obligations (ICAA section 121(1)). During court sessions, the family court, upon application by the party retaining the child, may order the party claiming return of the child not to make the child leave Japan if it finds any risk to the child caused by departure from Japan (ICAA section 122(1)). For the purpose of enforcing an order effectively, an indirect compulsory execution shall be obtainable (CEA section 172(1)) and under some conditions an execution by substitute of return of a child (direct compulsory execution) shall be available (CEA section 174(2) and IACC section 136). A petitioner but not obligor parent may attend at the time of handing over for preventing the minor from being frightened (IACC section 140). In some cases, a habeas corpus may be used for

513. *See* Shuji Zushi, 'Japan's 5-year Experience in Implementing the 1980 Hague Abduction Convention', International Family Law Journal 2019-2-80.
514. SK 16 Apr. 2020 CW.

returning a child. If the obligor parent continues to keep the child under his/her control despite the return order issued, the claiming parent is eligible to file a habeas corpus for returning the child (*see* paragraphs 436–440). In one case[515] where a mother lived with her son after taking him to Japan when he was 11 years of age and she resisted to obey the order of return of child to the United States finalized under sections 134(1) and 138 of the Implementation of the Hague Convention on the Civil Aspects of International Child Abduction Act 2013, a father filed a petition of habeas corpus for releasing him under restraint set out in section 2(1) of the Habeas Corpus Act 1948. The Supreme Court declared that it can be said that the boy of 13 years of age is in a situation where it is difficult for him to sufficiently obtain the multifaceted and objective information necessary to make a decision regarding whether he is going to stay with his mother, and that his mother unduly influences his emotions in making such decision. Therefore, there are exceptional circumstances where he cannot be said to be staying with his mother by his free will, and care for him by her falls under 'restraint' referred to in the Habeas Corpus Act. The Supreme Court came to the conclusion that the restrain of him by her has conspicuous illegality unless there are 'exceptional circumstances' where release of him from the care of his mother is found to be extremely unjust.

445. In some cases, abducting parents could be prosecuted for kidnapping minors (Cri. sections 224 and 226).[516] When a non-resident father with parental rights and responsibilities kidnapped by force a minor of 2 years of age under the care of its mother, the Supreme Court declared that he was guilty of the kidnapping of a minor because there was no necessity to take the minor away from the mother's care.[517] In another case where a father of Dutch nationality with parental rights and duties carried off two daughters, one of whom was hospitalized at the time of abduction, under peaceful and proper care by the mother, he was found to be guilty of kidnapping for transportation out of a country.[518] Some claim that abduction disputes should not be heard in the criminal court but rather in the family court due to the sensitive nature of such disputes.

§3. Administration of a Child's Property

I. Outline of Property Administration

446. A minor is not eligible to administer his/her own property because of his/her lack of capacity to enter into legal acts. To protect the interests of a minor, parents with parental rights and duties are responsible for administering (preserving

515. SD 15 Mar. 2018 Minshu 72-1-17.
516. Section 224 of the Criminal Code stipulates that a person who kidnaps a minor by force or enticement shall be punished by imprisonment with labour for not less than three months but not more than seven years and s. 226 which stipulates that a person who kidnaps another by force or enticement for the purpose of transporting another from one country to another country shall be punished by imprisonment with work for a definite term of not less than two years.
517. SK 6 Dec. 2005 Kagetsu 58-4-59.
518. SK 18 Mar. 2003 Kagetsu 58-4-371.

and utilizing) the minor's assets properly. A minor may dispose of his/her assets independently if the parents with those rights and duties have given him/her the assets unconditionally, or if conditions have been laid down, a minor can use the assets according to the purpose specified by the parents (Civ. section 5(3)). If a third party donates some property to a minor with the express condition that the parents must not take part in the administration of such property (Civ. section 830), an authorized person, appointed by either the third party or a family court, will be responsible for the administration of those assets.

447. The parents with parental rights and duties are entitled to utilize the property of their child properly and effectively at their own discretion if they consider it to be in the best interests of the child. In this respect, they can live in the house possessed by their child if to do so would be beneficial to maintaining the house. However, they are not allowed to use their child's assets for the purpose of meeting either their own interests or those of others.[519] In the event that damage is caused to the child's property as a result of the parents failing to exercise the same level of care as that which the parents would exercise over their own property the parents will lose the right to administer the property of their child thereafter (Civ. sections 827 and 835 and FAPA section 168(1)(i)(ii)).

II. Actions of Administration of Property

448. Parents with parental rights and duties are entitled to take any action necessary for the proper administration of their child's property, including transactions involving the property and the surrender of the right to succeed. They may also bring proceedings for and on behalf of the child in order to promote the child's interests in relation to the property (The Civil Litigation Proceedings Act section 31 and FAPA section 168(1)(2)).[520]

III. Joint Administration of Property by Parents with Parental Rights and Duties on Behalf of a Child

449. Generally, parents with parental rights and duties must jointly administer the property of their child. Where a legal action for and on behalf of the child is taken by one parent in the name of both parents without the other's consent, or if consent to perform a legal action is given to the child by one parent in the name of both parents without the other's consent, such action or consent will still be legally effective (Civ. section 825). However, this rule shall not apply to cases where the

519. SD 10 Dec. 1992 Minshu 46-9-2727.

520. Two different views have been expressed by the courts with respect to the matter of whether a minor is independently entitled to present a legal action to a court. One has held that a minor was eligible to file a petition if the dispute was attributed to the job contract made with the consent of the parents with parental rights and duties (Nagoya HD 19 Jun. 1963 Romin 14-5-1110) and the other stated that a minor was restricted from bringing proceedings independently from the viewpoint of protecting the interests of the minor (Nagoya HD 30 Jul. 1963 Romin 14-4-968).

aim of such an action is to create a legal relationship as a family member or where other parties involved in such an action are acting in bad faith.

450. Moreover, this rule will not apply to a case where one parent takes legal action in his/her own name without the consent of the other or where he/she gives the child his/her consent in a similar situation. Such action and consent will be void.[521] However, the action taken by one parent in such circumstances will be valid if the other party involved in the action is acting in good faith and is not negligent. In such a case, the other parent may subsequently ratify the action.

IV. Conflicts of Interests Between a Child and the Administrators of the Child's Property

451. Parents with the right to administer their child's property are not permitted to represent their child in the following situations: first, where the parents make a business deal with the child, and second, where the parents have the interests of two or more children to represent (Civ. section 826). In such circumstances, the parents must appoint a special representative for their child(ren) in order to ensure that the interests of each child are fairly represented. This rule also applies to any dispute affecting the family relationship.[522] An action that is pronounced to be a conflict of interests will be void. However, the child can ratify the action subsequently when he/she reaches the age of majority.[523]

452. Where a court is judging whether a particular action involves a conflict of interest for the parents involved, it will look to the objective appearance of the case rather than examine the subjective motives of the parents. Thus, where parents mortgage their child's property in order to borrow money in their own names, such action will be judged as involving a conflict of interest on the part of the parents and the action will be declared void; even if the purpose of the loan is to maintain the child financially.[524]

453. Other examples of cases where a conflict will be found between the interests of the parents who have the right to administer the property and those of the child are as follows: where the parents seek to acquire the assets of the child, or where the parents intend to transfer their property to the child including some burden with it, or where they agree to be liable for a debt jointly with the child. However, should the parents, while acting as agents of their child, give the child's property as security for the debt of a third party, no conflict of interest will be found as the parents will not gain any benefit from this act of representation.[525] However,

521. SD 29 Sep. 1967 Hanji 497-59.
522. In Osaka HD 31 Jul. 1959 Kamin 10-7-1624, where the validity of an adoption was disputed, the court found a potential conflict of interest between the parents and the child and thus ordered the parents to appoint a special representative for the child.
523. SD 11 Oct. 1960 Minshu 13-1-115.
524. SD 2 Oct. 1962 Minshu 16-10-2059.
525. SD 10 Dec. 1992 Kagetsu 45-4-90.

there would be a conflict of interest if the parents are guarantors or joint sureties.[526] Similarly, if a surviving parent acting as an agent of his/her child transfers to a third party a bill which is jointly owned with the child, this will not be interpreted as a conflict of interest.[527]

454. When the estate of a deceased person is being allocated, parents representing two or more minor heirs simultaneously will be judged as having a conflict of interest as between the heirs.[528] Where a surviving parent surrenders the child(ren)'s right to succession, on their behalf, over the deceased parent's estate, such an act will be regarded as a conflict of interest on the part of the surviving parent and thus declared void, unless he/she gives up his/her own right to succession at the same time.[529]

455. Where parents with the right to administer their child's property find themselves to be in a situation involving a conflict of interests, they must apply to the family court for the appointment of a special representative to act for and on behalf of their child in administering the property.[530] The family court usually appoints a special representative from a list of recommended individuals submitted by the parents. Consequently, the family court tends to limit strictly the powers and authority of the special representative in order to prevent him/her from becoming a puppet in the hands of the parents. When only one parent finds himself/herself to be in conflict with his/her right and the child's interests, the other parent and an appointed special representative will act jointly for and on behalf of the child.[531] If parents commence legal action on behalf of the child without the appointment of a special representative, the child can ratify such action upon reaching the age of majority.[532]

V. Settlement of Administration of Property

456. The parent(s), with parental rights and duties, must jointly settle the administration of their child's property in the following situations (Civ. section 828):

- Where the child attains the age of majority.
- Where the child dies.
- Where the parents lose either parental rights and duties or the right to administer the property.
- Where the parents resign from their post of administrator of the property or relinquish their post as parent with parental rights and duties.

---

526. SD 8 Oct. 1968 Minshu 22-10-2172.
527. SD 11 Dec. 1958 Kagetsu 11-2-47.
528. SD 24 Apr. 1973 Kagetsu 25-9-80.
529. A guardian will be in of a similar status (SD 24 Feb. 1978 Minshu 32-1-98).
530. The child is entitled to make an application of appointment of a special representative (FAPA ss. 168(1) and 118).
531. SD 25 Feb. 1960 Minshu 14-2-279.
532. SD 11 Oct. 1960 Kagetsu 13-1-115.

- Where parental rights and duties are transferred from one biological parent to the other sometime after a divorce.
- Where parental rights and duties are transferred from the biological parent(s) to the adoptive parent(s) upon the child's adoption, or vice versa in the case of dissolution of an adoption.

457. In settling the property, the parents with parental rights and duties may offset the expenses of bringing up the child and of maintaining the property against the value of the child's remaining property. On calculating the amount of the expenses to be offset, certain property will be excluded from the calculation if that property has been given by a third party as a gift to the child on the condition that it should not be included in the assets of the settlement (Civ. section 829). Any claim for expenses from the parents against the settlement of property must be made within five years from the time of the termination of their right to administer the property (Civ. section 832(1)). Where the parents' right to administer the property terminates and no legal representative for the child is appointed before the child attains the age of majority, that five-year period will commence from the time either when the child reaches full age or when a succeeding representative assumes office (Civ. section 832(2)). The parents will remain liable for any consequences arising from the administration of the child's property even after the termination of their right to administer unless they notify interested persons of that termination.

§4. Transfer of Parental Rights and Duties Between the Parents

I. Outline of Transfer

458. Unforeseen changes in a parent's circumstances sometimes lead to suggestions being made to transfer the parental rights and duties previously allocated to a single parent at the time of divorce. Such suggestions usually come from the parent without parental rights and duties, normally as a result of his/her absence, and who then claims that those rights and duties should now be transferred to him/her. The converse case, where the parent solely vested with those rights and duties compels the other to assume them, is much less frequently encountered.

459. Whereas the original allocation of parental rights and duties to a single parent can be made by the agreement of the parties, any subsequent transfer of those rights and duties can only take place with the approval of the family court, either through mediation or by a court determination (FAPA sections 39 and 244). Such procedural requirements are justified by the necessity of ensuring the child's welfare. Thus, any out-of-court agreement made between the parents is void. If a parent believes that the circumstances surrounding the child have changed, giving rise to the need to transfer the parental rights and duties, he/she must apply to the court for the transfer.

II. Procedure for Transfer of Parental Rights and Duties

460. A parent or relatives of the child (*see* Civ. section 725) are entitled to apply to the family court for the transfer of the parental rights and duties to the other parent (Civ. section 819(6) and FAPA section 168(1)(vii)). In order to protect the welfare of the child, any person looking after the child under an agreement with the parent currently holding the parental rights and duties may participate in this procedure (*see* FAPA sections 41 and 42). The family court will listen to the wishes and feelings of the child if he/she is 15 years or over, unless the court feels the child's own views are contrary to his/her own welfare (FAPA section 169(2)).

461. The most important criterion in the court's decision is the consideration of the child's welfare. In addition, the court will also take into account the surrounding circumstances of the case, particularly subjective factors; such as the genuine desire of the parent to take care of the child under his/her control and the wishes and feelings of the child;[533] and objective factors such as each parent's ability to look after the child; his/her financial capacity and resources; the age of the child, the nature of the relationships between the child and each parent; the general health of the parties, and the living environment of each parent. A family court will only transfer the parental rights and duties from one parent to the other if it is satisfied that the transfer will promote the welfare of the child, more than it could be promoted under the present situation.[534] In the majority of cases, the family courts tend to be in favour of preserving the status quo, unless the current situation is obviously detrimental to the child's welfare.[535]

§5. Removal and Suspension of Parental Rights and Duties

I. Outline of Removal and Suspension of Parental Rights and Duties

462. A family court will declare by a family court determination the removal or suspension of parental rights and duties if it finds that the parent(s) has abused those rights and duties or committed acts to harm the interests of their child. In other words, if a family court considers the parents' behaviour to be inappropriate and harmful to the welfare of the child, the parent(s) is in difficulty to resume their responsibilities of nurturing the child, or that the parent(s) are to be blamed according to the current social norms in order to protect the interests of the child, the court will then issue a determination to either remove or suspend the parental rights and

533. In Tokyo HK 27 May 1985 Kagetsu 37-10-75, a court primarily took account of the wishes and feelings of the children who were 11 and 12 years of age where the parents showed no difference in their respective abilities to bring them up.

534. Cf. Saitama FO 10 Jun. 2010 Kagetsu 62-12-100.

535. In some cases, this interpretation may cause an unfair result to one party since the parent could be allowed to keep the child if he/she has already created a 'fait accompli' by retaining the child under his/her care for some time (Osaka HK 19 Apr. 2000 Kagetsu 53-1-82).

duties, including the right to care and control over the child and the right to administer any property of the child (Civ. sections 834 and 834-2), or the right to administer the property (Civ. section 835).[536] If the family court finds a possibility that the cause for the removal will cease to exist within two years, it will not issue a determination of removal of the parental rights and duties (Civ. section 834). In addition to removal, suspension and/or resolution by section 28 of the Welfare of Children Act, a victim child may claim emotional damages against perpetrator parent.[537]

463. The child, relatives of the child, guardian or supervisor of the guardian of the child, a public prosecutor, or a director of a children's section of the local authority are eligible to apply to the family court for a determination either removing or suspending the parental rights and duties from the person in whom they are currently vested (Civ. sections 834 and 834-2, FAPA section 39 and WCA section 33-7). During the court procedure, the family court must provide an opportunity to the respondent parents to state their own views and, in addition, it must listen to the child's wishes if he/she is 15 years of age and over (FAPA section 169) The family court, if it considers necessary, may issue a determination provisionally suspending parental rights and duties or a determination appointing a tentative agent for the child, both of which are effective until a final court declaration to remove those rights and duties (FAPA section 105) has been made.[538]

464. In addition, an abuse case may be dealt with as a criminal case such as homicide (Cri. section), abandonment by a person responsible for their care and abandonment causing death or injury (Cri. sections 218 and 219),[539] assault (Cri. section 208), injury causing death (Cri. section 205), unlawful capture and confinement (Cri. section 220), unlawful capture or confinement causing death or injury (Cri. section 221),[540] compulsion (Cri. section 223), forcible sexual intercourse (Cri. section 177), constructive indecency through Compulsion 'Cri. section 178) and indecency by a person having custody of a person under 18 or sexual intercourse by a person having custody of a person under 18 (Cri. section 179).[541] In one case a

536. Since the mid-1970s, child abuse has gradually been recognized as a social problem. Especially in the 1990s, research and proposals on child abuse have been published by medical doctors, the bar association and several local governments. Moreover, special commissioners for the protection of children's right are appointed from commissioners belonging to the Commission for Protection of Human Rights in every district in order to investigate and resolve cases in which children's rights are claimed to have been infringed upon. Additionally, various kinds of assistance, including helpline and counselling services, operate on a voluntary basis and as a part of the welfare services of local governments.
537. Fukuoka HD 14 Feb. 2005 Hanta 1188-266.
538. In Osaka HK 28 Mar. 1994 Kagetsu 47-2-174, a court dismissed an appeal from a parent against an injunctive family court determination in which the court decided to suspend the parental rights and duties tentatively and appointed a lawyer as a representative for the child due to the parent's abuse of that child.
539. In a case of 'Shaken Baby Syndrome' a mother prosecuted for injury was declared not guilty (Osaka DD 7 Dec. 2020 CW).
540. Mito DD 25 May 1959 Kakei 1-5-1278.
541. In 13 Jan. 2021, Tsu district court sentenced a birth father to eight years imprisonment for taking pornographic photos of his 13-year-old child 348 times (Reuters: https://jp.reuters.com/article/idJP 2021011301001754).

daughter of 19 years of age had been sexually assaulted by her birth father for around six years; he was subsequently found not guilty of quasi-rape (Cri. section 178)[542] by reasoning that she was able to resist his assault[543] but the appellate court overturned the decision and sentenced him to ten years imprisonment.[544]

II. Removal of Parental Rights and Duties

465. A family court will issue a determination to remove parental rights and duties from the parents if it finds that the parents have abused or wilfully abandoned their child or it is obviously difficult for them to execute their parental rights and duties or it is obviously inappropriate to do so where the interests of the child are extremely damaged (Civ. section 834). A child, his/her relatives, his/her guardian or supervisor of the guardian, a prosecutor and a director of the children's section of a local authority are eligible to make an application to a family court for issuing a determination (Civ. section 834 and WCA section 33-7).

466. A family court will issue a determination to remove parental rights and duties from the parents on the basis that they have abused such parental rights and duties[545] if it discovers any physical abuse, sexual abuse,[546] neglect[547] or emotional abuse (*see* paragraph 66). In addition, the family court has declared the removal of parental rights and duties from the parents who unreasonably demanded a replacement of their minor from the childcare institution after the minor was sheltered because of cruelty by the parents against the minor.[548] However, a family court will not issue a determination to remove parental rights and duties if it finds a possibility that the abusive conduct will cease within two years (Civ. section 834). A common example is the case of cruelty to one's child in the name of discipline. It is not illegal for parents with parental rights and duties to inflict moderate and reasonable corporal punishment for the purpose of discipline (*see* Civ. section 822). However, if the mode and degree of the punishment inflicted by the parents are considered to be unacceptable from the standpoint of reasonableness, those parents will be liable for committing child abuse. A court held in one case that a father, vested with parental rights and duties, should be liable for abusing his right to care and control when he

542. Sections 177, 178 and 179 of the Criminal Code were revised in 2017. Cf. Section 179(1) A person who commits an indecent act upon another person under eighteen years of age by taking advantage of the influence arising from the fact of having custody of that person is punished in the same manner as prescribed in s. 176. (2)A person who engages in sexual intercourse, etc. with another person under eighteen years of age by taking advantage of the influence arising from the fact of having custody of that person is punished in the same manner as prescribed in s. 177.
543. Okazaki Branch of Nagoya DD 26 Mar. 2019 TKC (LEX/DB25562770).
544. Nagoya HD 12 Mar. 2020 (Nikkei 12 Mar. 2020 (https://www.nikkei.com/article/DGXMZO56706910S0A310C2CR8000/)).
545. *See* CAPA 2000 s. 2.
546. Hachioji Branch of Tokyo FO 16 May 1979 Kagetsu 32-1-166 (sexual abuse by a birth father) and Sasebo Branch of Nagasaki FO 23 Feb. 2000 Kagetsu 52-8-55.
547. Otsu FO 23 Dec. 1959 Kagetsu 12-3-141 (neglect case) and Kobe FO 29 Sep. 1980 Kagetsu 33-8-68 (desertion case).
548. Okazaki Branch of Nagoya FO 9 Dec. 2004 Kagetsu 57-12-82.

locked up his child, having tied his hands with wire, in a cupboard for two days in order to cure the child of his thieving propensity.[549]

467. When parent(s) vested with parental rights and duties fail to look after their child appropriately without any legitimate reason, they will be held culpable for an abuse of those rights and duties which will in turn be removed. In one case, a father lost his parental rights and duties by reason of abuse when he left the child at the home of its grandmother for seven years after the death of his wife.[550]

468. A family court under section 834 of the previous Civil Code used to declare the conduct of the parent(s) with parental rights and duties as gross misconduct if that conduct is measured against the current social norm and is found to be blameworthy and is detrimental to the welfare of the child. A declaration of gross misconduct leads to the removal or suspension of one's parental rights and duties. In many cases, a parent's adultery[551] and crimes committed by the parents will be classed as gross misconduct. However, according to a court, it was held that where a father and his child were living together with his lover, although his behaviour was to be blamed to some extent, would not come under the classification of gross misconduct unless it would be injurious to the child's welfare.[552] Furthermore, the courts seem to be unwilling to pronounce that a parent's past misconduct constitutes a ground for the removal or suspension of the parental rights and duties.[553] This interpretation will be applied to a case under revised section 834 of the Civil Code. Ultimately, 'gross misconduct' as a ground for removal of the parental rights and duties was deleted from section 834 as a result of revision in 2011.

III. Suspension of Parental Rights and Duties

469. Since the revision of section 834 in 2011, there have been two types of suspension of parental rights and duties. One is the tentative suspension of parental rights and duties which is still available under the current law, and the other is the suspension of parental rights and duties for up to two years (Civ. section 834-2). The latter was added to the Civil Code in 2011 based on the following understanding: the suspension procedure is a less hostile approach to abusive parents than the removal procedure and allows the intervening institution to maintain a relationship with the parents, the parents to predict what they must do within a decided period in order to reform their attitudes for caring for the child and to restore the relationship with the child, etc.

549. Mito DD 25 May 1959 Kakei 1-5-1278.
550. Kobe FO 29 Sep. 1980 Kagetsu 33-8-68.
551. Takada Branch of Niigata FO 29 Jun. 1968 Kagetsu 20-11-170.
552. Takamatsu HK 5 Nov. 1968 Kagetsu 21-2-168.
553. Okayama FO 6 Nov. 1964 Kagetsu 17-1-112.

470. In order to respond quickly to and to protect a child involved in a child abuse case (as an urgent resolution), a family court is empowered to issue a tentative suspension of parental rights and duties and/or appointment of a tentative agent to care for the minor as a preservative measure prior to issuing a final decision (FAPA section 105). A family court, in one case, issued a determination of tentative suspension of parental rights and duties until the final decision for removal of parental rights and duties was made and also appointed a lawyer as a tentative agent for the child when the parents refused to give consent to necessary and urgent medical treatment for the child.[554]

471. A family court will issue a determination to suspend parental rights and duties for up to two years if it finds that the parents find it difficult to execute their parental rights and duties or they are not the appropriate people to do so (Civ. section 834-2). A child, his/her relatives, his/her guardian or supervisor of the guardian, a prosecutor and a director of the children's section of a local authority are eligible to make an application to a family court for issuing a determination (Civ. section 8342 and WCA section 337).

472. Once the parental rights and duties are either removed or suspended, the appointment of a guardian of the minor becomes necessary, in relation to which the child parents, relatives of the child, other interested persons or a director of a children's section of the local authority are eligible to apply to the family court for a determination regarding the appointment of a guardian for the minor (Civ. sections 840 and 841, FAPA section 177 and WCA section 33-8).

473. When the misconduct that is alleged to be an abuse of parental rights and duties ceases, the parent or his/her relatives can apply to a family court to discharge the determination for removal or suspension of parental rights and duties (Civ. section 836).

IV. Resolution by Section 28 of Welfare of Children Act

474. In addition to the removal or suspension of parental rights and duties for the sake of the welfare of a minor, a resolution under section 28 of the Welfare of Children Act (hereinafter section 28 resolution) is available for the urgent protection of a minor victim. When public agencies such as local government discover a case of child abuse, they must take emergency steps for protecting and isolating the victim child from the perpetrator parents.[555] A director of a child guidance centre

554. Tsu FO 25 Jan. 2008 Kagetsu 62-8-83. As cases of medical treatment, Nagoya FO 25 Jul. 2006 Kagetsu 59-4-127.

555. The Welfare of Child Act s. 25 provides that any person suspecting child abuse should notify the welfare office of the local government or a child guidance centre. In practice, this measure does not function effectively.

may place the child tentatively under his/her control (WCA section 33), or the governor of the local government is entitled to admit the child into a special institution, such as a foster home or a children's home (WCA section 27(1)(iii)).

475. In the latter case, the governor may order emergency admission to protect the child from the parents even though he/she is formally required to obtain the approval of the family court for the admission. If this happens, the parents are able to claim that their child should be returned to their control since they still hold parental rights and duties (*see* WCA sections 27(4) and 47(2)). Accordingly, in some cases, the governor needs to petition for the removal or suspension of the parental rights and duties in order to assure the child's admittance to a children's home.

476. When the governor of a local authority has acknowledged the existence or a high possibility of misconduct by parents towards a minor and it judges that immediate action should be taken to rescue the minor, it is empowered to pass a resolution to place the minor in a safe and appropriate place on its motion with the consent of the parents (section 27 resolution) (WCA section 27(1) and (4)). If the parents do not consent to the resolution, the local authority is eligible to bring case to a family court seeking approval for passing the resolution without the consent of the parents (section 28 resolution) (WCA section 28 and FAPA section 235). This resolution must terminate within two years as a rule but it could be extended if the family court finds grounds for extension in light of the child's welfare (WCA section 28(2)).[556]

477. The welfare section of local authorities passes various types of resolutions for protecting minors abused by their parents. It places either the minor in a child-care institution[557] or with foster parents[558] for protection on grounds such as physical violence,[559] sexual abuse,[560] harmful conduct,[561] intentional neglect,[562] indirect violence causing the minor emotional damage,[563] failure to provide appropriate care to the minor.[564] For achieving further protection of the minor, the family court can

556. Osaka HK 12 Mar. 2009 Kagetsu 61-8-93.
557. Osaka HK 7 Sep. 2009 Kagetsu 62-7-61.
558. Kawasaki Branch of Yokohama FO 15 Oct. 2007 Kagetsu 60-7-84.
559. Osaka FO 2 Apr. 2001 Kagetsu 53-11-119 (a violent father) and Tokyo FO 5 Sep. 2005 Kagetsu 57-11-73 (a case of a violent stepfather).
560. Ichikawa Branch of Chiba FO 6 Dec. 2002 Kagetsu 55-9-70 (a case of a stepfather).
561. Miyakonojo Branch of Miyazaki FO 15 Nov. 2000 Kagetsu 54-4-74 (a case of Münchhausen Syndrome by Proxy).
562. Shizuoka FO 9 Jul. 2001 Kagetsu 54-2-138 (a case of a mother with an alcohol addiction).
563. Tokyo FO 14 Jul. 2008 Kagetsu 61-8-111. A minor of four years witnessed his brother being battered regularly by their parents for a long period and received serious emotional trauma.
564. Kishiwada Branch of Osaka FO 12 Nov. 1999 Kagetsu 52-4-36 (obsessive-compulsive disorder) and Sapporo FO 11 Jun. 2001 Kagetsu 53-12-88 (a case of a mother with emotional instability).

impose conditions to a determination such as a restriction against contact by the parents[565] or can issue a direction on how to reconstitute the family relationship under the supervision of a child welfare section (*see* WCA section 28(5)).[566]

V. Effects of a Determination for the Removal or Suspension of Parental Rights and Duties

478. During the period of marriage, one parent with parental rights and duties must continue to exercise those rights and duties if a family court issues a determination removing those rights and duties from the other parent. Where a family court orders either parents or a single parent, including an unmarried mother, to forfeit their parental rights and duties, guardianship will take place. A family court can appoint more than one guardian of a minor if it thinks it necessary on either an application by the already appointed guardian of a minor or on its own motion (Civ. section 840(2)).

VI. Removal of the Right to Administration of a Child's Property

479. If the parent(s) with parental rights and duties fails to properly exercise the right to administer the assets of the child, only this right to administer will be removed from the parent(s) (Civ. section 835).[567] A family court will decide whether or not the conduct of the parent(s) is appropriate from the viewpoint of protecting the child's property by taking account of all the circumstances, such as the parent's motive in disposing of the assets, the purpose of disposition of the assets,[568] the events surrounding the disposition of the assets, and the consequences of the parent's administration.[569] In one case, the family court declared that the right to administer the property of the child should be removed from a father who consumed the assets of a minor for his own sake such as for gambling and drinking alcohol.[570] In another case, the court interpreted that the right to administer the property of the child should be forfeited without considering the existence of misconduct of the parent when the parent was declared to be bankrupt.[571] However, as aforementioned, the parent(s) is eligible to use the property of the child for the purpose of meeting the expenses of maintaining the child.[572]

---

565. Kokura Branch of Fukuoka FO 27 Apr. 2006 Kagetsu 59-5-93.
566. Tokyo FO 14 Jul. 2008 Kagetsu 61-8-111.
567. Sasebo Branch of Nagasaki FO. 30 Mar. 1984 Kagetsu 37-1-124.
568. Kure Branch of Hiroshima FO 15 Dec. 1958 Kagetsu 11-3-155.
569. Tokyo HK 9 Feb. 1960 Kagetsu 12-11-125. In Tokyo HK 17 Sep. 1990 Kagetsu 43-2-140, a court held that the fact that an order declaring bankruptcy was issued against the parents should constitute a ground for the removal or suspension of the parent's right to administer the assets of the child.
570. Takamatsu FO 24 Jan. 2008 Kagetsu 62-8-89.
571. Tokyo HK 17 Sep. 1990 Kagetsu 43-2-140.
572. Cf. Sendai HK 24 Jul. 1950 Kagetsu 5-4-63.

480. The same procedures as those employed in removing all the parental rights and duties will similarly apply to the case of removing the parental right to administration of the child's assets. In some cases, where the removal of all the parental rights and duties is sought, a court may issue a determination depriving the parent(s) only of the right to administer the child's assets if it thinks appropriate.[573]

VII. Revocation of a Determination for Removal or Suspension of Parental Rights and Duties

481. When circumstances change after a family court has ordered the removal or suspension of parental rights and duties or the right to administer the assets of the child from the parent, the parent losing those rights, or his/her relatives, are entitled to petition for the revocation of the determination to the family court (Civ. section 836). If the family court declares a determination revoking the previous determination, the parental rights and duties will be restored to the parents; where guardianship has started, it will terminate at the time of issuing of the determination. The effects of the revocation do not operate retrospectively.

482. When a minor reaches the age of majority during the process of conducting hearings for the removal or suspension of the parental rights and duties, the case will be dismissed since the parental rights and duties will have terminated by reason of the minor having reached adulthood.[574]

§6. Resignation from the Status of a Parent with Parental Rights and Duties or Administrator of a Child's Property

483. Parents vested with parental rights and duties are not allowed to resign their post at their own discretion because they are regarded as holding their status not as a right but as an obligation to protect the child (Civ. section 837). However, where parents are unable to exercise their rights and duties fully by reason of illness, imprisonment, residence overseas or remarriage, they are eligible to apply for an approval of their resignation to a family court.

573. Sasebo Branch of Nagasaki FO 30 Mar. 1984 Kagetsu 37-1-124.
574. Sapporo HK 11 Dec. 1972 Kagetsu 26-1-32.

Chapter 7. Guardianship

§1. Outline of Protecting a Person with Insufficient Capacity

484. In 1999, a new scheme for protecting a person with insufficient capacity was introduced by means of a revision of the provisions of the Civil Code. Under the new scheme, guardianship by contract between a person and a would-be guardian became available in addition to statutory guardianship. Furthermore, tutorship was newly added to the protection scheme in order to provide more flexible and wide protections for persons with limited capacity (Civ. section 876-6).

485. It was often pointed out that a person with insufficient capacity and/or his/her relatives were reluctant to use the old scheme of guardianship and curatorship because of its poor availability, lack of flexibility, waste of time and money, and unwillingness of the parties to be registered as a person with limited capacity in the Family Registration Book. A reform of the scheme for protecting a person with insufficient capacity was also strongly advocated in anticipation of the rapid increase of the elderly population which would, in turn, give rise to issues such as respect for a person's right to self-determination and the utilization of his/her remaining capacity. Eventually, the law was changed in 1999. The new law provides wider and flexible measures for protecting a person with limited capacity such as allowing for a legal person to be appointed as a guardian and the head of a local authority to be able to make an application for guardianship (section 32 of the Welfare of the Elderly Person Act, section 51-11-2 of the Mental Health and Welfare of the Mentally Disabled Act 1950 and section 28 of the Welfare of Persons with Intellectual Disabilities Act 1960). Concurrently, the law governing guardianship of minors was revised. After the new guardianship scheme began to operate, some faults which have caused various inconveniences for the users have been revealed. In 2019, the Ministry of Justice decided to revise this scheme as soon as possible in order to provide more user-friendly services, and eventually 208 Acts were simultaneously revised to improve the opportunities for a ward to be employed in 2019.[575]

§2. Guardianship of an Adult

I. Outline of the Procedure of Statutory Guardianship of an Adult

486. A family court can appoint a suitable person as a guardian of an adult by considering all the circumstances of a case,[576] and a family court can appoint concurrently more than one guardian of an adult ward (a family court can appoint by its own motion a guardian of an adult additionally to the guardian who has been

575. The Revising the Provisions Restricting Employment of the Wards and Improving the Interests of Wards Act 2019.

576. Yukiko Inubushi, 'Section 843', in Fujio Obo and Jun Nakagawa ed., *Japanese Civil Law Annotated*, vol.25, 2nd ed (rev.). Yuhikaku, 2004, pp. 313–315.

appointed if it thinks necessary (Civ. section 843(1)), a legal person can be appointed as a guardian of an adult, a family court has the power to determine the scope of a guardian's authority, and a family court has a statutory power to intervene into the transaction of a ward's home. Moreover, the provisions clarify the factors to be considered at the time of appointment of a guardian of an adult such as the ward's wishes and the interests of the ward and a guardian of an adult, etc. (Civ. section 843(4)).

487. The procedure for the commencement of a guardianship of an adult can be triggered on the basis of either of the following two grounds: if a person continuously has an impairment of, or a disturbance in the functioning of, the mind or brain and is lacking in sufficient capacity to understand the nature and quality of his/her acts (Civ. section 7) or if a guardian resigns from his/her office (Civ. sections 844 and 845).

488. The following persons are eligible to make an application for the appointment of a guardian of an adult; a person with a mental health condition, his/her spouse, a relative within the fourth degree, a prosecutor, a guardian of a minor, a supervisor of the guardian of a minor ward, a curator, a supervisor of a curator, a tutor, a supervisor of a tutor (Civ. section 7), the head of a local authority (section 81 of the Social Security Act, section 32 of the Welfare of the Elderly Act, and section 51-11-2 of the Welfare of the Mental Health and Mental Disabled Act),[577] a prospective guardian by contract, a guardian by contract, and a supervisor of the guardian by contract (GCA section 10(2)). No consent from a person with a mental health condition is required for the application, but a family court must hear a statement by the person with a mental health condition in the case of an application for guardianship (FAPA section 120).

489. On an application, a family court will decide on the guardianship of an adult and assign a guardian(s) to an adult ward by issuing a family court determination by considering the mental and physical conditions of the ward, the financial situation and property of the ward, an occupation and career background of the would-be guardian, the interests of the ward and guardian, a view of the ward and all the relevant circumstances (Civ. section 843(4) and FAPA section 120). As a general rule, a family court must hear expert evidence in order to issue or discharge a determination (FAPA section 119). A family court can appoint a legal person as a guardian such as a charitable company, a bank or any other professional institution (Civ. section 843(4)). Moreover, a family court can appoint more than one guardian if it thinks necessary (Civ. section 843(3)). Recently, in order to encourage people to use the guardianship system,[578] an ordinary person, not a professional in the area of guardianship, who has attended a course provided by a local authority or other organization specialized in guardianship can be appointed by a family court as a volunteer guardian (*see* section 32-4 of the Welfare of Elderly People Act 1963).

577. Osaka FO 8 May 2002 Kagetsu 55-1-106 (applicant is a mayor of a city).
578. *See* s. 1 of the Encouraging Use of Guardianship of Adult Act 2016.

490. A family court must not assign as a guardian the following persons: a minor, a bankrupt person, his/her spouse or his/her lineal relative by blood who has brought or is bringing a legal claim against the ward,[579] a statutory representative, curator and tutor who was dismissed by a family court, and a missing person (Civ. section 847). A family court, by its own motion or on an application by a supervisor of the guardian, a ward, a relative of the ward or a prosecutor, can dismiss the guardian from his/her office if it discovers any inappropriate administration such as irregularities in the conduct of the guardian and/or gross misconduct of the guardian (Civ. section 846).

491. When a family court issues a determination to assign a guardian of an adult, it must commission the relevant Regional Legal Affairs Bureau to register the guardianship of the adult in the Registration of Guardianship Book (the Registration of Guardianship Act 1999 section 4).

492. As for the discharge of a determination, a family court must discharge a determination of guardianship if a ward regains a normal state of mental health and on an application by a ward, his/her spouse, a relative within the fourth degree, a guardian, a supervisor of the guardian or a prosecutor (Civ. section 10).

493. A guardian can resign from his/her responsibilities with the approval of the family court if he/she can prove reasonable grounds for resignation (Civ. section 844). Where no guardian is in office due to resignation, the resigning guardian must apply swiftly to a family court to appoint a new guardian (Civ. section 845). For instance, a guardian claiming that he/she cannot look after the ward properly because he/she lives too far from the ward's residence or has difficulties in administering the assets of the ward due to an illness will be regarded as reasonable grounds for resignation (Civ. section 844).

494. The family court may dismiss the guardian from his/her office if it discovers that the guardianship is being conducted contrary to the interests of the ward (Civ. section 846). The grounds for dismissal are as follows:

- irregularities in the conduct of the guardian which will directly or indirectly cause damage to the interests of the ward;
- gross misconduct of the guardian which will infringe upon the interests of the ward;[580] and
- any other facts which are regarded as inappropriate for the administration of guardianship.[581]

579. Amagasaki Branch of Kobe FO 18 Jul. 1974 Kagetsu 27-5-134, but the court will not consider such act to constitute a ground for ineligibility as a guardian if the act is not substantially against the interest of the ward (Osaka HK 8 Feb. 1977 Kagetsu 29-9-82).

580. According to the court, the mere fact that the guardian is indicted for fraud and blackmail will not constitute a ground for dismissal, but it will be a ground if such an act has directly caused disadvantage to the ward (Osaka HK 26 Sep. 1960 Kagetsu 12-11-128).

581. For instance, the court found grounds for dismissal when a guardian mortgaged the ward's assets for his/her own debt (Osaka HK 1 Jul. 1957 Kagetsu 9-7-29), on the death of the ward's parent, a

A guardian will be liable for damages to a ward if he/she fails to resume the guardianship with reasonable care.[582] In addition, a guardian shall be prosecuted for embezzlement in the pursuit of social activities (Cri. section 253) or deception (Cri. 246) when he/she abuses his/her authority as a guardian and causes financial damages against a ward.[583] For protecting the interests of a ward, the Japan Bar Association commenced an insurance system in 2019 for guaranteeing compensation up to JPY 30 million in the case of embezzlement by an attorney of the property of a ward.

495. The following people are eligible to start the procedure to dismiss a guardian: the ward, the supervisor of the guardian, the relatives of the ward, a public prosecutor (Civ. section 846) and the director of the child guidance centre (WCA section 33-9). In addition, a family court, by its own motion, may dismiss the guardian by examining the report issued by the family court welfare officer (Civ. section 846). Moreover, a family court is able to take a preservative measure, if it is deemed necessary, for protecting the interests of the ward (FAPA section 127).

496. The guardianship will terminate on the death of either the guardian or the ward. On termination of guardianship, the guardian or an heir of the guardian must prepare a full report within two months on the fluctuation of the assets of the ward (Civ. section 870). He/she is required to hand the report to the newly appointed guardian and the ward or the heir of the ward after making the report in the presence of any appointed supervisor (Civ. section 871). If the report is not drawn in the presence of the supervisor of the guardian, it will be void. However, if the supervisor of the guardian is not co-operative, the guardian can make the report independently. In the case of the guardianship of a minor ward, the ward may set aside the contract with the guardian or the heir of the guardian when the completion date of the account is after the ward has attained the age of majority (Civ. section 872). On the death of a ward, a guardian can take an action necessary for preserving property of the estate of a deceased, liquidate debts of the deceased and make a contract of funeral of the deceased if necessary unless contrary to the intention of the successors and until the time when the successors shall be able to administer the estate (Civ. section 873-2).

---

guardian spent the ward's automobile insurance money (Utsunomiya FO 15 Dec. 1972 Kagetsu 25-7-51), and a guardian was imprisoned after having left the care of the ward to the guardian's mother (Fukuoka FO 26 May 1967 Kagetsu 19-12-65).

582. Tokyo DD 25 Jan. 1999 Hanji 1701-85.

583. *See* Sendai DD 2 Feb. 2917 CW (an uncle embezzled more than 70 million yen belonging to the ward), SK 9 Oct. 2012 CW (an adoptive father of a ward), SK 18 Feb. 2008 CW (a grandmother of a ward), and an attorney was prosecuted for embezzlement in the pursuit of social activities in 2019 (https://jlfmt.com/2021/03/18/46720/). It is often asserted that a relative guardian may abuse his/her authority as a guardian.

II. Conflicts of Interests Between a Guardian and a Ward

497. A similar procedure for conflicts of interests between parent and child can be applied to the relationship between a ward and guardian (Civ. sections 860 and 826). For the purpose of protecting the interests of the ward, a supervisor can be appointed to act for the ward or to give the ward consent to act (Civ. section 851(4)). Alternatively, a special representative can be nominated to do so. The courts, for instance, consider a conflict of interests to be present where there is a conveyance or gift of assets between the guardian and the ward or a transfer of assets between the ward and the guardian's cohabitee.[584] Yet, this is not the case if the interests only conflict on a superficial level and not substantially. For instance, the court declared there to be no conflict of interest when a guardian (the surviving parent) and the ward (the child of the guardian) jointly surrendered their rights to succeed.[585] The ward is entitled to set aside any conveyances of assets to the guardian or the acquisition of any rights by the guardian which a third party may have held against the ward (Civ. section 866), on the basis that a conflict of interests exists.

III. Details of Guardianship of an Adult

498. A guardian is required to complete the following procedures before he/she represents a ward. First, he/she must promptly investigate the assets of the ward and make the full inventory, one of which should be submitted to the family court within one month after his/her assignment (Civ. section 853(1)).[586] Second, if a guardian has a supervisor, he/she must report any claim against and/or any obligation towards the ward (Civ. section 855). Third, he/she must make an annual budget for the care of the ward and the administration of the ward's assets (Civ. section 861).

499. A guardian must specify the ward's assets in an inventory together with details of their type, number, value and whereabouts. A supervisor of the guardian must be called to take such inventory, otherwise it will have no effect unless it is subsequently ratified by the supervisor (Civ. section 853(2)).

500. The failure on the part of the guardian to investigate the ward's assets and make an inventory will not constitute a ground for his/her dismissal, but it may be taken into consideration when an application for dismissal is made.

501. During the period of investigation and taking inventory, the interests of the ward may be infringed upon if the guardian is free to act as the ward's representative. In order to protect these interests, therefore, the guardian must only undertake urgent and necessary acts, although this rule will not defeat a claim by a bona

584. SD 22 May 1970 Minshu 24-5-402.
585. SD 24 Feb. 1978 Minshu 32-1-98.
586. The family court may extend this period if it thinks necessary on consideration of all the circumstances (Civ. s. 853(1)).

fide third party (Civ. section 854). For instance, an urgent and necessary act could include the guardian repairing a derelict house owned by the ward to prevent it from collapsing.

502. As for property claims between a guardian and ward, the guardian must notify such claims to his/her supervisor before starting his/her investigation, or include details of the claim in the inventory where no supervisor has been appointed (Civ. section 855(1)). Otherwise, his/her claim will be lost (Civ. section 855(2)).

503. The guardian must submit a report on the management of guardianship at the request of the family court or a supervisor of the guardian. Although the guardian will not be sanctioned if he/she fails to do so, the family court may dismiss the guardian if he/she does not submit a report on the budget at its request or that of the supervisor of the guardian (Civ. sections 863 and 846).

504. The guardian of an adult may act as a legal representative with respect to the property of the ward and may administer the ward's assets and finances (Civ. section 859). In addition, he/she may be a representative in litigation on behalf of the ward. All acts carried out by a ward are voidable; either the ward or the guardian of an adult ward can revoke the acts (Civ. sections 9 and 120(1)). Meanwhile, a ward can validly carry out minor acts such as the payment of electricity, purchasing foods and daily necessities independently (Civ. section 9). For the purpose of protecting the interests of the ward, the guardian of an adult must obtain the approval of a family court to make a contract for the transfer or lease of the ward's home (Civ. section 859-3).

505. Since a guardian has wide powers over the ward's assets, his acts relating to them will be treated as valid. In this respect, neither the guardian nor the ward can defeat the claim of a bona fide third party against any act undertaken by the guardian whether or not it in his own interests. In the case of an act committed by an unauthorized agency prior to the time of the appointment of the guardian, he/she may refuse the subsequent ratification if he/she can prove that the refusal would not be against the fair and equitable principle in light of all the circumstances.[587] On the other hand, a person who has acted as a de facto representative for the ward and is later appointed as a guardian, is not allowed to refuse a subsequent ratification, except where there is a conflict of interest between the ward and the guardian[588] or special circumstances exist.[589]

506. A guardian is not entitled to represent the ward in relation to such acts affecting family relationships, except for giving consent for adoption (Civ. section 797). Accordingly, in the case of a divorce, the guardian must participate in the divorce litigation not as a representative of the mentally unsound ward but as a party

587. SD 13 Sep. 1994 Minshu 48-6-1263.
588. SD 18 Feb. 1972 Minshu 26-1-46.
589. SD 9 Nov. 1995 Hanji 1557-74.

to the litigation (PALA sections 13 and 14).[590] If a minor ward is an unmarried parent, the guardian also exercises the parental rights and duties over the child of the ward (Civ. section 867).

507. Unlike the old scheme, the family court can appoint more than one person to act as guardian of an adult ward on the application by either the guardian of an adult ward, relatives of the ward, or any interested person if necessary for protecting the ward (Civ. section 843(3)). In such instance, a family court can determine or revoke by its own motion how the guardians of an adult should resume their office individually or jointly (Civ. section 859-2(1)).

508. A guardian of an adult ward must conduct his/her guardianship of his/her ward properly by respecting the wishes and mental and physical state of the ward (Civ. section 858). For the benefit of a ward, a guardian is entitled to administer and open the mail of the ward (Civ. sections 860-2 and 860-3). In terms of the legal acts that a guardian of an adult ward can carry out in respect of taking care of the ward, the guardian is entitled to make a contract for the receipt of ordinary medical treatment and for admission to a medical institution for the benefit of the ward. However, since a guardian of an adult ward has no authority to consent to invasive medical treatment on behalf of the ward, he/she often faces difficulties in performing his/her duties efficiently. A guardian of an adult is not allowed to deal with highly personal matters of the ward such as issuing a last will because the ward's intention must be primarily respected in such an act.

509. The guardian must obtain consent from his/her supervisor to allow the ward to start a business or act in such a way that is likely to affect the ward's assets (Civ. section 864). These acts include taking on debt, conveying real estate, making gifts, accepting or surrendering the right to succeed, filing a petition, rebuilding, or making a long-term lease/tenant contract (Civ. section 13(1)). If the guardian represents the ward or gives the ward consent without obtaining the approval of the supervisor, the ward or the guardian himself/herself can set aside the act or the consent (Civ. section 865). However, in order to protect the interests of the other party involved in such a case, such other party may remind the ward or the guardian of their obligation (Civ. section 20) or request the guardian to later ratify the act.

510. A guardian must always act with reasonable care (Civ. section 869).[591] If he/she fails to administer the assets of a ward with reasonable care, he/she will be responsible for damages in tort.[592] When conflicts between a ward and a guardian's interest arise and a supervisor of the guardian is not in office, a special representative will be appointed by a family court (Civ. sections 860 and 826).

---

590. SD 25 Jul. 1958 Minshu 12-12-1823.
591. Fukuoka HK 10 Sep. 1954 Kagetsu 6-9-39. In the case where a railway company brought a litigation against a wife and son of a 91-year-old man with dementia by pointing to their failure to conduct proper care when claiming compensation for damages caused by him, the Supreme Court dismissed this case by stating that the wife and the son did not fall under the category of a person responsible as guardian (Civ. ss. 714 and 858) (SD 1 Mar. 2016 Hanta1425-126).
592. Tokyo DD 25 Jan. 1999 Hanji 1701-85.

511. A guardian may be responsible for any damage caused by his/her failure to use reasonable care. A guardian is unpaid because of the public nature of his/her task. However, family courts may decide to grant the guardian a reasonable reward by considering all the circumstances of the case (Civ. section 862). Family courts may calculate the amount of such reward by taking into account the following matters: the content of the will issued by the ward's deceased parent; the social status and financial situation of the ward; and the nature of the work undertaken by the guardian.[593] The reward may succeed to the heirs of the guardian in the event of his/her death. The guardian is also entitled to add to the annual budget for the guardianship the amount of expenditure that he/she has incurred in carrying out his/her duties (cf. Civ. section 861).

IV. Supervisor of Guardianship (Applicable in Both the Cases of Adult and Minor Guardianships)

512. Where it thinks necessary, a family court can appoint a supervisor of the guardian by its own motion or on an application by the ward, his/her relatives or guardian (Civ. section 849). This applies to a case where a supervisor of a guardian of a minor has not been appointed. In the case of a minor ward, a person (usually the parents of a minor) who is entitled to appoint a guardian of a minor ward can also assign a supervisor of the guardian in his/her last will (Civ. section 848). In the interests of the ward, a spouse, lineal relatives and siblings of the guardian are not eligible to be a supervisor (Civ. section 850).

513. The supervisor is responsible for controlling the guardian, if necessary, in the following manner:

- being present when at the time of his/her appointment, the guardian investigates the assets of the ward and makes a full inventory of such assets (Civ. section 853(2));
- being present when the final accounts of the guardianship are drawn up upon its termination (Civ. section 871);
- accepting a notice from the guardian relating to the rights and debts as between the ward and the guardian (Civ. section 855(1));
- giving the guardian consent relating to the matters stipulated in section 13(1) of the Civil Code such as care of the ward, business activities of the ward, and transactions of any substantial assets of the ward (Civ. section 864);
- requiring the guardian to submit reports on the administration of guardianship, any guardianship affairs, the state of the ward's assets, or an inventory of the ward's assets (Civ. section 863(1));

  applying to a family court to obtain any necessary remedies to ensure the proper management of the ward's assets (Civ. section 863(2));

593. *See* Tokyo FO 29 May 1973 Kagetsu 26-3-63 (an adult ward case) and Kumamoto FO 20 Jan. 1982 Kagetsu 35-8-123 (a minor ward case).

- applying to a family court for the appointment of a new guardian in the event that the guardian is deceased, dismissed or resigns his/her post (Civ. section 851(1)(ii));
- applying to a family court for the dismissal of the guardian (Civ. section 846);
- representing the ward where a conflict of the interests occurs between the ward and the guardian (Civ. section 851(1)(iv)); and
- taking any necessary steps for the benefit of a ward in an urgent situation (Civ. section 851(1)(iii)).

514. The supervisor of a guardian must use reasonable care in carrying out his/her task (*see* Civ. sections 852 and 644). He/she may resign his/her office upon demonstration of a legitimate reason to do so (Civ. sections 852 and 844). He/she can be dismissed by a decision of the family court if he/she is found to have committed irregularities or gross misconduct during the course of his/her supervision[594] upon an application made by the following persons; the relatives of the ward; a public prosecutor; other supervisors of the guardian and the ward provided he/she has the capacity to understand the meaning and effects of his/her conduct (*see* Civ. sections 852 and 846).

V. Guardianship and the Family Court

515. In order to protect the interests of the ward, the family court may exercise control over the administration of the guardianship (Civ. section 863). The family court may take its own measures to protect the property of the ward by ordering the guardian to investigate and present a full inventory of the assets of the ward and submit a report on the administration of guardianship. In addition, if the family court decides to permit the property of a ward to be held in trust under a guardianship support trust scheme, it can direct a trust bank to make payment to a bank account administered by the guardian. Furthermore, the family court may direct the guardian to take necessary actions[595] or dismiss the guardian on its own motion.[596] Meanwhile, a family court shall be responsible for damages to a ward's property caused by misconduct of the guardian if it mistakenly appointed him who abused his authority as a guardian or fails to properly supervise him.[597]

594. Naha FO 14 Aug. 1980 Kagetsu 33-7-64.

595. In Hachinohe Branch of Aomori FO 28 Dec. 1968 Kagetsu 21-6-64, the family court ordered a guardian to apply for the appointment of a supervisor for a minor orphan, to present the documents relevant to the administration of guardianship, and gave detailed directions concerning the care and control of the ward.

596. Asahikawa family court made a determination dismissing the guardian by its own motion on suspicion that the guardian had embezzled the property of the ward (6 Aug. 1970 Kagetsu 23-2-101).

597. Hiroshima HD 20 Feb. 2012 CW.

§3. Guardianship of a Minor

I. Procedure for Appointment of a Guardian of a Minor

516. Parent(s) of a minor who holds the right to administer the assets of the minor as parental rights and duties can appoint a guardian of a minor ward in his/her last will (Civ. section 839(1)). A family court has the power to issue a determination to assign a guardian of a minor ward on the application of a ward, his/her relatives, any interested person (Civ. section 840(1)), a director of a child guidance centre (WCA section 33-8) and the welfare division of a local authority (section 81 of the Social Security Act). Parents must apply to a family court for the appointment of a guardian of a minor ward without any delay in the event that they resign from the status of parents with parental rights and duties or from the status of parents with the authority to administer the assets of the minor, or where they are either suspended or dismissed from their office as parents with those attendant rights and duties (Civ. section 841). In the case of adoption, guardianship starts on the death of the adoptive parents. A birth parent will not automatically reassume his/her former parental rights and duties[598] and a guardian will be appointed instead.[599] If a divorced adoptive parent with these rights and duties dies, the surviving adoptive parent will reassume these rights and duties.

517. In the case where a deceased parent has appointed a guardian by a will and a surviving parent only has the right of care and control over the child, he/she can exercise that right while the guardian is responsible for administering the assets of the ward. If the surviving parent dies, the guardian is vested with all the rights and duties over the ward. Such guardianship is effective on the death of the testator (Civ. section 985).

518. Similar to a guardian of an adult, a family court can appoint additional guardians on application by a person stipulated in section 840(1) of the Civil Code, by a supervisor of the guardian or by its own motion if it thinks it necessary (Civ. section 840(2)). A family court must consider the emotional and physical conditions of a ward, the financial situation and property of the ward, the occupation and career background of a prospective guardian, the interests of the ward and guardian, the wishes of the ward and all other relevant circumstances (Civ. section 840(3) and FAPA section 178).

519. Where more than one guardian is appointed, they will assume guardianship jointly (Civ. section 857-2(1)). A family court can assign specified guardians to conduct the administration of the ward's property or order the guardians to share the office (Civ. section 857-2(2) and (3)). A third party can express his/her intention for the purpose of making a legal transaction and such expression of intent will be valid to one of the guardians if more than one person is appointed as a guardian (Civ. section 857-2(5)).

598. Tokyo HK 2 Sep. 1981 Kagetsu 34-11-24.
599. Tokyo HK 26 Apr. 1991 Kagetsu 43-9-20 and Tokyo HK 30 Sep. 1999 Kagetsu 52-9-97.

520. As further protection for the ward, a family court must appoint a supervisor of the guardian, where necessary, on application by the ward, the relatives of the ward, a previously appointed guardian or on its motion (Civ. section 849).

521. On the death of a parent who has solely assumed parental rights and duties after a divorce, the surviving parent will take over those responsibilities instead of a guardian being appointed, provided the family court considers the former arrangement to be for the benefit of the child.[600] This rule will apply to cases where a guardian has already been appointed.[601]

522. The requirements and procedures of appointing a guardian are similar to those concerning the appointment of a guardian of an adult.

II. Details of Guardianship of a Minor

523. A guardian of a minor ward whose rights and duties are equivalent to those of a parent with parental rights and duties is entitled to take care of a minor and to administer the minor's assets (Civ. sections 857).[602] In the case where a parent(s) has lost the authority to administer the minor's assets, he/she can only care for the minor, while a guardian legally administers the minor's assets (Civ. section 868). The guardian must obtain consent from his/her supervisor, if already appointed, where the guardian intends to alter the decision made by the parents relating to education and residence, as well as where he/she approves, revokes or restricts any business undertaken by the minor (Civ. section 857). Where a conflict of interest exists between the guardian of a minor ward and the minor, an ad hoc representative must be appointed if a supervisor of the guardian is not appointed (Civ. sections 860 and 826).

524. A guardian of a minor ward must follow a similar procedure to that which is required for a guardian of an adult. When the ward reaches the age of majority, he/she is entitled to invalidate any contract concluded with either the guardian or his/her successor as part of the process of terminating the guardianship (Civ. section 872). This rule will apply to any unilateral legal act made between those persons.

525. For an illegitimate child whose paternity has not been acknowledged, guardianship will start when his/her mother dies. However, guardianship will not take place where the father acknowledges paternity of the child after the death of

600. Sapporo HK 10 Aug. 2001 Kagetsu 54-6-97 decided to appoint the uncle of a child as guardian rather than assign to the father parental rights and duties by considering all the circumstances and the interests of the child.
601. Kanazawa Branch of Nagoya HK 23 Mar. 1977 Kagetsu 29-8-33.
602. When a minor has his/her own child, a guardian of the minor will assume the parental rights and duties over the child (Civ. s. 867).

the mother, or the mother of the child dies after the father has acknowledged paternity.[603] In one case, a family court vested the father with parental rights and duties after acknowledgement of paternity was confirmed on the grounds of section 819(4) and (5).[604] If the father dies after he has obtained these rights and duties through acknowledgement of paternity, the surviving mother may make a claim to have such rights and duties transferred to her under section 819(6) with any necessary modifications.

526. Guardianship will terminate on the death of either the guardian or the ward, and will also terminate when the ward reaches the age of majority.

§4. CURATORSHIP

I. Outline of Curatorship

527. Curatorship is equivalent to the quasi-incompetent scheme in the previous Civil Code. The new scheme is different from the old one in that a curator: has the authority to invalidate the effects of actions taken by a ward (a person under curatorship) without the curator's consent (Civ. section 13(4)); is authorized by a determination of a family court to represent the ward in legal matters as specified by the family court (Civ. section 876-4(1)); and must consent to a legal act undertaken by the ward with respect to 'important assets' (such as transaction of the ward's real property or intellectual property) (Civ. section 13(1)(c)). A ward, a person stated in section 11 of the Civil Code, a curator or the supervisor of a curator is eligible to make an application for representation, provided the applicant has obtained consent from the ward (Civ. sections 12, and 876-4(2)).

II. Procedure for Curatorship

528. A person with a mental health condition, his/her spouse, a relative within the fourth degree, a public prosecutor, a guardian, a supervisor of the guardian, a tutor, a supervisor of a tutor (Civ. sections 11 and 876), the head of a local authority (section 81 of the Social Security Act, section 32 of the Welfare of the Elderly Act, and section 51-11-2 of the Welfare of the Mental Health and Mental Disabled Act), a mandatary (a prospective guardian by contract), a guardian by contract, or a supervisor of the guardian by contract (GCA section 10(2) and FAPA section 39) can apply to court for a determination to commence the curatorship of a person who is extremely lacking in sufficient capacity to understand the nature and quality of his/her acts as a result of suffering from mental health problems. A temporary curator must be appointed by a family court if a conflict of interests exists between a curator and the ward in the absence of a supervisor of the curator (Civ. section 876-2(3)).

603. Cf. Osaka FO 21 May 1982 Kagetsu 35-11-98.
604. Tokyo FO 25 Dec. 1963 Kagetsu 16-6-175.

529. A family court must revoke a determination of curatorship on an application by a ward, a spouse of the ward, a guardian of a minor ward, a supervisor of a guardian of a minor ward, a curator or a supervisor of the curator or a public prosecutor if the ground for curatorship ceases to exist (Civ. section 14). A curator will be dismissed from his/her office by a family court if his/her conduct is judged as being against the interests of the ward (Civ. section 876-2(2)).[605]

530. With respect to the appointment, resignation, dismissal, new appointment, and ineligibility of a curator, the provisions relating to a guardian will be applied *mutatis mutandis* (Civ. sections 876-2(2)).

III. Curatorship and Legal Effects

531. A curator has the authority to give his/her consent to the ward with respect to the issues stated in section 13 of the Civil Code, and both the curator and the ward can revoke any legal act carried out by the ward without the consent of the curator (Civ. sections 13(4) and 120(1)). Neither the ward nor the curator will be allowed to revoke the act if the ward misrepresented himself/herself as having full legal capacity (Civ. section 21).[606] A ward can apply to a family court to issue permission in lieu of the curator's consent if the curator unreasonably refuses to consent (Civ. section 13(3)).

532. A family court can issue a determination on the scope of matters to which a curator should consent and on the extent of representation of a curator, and it can revoke either part or all of the previous determination on those matters according to the state of the ward (Civ. sections 876-4(3) and 14(2)).

533. While a ward can validly carry out minor acts such as the payment of electricity, purchasing food and daily necessities without the consent of a curator (Civ. section 9), he/she must obtain consent from a curator in the following matters:

- he/she receives or uses any principal;
- he/she borrows money or guarantees an obligation;
- he/she obtains or relinquishes any right regarding real estate or other valuable property;
- he/she brings legal action;
- he/she makes a gift, any settlement or agrees to arbitrate (referring to the agreement to arbitrate as provided in section 2 of the Arbitration Act 2003);
- he/she accepts or renounces any inheritance or division of estate of a deceased person;
- he/she refuses an offer of a gift, renounces any bequest, accepts the offer of gift with burden or accepts any bequest with burden;

---

605. *See* Osaka HK 9 Dec. 1998 Kagetsu 51-5-45.

606. Nagoya HK 25 Jun. 1992 Hanta 801-172. Nagoya DD 7 Oct. 1992 declared that the act of merely keeping silent by a ward should not constitute the ground under s. 21.

- he/she effects any new construction, renovation, expansion, or major repairs of his/her home; or
- he/she makes any lease agreement with a term which exceeds the period set forth in section 602 of the Civil Code (Civ. section 13(1)(j)).

534. A curator has responsibilities to respect the wishes of the ward and consider the emotional and physical state of the ward in performing his/her office (section 876-5(1)).

IV. Supervision of the Curator

535. For the purpose of protecting a ward, a family court will appoint a supervisor of a curator by its own motion or on an application by the ward, his/her relatives or a curator by applying *mutatis mutandis* the procedure for the assignment of a guardian (Civ. section 876-3(1)). The provisions concerning the supervisor of a guardian of an adult will be applied *mutatis mutandis* to a supervisor of a curator except in a case of necessary disposition in an emergency occasion (Civ. sections 876-3(2), 876-5(2) and (3)).

§5. Tutorship

I. Outline of the Tutorship Scheme

536. Tutorship is a new scheme which aims to protect and promote the interests of a person whose capacity is to some extent insufficient due to dementia, being intellectually disabled or having mental or psychiatric impairment, but which also enables that person to utilize his/her surviving capacity to the extent possible.

II. Procedure for Commencement of Tutorship

537. When a person is lacking in sufficient capacity to understand the nature and quality of his/her acts because of mental problems, that person, his/her spouse, his/her relative within the fourth degree, a guardian, a supervisor of the guardian, a curator, a supervisor of the curator, a prosecutor or the head of a local authority can make an application to a family court. A family court can issue a determination of tutorship provided it has obtained the consent of the person with insufficient capacity if the application is not made by him/her (Civ. sections 15(1) and (2), 876-6, section 32 of the Welfare of the Elderly Act, and section 51-11-2 of the Welfare of Mental Disabled Act). In one case, the court rejected an application of tutorship on the grounds that the subject of the application, who was mentally retarded and suffered from schizophrenia, had not agreed to the application since he did not understand the meaning of an application for tutorship.[607] A family court can assign a tutor by its motion (Civ. section 876-7). A tutor must administer the tutorship by considering the physical and mental state of the ward.

538. When a ground for tutorship stipulated in section 15(1) of the Civil Code ceases to exist, a family court will issue a determination to terminate the tutorship partly or totally on an application by the ward, his/her spouse, any relative within the fourth degree, the guardian of a minor ward, the supervisor of the guardian of a minor ward, the tutor, the supervisor of the tutor, or a public prosecutor (Civ. section 18(1)).

III. Tutorship and Legal Effects

539. A family court will vest the right to consent, revoke and represent in a tutor with respect to specified matters on the request of persons such as the ward, his/her spouse, his/her relatives within the fourth degree, a guardian, a supervisor of the guardian, a curator, a supervisor of the curator, a public prosecutor, a tutor and a supervisor of a tutor after acquiring the consent of the ward (Civ. section 876-7). In the case of an application for representation, an applicant must obtain consent from the ward (Civ. section 876-9(2)). Unlike the right to represent, the right of the tutor to consent and revoke will be effective in relation to the matters prescribed in section 13(1) of the Civil Code (Civ. section 17(1)).

540. The provisions regarding matters such as the duties, disqualification, dismissal and resignation of a guardian and the termination of guardianship will apply to a tutor (Civ. sections 876-7(2) and 876-10). When conflicts of interests exist between a ward and a tutor and a supervisor of the tutor is not appointed, a family court will appoint an ad hoc tutor on the application of a tutor (Civ. section 876-7(3)).

IV. Supervision of Tutorship

541. A family court will assign a supervisor of a tutor whose tasks are the same as those of a supervisor of a curator, by its motion or on the application of the ward, his/her relatives or the tutor (Civ. sections 876-8(1) and (2), and 876-3(2)).

607. Sapporo HK 30 May 2001 Kagetsu 53-11-112.

§6. Guardianship by Contract: A Contract of Mandate and the Registration of Guardianship Act

I. Outline of the Guardianship by Contract Scheme

542. In addition to statutory guardianship, the guardianship by contract scheme was newly enacted for protecting the interests of a person lacking in sufficient capacity (the Guardianship by Contract Act 1999). This scheme has two main characteristics. First, a person can appoint a guardian in advance by contract in preparation for the eventuality that he/she loses the capacity to make decisions due to mental problems (a person with intellectual (or mental) problems is still eligible to enter into such contract as long as he/she has the capacity to understand and judge appropriately), and second, a family court can appoint a supervisor of the guardian by contract and supervise him/her in order to provide greater protection for the ward (*see* GCA sections 4 and 7). Under this scheme, it can be said that the ward's right to self-determination will be respected more so that a guardian can be appointed by the ward himself/herself, in contrast to the statutory guardianship scheme, whereby a guardian can be appointed by a family court without any knowledge of the ward. More protective measures are also available to the ward through a family court intervention.

II. Procedure of Appointment of a Guardian by Contract

543. A person can vest in another person, by a contract of mandate, the right to representation for the purpose of looking after him/her and administering his/her assets when he/she loses the capacity to decide appropriately due to mental impairment (GCA section 2(1)(a)).[608] A notary public will execute a notary deed of guardianship by a contract of mandate and register it at the registration office (GCA section 3 and the Registration of Guardianship Act 1999 section 5). Since no professional qualification is required for a guardian by contract, any person such as a relative of the person, a lawyer and even a corporation is eligible to be a guardian.

544. A person can make any provisions by contract unless these are against public policy. The guardianship may include the acts of administering the assets of the ward, of taking care of the ward and representing the ward in litigation. The precise scope of representation should be clearly described in the notary deed (*see* GCA section 3).

III. Commencement of Guardianship by Contract

545. When a person loses his/her capacity after a contract is registered, a family court will appoint a supervisor of the guardian by contract on an application by such

608. When a person lacks the capacity to make a contract, the contract shall be void (Tokyo DD 6 Jul. 2006 Hanji 1965-75).

person, his/her spouse, a relative within the fourth degree and a mandatary for the purpose of commencing the guardianship by contract. A family court must obtain consent from the person before giving effect to the contract, if the application is not made by the person but by the spouse, a relative or a mandatary (GCA section 4(3)). When a supervisor of a guardian by contract is appointed, the mandatary becomes a guardian by contract. Then the guardian by contract can start resuming his/her office according to the provisions of the contract.

546. However, a family court can refuse the appointment of a supervisor of the guardian by contract in the following instances (GCA section 4(1)):

– if the ward is a minor who should be primarily cared for by his/her parents with parental rights and duties;
– if the court considers that the continuation of a guardianship, curatorship or tutorship is necessarily in the best interests of the ward; or
– if a mandatary is judged as inappropriate for guardianship on the grounds that the mandatary is: (1) a minor; (2) a legal representative, curator or tutor who has been dismissed by the family court; (3) bankrupt; (4) a person whose whereabouts are unknown; (5) a person who has brought or is bringing a claim against the person to be protected (a prospective ward), his/her spouse, his/her lineal relative by blood; or (6) a person who has committed irregularities in the conduct and/or gross misconduct against the prospective ward (*see* GCA section 4(1)(c) and Civ. section 847).

547. Both natural and legal persons are eligible to be a supervisor of the guardian by contract. However, a spouse, a lineal relative by blood and siblings of a guardian by contract or of a mandatary are not eligible to be a supervisor of guardian by contract (GCA section 5). A family court can appoint an additional supervisor of a guardian by contract on the application of any of the persons mentioned above or by its motion if it thinks necessary (GCA section 4(5)). A lawyer, a specialist in social welfare, and corporations engaged in the welfare business are regarded to be suitable as a guardian by contract.

IV. Duties of a Guardian by Contract and a Supervisor of the Guardian by Contract

548. When a guardianship starts, a guardian by contract will perform his/her tasks according to the contractual provisions. As long as the contract is not against public policy, the parties can make agreements on any kinds of activities relating to legal and de facto matters of a prospective ward. Matters for the legal representative include administering the assets of the ward such as transacting real estate, drawing money from the ward's bank account and carrying out legal acts concerning care of the ward, such as making a medical contract with a hospital and caring contract with a nursing home. For instance, a guardian by contract filed a suit seeking the rescission of a contract and the return of the proceeds of unjust enrichment where the ward made a contract to purchase a temple bell worth about JPY 300 million.[609] A guardian by contract must respect the wishes of the ward and consider the emotional and physical condition and the living circumstances of the ward (GCA section 6).

549. When guardianship by contract commences at the time of the appointment of a supervisor of the guardian by contract, the supervisor of a guardian by contract must supervise the guardian by contract and he/she must submit reports on the administration of guardianship by contract to a family court on a regular basis (GCA section 7(1)(i) and (ii)). If the supervisor thinks it necessary, he/she can require the guardian by contract to report on the administration of guardianship and investigate any guardianship affairs and the state of the ward's assets (GCA section 7(2)). A family court, if it thinks necessary, can also order the supervisor of the guardian by contract to report on the administration of guardianship by contract, to investigate the guardianship affairs and the state of the ward's assets and to take any necessary action for the benefit of the ward (GCA section 7(3)).

550. In the case of emergency concerning a guardian by contract, such as illness, a supervisor of the guardian by contract can take any necessary action within the scope of power of the guardian by contract (GCA section 7(1)(iii)). If a conflict of interest exists between a ward and a guardian by contract, a supervisor of the guardian by contract can act as a proxy for the ward (GCA section 7(1)(iv)).

V. Termination of Guardianship by Contract

551. Either a prospective ward or a mandatary can terminate the contract before the appointment of a supervisor of the guardian by contract by way of a deed in which a notary public notarizes the authenticity of the signatures or seals of the ward and the mandatary (GCA section 9(1)). After the appointment of a supervisor of the guardian by contract, the ward and guardian by contract can discharge the contract with the approval of a family court by demonstrating legitimate cause for terminating the contract (GCA section 9(2)).

552. On application by the ward, his/her relative, a supervisor of the guardian by contract or a public prosecutor, a family court will dismiss the guardian by contract from his/her services if it thinks that the guardianship by contract is being conducted in a way that is contrary to the interests of the ward due to irregularities in the conduct and/or gross misconduct of the guardian by contract (GCA section 8).[610]

---

609. Osaka DD 4 Mar. 2011 Hanji 2114-87.

610. The conduct which occurred before the time of appointment of a guardian by contact shall not constitute misconduct under this s. (Nagoya HK 5 Apr. 2010 Court Website).

553. Guardianship by contract will terminate on the following grounds: the commencement of statutory guardianship, the death of a ward or a mandatary, adjudication of bankruptcy of the guardian by contract, or the determination of guardianship issued by a family court for the guardian by contract. Termination of guardianship by contract must be registered (*see* below).

554. Even after a guardianship by contract is registered, a family court can issue a determination to commence statutory guardianship, curatorship or tutorship on an application by the ward, his/her spouse, his/her relative within the fourth degree, a public prosecutor, a mandatary, a guardian by contract or a supervisor of the guardian by contract, provided it thinks it especially necessary for protecting the interests of the ward (GCA section 10(1), (2) and Civ. section 7).[611] Such special necessity may be found in circumstances where the guardianship by contract is judged to lack protection for the ward under all the circumstances, such as an ambiguity in the scope of agency, unreasonably high fees for the guardian by contract and other grounds stipulated in section 4(1) of the Act.[612] Guardianship by contract will terminate when a determination to commence statutory guardianship is issued by a family court even after the appointment of a supervisor of the guardian by contract (GCA section 10(3)).

555. If a determination to commence statutory guardianship is issued before the appointment of a supervisor of the guardian by contract, the statutory guardianship and the guardianship by contract will exist in parallel. In such a case, a family court will appoint a supervisor of the guardian by contract and revoke the determination for statutory guardianship unless it considers that the latter will serve to protect the interests of the ward more (GCA section 4(1)(b) and (2)).

556. The ward, his/her relatives and other interested persons must apply for registration of the termination of a guardianship by contract unless a family court issues a determination to terminate the guardianship by contract (the Registration of Guardianship Act section 8(2) and (3)). Otherwise, termination of guardianship will not be effective against a bona fide third party unless and until the termination of guardianship is registered (GCA section 11). In addition, for the sake of protecting a third party who transacts with a guardian by contract, he/she is entitled to request the ward, his/her relative within the fourth degree, a guardian by contract and a supervisor of the guardian by contract to submit the certification of registration issued by the registration office showing the scope of agency for the ward (*see* RGA section 10).

611. Sapporo HK 25 Dec. 2000 Kagetsu 53-8-74 dismissed an application for tutorship on this ground.
612. Osaka HK 5 Jun. 2002 Kagetsu 54-11-54 (curatorship case).

§7. Registration of Guardianship

557. A family court must notify the registration office of a determination to commence statutory guardianship, which must, in turn, be registered in the Guardianship Registration Book (RGA section 4 and FAPA section 116). In the case of a guardianship by contract, the procedure is as follows: a notary deed of contract is registered in the Guardianship Registration Book and when the ward loses sufficient capacity, the ward, his/her relatives, a mandatary applies to a family court to appoint a supervisor of the guardian (RGA section 5 and the Notary Public Act section 57-3). A relative of the ward and other interested persons are entitled to make an application to revise any particulars that are registered in the Guardianship Registration Book when the particulars such as the family name have changed (RGA section 7(1) and (2)).

§8. Certificate of Registration

558. A guardianship registration file should be kept at the local branch of the Ministry of Justice (RGA section 2). A clerk of the registration section can issue a certificate of registered matters (RGA section 10). Only the following persons are eligible to apply for a certificate; a ward, a guardian of an adult, a supervisor of the guardian of an adult, a mandatary, a guardian by contract, a supervisor of the guardian by contract, the ward's spouse, a relative within the fourth degree, a guardian of a minor ward or a civil servant with a legitimate ground for making an application relating to official use (RGA section 10). A person who has engaged in a transaction with the ward can only request the ward or the other persons listed above to submit the certificate. In the case where the ward pretends to be a competent person by not submitting the certificate and conducts transactions, the ward is not allowed to discharge his/her act (Civ. sections 20 and 21).

559. A certificate of registration will certify the scope of agency and the other details of the guardianship. When the guardianship terminates, the registered matters will be recorded in the Discharge of Registration File and only the persons stated in the provision are eligible to apply to a clerk of the registration section to issue a certificate of discharge of registration (RGA sections 9 and 10(3)).

Chapter 8. Kinship

560. Section 725 of the Civil Code stipulates that the following persons shall be relatives: (1) a relative by blood within the sixth degree; (2) a spouse; and (3) a relative by affinity within the third degree.

561. Relatives are eligible to make an application to a family court with respect to the issues relating to incapacity of a person (*see* paragraphs 112-114), legal effects of marriage (*see* paragraphs 171 and 176), acknowledgement of paternity (*see* paragraph 295), adoption (*see* paragraph 354), disputes on parental rights and duties (*see* paragraphs 460, 463, 465, 471, 472, 473 and 481), guardianship (*see* paragraphs 488, 490, 492, 495, 507, 512, 514, 516 and 520), guardianship by contract (*see* paragraphs 545, 552, 554, 556 and 557), curatorship (*see* paragraphs 528 and 535), tutorship (*see* paragraphs 537, 538, 539 and 541).

562. Relatives have rights and duties in the following matters such as maintenance (*see* paragraphs 574 and 802), marriage (*see* paragraph 174), cohabitation (*see* paragraph 242), special adoption (*see* paragraphs 387 and 388), fostering (*see* paragraph 390), guardianship (*see* paragraph 558), guardianship by contract (*see* paragraph 547), succession (*see* paragraphs 625, 641, 643, 651, 652 and 658), will (*see* paragraph 706) and the estate of a deceased (*see* paragraphs 788 and 802).

563. A matter of maintenance among relatives is explained in note 172 (*see* paragraph 159). In addition to rights and duties under the Civil Code, relatives may be in a position to maintain other relatives by section 4 of the Social Welfare Act 1950.

564. In the case of criminal matters, relatives may be in special position according to section 244 of the Criminal Code stating that a person who commits the crime prescribed under section 235(theft) or section 235-2 (taking unlawful possession of real estate) or attempts thereof against a spouse, lineal blood relative or relative living together, shall be exculpated and a person who commits the crime prescribed under the preceding paragraph against a relative other than those provided in the paragraph, shall not be prosecuted without a complaint. In addition, the crimes include fraud (Cri. section 246), computer fraud (Cri. section 246-2), breach of trust (Cri. section 247), quasi-fraud (Cri. section 248), extortion (Cri. section 249), embezzlement (Cri. section 252), embezzlement in the pursuit of social activities (Cri. section 253) and embezzlement of lost property (Cri. section 254).

565. In the case of legal proceedings, relatives shall be treated specially by the procedural law. Subsection of section 10 of the Family Affairs Proceedings Act 2011 stipulates that in the following cases, a judge shall be disqualified from performing the judge's duties; provided, however, that in the case set forth in item (vi), this shall not preclude a judge from performing the judge's duties as a commissioned judge based on a commission from another court: item (i) where a judge or the judge's spouse or a person who was the judge's spouse is a party to the case or any other person who is to be subject to adjudication (meaning a person who is to be subject to adjudication when a ruling is made (excluding a ruling to dismiss a petition); the same shall apply hereinafter), or is related to such party or person in relation to the case as a joint obligee, joint obligor or obligor for redemption; item (ii) where a judge is or was a blood relative within the fourth degree or relative by marriage within the third degree of, or relative living together with, a party to the case or any other person who is to be subject to adjudication.

566. As for ordinary civil litigation, a judge shall be disqualified from doing his/her duties where the judge or his/her spouse or person who was his/her spouse is a party to the case, or is related to a party in the case as a joint obligee, joint obligor or obligor for redemption or where the judge is or was a party's relative by blood within the fourth degree, relative by affinity within the third degree or relative living together (section 23 of the Civil Litigation Proceedings Act 1996).

567. In the criminal case, a judge shall be disqualified from execution of his/her duty when the judge is or was a relative of the accused or the victim (section 10(2) of the Criminal Proceedings Act 1948).

Part III. Matrimonial Property Law

Chapter 1. Rights and Obligations of Spouses

§1. General Principle

568. According to the general principles of matrimony as set out in section 24 of the Constitution, spouses should be treated equally.

§2. Household Expenses

I. Sharing of Household Expenses

569. Spouses should support each other in order to maintain their everyday lifestyle (Civ. sections 752 and 760). Either section 752 or 760 may apply in a dispute over the financial matters of matrimonial life. In general, the family court settles the issue of sharing living expenses during a marriage on the basis of section 760.[613] It is usually interpreted that living expenses include the expenses for minors and dependent adult children.

II. Household Expenses to Be Shared Between Separating Spouses

570. Where a couple has separated, they still have a duty to support each other in accordance with their mutual obligation which arises from their marriage. However, the degree of support to be offered by a separating couple may change according to individual situations. In general, if the relationship of a couple has seriously broken down, the degree of support may be reduced. The family court will calculate the degree of maintenance by taking into account the circumstances surrounding the matrimonial breakdown, the cause of breakdown, the financial capacity and resources of the spouses, and the present state of affairs of both the parties.[614] Accordingly, a spouse may be exempted from sharing financial obligations if he/she does not have enough resources to live independently.

---

613. Section 760 may apply to a dispute between cohabitants (SD 11 Apr. 1958 Minshu 12-5-789).
614. Tokyo HK 6 Oct. 1962 Kagetsu 15-3-115.

571. If a claimant is primarily responsible for the separation, he/she may only claim, from the other spouse, financial support for his/her dependent child and/or for maintaining a minimum standard of life. In one case where the spouse who has caused the separation filed for divorce and claimed financial support from the other spouse, the court declared that the claim should not be accepted as the fact that the former was bringing divorce litigation was evidence that the relationship had broken down, and so the responsibility to support had also terminated.[615] In another case, the court dismissed the claim by a wife responsible for separation stating that the claim shall be an abuse of the right or against the principle of good faith since the husband takes care of their child and continues paying the loan for the matrimonial house where she lives.[616] Meanwhile, if both parties are responsible for the breakdown of the marriage, the degree of maintenance will be calculated by the standard stipulated in the Public Assistance Act 1950.[617] On the other hand, if the respondent is responsible for the separation, it is generally interpreted that the claimant may demand an amount to maintain a standard of life similar to that of the respondent. If both parties have equally contributed to the marital breakdown, there is no requirement for either party to provide maintenance to the other in order to achieve an equal standard of life.

III. Reimbursement of Amounts Which Have Already Been Paid for Maintenance

572. Similar to the position of financial support among relatives discussed earlier, maintenance between separating spouses raises a number of issues. For instance, it is often observed that a wife must borrow money from a third party in order to pay her living expenses during the period of separation when her husband fails to provide financial support. This may be interpreted as the husband having evaded his own matrimonial responsibilities at the expense of his wife. For the purpose of justice, the court may calculate the amount which should have been paid by the husband to satisfy his maintenance obligations during the time of separation.[618] In addition, when the courts assess the division of matrimonial property in the event of divorce, they may take account of the amount each spouse contributed to maintenance during the period of separation.[619]

573. Various views are expressed on when the obligation of maintenance commences; when separation starts, when one party claims maintenance from the other, when the application for family court mediation of maintenance is accepted by the family court, or when one becomes aware of his/her obligation. The obligation of maintenance terminates either when the couple gets divorced or when they start to live together.

615. SK 9 Jun. 2005 Kagetsu 58-3-104.
616. Tokyo HK 31 Jan. 2021 Hanta 1471-33.
617. Sapporo HK 25 Feb. 1991 Kagetsu 43-12-65.
618. Miyazaki Branch of Fukuoka HK 12 Jan. 1987 Kagetsu 39-10-86 and Miyazaki FO 12 Feb. 1993 Kagetsu 46-5-32.
619. SD 14 Nov. 1978 Minshu 32-8-1529.

IV. Factors and Methods of Assessment

574. When the family court assesses the amount of maintenance, it takes into account all the circumstances of the separating couple. This includes the annual income of both spouses, the social welfare benefits of the claimant, the living expenses of the respondent, financial situation of the spouse's relatives[620] and the misconduct of either spouse.[621]

575. There are three ways in which the family court may assess the amount of maintenance: (1) by estimating the minimum amount of support according to the guidelines on living expenses laid down by the Ministry of Health, Labour and Welfare, with some adjustments; (2) by broadening the criteria set out in the guidelines of the Ministry of Health, Labour and Welfare; and (3) by assuming that both should enjoy a similar standard of life. It is often the case that the first option will be applied if the matrimonial relationship has irretrievably broken down while the third approach may apply if there is a reasonable prospect of reconciliation. Recently, the court often assesses the amount by using the tariff with some adjustment to take account of all the circumstances of a case.[622]

V. The Procedure for Claiming Maintenance

576. When a couple cannot reach an agreement on maintenance, they may seek family court mediation prior to applying for family court determination. The family court may issue a determination of maintenance. The determination, once made, may be revised due to a change in the circumstances such as the rise of commodity prices.

577. If one party urgently requires part of the household expenses to be paid for by the other due to financial difficulties, the family court may take a preservative measure on the application by the spouse (e.g., a provisional determination for seizure of the property of the other spouse) before issuing a final determination on maintenance (FAPA section 105). For instance, the court can approve one spouse to exercise his/her right to intervene in a preferential transaction taken by the other spouse where the latter is clearly suspected of attempting to avoid his/her obligation through the disposition of his/her property.[623]

620. Tottori FO 21 Nov. 1975 Kagetsu 28-10-59.
621. Tokyo FO 31 Jul. 2008 Kagetsu 61-2-257.
622. Osaka FO 3 Sep. 2008 TKC (no. 25450867). The tariff is not an official document but is a guideline made by a research group for family disputes (Hanta 1111-285).
623. SD 21 Sep. 1971 Minshu 25-6-823.

§3. Sharing Household Expenses

578. Although the Civil Code adopts a separate property regime as a general rule, a husband and a wife will be jointly liable for transactions of necessity made by either spouse with a third party (Civ. section 761). The question that arises is which transactions should be defined as those of necessity. Necessity is decided according to individual circumstances; the social status of the family, the financial resources of the family and the nature of the transaction.[624] For instance, where a wife bought an English language learning kit worth three times more than her husband's income for their six-month baby, the court held that the kit was 'expensive' and not 'necessary' for that family.[625] Generally, it is interpreted that a large debt even arising from everyday expenses or a disposition of real property will not be regarded as a transaction of necessity.[626] In cases concerning a TV license contract with Nippon Hoso Kyokai (NHK) (near equivalent of the BBC in the UK), the court has in the past decided that a husband and wife should be jointly liable to pay the TV license fee on the basis of a contract made by one spouse without the knowledge of the other,[627] but has also dismissed a claim by NHK on the basis that there was no joint liability.[628] In 2011, however, the Supreme Court repealed the decision by Sapporo District Court.[629]

579. As to the nature of joint liability in the context of transactions of necessity, one principle states that a couple represents each other and can assume liability on behalf of the other. If one spouse makes a contract with a third party as a transaction of necessity and the contract is beyond the power of the agent spouse, the other spouse will still be jointly liable for the performance of that contract as long as the third party can prove to have a reasonable ground for believing that the content of the contract was within the range of a transaction of necessity (Civ. section 110). The other principle asserts that a couple will usually have joint liability for transactions of necessity and clauses on ordinary ostensible agency will only apply if the legal act (contract) was beyond the power of the agent spouse when it was made.

§4. The Matrimonial Home

580. When one spouse makes a contract of tenancy for the matrimonial home under his/her name, the other will also be entitled to enjoy the status of tenant for that home in the absence of any contrary intention. Accordingly, it is often difficult for a landlord or a third party to evict a spouse from the matrimonial home as long as he/she continues to pay the rent. In addition, in practice, such a tenancy may pass

624. SD 18 Dec. 1969 Minshu 233-12-2476.
625. Tokyo Summary CD 26 Dec. 2002 TKC (LEX/DB28080957). Opposite decision in a similar case (Tokyo DD 2 Dec. 1998 Hanta 1030-257).
626. SD 19 Jul. 1968 Hanji 528-35.
627. Sapporo HD 5 Nov. 2010 Hanji 2101-61 and SK 31 May 2011 TKC (LEX/DB25471220).
628. Sapporo DD 19 Mar. 2010 Hanji 2073-98.
629. SK 31 May 2011 (TKC data base no. 25471220).

from one spouse to the other in the event of divorce and may even be handed down to a surviving spouse on succession. These rules will apply to the case of cohabitants.[630]

581. No special provision for dealing with a dispute between spouses over the matrimonial home is incorporated in the Civil Code. As a result, when the home is registered under one party's name (owner spouse), the other (non-owner spouse) has often no effective measures of preventing the former from disposing the matrimonial home. A non-owner spouse has no means of defeating a claim by a bona fide third party who has trusted the registration of that home by reason of the protection of third party' interests. Meanwhile, in the area of succession, an heir spouse shall be eligible to continue to occupy a matrimonial home at the time of succession and he/she shall be given a status prior to other heirs in the process of dividing the property of a deceased. Moreover, the matrimonial home shall be dealt with differently from the other property of a deceased spouse (*see* paragraphs 793ff).[631]

§5. Transactions Between Spouses

582. The Civil Code stipulates no special provisions for transactions between spouses. It is merely stated in section 754 that a spouse is entitled to set aside a contract made during the marriage as long as the marriage continues. However, the court has held that this section would not apply in a case where the relationship between the couple has broken down.[632]

630. SD 28 Apr. 1967 Minshu 21-3-780.
631. *See* s. 1028 of the Civil Code.
632. SD. 6 Mar. 1958 Minshu 12-3-414 and SD 2 Feb. 1967 Minshu 21-1-88.

Chapter 2. Division of Matrimonial Property

§1. Division of Matrimonial Property and Compensation for Distress Caused by Divorce

583. In the event of divorce, a husband and wife must settle their financial matters. The way of dealing with these issues is particularly crucial for one party – usually the wife – who is likely to face financial difficulties after the divorce. Before the divorce law reform in 1947, a wife was entitled to claim damages in tort (Civ. section 709) which included compensation for distress caused by the divorce in order to alleviate her difficult economic position. Under the current law, the new provision for the division of matrimonial property on divorce operates with the purpose of securing the post-divorce life of a vulnerable spouse (Civ. section 768).[633] Now, either spouse is eligible to exercise these two measures for adjusting the matrimonial property on divorce. These measures can also apply to a dispute between cohabitees.[634]

584. It is widely supported by lawyers that the division of the matrimonial property on divorce has three purposes: first, it aims to reallocate the matrimonial property that a couple has jointly obtained during the marriage; second, it provides either party with post-divorce maintenance (in fact, there is no single provision of alimony in the Civil Code); and third it includes the payment of additional allowances for any distress caused by the divorce, a different aim from the compensation under section 709. Accordingly, the court can take account of these purposes when it assesses the division of the matrimonial property on divorce.

§2. Various Types of Division of the Matrimonial Property

I. Reallocation of Matrimonial Property

585. There are generally three categories of parties involved in disputes over the division of matrimonial property: an employed spouse and a full-time stay-at-home spouse; a husband and wife engaged in the business of retailing or farming usually with no independent income; or a couple both employed either full-time or part-time.

586. In the first category, most stay-at-home spouses can neither acquire their own assets nor jointly contribute to the matrimonial property with their spouses under the separate property regime (Civ. section 762) as they will have had no separate income during the marriage. Consequently, they are not entitled to claim their part of the matrimonial property. However, such results are regarded as unfair to

633. Some academics assert that when a dispute concerning the matrimonial property arises, s. 768 applies to a divorcing couple while s. 762 applies to a married couple.

634. Civ. ss. 709 and 760 applied in SD 11 Apr. 1958 Kagetsu 10-4-21 and Civ. s. 768 in Kokura Branch of Fukuoka FO 25 Aug. 1971 Kagetsu 25-1-48.

most stay-at-home spouses and the court will usually assess the share of the matrimonial property on divorce by taking into account the principles of the community property regime.

587. When the court assesses the division of the matrimonial property, it considers the fact that one spouse, for instance, the husband, acquires his own assets during the marriage with his wife's assistance and contribution through her domestic chores. In addition, it can hold the view that the wife should be rewarded for her contribution if she maintains her husband's assets and property or even increases the value of such property that he alone had acquired before the marriage or during the marriage.[635]

588. Second, in the case where both spouses jointly work for their family business, such as retailing, but one spouse – for instance, the wife – does not obtain her income or works unpaid for her husband, the court will divide the matrimonial property according to the degree of her contribution. According to one precedent, the court gave a divorcing wife approximately 40% of her husband's assets in recognition of her contribution in the management of his factory.[636] Furthermore, the court has granted the wife a portion, equivalent to her statutory share as the surviving spouse, by reason of the fact that she was mainly engaged in her husband's farming business with no payment.[637] Moreover, the court held in one case, where a wife worked unpaid in her father-in-law's livestock business, that she could claim payment from her father-in-law as part of the division of the matrimonial property if she had made a substantial contribution to his assets.[638] In another case, the court declared that the wife's share in the matrimonial property should be assessed by considering the average wage of a female employee under the same circumstances. In this case the wife worked from 6.00 am until 11.00 pm in a textile factory owned by her husband's family before eventually seeking a divorce due to 'bride bullying'.[639]

589. For a couple engaged in paid employment, the court has held that it will divide the matrimonial property according to the amount that each spouse has substantially contributed to their property and other assets, despite the name under which the property is registered.[640] In this case, a husband earned slightly more income than his working wife because she spent more time taking care of their children, and so, the court reallocated the matrimonial property on an equal basis as it held that there was no difference between the husband's and the wife's contribution to their property.

635. Tokyo HD 16 Dec. 1980 Hanta 437-151.
636. Osaka FO 12 Apr. 1966 Kagetsu 18-11-60.
637. Niigata FO 26 Dec. 1967 Kagetsu 20-8-72.
638. Yatsushiro Branch of Kumamoto DD 5 Jul. 1977 Hanji 890-109.
639. Ichinomiya Branch of Nagoya DD 26 May 1978 Hanji 937-64.
640. Hiroshima HK 7 Jul. 1980 Kagetsu 34-5-41.

II. Cohabitation and Division of Matrimonial Property

590. As mentioned earlier, section 768 which provides for the division of the matrimonial property can apply to cases involving cohabitees. If one cohabitee contributes to the family property, similarly to a married couple, he/she is entitled to claim a portion of that property in the event of the dissolution of the relationship. In one case, where the cohabitee 'wife' had mainly worked to manage a restaurant owned by her cohabitee husband and had taken care of six 'step-children' for the eleven years of cohabitation, the court held that the cohabitee 'wife' should be awarded 40% of the family property.[641] Meanwhile, as a surviving cohabitee is not eligible to claim a portion of the estate of his/her deceased cohabitee, the family court, which once interpreted the dissolution of cohabitation by death equivalent to the dissolution of marriage by divorce, can distribute some portion of that estate to the surviving cohabitee by analogy to section 768.[642] However, the Supreme Court has rejected this interpretation.[643] However, the court has applied section 762, which provides for matrimonial property, instead of section 768, to a case where it assessed the contribution made by each cohabitee to their property.[644]

§3. How to Divide the Matrimonial Property

I. General Principle for Division

591. The court divides the matrimonial property by considering all the circumstances of the marriage (Civ. section 768). Accordingly, the court can allocate the matrimonial property to each spouse not only as an adjustment to the property but also as alimony and compensation for distress caused by the divorce. In general, the court assesses each spouse's portion on the following principle: as a rule, the spouses have an equal share of the matrimonial assets as most spouses acquire their property jointly during marriage. In addition, the court will grant each spouse a substantially fair quota of their property by considering the nature of the marital relationship and the degree of contribution in acquiring and maintaining the family property.

II. Property to Be Divided

592. Any property jointly acquired by spouses during marriage will be divided on the dissolution of the marriage. It is commonly observed that even the property registered in the name of one spouse can be regarded as matrimonial property by

641. Kokura Branch of Fukuoka FO 25 Aug. 1971 Kagetsu 25-1-48.
642. Osaka FO 23 Mar. 1983 Kagetsu 36-6-51. But *see* Osaka HK 20 Feb. 1992 Kagetsu 45-1-120.
643. SK 10 Mar. 2000 Minshu 54-3-1040.
644. Osaka HD 30 Nov. 1982 Kagetsu 36-1-139. If a cohabitee becomes an obligor to divide the 'matrimonial property' because of dissolution of cohabitation, his/her heir shall succeed the obligation of division of the property at the time of death of the obligor cohabitee (Oosaka HK 15 Nov. 2011 Hanji 2154-75).

reason of the fact that the other often contributed to acquiring or building up that property. Such items are usually the matrimonial house and bank deposits.

593. It is generally understood that severance pay can be divided after it has been paid to one spouse.[645] In addition, when one spouse will retire in the foreseeable future, the court can divide his/her severance pay with the other spouse at the time of divorce[646] or at the time of retirement.[647] However there are various interpretations on how to evaluate the amount of the payment: the courts have, for instance, calculated the relevant portion of future severance pay by considering the length of cohabitation[648] as well as by using a special equation.[649] Unlike the US, no cases have ever been reported where a qualification, such as that of a medical doctor or a lawyer, has been divided between spouses in a case of divorce.

594. In the case of pension, what happens to either spouse in the event of a divorce after the implementation of the new 2007 pension scheme? As a general rule, persons are required to join the National Pension Scheme by paying a regular contribution which will provide a basic pension payment to the contributor whose age is 65 years or more. This is the basic pension for an individual contributor. In a case where a divorcing spouse is employed and belongs to an additional employment pension scheme, while the other is a house husband/wife and not employed, the latter is entitled to claim half of the former's pension which will be calculated according to the number of years married (the Employee Pension Insurance Act sections 78-13 and 14). In other cases where both spouses are employed and have joined a pension scheme individually, the spouse whose amount of pension is less than the other's will be entitled to claim half of the difference between the two pensions (the Employee Pension Insurance Act sections 78-2 and 3). When the parties fail to reach an agreement, either of the them can make an application to the family court (the Employee Pension Insurance Act section 78-2(2)).

III. Division of Matrimonial Property and Household Expenses (*See* Section 760)

595. Where a husband vacates the matrimonial home, leaving his wife to manage on her own during the period of separation, the question often arises as to whether she can include, in her portion of the division of the matrimonial property, the amount of household expenses that her husband should have paid as part of his marital responsibilities. It is generally observed that the court can adjust the division of the matrimonial property by taking account of this amount as one of the factors in a particular case.[650]

645. Tokyo HD 8 Sep. 1983 Hanji 1095-106 where the court divided the husband's severance pay to the wife because of her age (53 years of age at the time of divorce).
646. Tokyo DD 3 Sep. 1999 Hanji 1700-79.
647. Osaka HD 23 Jan. 2007 Hanta 1272-217.
648. Yokohama FO 26 Dec. 2001 Kagetsu 54-7-64.
649. Osaka HD 23 Jan. 2007 Hanta 1272-217.
650. SD 14 Nov. 1978 Minshu 32-8-1529.

596. There are two interpretations concerning the point in time when responsibility to share the household expenses starts. First, it may be the time that one spouse is or could have been aware that the other spouse is in need of being supported.[651] Alternatively, it may be the time that one spouse claims financial support from the other.[652]

IV. Financial Support after Divorce (Alimony)

597. As mentioned above, the court can grant financial support to one spouse after divorce as part of the division of the matrimonial property despite there being no provision for alimony in the Civil Code. While the court is unlikely to give long-term financial support, it may grant a lump sum to an elderly claimant by taking account of his/her remaining years. In one case, the court held that a husband should continue to pay 30% of his monthly wage to his divorced wife for three years during which she was expected to acquire the ability to live independently.[653] In another case where a couple had no common property despite being married for forty years, the court estimated the living expenses of one spouse after divorce by considering the average lifespan.[654] Recently, the courts have shown a trend of granting more financial support to one spouse if there is a long period of separation and the spouse seeking divorce was responsible for the separation.[655]

V. Other Relevant Issues

598. In some cases, the question may arise as to whether the division of the matrimonial property is preferential. Where a third party, retaining a chose in action against a husband, tried to set aside the effect of dividing the matrimonial property, he/she was able to assert that the act of dividing the matrimonial property should be considered to be a preferential transaction. The court agreed but stated that it would be a preferential transaction only if the division of the property was regarded as unreasonably large so as to be a sham disposition of the assets.[656] Accordingly, under such circumstances, the court prefers to protect a third party rather than a spouse.

599. Unlike the above case, where one spouse discovers that the other spouse will transfer or has transferred most of his/her property to a third party in order to escape from the obligation of dividing their matrimonial property, the former is

651. Hiroshima HK 17 Jul. 1975 Kagetsu 28-4-92.
652. Tokyo HK 26 Dec. 1985 Hanta 603-80.
653. Tokyo HD 30 Nov. 1972 Tokyo-Komin-jiho 23-11-177.
654. Tokyo HD 22 Nov. 1989 Kagetsu 42-3-80.
655. Nagoya HD 28 May 2009 Hanji 2069-50 but Tokyo FD 31 Aug. 2007 Kagetsu 61-5-55.
656. SD 19 Dec. 1983 Minshu 37-10-1532 SD 9 Mar. 2000 Minshu 54-3-1013.

entitled to claim that the latter has made or is about to make a preferential transaction, as long as the parties are aware that a divorce decree is expected to be declared in the very near future or the third party knows the real intention of the transaction.[657]

600. When one spouse finds that the other spouse has insufficient property for the purpose of division of matrimonial property, but he/she has a chose in action against a third party, the former can make a claim for the subrogation of the latter's rights against the third party unless or until that chose in action is confirmed or given a due date for performance.[658] Meanwhile, where a third party has a chose in action against one spouse who is eligible to claim division of matrimonial property, that third party can only make a claim in respect to the subrogation of that spouse's rights against the other spouse if the former spouse claims his/her right to division of matrimonial property against the other spouse.

601. In order to ensure a share of the matrimonial property on divorce, the following measures are available: a provisional resolution before finalizing a settlement agreement through family court mediation (FAPA section 266); preservative measures such as an attachment before a family court determination is issued (FAPA section 105).

§4. Compensation for Distress Caused by Divorce

602. In addition to dividing the matrimonial property, a spouse is entitled to claim compensation from the other spouse for distress caused by the divorce (*see* paragraph 240). While the court will assess the share of the matrimonial property by taking account of any emotional damage caused by the divorce (Civ. section 768), a spouse can also claim compensation for distress under the law of torts (Civ. section 709). The reason that section 709 is available is to financially protect the vulnerable party since often a simple division of matrimonial property provides insufficient financial support after the divorce. Furthermore, under section 709, the court is authorized to exercise a wider discretionary power in estimating the amount of compensation in order to achieve a just and fair result for both parties.

603. It is generally understood that a party who claims compensation under section 709 is required to prove that he/she has suffered from misconduct, committed either intentionally or unintentionally by the other spouse during the marriage and that such misconduct resulted in the divorce. Some lawyers describe the distinction between compensation for emotional damage under sections 709 and 768 by the fact that the former concerns distress brought about by the wrongful act of one party (e.g., adultery or violence) while the latter concerns injured feelings of a party as a result of being forced to give up their marriage.

657. Kyoto DD 19 Jun. 1992 Hanta 813-237.
658. SD 11 Jul. 1980 Minshu 34-4-628.

604. Under section 709, a spouse is not only entitled to claim compensation from the other spouse but also from third parties who have wrongfully contributed to the marital breakdown.[659] For instance, where a husband has committed adultery which leads to divorce, the wife can take proceedings in tort against her husband and his mistress as joint tortfeasors.[660] However, the Supreme Court held in 2019 that a spouse shall not be entitled to claim compensation for divorce from the third person who had affair with his/her spouse unless there exist special circumstances.[661] Furthermore, if divorce is caused by the unreasonable intervention in the marriage by the parent(s) of one party, the other can claim compensation from them.[662]

605. It is widely accepted that a 'wronged' spouse is entitled to file a petition for emotional damage under section 709. However, children cannot take similar proceedings against their parents unless special circumstances exist. In a case where some children sued their father's mistress for emotional damages, the Supreme Court held that she would not be liable to pay compensation for their injured feelings since the father voluntarily stayed away from them, and she did not intentionally prevent him from having access to them.[663]

§5. Division of Matrimonial Property and Compensation for Distress Caused by Divorce

606. As sections 768 and 709 are available to a divorcing couple, one question that may arise is which section a divorcing couple should use to acquire financial protection. In other words, can a divorcing party bring proceedings in tort – i.e., a claim for compensation for injured feelings – against the other party after he/she has been granted a portion of the matrimonial property? Some lawyers assert that in order to protect a divorcing party, he/she is entitled to claim a share of the matrimonial property and file a petition for compensation for the following reasons: first, the proceedings under section 768 do not require the respondent to be deemed guilty, unlike under section 709; second, the former will be dealt with by a family court while the latter is a matter for the ordinary court; and third, the former has a limitation period of two years without interruption but the latter has a limitation period of under three years. However, others have stated that a divorcing spouse should not be eligible to claim compensation for distress caused by divorce if he/she has already obtained a share of the matrimonial property. They point out that the division of the matrimonial property is assessed by taking into account the guilt of the respondent and one procedure would be much more convenient for both parties.

659. SD 30 Mar. 1979 Minshu 33-2-303.
660. Cf. SD 24 Nov. 1994 Hanji 1514-82 and Tokyo HD 19 Oct. 1976 Hanta 350-308.
661. SD 19 Jan 2019 Minshu 73-2-187.
662. Cf. Takamatsu HD 20 Aug. 1960 Kagetsu 13-5-133.
663. SD 30 Mar. 1979 Minshu 33-2-303.

Otherwise, the parties would have to go to the family court for a petition on the division of the matrimonial property under section 768 and to the ordinary court for emotional damages under section 709.

607. The Supreme Court has held that a divorcing party would be entitled to bring proceedings in tort in addition to claiming a share of the matrimonial property as the latter was considered to be insufficient compensation for injured feelings.[664] Therefore, a divorcing spouse can claim separately for the division of the matrimonial property and compensation for emotional damages. However, after implementation of the Personal Affairs Litigation Act 2004, if a couple decide to divorce but cannot reach an agreement on financial matters through family court mediation, they can file a divorce petition to a family court with the matter of dividing the matrimonial property and of claiming compensation for emotional damages in tort as an additional disposition to divorce litigation (PALA sections 17 and 32).

§6. Division of Matrimonial Property and Taxation

608. Usually, division of the matrimonial property at the time of divorce will not be charged as a gift between spouses because it is regarded as an allocation of their own property. However, if the amount is considered excessively large, it will be charged as a gift.[665] In one case, the court decided that an agreement between two spouses on the matrimonial property should be rendered void by reason of mistake, if one spouse wrongly believed that the division would not be charged and had notified the other that he/she would not pay any tax in respect to the property transaction.[666] The court in another case declared that a transaction of real property between divorcing spouses, either as financial support after divorce or as compensation for distress caused by the divorce would be subject to tax on account of acquiring real estate.[667]

664. SD 21 Feb. 1956 Minshu 10-2-124 and 23 Jul. 1971 Minshu 25-5-805.
665. *See* s. 9-8 of the Regular Memorandum on the Inheritance Tax Act with respect to acquisition of property as division of matrimonial property by divorce or annulment of marriage.
666. SD 14 Sep. 1989 Hanji 1336-93.
667. Tokyo DD 22 Sep. 1970 Hanji 606-27.

Chapter 3. The Legal Matrimonial Regime

§1. General Principles

609. The Civil Code adopts a separate property regime under which property and assets owned by each spouse before and during marriage will belong to that party individually (Civ. section 762(1)). Meanwhile, the property and assets acquired during marriage will be presumed to be common property unless either spouse can clearly prove himself/herself to be the distinct owner (Civ. section 762(2)).

610. Comparatively few cases concerning the separate property regime have been reported because of the following reasons: a couple is, in fact, unlikely to dispute over their matrimonial property as long as their marriage goes well and when their marriage is in crisis such as in the case of a divorce, section 768 may apply to the resolution of disputes over financial matters. In this sense, it could be said that section 762 merely stipulates the basic principle with respect to the matrimonial property.

611. In practice, for the purpose of achieving fairness and equality among spouses, various interpretations have been voiced among lawyers in accordance with the principles of the separate property regime. According to an early interpretation, where a spouse claimed a share in the assets placed in the other's name during the marriage, he/she was required to prove that he/she actually obtained that asset by himself/herself or made a joint contribution to it. However, it was usually difficult for him/her to fulfil such requirements. Accordingly, under the recent interpretation, the respondent spouse must also undergo a similar process as the claimant spouse of proving either that he/she actually gained that asset by himself/herself or that the claimant spouse had made no contribution to it. In other words, the burden of proof has passed from the claimant to the respondent in order to protect the interests of a financially vulnerable spouse.

612. The court has made it clear that a decision on the extent of each spouse's ownership of the matrimonial property should not be made according to the formalities of property registration, but rather to the degree of substantial contribution that each spouse has made to the property,[668] while as a general rule it upholds the principles of the separate property regime.[669]

613. The process of acquiring the matrimonial property is often complicated. As a result, despite section 762 being laid down on the basis of the separate property regime, the philosophy of common property may be applied in order to achieve fairness and equality among the parties.

---

668. SD 14 Jul. 1959 Minshu 13-7-1023.
669. *See* SD 6 Sep. 1961 Minshu 15-8-2047.

614. Where both spouses are employed, they can generally retain the property acquired in their own names. However, in order to achieve fairness and equality, the court may deal with an individually owned asset as if it was common property after considering all the circumstances. For instance, where a working wife made a financial contribution for acquiring the matrimonial house, which was registered in her husband's name, the court declared that she should be regarded as joint owner with a right to share half of that house because of her substantial contribution, unless special circumstances existed.[670] In addition, where a cohabiting couple purchased real property with the income arising from their joint family business and had it registered in the cohabiting husband's name, the court pronounced that the real property should belong to the couple jointly, unless a specially provided statement against joint ownership existed.[671] Since this approach can apply to a dispute over a bank account, a working spouse is eligible to claim his/her share of the bank account of the other spouse as a quasi-owner.[672]

615. Where a housewife makes a certain contribution to acquiring the matrimonial assets registered in her husband's name, the courts seem to hold different views. A court declared in one case that a husband can hold sole ownership of the house notwithstanding the wife's contribution if he purchased it with his own mortgage and his good reputation.[673] However, a recent case showed that a housewife was usually eligible to claim a certain portion of the property which had been obtained under her husband's name because she was presumed to have made a substantial contribution in acquiring and maintaining this matrimonial property.[674] Furthermore, if surplus is produced from the money that a husband has provided a wife for the family budget owing to her appropriate management of the family budget, it will be dealt with as common property.[675]

§2. Protection for Third Persons

616. Under the separate property regime, if a third party is involved in a transaction with the property, of which ownership has been registered in the name of one spouse, he/she can usually trust the registration description which states the owner of the property. However, in some cases, the other spouse may be the real owner of that property in spite of the registration description due to practical reasons of the property registration scheme. Accordingly, in order to achieve justice for the parties involved in such cases, a bona fide third party will be protected when committing to the transaction, although this does not extend to a third party acting in bad faith (*see* Civ. sections 94(2) and 177).[676]

670. Sapporo HD 19 Jun. 1986 Hanta 614-70.
671. Osaka HD 30 Nov. 1982 Kagetsu 36-1-139.
672. Yokohama DD 24 Mar. 1977 Hanji 867-87.
673. Osaka HD 10 Apr. 1973 Hanji 710-61.
674. Tokyo DD 28 Aug. 1992 Kagetsu 45-12-102.
675. Tokyo DD 12 Jul. 1984 Hanji 1150-205.
676. A fictitious declaration of intention made in collusion with the other party is null and void (Civ. s. 94(1)) and the nullity of a declaration of intention as mentioned in the preceding paragraph cannot

617. Where a third party intends to seize a couple's common property on the ground that one of them is a debtor, he/she is only eligible to seize a share of the common property which is equivalent to his/her claim (credit). Accordingly, if the third party seizes the whole common property, a non-debtor spouse can take an action independently for seeking a stay of execution and annul the execution in order to recover his/her legitimate share.[677]

---

be asserted against a bona fide third party (Civ. s. 94(2)). The acquisition or loss of, or any alteration in a real right over immovable property cannot be asserted against a third party until it has been registered in accordance with the provisions of law concerning registration of property (Civ. s. 177).

677. Tokyo DD 16 Apr. 1975 Hanta 326-249.

Chapter 4. The Conventional Matrimonial Regime

618. Prenuptial settlements are available to a couple wishing to marry (Civ. sections 756 to 759) but no special provision on postnuptial settlements is stipulated in the Civil Code. Few couples use the prenuptial settlement scheme due to its strict procedures and inconveniences. As a result, the Deliberative Council on the Legal System proposed in 1975 that the conventional matrimonial clauses should be amended in order to be more accessible to the parties.

619. A valid prenuptial settlement will be effective under the conditions that first, a couple must agree on the details of the settlement before the registration of their marriage, second, they must have the contents of the agreement recorded at a local legal affairs bureau (the Registration of Foreign Juristic Person and Ante-Nuptial Settlement Act 2011 sections 5, 6 and 7) and third, they are not allowed to review the contents after marriage.

620. If a spouse fails to administer the assets recorded in the prenuptial settlement properly, the other can apply to the family court to have him/her administer the assets for himself/herself. In addition, where the recorded assets are owned jointly, the other may apply to the family court for a division of the assets if he/she thinks it necessary (Civ. section 758(3)). However, in order to achieve those aims, a prenuptial agreement must have been made. In one case where a wife claimed to become an administrator and to possess part of the assets that were registered in her husband's name but acquired jointly, the court dismissed her claim because of the lack of a prenuptial agreement.[678]

621. Neither spouse can defeat a claim from third parties concerning the assets unless the above-mentioned review and/or other changes with respect to the assets have been recorded under the prescribed procedures (Civ. section 759). As for taxation, a court has decided that the tax authority is entitled to levy a tax on the whole income gained by one spouse notwithstanding the fact that the spouses have agreed to share equally the assets acquired by them in the registered prenuptial agreement.[679]

622. The couple must have the capacity to enter into legal acts at the time of making the prenuptial settlement. In general, they may reach any agreement on the contents of the settlement unless it is against public policy or the equality principle in Article 24 of the Constitution.

678. Fukuoka HK 17 Sep. 1964 Kagetsu 17-1-79.
679. Tokyo DD 16 May 1988 Hanji 1281-87 and SD 3 Dec. 1991 Zeimusoshoshiryo 187-231.

Part IV. Succession Law

Chapter 1. Intestate Succession

§1. The Opening of the Succession

I. Death

623. Japanese succession law, which constitutes the fifth part of the Civil Code, states that succession shall take effect only at the time of death of a natural person (Civ. section 882). Under the old family law, in which 'succession' before death also operated, it sometimes happened that the head of, for instance, an '*Ie*' household retired from his post during his lifetime thus transferring all rights and duties concerning the property of the '*Ie*' household to his eldest son (a single heir apparent). This system was abolished in 1947 and the sole ground of opening the succession under current law is a natural person's death (*see* Part I Chapter 1 §1. Definition of a Person).

II. Missing Persons and Absentees

624. The law relating to the opening of succession in respect of missing persons and absentees is similar to that governing the death of a person (*see* Part I Chapter 1 §3. Absentees).

§2. The Heir

I. Capacity to Succeed

625. In general, only a natural person who has the capacity to hold rights and duties is eligible to become an heir. However, a legal person may become a beneficiary of the whole rights and duties of the deceased (Civ. section 990).[680] Furthermore, if a relative of a deceased had made a significant contribution by devoting himself/herself to the voluntary care of the deceased or to maintenance and acquisition of the property for the deceased, he/she can claim the amount of money as a relative as special contributor to the heirs (Civ. section 1050(1)).

680. A legal person can be a beneficiary of a universal gift by a will.

626. Since all rights and duties of a deceased person will be transferred to his/her heir(s) at the time of his/her death, without interruption, the heir(s) must be alive at the time of the death. Accordingly, two questions arise; first, whether an unborn child is entitled to succeed and, second, what happens if the order of death in time of a deceased person and his/her heir(s) is not clear (*see* Part I Chapter 1 §3. Absentees).

627. In the former case, section 886(1) provides that an unborn child is deemed to have already been born with respect to succession, but section 886(2) states that subsection (1) shall not apply if the unborn child is stillborn. Some lawyers assert that a representative of an unborn child is entitled to take part in the division of the deceased person's estate since the likelihood of birth is generally high. However, the courts hold that the unborn child is only entitled to claim his/her portion of the estate retrospectively after his/her birth. To avoid unnecessary disputes among successors, it is claimed that division of a deceased person's property by consent should be postponed until the birth of the unborn child.

II. Commorientes

628. When persons, for instance parents and their children, die on the same occasion and at the same time, no succession takes place among them. Where the times of death are not clear, they are presumed to have died at the same time, and succession therefore becomes ineffective (Civ. section 32-2 and *see* Part I Chapter 1 §3. Absentees). In such a case, however, representation may take place.

III. Unworthiness to Succeed

629. The heir apparent holds the primary right to succeed among family members of the deceased. To prevent the heir apparent from being forced to surrender his/her right to succeed, a person cannot give up his/her status as an heir apparent prior to the opening of the succession. The heir apparent can forfeit his/her status if certain conditions are met.

A. *Disqualification of Succession*

630. If a person commits grave misconduct or there are irregularities concerning the succession, he/she can be deprived of his/her status of heir apparent. Grounds for forfeiture of such status are as follows (Civ. section 891):

(i) When a person has been sentenced to punishment for having intentionally caused or attempted to cause the death of either the deceased and/or any person who has priority or equal rank in terms of succession.

(ii) When a person, knowing that the deceased has been killed by homicide, has failed to alert the authorities of the perpetrator's identity (making a 'complaint' or bringing an 'accusation'), unless he/she has no capacity to discern right from wrong or the perpetrator is his/her spouse or lineal relative by blood.
(iii) When a person has, by fraud or duress, prevented a deceased person from making, revoking or revising a will relating to the succession.
(iv) When a person has, by fraud or duress, induced a deceased person to make, revoke or revise a will relating to the succession.
(v) When a person has forged, altered, destroyed or concealed the will of a deceased person relating to the succession.[681]

The court requires two factors to disqualify a person from succession: for example, any act described under item (v) must be established, and such act must have been committed to obtain an unjust profit.[682]

When an heir apparent is deprived of his/her status after the opening of the succession, he/she will retrospectively be treated as a person with no rights and duties concerning such succession from the time of its opening. Accordingly, any legal acts performed by that person during the period between the opening of the succession and the forfeiture of their status of heir apparent will be void.

B. Disinheritance

631. A person may apply to the family court for a determination depriving his/her forced heir of all rights and duties relating to the succession on the basis of the following grounds (Civ. section 892):

(i) where the person has been treated with cruelty by a forced heir or has been grossly insulted by him/her; or
(ii) where the person discovers other serious misconduct committed by a forced heir.

For the purpose of disinheritance, acts of 'cruelty' or 'gross insult' must be directed against the person to be succeeded. However, 'serious misconduct' need not be directed against the person to be succeeded as long as it causes damage to him/her.[683] In general, the court may order disinheritance if it finds a forced heir has caused the breakdown of the family relationships in terms of succession.[684] It will evaluate, in light of social norms, the gravity of the act when deciding whether deprivation of the right to succeed is appropriate.[685] For instance, the court has stated

681. According to SD 3 Apr. 1981 Minshu 35-3-431, a minor alteration merely concerning the formalities of a will would be acceptable if the alteration attempted to clarify the intention of a deceased.
682. SD 28 Jan. 1997 Minshu 51-1-184.
683. Tokyo FO 19 Nov. 1971 Kagetsu 25-1-87.
684. Itami Branch of Kobe FO 17 Oct. 2008 Kagetsu 61-4-108.
685. Kanazawa Branch of Nagoya HK 16 May 1990 Kagetsu 42-11-37.

that, where a child neglected her parents when they were suffering from ill-health, or otherwise abused them, these acts should be construed as 'cruelty' and 'insult'.[686] It further held that the fact that a forced heir had committed several crimes which caused emotional and financial damages against his parent would be regarded as 'serious misconduct' for the purpose of disinheritance.[687]

632. Before the opening of the succession, the person to be succeeded may apply for mediation, or a determination of the family court to settle disinheritance cases. Where a person to be succeeded states his/her intention to disinherit in a will, a testamentary executor will take similar steps and the family court can then make a determination of disinheritance. For instance, where a separating husband made clear in his will that his wife should not be eligible for his pension because he believed that she had merely married him for his money, the court granted an application of disinheritance issued by a testamentary executor.[688]

633. A person to be succeeded may apply to the family court for a revocation of disinheritance at any time (Civ. section 894). In addition, this will apply to a case where a person to be succeeded states his/her intention to revoke a disinheritance in his/her last will (Civ. section 893). Once revocation is granted, the forced heir will be retroactively treated as a legitimate heir.

§3. The System of Descent

I. The Classes of Heirs

634. Heirs include a spouse, child(ren), ascendants, siblings of a deceased person, and successors by representation (Civ. sections 887, 890 and 889). The order of heirs is as follows; a spouse is always entitled to succession, the child(ren) of the deceased is next in line. Where there are no children, lineal ascendants are eligible to succession; however, those nearer in degree are preferred to persons standing in a more distant degree of relationship. The deceased's sibling(s) is next in succession (Civ. section 889(1)(ii)).

A. Surviving Spouse

635. Under the current family law of 1947 in which the sexual equality principle was incorporated, both spouses may hold the right to succeed each other. Moreover, the status of a spouse in terms of succession was further strengthened following the revision of section 900 of the Civil Code in 1980.

---

686. Tokyo HK 12 Apr. 1992 Hanji 1448-130.
687. Kyoto FO 28 Feb. 2008 Kagetsu 61-4-105.
688. Hiroshima HK 27 Sep. 1991 Kagetsu 44-5-36.

636. As mentioned in Part III (in particular Chapter 2 – Division of Matrimonial Property), in order to achieve the financial equality of both spouses, various interpretations of the Civil Code provisions have been proffered by lawyers. This is true not only in the case of divorce but also in the case of disputes between spouses and third parties. In this respect, some lawyers assert that a surviving spouse may make final adjustments relating to the matrimonial property by securing his/her share to the estate of the deceased spouse.

637. A spouse is always eligible to be an heir apparent (Civ. section 890). In the case of intestacy, the spouse's share in the succession is as follows:

- one-half of the estate of the deceased spouse where children are heirs apparent simultaneously (Civ. section 900(1) (i));
- two-thirds of the estate of the deceased spouse where lineal ascendants are heirs apparent simultaneously (Civ. section 900(1) (ii)); or
- three-quarters of the estate of the deceased spouse where siblings of the deceased are heirs simultaneously (Civ. section 900(1) (iii)).[689]

638. A cohabitee has no right to succeed his/her deceased cohabitee, but he/she is eligible to apply to the family court for a determination granting his/her share to the estate of the deceased only where no heirs apparent exist (Civ. section 958-2).

B. Descendants

639. Among the relatives by blood, children are heirs apparent as a primary group. Their share in the succession is one-half of the estate (Civ. section 900(1) (i)). Where there are two or more children, their respective shares will be equal, regardless of their sex, age or status as biological or adopted children.

640. However, the share of half-blood siblings will be half that of full-blood siblings in the case of succession among siblings (Civ. section 900(1) (iv)). Regarding the share of an illegitimate child, it has been voiced in many quarters that it violates the equality principle laid down in Article 14 of the Constitution. The lower court has, on one occasion, declared section 900(1) (iv) to be in violation of the equality principle, constituting unreasonable discrimination against an illegitimate child.[690] However, that decision was dismissed by the Supreme Court, which stated that the issue should be dealt with by parliament.[691] As mentioned in paragraphs 86, 87 and 280, the Supreme Court finally declared such discriminatory provision violates the equality principle of the Constitution in 2013.

689. Before 1980, the share of a spouse in the event of succession was one-third, one-half and two-thirds for item (i), item (ii) and item (iii) of Civ. s. 900(1) respectively.

690. Tokyo HK 23 Jun. 1993 Kagetsu 45-6-104.

691. SK 5 Jul. 1995 Minshu 49-7-1789 and SK. 21 Sep. 2009 Kagetsu 61-12-55. It was reported in July 2010 that the Petit Bench of the Supreme Court transferred a case to the Grand Bench, which suggested that the Supreme Court would revise the precedents in the near future.

C. Ascendants

641. Among the relatives by blood, lineal ascendants in the nearer degree will follow in the succession if there are no children (Civ. section 900(1)(ii)). Paternal and maternal ascendants in the same degree will be treated equally in the succession. For instance, where there are paternal parents but only the maternal grandparents are alive, the paternal parents will be entitled to succession as eligible ascendants. Where bilateral parents exist, each of them will be granted an equal share of the estate. Collateral ascendants of the deceased have neither the right to succeed nor to become successors by representation (Civ. sections 889(2) and 887(2)).

D. Collaterals

642. Siblings of the deceased will become heirs apparent if neither lineal descendants nor lineal ascendants of the deceased exist (Civ. section 900(1) (iii)). Half-blood siblings are entitled to half the share of full-blood siblings in the estate of a deceased (Civ. section 900(1) (iv)). Children of siblings are entitled to claim their share of the estate as successors by representation.

II. Representation

643. In general, where the child of a deceased person has died prior to the opening of the succession, or he/she has lost the right to succeed (Civ. sections 891 or 892), his/her children will become successors by representation. This applies to the siblings of a deceased and the children of a deceased sibling may also be eligible to become successors by representation. The representation system aims to secure the interests which such children might reasonably have expected to receive, to achieve fair and just financial settlement among relatives by blood of the deceased, and to transfer the estate of a deceased along the bloodline. When a testator states in the will that he/she shall make a specified successor 'to inherit an asset' but that successor dies before the opening of succession, succession by representation shall take effect unless the testator evidently intends to transfer the asset to the successor by representation.[692]

644. The scheme of representation has been revised several times. Major revisions were made in 1962 and 1980. Before 1962, there was controversy over whether successors by representation would hold the right to succeed by representation as an inherent right or whether the right would derive from the rights of succession as enjoyed by his/her deceased or disqualified parents. In 1962, it was made clear that the right should be peculiar to successors by representation. In addition, successors by representation would not hold the right to succeed if their ascendants

692. SD 22 Feb. 2011 Minshu 65-2-699.

(usually parents) had surrendered their rights to succeed. After the revision in 1980, only nephews and/or nieces of the deceased have the right to succeed by representation (Civ. section 889(2)). This revision is perhaps reflective of recent social changes. Relationships among relatives have been prone to weakening due to an increasing number of conjugal families; this led lawyers to recognize that it would become increasingly difficult to search for people eligible for succession by virtue of representation.

A. *Requirements for Succession by Representation*

1. Who Is Eligible to Be a Successor by Representation?

645. Lineal descendants of the deceased person's children (usually grandchildren of the deceased) can be successors by representation (Civ. sections 887(2) and (3)). Accordingly, a child whose parent had been adopted by the deceased will be a successor by representation so long as he/she was born after the parent's adoption. However, if he/she is born before the parent's adoption, he/she is not entitled to succession by representation since he/she is not considered as the lineal descendant of the deceased.[693] Where there are neither lineal descendants nor ascendants, the children of a deceased person's siblings who are also deceased are eligible to be successors by representation (Civ. section 889(1) (ii)).

2. When Does a Successor by Representation Come into Existence?

646. A successor by representation is deemed to exist at the opening of the succession, but this interpretation creates a problem. For instance, should a person lose his/her right to succeed on the grounds laid down in sections 891 or 892 of the Civil Code, he/she could adopt a child prior to the opening of the succession for the sole purpose of using the child as a 'puppet', who will be eligible to be a successor by representation. Through his/her adopted child, the former heir can benefit from the estate of a deceased person. If at the opening of the succession, the successor by representation is dead or has lost the right to succeed on certain grounds (Civ. sections 891 or 892), his/her lineal descendant (usually a child) becomes a successor by representation (Civ. section 887(3)).

693. Osaka HK 10 Aug. 1989 Hanta 708-222 expressed a different interpretation in the following case: a deceased person adopted the husband of his daughter who had already had a child two weeks before the time of adoption. The couple had a child after the adoption and the husband died prior to the death of the deceased person. In this case, the successors were the daughter of the deceased as an heir apparent and the child born after the time of adoption as a successor by representation. The court declared that the child born before the adoption should also be considered as a successor by representation because she was the lineal descendant of the deceased through her maternal line and fairness should be achieved between the children in this case.

B. Effects of Succession by Representation

647. A successor by representation holds the same right to succeed a deceased person or disqualified heir of the deceased person in terms of both the order of succession and the share of the estate. For instance, where a married person with two children dies, and one of the children has died leaving three children, the surviving spouse will take half of the estate, the surviving child will have one-fourth of the estate and the three grandchildren will each obtain one-twelfth of the estate at the time of the opening of the succession (Civ. section 900).

III. The Anomalous Succession

648. The scheme of anomalous succession is not incorporated into Japanese succession law, since under the current law all rights and duties of a deceased person are transferred to successors at the opening of the succession (Civ. section 896). However, there are two exceptions relating to highly personal property (which will be discussed separately later) and the ownership of property used for ancestral worship such as the family tree, utensils of religious rites, tombs and burial grounds. The family tree is a special diagram showing the relationships within the '*Ie*' household across various generations. Utensils of religious rites include Buddhist memorial tablets and Buddhist family altars.

649. The person primarily responsible for ancestral worship will succeed the property used for such worship, which is excluded from the estate of a deceased person.[694] A person to be succeeded may appoint the successor of property used for ancestral worship. In case no appointment is made,[695] a successor will be decided in accordance with local custom. If there is no clear custom, he/she may be appointed by a family court determination (Civ. section 897(2)).[696] While an eldest son or a surviving spouse will assume this position in many cases, once a dispute arises among the parties, a court will issue a determination by considering the closeness of the relationship between the deceased person and a person to be appointed to succeed the property in question.[697]

694. Ashes or remains will belong to the person who is primarily responsible for ancestral worship (Tokyo FO 20 Mar. 2009 Kagetsu 62-3-67 SD 18 Jul. 1989 Kagetsu 41-10-128).

695. Where a deceased person has made a gift of major property to one of his children in expectation that the child will succeed his family business, such gift may be interpreted as a demonstration of his intention to appoint a successor of ancestral worship (Nagoya HK 19 Apr. 1984 Kagetsu 37-7-41).

696. Factors taken into account when making appointments include the following; the relationship with the deceased person, the intention of the deceased person and the prospective successor, living conditions of the prospective successor and the fact that the prospective successor has already committed to ancestor worship (Tokyo FO 31 Oct. 2007 Kagetsu 60-4-77). The family court appoints a person who is considered to have had the closest relationship with the deceased person (Isahaya Branch of Nagasaki FO 31 Aug. 1981 Kagetsu 40-5-161). In this respect, the family court can appoint a non-relative to be in charge of ancestral worship if it finds these conditions are satisfied (Takamatsu FO 15 Jul. 1992 Kagetsu 45-8-51).

697. Fukuoka HK 5 Feb. 2007 Hanji 1980-93.

650. Since property for ancestral worship is not regarded as part of the deceased person's estate, it is excluded from those assets distributed by the process of succession. Indeed, in the case of tomb and burial grounds, the market value is generally extremely high due to the recent shortage of cemetery land. Accordingly, some lawyers believe it to be unfair to other successors in some cases where the successor of ancestral worship could through the anomalous succession regime gain valuable property without any financial obligation.

IV. Adopted Descendants

651. In terms of succession, children adopted by contract or by special court determination will be treated as heirs apparent amongst blood relatives of the deceased person (Civ. section 809). Provisions relating to succession by representation also apply to adopted children. Adopted children by contract may succeed their adoptive parents and birth parents since the relationship between adopted children and their birth parents and relatives remains even after the adoption. However, adopted children by special court determination may succeed only their adoptive parents because their legal relationships with their birth parents and relatives terminate at the time of adoption (Civ. sections 817-2(1) but 736). These provisions may apply to adoptive parents, birth parents and the relatives of adopted children. Accordingly, when an adopted child by contract dies, both adoptive parents and birth parents are eligible to succeed him/her. Sometimes, it may happen that in the case of adoption by contract, the birth parents' right to succeed will be given priority over succession by representation of the surviving parents of the deceased adoptive parents (adoptive grandparents).

V. Relative as Special Contributor

652. When a relative (not an heir) of a deceased had made a significant contribution by devoting himself/herself to the voluntary care of the deceased or to maintenance and acquisition of the property for the deceased, he/she is eligible to claim the amount of special contribution as a relative as special contributor to the heirs after the time of opening of succession (Civ. section 1050(1)).

653. If the parties fail to, or cannot agree the payment, a relative as special contributor is eligible to apply to a family court to decide the amount of special contribution within six months after he/she acknowledges the opening of succession or within one year from the time of the opening of succession (Civ. section 1050(2)). On an application by a relative as special contributor, a family court shall finalize the amount by considering all the circumstances including the degree of contribution and the assets of the deceased (Civ. section 1050(3)). An heir shall be obliged to make payment according to his/her share as an heir (Civ. section 1050(5)).

§4. THE RIGHTS OF THE STATE UPON *BONA VACANTIA*

I. A Legal Person for Administering the Estate of a Deceased Person

654. Where it is unknown whether or not a successor exists, the estate of a deceased person will constitute a legal person (Civ. section 951). 'Unknown' in this provision indicates not only a situation where it is not clear whether a successor exists but also refers to cases in which it is evidently confirmed that no successor exists. Where a successor is merely missing, an issue of absenteeism may arise. In order to administer the estate of a deceased person properly, the family court may appoint an administrator on the application of either a person with a legal interest or a public prosecutor. The court must then give public notice of the administrative appointment without delay (Civ. section 952(1)).

655. The administrator is responsible for representing the deceased person's personified estate and is responsible for administrating the estate according to the guidelines laid down in sections 27–29 of the Civil Code. The administrator must first prepare an inventory of the estate. He/she must then take necessary measures in order to preserve the estate as ordered by the family court and may act in excess of the powers specified in section 103 of the Civil Code[698] with permission from the family court. Finally, he/she is required to furnish adequate security for the management and return of the estate.

656. From the time the public notice is given by the family court of the administrator's appointment, he/she must preserve the estate of the deceased. When the existence of a successor is not confirmed within two months after the public notice has been issued, the administrator can give public notice to all obligees and all beneficiaries, inviting them to claim their rights within a specified period (that period should be more than two months) (Civ. section 957). Where it is still unknown whether a successor exists after the period of two months as prescribed in section 957, on an application by the administrator or a public prosecutor, the family court must give public notice calling upon successors to assert their rights within a specified period of more than six months (Civ. section 958). If no one claims the right to succeed during that period,[699] no person is allowed to assert his/her right to succeed as an heir afterwards, and if no one has notified the administrator of his/her right as an obligee or a beneficiary during that period, no person can exercise his/her rights at a later date (Civ. section 958-2).

657. Where a successor appears during the periods prescribed in section 957, the legal person (i.e., the estate) is deemed never to have existed, but all acts done by the administrator within the scope of his authority are considered valid (Civ. section

698. Section 103 stipulates that a representative whose authority is not specified only has authority to undertake the following acts: (1) acts of preservation; and (2) acts of making use of or improving the thing or the right which forms the subject-matter of the representation, only in so far as the nature of such thing or right is not altered thereby.
699. This period will not be extended (SD 30 Oct. 1981 Minshu 35-7-1243).

955). The administrator's authority terminates when a successor accepts the succession (Civ. section 956(1) and *see* Civ. sections 920 and 922), and on the occurrence of such event, he/she must provide the successor with an account of the administration without delay (Civ. section 956(2)).

II. A Person Who Has Provided Special Care and Devotion to a Deceased Person

658. Under the old law, in the absence of a successor, the whole estate of a deceased person belonged to the state treasury (*see* paragraph 665).[700] Due to the fact that in the past, few people made wills, cohabitees or de facto adopted children could not succeed the estate of a deceased person, and the state would eventually acquire it. After 1962, in order to protect the interests of such people and also to respect the implied intention of an intestate deceased person, had he/she written a will,[701] certain persons can apply to the family court to claim his/her share of the estate of a deceased person. It must be noted that the person providing special care and devoting time to a deceased person differs from a relative as special contributor of section 1050(1) of the Civil Code (*see* paragraphs 652, 653 and 813).

A. *Who Is Eligible to Be a Claimant*

659. The family court may, at its discretion, decide who is eligible to be a claimant among those who have cohabited with, have provided special care and devotion to or have enjoyed a special relationship with the deceased person. The court may also make a determination to give such persons the whole or part of the estate of the deceased following its liquidation (Civ. section 958-2).[702] In many cases, an applicant has done something special for the interests of a deceased or had special relationship with him/her before the death. In a case where an applicant has done something special for a deceased such as performing funeral duties or maintaining the graveyard properly after the death of a deceased, a court will not refuse an application but usually imposes heavy conditions for accepting an applicant to be an eligible claimant.[703]

660. For instance, the following people have been declared as falling within this category: the de facto adopted child who has shared 'joys and sorrows' for more than thirty years with a deceased person,[704] a person who has supported the

700. The Mainichi 8 Jan. 2019 reported that the total amount of 52.5 billion Yen belonged to the treasury due to the absence of successor in 2017. In this connection, the number of administrators appointed by the court increased from 16,751 in 2012 to 21,130 in 2017 (https://mainichi.jp/articles/20190107/k00/00m/040/290000c).
701. Nagasaki FO 26 Jan. 1990 Kagetsu 42-9-41.
702. The court seems reluctant to accept acts by any person after the time of the deceased person's death as 'special care and devotion' (Odawara Branch of Yokohama FO 26 Dec. 1980 Kagetsu 33-6-43).
703. *See* Tokyo HK 15 Jun. 2014 Hanta1418-145 and Tokyo HK 21 May 2014 Hanta 1416-108.
704. Osaka FO 11 Mar. 1965 Kagetsu 17-4-70.

deceased – for example, her former teacher – not only financially but also emotionally for a long period of time,[705]or an employer who has supported the disabled deceased for many years in everyday life and paid wages beyond the worth of his labour by which he obtained a fair amount of assets.[706] A legal person is also entitled to apply to the family court; for example, the school where a deceased person devoted his life as a leading member of staff,[707] the temple of the parish to which the deceased person belonged,[708] the nursing home that looked after the deceased person,[709] the local authority that provided the deceased person with various care services,[710] or the local authority responsible for managing the nursing home where the deceased person resided for a long time.[711] A successor who has renounced succession once can claim his/her share as a person in this category[712] as long as he/she meets the above-mentioned eligibility requirements. In addition, a third person can claim reimbursement of the amount incurred in maintaining or performing funeral of a deceased as quasi-contract (Civ. section 702) in the process of administrating the estate of a deceased (Civ. section 957(1)).[713] However, such person sometimes fails to claim reimbursement during the period of two months due to hesitating to make the claim against heirs who are in grief and facing a difficult situation following the death of a family member. In such cases, the person may be interpreted to be a person who has provided special care and devotion to a deceased person in order to achieve a fair outcome.

661. If a person applies to the family court for a determination declaring him/her as a person in this category but dies prior to its issue, his/her heir apparent may succeed to his/her status.[714] Conversely, if such person has not made such an application, his/her heir apparent is not entitled to succeed to his/her rights.[715]

B. The Criteria for Issuing a Determination: Reasonable Grounds

662. The family court may, in its discretion and taking into account all relevant circumstances, issue a determination giving the whole or part of the deceased person's estate to the applicant if it considers there are reasonable grounds for doing so. Factors to be taken into account include; the relationship between the deceased

705. Osaka FO 23 Dec. 1963 Kagetsu 16-5-176.
706. Osaka HK 15 Feb. 2019 FCJ 24-91.
707. Kobe FO 24 Apr. 1976 Hanji 822-17.
708. Tokyo FO 12 Aug. 1965 Kagetsu 18-1-96.
709. Ishigaki Branch of Naha FO 30 May 1990 Kagetsu 42-11-61.
710. Chichibu Branch of Urawa FO 15 Jun. 1990 Hanji 1372-122.
711. Kumamoto FO 3 Mar. 1964 Kagetsu 17-8-75.
712. Okayama Branch of Hiroshima HK 20 Jul. 2006 Kagetsu 59-2-123.
713. *See* Nagasaki FO 26 Jan. 1990 Kagetsu 42-9-41.
714. Osaka HK 5 Jun. 1992 Kagetsu 45-3-49.
715. Hiroshima FO 8 Jan 1973 Kagetsu 25-10-92.

and an applicant, how much financial and emotional support the applicant had provided for the deceased, whether the applicant had held a substantive memorial service for the deceased[716] and any misconduct by the applicant against the deceased.[717] In the case of a cohabitee, the court acknowledged the cohabitee's contribution to making the property of a deceased, but it dismissed the application as a claimant stating that it is against justice because she forged the will of the deceased in order to defraud the estate of the deceased.[718]

C. The Procedure of Issuing a Determination

663. A person who claims to be within this category must apply to the family court for the issue of a determination allocating his/her share of the deceased person's estate no later than three months after the expiry of the period stated in the last public notice by the family court (Civ. section 958-2(2)).[719] The family court can distribute the residuary, after the liquidation of the deceased person's estate according to the criteria mentioned in paragraph 662.

664. However, a conflict may arise concerning the right of persons within this category: according to section 255 of the Civil Code, if a co-owner dies in the absence of a successor, his/her share is transferred to the other co-owners. What happens in this scenario if a person applies to the family court requesting the distribution of a share of the deceased person's estate by reason that he/she is within the relevant category? The Supreme Court stated that, in such a case, section 985-3 will apply prior to section 255 and as a result any person may claim their share of the deceased person's estate provided such person is accepted by the court as being within this category.[720]

III. Devolution of the Estate to State Treasury

665. Where there is neither a successor nor a person prescribed in section 958-2(1), or where some property is left after the estate of a deceased person has been allocated to the claimants, the remaining property devolves to the State Treasury (Civ. section 959). Once the property belongs to the State Treasury, any legal person relating to the succession is terminated.[721]

716. Osaka HK 24 Dec. 1969 Kagetsu 22-6-59.
717. Tokyo HK 19 Aug. 2008 Kagetsu 62-3-60.
718. Tokyo HK 8 Apr. 2013 Hanta 1416-114.
719. SK 20 May 2005 Kagetsu 57-11-52.
720. SD 24 Nov. 1989 Minshu 43-10-1220.
721. SD 24 Oct. 1975 Minshu 29-9-1483.

§5. ACCEPTANCE AND RENUNCIATION OF SUCCESSION

I. Outline of Acceptance and Renunciation of Succession

A. The Right to Determination of a Successor

666. Under the current law, full rights and duties of the deceased necessarily belong to heirs apparent at the time of the succession. In some cases, a successor can face financial difficulties at the time of the succession due to the fact that the deceased person's debts far exceed the estate. In such a case, however, the successor will in general prefer to surrender all the rights and duties of the deceased rather than risk being in debt. Similarly, a third party involved in the succession, such as a creditor of the deceased person's debts may also need to confirm whether a successor will acquire all the rights and duties of the deceased. In order that the interests of the parties concerned are protected, a successor may decide whether to accept unconditionally, accept with the benefit of inventory or entirely renounce the succession. If he/she accepts unconditionally, a successor assumes all the rights and duties of the deceased. If the successor opts for acceptance with the benefit of inventory, he/she can be relieved of the responsibility if the debt is greater than the estate.

B. The Period of Consideration

667. An heir apparent must express his/her intention of unconditional acceptance, acceptance with the benefit of inventory, or renunciation within three months from the time when he/she becomes aware of the opening of the succession in favour of him/her (Civ. section 915).[722] Acceptance with the benefit of inventory or renunciation requires the heir apparent to submit, together with an inventory of the estate, a statement of his/her intention to the family court within the period prescribed in section 915(1) (*see* Civ. sections 924 and 938). An heir apparent is considered an unconditional successor unless he/she expresses his/her intention to accept with the benefit of inventory or to renounce within the consideration period of three months (Civ. section 921(1)(b)).

668. In some cases, the definition of 'the time when he/she becomes aware of the opening of the succession in favour of him/her' may place the successors at an unexpected disadvantage. In order to protect the interests of the successors, the Supreme Tribunal has declared that the consideration period starts from the time when the successor becomes aware not only of the opening of the succession in favour of him/her but also that he/she is 'actually' a legitimate successor.[723] Furthermore, it has held that the period would not commence if the successors believed, in good faith, that they were not successors due to their belief that no estate of the

722. In the case of a person with limited capacity, this applies to his/her statutory representative (Civ. s. 917).
723. STD 3 Aug. 1926 Minshu 5-679.

deceased person existed.[724] If the heir apparent dies without expressing his/her intention of unconditional acceptance, acceptance with the benefit of inventory, or renunciation, the consideration period for an heir of the deceased heir starts from the time when the heir becomes aware of the fact of the opening of the succession in favour of him/her (Civ. section 916).[725]

669. The Supreme Court has declared that a successor would be eligible to renounce the succession about one year after its opening where he/she was aware of the fact that he/she had succeeded the deceased, but subsequently he/she acknowledged the debts of the deceased by the court notice after the expiry of the consideration period.[726] In this case, the Supreme Court has laid down the following criteria: (1) the successor genuinely believed that no estate of the deceased person existed; or (2) the successor reasonably believed that he/she had no share of the estate. The court also noted that it could hardly be expected of a successor that he/she investigate the estate, by virtue of the relationship between a successor and a deceased person. If either such criteria are met, the consideration period will start from the time when a successor becomes aware, or should reasonably be aware, that there exists an estate to which he/she is the successor either wholly or in part. In this respect, the Supreme Court has clarified that it will apply this rule in accordance with these two conditions.

670. In another case in the lower courts, it was decided that the period of consideration should start from the time when a successor discovers his misunderstanding relating to the order of the succession after the expiry of the original period. The statement of renunciation may then be issued within three months from that time.[727] Similarly, the court applied this rule to a case where after the successors completed the distribution of the deceased's property, one successor discovered that the deceased held joint and several sureties for one of the successors.[728] Where a successor is in a position to know the financial situation of the deceased as a result of everyday contact, he/she must investigate whether the deceased person has acquired any debt. Accordingly, the consideration period starts from the time when he/she inquires into the existence of the deceased person's debts.[729]

C. Withdrawal and Revocation of Acceptance and Renunciation

671. Section 919(1) stipulates that unconditional acceptance, acceptance with the benefit of inventory, or renunciation cannot be revoked. At the same time, it has

---

724. Order of the Supreme Tribunal (Taishinin Kettei) (STK) 3 Mar. 1932 Shimbun 3393-17.
725. SD 9 Aug. 2019 Minshu 73-3-293.
726. SD 27 Apr. 1984 Minshu 38-6-689.
727. Sendai HK 9 Nov. 1984 Kagetsu 37-6-56. In addition to the discovery of the misunderstanding of the order of the succession, he/she must be aware of his/her entitlement to the whole or part of the rights and debts relating to the succession (Takamatsu FO 13 Feb. 1989 Kagetsu 41-9-120).
728. Osaka HK 9 Feb. 1998 Kagetsu 50-6-89.
729. Fukuoka HD 14 May 1987 Hanji 1250-49.

been established that such acts may be revoked on the general grounds of revocation prescribed in the Civil Code, through the issuing of a statement to the family court (Civ. section 919(2)). For instance, where a minor commits such an act without the consent of his/her statutory representative or where a person expresses his/her intention of acceptance or renunciation under duress or fraud, the acceptance or renunciation may be revoked within six months of the time when he/she can exercise the right to ratify it, or within ten years from the time when he/she has accepted or renounced the succession (Civ. section 919(3)).

672. A successor is free to renounce succession within the specified period after the succession is opened. Accordingly, a third party, such as a creditor of the successor, is not entitled to dispute the validity of the act of renunciation by asserting that the act constitutes preferential assignment causing him/her to incur loss.[730]

D. Administering the Estate of a Deceased Person During the Period of Consideration

673. During the period of consideration, a successor must manage the estate of a deceased person with the same care he/she would exercise in respect of his/her own property until he/she accepts or renounces the succession (Civ. section 918(1)).

II. Unconditional Acceptance of the Succession

A. Unconditional Acceptance

674. Unconditional acceptance will take effect either by an expression of such intention by the successor or by the following events:

- Where a successor disposes of the whole or part of the estate knowing either of the opening of the succession for his/her benefit, or the death of the deceased person[731] (Civ. section 921(1)(i)). Disposition by a successor includes not only legal acts such as transfers but also de facto acts such as restoring the deceased's property. In addition, a successor must regard himself/herself as a genuine successor.[732] However, in practice, it is interpreted that the distribution of mementos of the deceased or the payment of a funeral from the deceased's assets does not constitute a disposition by a successor by virtue of the nature of the act.[733]
- Where three months have elapsed from the time when a successor has become aware of the opening of the succession for his/her benefit (Civ. section 921(1)(ii)). If that period has elapsed due to the fact that a successor has not expressed his/

730. SD 20 Sep. 1974 Minshu 28-6-1202.
731. SD 27 Apr. 1967 Minshu 21-3-741.
732. Tokyo HK 27 Jan. 2000 Kagetsu 53-7-124.
733. Osaka HK 3 Jul. 2002 Kagetsu 55-1-82.

her intention either to accept with the benefit of inventory or to renounce the succession, and failure to do either is a direct result of fraud or duress, unconditional acceptance will not take effect.[734]

- Where it is discovered that, even after a successor has accepted with the benefit of inventory or renounced the succession of the deceased, he/she has concealed or secretly appropriated the estate of a deceased person, either wholly or in part, or has failed in bad faith to make entries in the inventory (Civ. section 921(1)(iii)). For the purpose of this section, to conceal indicates that a successor has placed or kept the property of a deceased person in a place where it cannot easily be discovered; to appropriate secretly means using the property for his/her own interests and thus knowingly damaging the interests of the deceased person's creditors.
- Failure in bad faith to make entries in the inventory is interpreted as a strong intention on the part of the successor to conceal. This applies to cases where the successor fails to omit, not only the property of a deceased person but also the debt of that person from the inventory.[735]

675. Once unconditional acceptance takes effect, a successor will succeed unconditionally the whole rights and duties of a deceased person (Civ. section 920). However, a successor can dispute the validity of unconditional acceptance by pointing to the fact that the act of unconditional acceptance was mistakenly made due to false documents concerning the assets of the deceased having been issued by a third party.[736]

III. Acceptance with the Benefit of Inventory

A. Procedures of Acceptance with the Benefit of Inventory

676. Under the scheme of acceptance with the benefit of inventory, a successor's liability in respect of the deceased person's estate is only up to the amount of assets that he/she receives. Furthermore, his/her property does not merge with the estate of a deceased person. In this respect, a successor can avoid being indebted by virtue of the succession, where he/she is unsure as to the value of the assets and liabilities left by the deceased.

677. As for the procedure, all successors must unanimously accept the benefit of inventory at the time of the succession (Civ. section 923). Consequently, acceptance with the benefit of inventory will not be effective if one of the successors does not agree to it. If a successor desires to accept with the benefit of inventory, he/she is required to submit a statement of this acceptance to the family court together with

734. STD 9 Mar. 1908 Minroku 14-241.
735. SD 20 Mar. 1986 Minshu 40-2-450.
736. Takamatsu HK 5 Mar. 2008 Kagetsu 60-10-91. In this case, the creditor issued false documents of the deceased so that successors were treated as having unconditionally accepted by mistake.

an inventory of the estate prepared by him/her within the period prescribed in section 915(1)(i) (Civ. section 924 and FAPA section 39). Where a ground of unconditional acceptance exists for one of the successors, each successor is liable to a creditor of the deceased person for the amount that he/she would have assumed had he/she accepted unconditionally.[737]

B. Effects of Acceptance with the Benefit of Inventory

678. A successor in this category will be liable to a creditor of a deceased person only up to the amount that he/she has acquired through the succession (Civ. section 922). Accordingly, he/she is not obliged to offer any amount at his/her expense from his/her personal assets if the estate of a deceased person is insufficient to cover the debts, unless it takes effect as a result of mistaken payments to the creditor (Civ. section 705).[738]

C. Administration and Liquidation of the Estate of a Deceased Person

679. Where a successor has accepted with the benefit of inventory, unlike unconditional acceptance in which the estate of a deceased person is merged with the assets of a successor, the estate is liquidated independently. Consequently, if the successor holds the rights and duties of the deceased person apart from the succession, these continue to be effective even after liquidation (Civ. section 925). A successor who has accepted with the benefit of inventory must administer the estate of a deceased person with the same standard of care as would be employed in respect of his/her own property (Civ. section 926).

680. In the case where there are more than two successors, the family court must appoint one of them as the administrator of the deceased person's estate (Civ. section 936(1) and (3)). The administrator is entitled to act as a statutory representative for all successors in the event of litigation arising from that estate.[739]

681. For the purpose of liquidating the estate of a deceased person, the following procedures must be taken:

(1) The total amount of the deceased person's debts and the number of creditors must be confirmed.
(2) The successor who accepts with the benefit of inventory must, within five days of the acceptance, give all creditors and beneficiaries a public notice in which it should be stated that acceptance has been made and which should invite

737. Toyama FO 23 Oct. 1978 Kagetsu 31-9-42.
738. Section 705 stipulates that if a person, who has effected an act of performance, thereby purporting to discharge an obligation, was aware at the time that no such obligation existed, he/she cannot demand the return of the subject-matter of such act of performance.
739. SD 9 Nov. 1972 Minshu 26-9-156.

them to present claims within a specified period of more than two months (Civ. section 927(1)). If any of the successors in this category are aware of a creditor, the administrator must inform such a creditor individually in addition to issuing the public notice. However, the successor is not obliged to investigate the existence of a creditor.[740]

(3) If necessary, the successor (or the administrator) must sell the whole or part of the estate. In such a case, he/she usually effects the sale through an official auction but may alternatively have the estate valued by an appraiser appointed by the family court (Civ. section 932).

(4) After the period of public notice and upon completion of the sale or appraisal, the successor (or the administrator) makes payment from the estate to creditors who have presented their claims and to all other known creditors in amounts proportionate to their respective claims. However, the right of creditors who have priority must not be compromised (Civ. section 929).

(5) If a creditor or beneficiary is unable to acquire his/her legitimate share of the estate by virtue of the fact that the successor (or the administrator) has either failed to give proper public notice (as prescribed in section 927) or allocated the estate to other creditors or beneficiaries during the period of public notice, he/she is entitled to claim damages from the successor (Civ. section 934(1)). In addition, he/she is eligible to claim reimbursement from creditors or beneficiaries who have obtained any benefit in bad faith (Civ. section 934(2)).

IV. Renunciation of Succession

A. *Outline of Renunciation*

682. In theory, the whole rights and duties of a person will be transferred without interruption to his/her heirs apparent on his/her death. However, in order to protect the interests of heirs apparent, they may renounce the succession, on submission of the relevant statement to the family court, no later than three months from the opening of the succession (Civ. section 915(1)). Once the statement is issued, he/she will be deemed not to have been a successor from the opening of the succession (Civ. section 939). Where there are more than two heirs apparent, unlike acceptance with the benefit of inventory, an heir is eligible to renounce individually.

683. The purpose of renunciation is to protect the interests of the successor of the deceased whose debts exceed his/her estate, and to respect the freedom of that person to decide whether or not to become a successor. In addition, successors often opt for renunciation for the purpose of achieving substantial equality among them since the legitimate children of the deceased are eligible to claim equal shares in the estate of their parent (Civ. section 900(1)(d)). If this rule of equality applies without taking into account the individual circumstances of each case, it can cause unfair results and create difficulties among successors.

740. Tokyo DD 16 Feb. 2001 Hanji 1753-78.

684. For example, the eldest child may work, virtually unpaid, on his/her parent's farm for a long period of time and consequently sacrifice the opportunity of obtaining higher education. Yet the other children may find employment in the business world after obtaining the necessary qualifications, with the financial support of their parents. If the claim of those children, on the basis of the equality rule, is approved and the estate is distributed among the children, it can cause extreme unfairness to the eldest child. In such a case, the person inheriting the family business will, through renunciation by the other successors, be able to possess the whole estate in terms of securing the management of the business, while ensuring a fair outcome for the other successors.

685. In order that similar results are achieved, two measures are available in practice. First, all successors with the exception of one may declare during the process of dividing the property of a deceased that they have no share of the estate. As a result, the one successor is able to possess the whole estate. Second, after the acceptance of the succession, all successors except one may issue a document stating that they are not entitled to their share of the estate because they have already benefited from a gift by the deceased prior to the opening of the succession (cf. Civ. section 903).[741]

B. Procedures of Renunciation

686. For the purpose of renunciation, a successor must submit a statement of renunciation to the family court (Civ. section 938). Renunciation prior to the opening of the succession is not allowed in order that the interests of a successor may be protected. In some cases, there may be some benefit in allowing a successor to renounce succession prior to the opening of the succession but the family court usually rejects this interpretation due to the lack of a legal basis.[742]

687. The statement of renunciation must be made within three months of the opening of the succession (Civ. section 915). During this period, a successor can investigate the estate of a deceased person but is not required to issue an inventory of that estate. On the submission of the statement of renunciation, the family court will confirm by way of a family court determination whether the statement has been issued in accordance with the real and true intention of the successor (FAPA section 39). In practice, the family court does not require a successor to be interviewed or to sign the statement in person as long as the family court can find that the statement was issued with a genuine intention on the part of the successor.[743] For

741. Tokushima FO 16 Aug. 1978 Kagetsu 31-6-44 pronounced that this measure was acceptable as long as the parties agreed to submit such document of which content was false, and interpreted that the act of submission indicated either a de facto renunciation or a gift of the successors' share to one particular successor.

742. Tokyo FO 8 Sep. 1977 Kagetsu 30-3-88.

743. SD 21 Dec. 1954 Minshu 8-12-2222.

example, in one case, the family court regarded as sufficient a statement that a successor told a family court welfare officer he had no intention of succeeding, was ready to accept a decision by the court, and was unwilling to be involved in the case.[744] Where there are more than two successors, each of them may renounce the succession individually. A successor may not renounce a portion, or a specified part of the estate since renunciation takes effect in respect of the whole estate.

688. For a renunciation to be valid, the following requirements must be met. First, it will only be effective if a successor solely declares his/her intention to renounce. Second, a person with limited capacity is not eligible to renounce but his/her statutory representative can do so. In the case of a minor, there are two questions to be answered. Where a mother and her minor succeed the father of the minor, is she eligible to renounce on behalf of the minor? Some argue that representation by the mother may conflict with the interests of the minor if, after renunciation, she is able to obtain the whole estate. Furthermore, where there are two or more minor successors, the mother will be prohibited by law from representing both parties for the purpose of renunciation (Civ. section 108). The Supreme Court declared that, in such a case, she would be entitled to represent her children in respect of renunciation if she jointly renounced the succession.[745]

689. Since the right to renounce is exclusive to a successor, no one can force him/her to exercise it or refrain from exercising it, against his/her free will. Accordingly, for instance, a creditor was not eligible to challenge the validity of a successor's renunciation as a preferential course of action where the debt of the deceased far exceeded the estate.[746]

690. A successor is not allowed to revoke a renunciation once it is made (Civ. section 919(1)). However, if the grounds for revocation prescribed in the Civil Code can be established, then renunciation may be set aside (Civ. section 919(2)). This applies where renunciation is claimed to be void. The courts have pronounced that renunciation was voidable by reason of fraud[747] and void on the ground of mistake.[748] Due to the different nature of individual cases, one court has stated that renunciation should be void because it was made mistakenly by false information,[749] while another has declared that a claim that the renunciation was void by reason of mistake should be regarded as an abuse of rights.[750]

744. Tokyo FO 1 May 1992 Kagetsu 45-1-137.
745. SD 24 Feb. 1978 Minshu 32-1-98.
746. SD 20 Sep. 1974 Minshu 28-6-1202.
747. Tokyo HD 22 Jul. 1952 Kagetsu 4-8-94.
748. SD 27 May 1965 Kagetsu 17-6-251.
749. Fukuoka HD 26 Aug. 1998 Hanji 1698-83.
750. Tokyo HD 25 Apr. 1988 Hanji 1278-78.

C. Effects of Renunciation

691. Since renunciation takes effect retrospectively as at the opening of the succession, a person who has renounced the succession will be deemed not to have been a successor from that time (Civ. section 939). Accordingly, the descendant of a successor who has renounced the succession is not eligible to be a successor by representation. Renunciation will affect the share of each successor. For instance, where there exists a surviving spouse and more than two children, the share of one of the successors is, on renunciation, merged into the remaining portion of the rest, while the portion for the surviving spouse remains the same (Civ. section 900(1)(i)). If a surviving spouse renounces the succession, her/his portion is merged with that of the children.

692. A successor may die without accepting or renouncing the succession. In such a case, the successor of a deceased successor is eligible to decide whether to accept or renounce each succession individually. Thus, if he/she renounces the latter succession, he/she will not be the successor of either the former or latter succession. If he/she renounces the former succession, he/she will not succeed the former, but he/she will remain eligible to either accept or renounce the latter.

Chapter 2. Testamentary Succession

§1. Introduction

693. There are two different views on testamentary succession among lawyers. One interprets it as the procedure under which a person is able to dispose of his/her own property by his/her free will, even after the time of his/her death. In other words, it reflects the principle of self-determination. The other opinion, however, regards testamentary succession as an exceptional case outside that principle. As a result, under the current interpretation of the Civil Code, no person can usually enforce his/her intention after death because he/she ceases to exist as a legal subject. Accordingly, the fact that the will of a deceased person may be effective even after his/her death shows that it is an exceptional case of the principle of self-determination.

694. Strict formalities and requirements apply when dealing with a will (Civ. section 960).[751] The act of making a will is considered special *(acte à cause de morte)* with the objective that it will take effect after the death of the testator. If the requirements and formalities are met, a will is effective without the acceptance of a beneficiary (*acte unilateral*). A will may be withdrawn or revoked before the death of a testator.

695. Historically, intestate succession has appeared more frequently in society than testamentary succession. Nowadays, however, the number of people making a will has increased and subsequently applications to the family court for granting probate of a will has risen for decades. Such an increase may reflect the changing social trend in senior people making wills in order to reward the person who has looked after them during the later stage of life. Succession, through this type of will, is called 'succession as reward' and reflects a 'give and take' attitude between the testator and beneficiary.

696. In addition, due to a rise in the value of real property during the period of rapid economic growth and the subsequent bubble economy, a number of people became more aware of the necessity of making arrangements for property after death to prevent disputes among their relatives. Such views illustrate the attitude that property, even among family members, should be considered individual, not communal. This individualistic view appears to form the backdrop to the trend of an increasing number of people making a will.

§2. The Capacity to Make a Will

697. A person aged 15 years or over is eligible to make a will (Civ. section 961). Where a person is of full age, he/she is qualified to make a will if he/she has the

751. It is generally supported that the true intention of a testator will take priority (*See* SD 24 Dec. 1974 Minshu 28-10-2152).

capacity to understand the meaning and effect of his/her act.[752] As a result, a person under guardianship may independently make a will in the presence of two medical doctors as long as he/she has the capacity to do so (Civ. section 973(1)).[753] A person under curatorship or tutorship is entitled to make a will without consent by the curator or tutor (Civ. section 962). A will made by a person with a mental health condition will be void or a will made under duress or fraud will be voidable. The capacity to make a will is required at the time of its creation and a subsequent loss of capacity on the part of the testator will not affect the validity of the will.

698. For the purpose of deciding whether a testator has the capacity to make a will, a court will take into account all the circumstances of the case including any diagnosis by a medical doctor, the ability of the testator to communicate, the process of making a will and the rationality of the content stated in a will.[754]

§3. DIFFERENT TYPES OF WILLS

699. There are seven types of will under the current law:

(1) A will by ordinary procedure:
   - (a) A will by holographic document (Civ. section 968)
   - (b) A will by notary document (Civ. section 969)
   - (c) A will by secret document (Civ. section 970).

(2) A will by special procedure:
   - (a) A will of a person in imminent danger of death (Civ. section 976)
   - (b) A will of a person isolated on account of a contagious disease (Civ. section 977)
   - (c) A will of a person in imminent danger of death on board a distressed ship (Civ. section 979)
   - (d) A will of a person on board a ship (Civ. section 978).

(3) A will to specify a particular property for succession
   - (a) This type of a will is added in 2018 for the purpose of distribution of the estate (*see* Civ. section 1014).
   - (b) A will shall be a will to specify a particular property for succession if a testator makes a will in which he/she specifies the property to be allocated to an heir or heirs as a means of distributing his/her estate.
   - (c) This type of a will can be made by any type of will such as holographic document etc. with some restriction (Civ. section 1014(2)).

752. *See* Osaka HD 26 Jun. 1990 Kagetsu 43-8-40. Even in the cases of senile dementia, the courts have declared wills by notary document to be valid (Nagoya HD 28 May 1997 Hanta 960-249).

753. Okazaki Branch of Nagoya DD 27 May 1993 Kagetsu 46-7-79.

754. Tokyo DD 7 Jul. 2004 Hanta 1185-291, Osaka HD 26 Apr. 2007 Hanji 1979-75 and Tokyo DD 25 Jul. 2006 Hanji 1958-109.

I. A Will by Holographic Document

700. In respect of the formalities of this type of will, a testator must write the whole text by hand, the date and his/her full name and must affix his/her seal.[755] Consequently, a will written by typewriter or word processor or a will recorded by tape recorder will not be effective. As long as a testator writes a will by hand, no particular form of words, language or symbols need to be used. A testator is not required to write the whole text of an inventory attached to the main document of a will by hand except his/her full name and must affix his/her seal on each page if any (section 968(2)). Furthermore, there are no restrictions as to the materials on which the will may be handwritten, or the tools (pencil or ink) that may be used. Where someone writes part of the will on behalf of the testator, that part will be void unless it substantially affects the will.[756] If a will is several pages long, it will be valid if those pages combine to create a single will, which will be judged based on the entries, the type of paper and seal.[757]

701. A person's commonly known name, stage name or nom de plume may be used. Indeed, a surname is effective by itself if a testator can be identified by it.[758]

702. The date of a will may be worded to describe a particular time in order to assure the validity of a will. Consequently, the following description will not be effective since it is difficult to confirm the actual date that the will was made: January 2022 (as only the month and year is stated) or the lucky day of January 2022.[759] However, 'my sixtieth birthday' or 'the first day of the year of 2022' will be valid. In the case where a testator writes the date several days after actually making the will, it will still take effect unless the lapse of time is considered unreasonably long.[760]

703. When a testator intends to insert, delete or alter part of a will including the text of an inventory, he/she must clearly indicate the section to be amended, whether it is to be an insertion, deletion or alteration, add his/her signature and affix his/her seal at the place of the amendment (Civ. section 968(3)). Failure to satisfy such requirements will cause the part of the will to be void unless it is a minor error, such as a misspelling. Where a will is void by reason of its failure to meet the said requirements, it may be converted into a different legal act. For instance, in the case where a will, in which a testator intended to transfer his/her estate to a person, was

755. For the purpose of making a will, a thumb print is generally acceptable (SD 16 Feb. 1989 Minshu 43-2-45). However, 'Kao' which is a special signature drawn in the traditional way, is not accepted as a seal (SD 3 Jun. 2016 Kinyushoji-hanrei 1501-8).
756. In one case where someone merely helped a testator to handwrite a will, the Supreme Court declared the will valid (SD 8 Oct. 1987 Minshu 41-7-1471).
757. SD 22 Jun. 1961 Minshu 15-6-1622.
758. STD 3 Jul. 1915 Minroku 21-1176.
759. SD 29 Nov. 1977 Kagetsu 30-4-100.
760. SD 9 Apr. 1977 Kagetsu 29-10-132.

pronounced void due to a failure to satisfy the formalities, the court considered it a valid gift *causa mortis* (*donatio mortis causa*).[761]

704. This type of will can be made without cumbersome procedures but it is not always secure, as a result of which, it may be vulnerable to alteration, concealment or disposition by a malicious party and may bring about disputes regarding its interpretation among the parties due to ambiguity or failure to adhere to the requisite formalities.

II. A Will by Notary Document

705. This type of will is made by a notary public on behalf of a testator. It is available to a testator who, for example, wishes to make the will secure or is an illiterate person, as the will must be kept safe despite there being few possibilities for alteration or forgery. However, making such a will requires a fee and its content will be known to the notary public and two witnesses.

706. In order to validate a will, two or more witnesses must be present at the time of its creation. Only a person with the capacity to enter into a legal act is eligible to be a witness. However, there are persons who are not eligible to be witnesses. These persons include a minor, an heir apparent or beneficiary, his/her spouse or lineal relatives by blood, the spouse of a notary public or his/her relatives within the fourth degree, clerical staff or other staff of the notary public office (Civ. section 974).[762]

707. The aim of this requirement is for the witnesses to attest the identity of a testator, his/her testamentary capacity, the existence of his/her oral declaration, the genuineness of his/her intention, and to monitor the drawing of the will by the notary public. Since the whole process must be attested, the will will be void if one witness is not present or only participates in part of the process, or if there is initially only one witness.[763] However, a will should be valid as long as it is made in the presence of eligible witnesses notwithstanding the fact that a person without eligibility as a witness is present during the time the will is made.[764] In addition, if a witness fails to confirm the details of an oral declaration by a testator, the will shall be void.[765]

708. An oral declaration requires a testator to verbally state the content of a will to a notary public. It will be valid if a testator declares, 'the content of the will has been stated in the document' after handing the document to the notary public.[766]

761. Tokyo DD 3 Aug. 1981 Kagetsu 35-4-104.
762. SD 25 May 1972 Minshu 26-4-747. A person with vision impairments may be eligible as a witness in certain circumstances (SD 4 Dec. 1980 Minshu 34-7-835).
763. SD 14 Jun. 1977 Kagetsu 30-1-69 but an exceptional case (SD 13 Mar. 1998 Kagetsu 50-10-103.
764. SD 27 Mar. 2001 Minshu 53-10-98.
765. Kure Branch of Hiroshima DD 31 Aug. 1989 Kagetsu 42-5-97.
766. STD 10 Jul. 1934 Minshu 13-1341.

Subsequently, the notary public must draw up the will and then read it to the testator. The will then remains valid despite the procedure being changed if it can be confirmed that the genuine intention of the testator has been adhered to following his/her oral declaration.[767]

709. However, the court in one case did not regard a valid oral declaration to include a testator who laid in bed and nodded slightly to some questions put by a notary public.[768] If part of the oral declaration of a testator with a speech defect is interpreted by a third party, the oral declaration will be valid unless the testator's genuine intention has been evidently distorted.[769] A testator need not orally declare the whole details of a will, he/she is merely required to specify the property concerned in the will and may later submit a memorandum on these details.[770] An assistant of a notary public may write down the oral declaration of a testator under the direction of the notary public.

710. Once the notary public has noted the oral declaration of a testator and has recited it to the testator and the witnesses, the testator and witnesses must sign and affix their seals to the will as proof of having attested it. Where a testator is unable to sign, a notary public may add an entry of this fact in substitution of the signature (Civ. section 969(1)(iv)).

711. At the last stage of the procedure, the notary public will make an entry that he/she has complied with the formalities and then sign and affix his/her seal to the will (Civ. section 969(1)(v)).

712. Since a notary public must confirm the will by reading it to the testator and witnesses under the old procedure, a person with a hearing impairment was not eligible to make such a will because of his/her difficulties in verbal communication. For the benefit of such persons, a new provision was introduced in 1999 which stipulated that a person with a hearing impairment could make a will by notary document with the help of a sign language interpreter including speech reading, touch reading and Braille (Civ. section 969-2). This new approach will apply to cases involving a will by a secret document, a will of a person in imminent danger of death, and a will of a person in imminent danger of death on board a distressed ship (Civ. sections 972, 976 and 979, *see* Part IV Chapter 2 §3 III, IV and V).

713. A testator is required to state the content of a will to a notary public with the help of the interpreter or by communicating by writing with the notary public in the presence of two witnesses. The notary public must draw up the will and then confirm its content with the help of an interpreter or by written communication. Writing as a means of communication is available in the case of other types of wills (Civ. sections 969-2 and 969(1)(iii)).

767. SD 20 Dec. 1968 Minshu 22-13-3017.
768. SD 16 Jan. 1976 Kagetsu 28-7-25.
769. Osaka HD 31 Mar. 1982 Kagetsu 35-7-66.
770. SD 5 Jul. 1979 Hanji 942-44.

714. The original copy of a will by notary document is kept at the notary public office for at least twenty years. A testator or successor may apply to the office for the will itself to be delivered or a complete copy to be issued (Notary Public Act 1908 sections 47 and 51). A Japanese consul can undertake the duty of a notary public for the purpose of making a will by notary document or secret document (mentioned later) in respect of a Japanese citizen living abroad (Civ. section 984).

III. A Will by Secret Document

715. This is the term given to a testator who intends to keep the content of a will confidential but to make its existence known to the persons concerned. In order to make a will of this type, the following requirements must be satisfied (Civ. section 970(1)):

- A testator must sign and affix his/her seal to the document. The document may not only be written by a testator but also by a third party under the testator's direction. Furthermore, the document will be valid whether written by typewriter or word processor. A testator need not necessarily state the date in the will since a notary public will make an entry of the date on the cover of the document.
- A testator must close that document with a seal.
- On presenting the sealed document to a notary public and at least two witnesses, the testator must orally confirm that it is his/her own will and state his/her name and address. If a third party has dictated the will on the testator's behalf, he/she must declare the name and address of that person. Where a testator is unable to speak, he/she must produce a statement written by himself/herself in the presence of a notary public and at least two witnesses or he/she can make a statement with the assistance of an interpreter (Civ. section 972(1)). In the latter case, a notary public must make an entry on the sealed document to that effect (Civ. section 972(2)). The written statement must indicate that the document is his/her own will or where a third party has dictated the will, it must state the name and address of that person. A notary public will then add an affirmation to the cover of the sealed document stating that the testator has made the will in compliance with the formalities laid down in section 972(1).
- A notary public makes an entry of the date on which the document and declaration was presented on the cover of the sealed document. Then, the notary public, the testator and the witnesses sign and affix their seals to the cover.

716. A will by secret document will not take effect if it fails to meet the formalities prescribed in the Civil Code. However, if there is such a violation, it may be effective as a will by holographic document if it fulfils the formalities laid down in section 968.

IV. A Will of a Person in Imminent Danger of Death

717. A will of this type is made by a person who faces imminent danger of death through illness or other causes. The following procedures are taken in this instance (Civ. section 976):

- a testator, in the presence of three witnesses, must orally declare the tenor of the will to one of them;
  the witness to whom oral declaration is made will then write the tenor in a document and read it to the testator and other witnesses;
- those witnesses will attest the document by signing and affixing their seals to the document.

718. It is not necessary to state the date of the will.[771] The will will be confirmed by the family court on application by either one of the witnesses or any interested persons within twenty days of its creation. The family court may declare the will valid if it is convinced that it reflects the testator's genuine intention.

V. A Will of a Person in Imminent Danger of Death on Board a Distressed Ship

719. Where a person is in imminent danger of death due to a shipwreck, he/she may make a will through the following procedure (Civ. section 979). A testator may orally declare the tenor of a will to at least two witnesses. The witnesses must sign and affix their seals to the written document. In addition, one of the witnesses or an interested person must apply to the family court, without delay, to confirm the document as a valid will. If this procedure is not followed, the will shall have no effect.

VI. A Will of a Person Isolated on Account of a Contagious Disease

720. Where a person is quarantined by the authorities due to a contagious disease, he/she may make a will in the presence of a policeman/woman one other witness (Civ. section 977).

VII. A Will of a Person on Board a Ship

721. A person on board a ship may make a written will in the presence of the captain or one of the ship's clerical staff and at least two other witnesses (Civ. section 978).

722. In the case of a will by sections 977, 978 and 979, a testator, witnesses and officers must sign and affix their seals to the will and they must record the reason

771. SD 17 Mar. 1972 Minshu 26-2-249.

when they cannot do so (Civ. sections 980 and 981). Person with a hearing impairment could make a will with the help of a sign language interpreter including speech reading, touch reading and Braille (*see* paragraph 697). A will by special procedure will be invalidated if the testator survives for six months after he/she becomes able to make a will by ordinary procedure (Civ. section 983).

§4. A Joint Will

723. Under the Japanese Civil Code, a joint will is prohibited as it is likely to cause the legal relationships between the parties concerned to become complex and confused (Civ. section 975). Accordingly, where a husband and wife make a joint will by holographic document under their married name, but the latter fails to sign the document, the will cannot be saved in the form of the husband's sole will and is altogether void due to a violation of section 975.[772] However, if, for instance, the document consists of four pages, which can be clearly separated into three pages for the husband and one page for the wife, the will is valid if each part is made in compliance with the proper formalities.[773] Furthermore, where a husband and wife have both signed and affixed their seals to the document, a court has stated that the will shall be valid despite the tenor only covering the husband's estate and not that of the wife.[774]

§5. Revocation of a Will

724. A will is effective on the death of a testator or, in the case of a will under condition precedent, when the condition is met (Civ. section 985). However, a testator may revoke the whole or part of the will at any time before his/her death if it is in accordance with the rules stipulated in section 967(Civ. section 1022). In order to respect the testator's last wishes, he/she is not allowed to waive the right to revoke the will (Civ. section 1026). A will may be revoked if it has been made under fraud or duress.

I. Method of Revocation

725. The formalities required to revoke a will are the same as those required to create it. For instance, a testator may set aside a previous will on the formation of a new will by merely satisfying the same formalities. In fact, he/she can revoke the original will by holographic document on the creation of a new will by secret document if the correct formalities are met.

---

772. SD 11 Sep. 1981 Minshu 35-6-1013.
773. SD 19 Oct. 1993 Kagetsu 46-4-27.
774. Tokyo HK 27 Aug. 1982 Kagetsu 35-12-84.

726. In addition, an implied revocation can also take effect. Section 1023 indicates that if a previous will is inconsistent with a subsequent will, the former is to be regarded as having been revoked by the latter. Furthermore, this section states that if the tenor of a will is incompatible with any disposition or legal act undertaken by a testator after making the will, that part of the will will be revoked. For instance, a gift by will will be revoked if a testator has transferred the gift to a third party after having made the will. Where a testator adopted a beneficiary on the agreement that she would be looked after by the latter in the future, in exchange for property as a reward, the court declared that a gift by will would be revoked if the adoption was dissolved.[775]

727. When a testator intentionally destroys part of a will, for instance, drawing an oblique line on the will, such part will be regarded as having been revoked, as is the case when the subject-matter of a gift by will is intentionally destroyed (Civ. section 1024).[776]

II. Revival of a Will

728. Unless a will is revoked under fraud or duress, it may not be revived in order to avoid ambiguity concerning the testator's intention (Civ. section 1025). However, some assert that the revival of a revoked will should be accepted if a testator is genuinely considered to have done so by emphasizing that his/her latest intention must be respected. In the case where a person without sufficient capacity has revoked a will, he/she cannot revive it. However, the Supreme Court declared that a first will should be revived when a second will revoking the first one was lawfully revoked by a third one indicating revival of the first one.[777]

§6. Provisions in a Will and Gifts by Will

I. Provisions in a Will

729. Provisions in a will shall only be effective if they are related to the following matters:

- acknowledgement of paternity of an illegitimate child (Civ. section 781(2));
- appointment of a guardian or a supervisor of a guardian (Civ. sections 839(1) and 848);
- gifts by will (Civ. section 964);
- matters relating to gifts by will (Civ. sections 988, 992, 994(2), 995, 997, 1000 and 1002(2));

775. SD 13 Nov. 1981 Minshu 35-8-1251.
776. SD 20 Nov. 2015 Minshu 69-7-2021.
777. SD 13 Nov. 1997 Minshu 51-10-4144.

- disinheritance of an heir apparent and subsequent revocation of any disinheritance (Civ. sections 893 and 894);
- determination of each successor's portion and delegation of this decision to a third party (Civ. section 902);
- exemption of a successor from surrendering anything acquired in accordance with the hotchpot rule (Civ. section 903(3));
- determination of the method used to allocate a deceased person's estate and delegation of this decision to a third party (Civ. section 908);
- prohibition of allocating a deceased person's estate (Civ. section 908);
- specification of a liability of warranty among successors (Civ. section 914);
- appointment of an executor or delegation of such appointment and other matters relating to the executor to a third party (Civ. sections 1006, 1016 and 1017);
- revocation of a will (Civ. section 1022);
- appointment of a person responsible for ancestor worship (Civ. section 897);
- an act of founding an association and foundation (General Incorporated Associations and General Incorporated Foundations Act 2006 section 152(2));
- an act of creating a trust (Trust Act 2006 section 3(1)(ii); and
- changing the beneficiary under an insurance policy (Insurance Act 2008 sections 44 and 73).

II. Gifts by Will

730. On the death of a testator, his/her successor is generally responsible for allocating gifts to beneficiaries (legatee/devisee).[778] Occasionally, if a beneficiary receives the whole or part of the rights and duties concerning the testator's estate,[779] an administrator appointed by the family court (Civ. section 952) or only an executor may allocate gifts to beneficiaries (legatee/devisee) after taking over the office on behalf of the successor (Civ. sections 1015 and 1012(2)). Under the current law, an unconditional or conditional gift is available by a will (Civ. section 964).

A. A Particular Gift by Will

731. To effect a particular gift by a will, a testator must specify the asset to be given to the beneficiary in the will, which should be worded to reflect his/her intention to leave any real property to his/her spouse. In the case of money or other property, which is not usually considered specific, a testator may treat it as particular property if he/she is able to highlight it.

---

778. The Civil Code stipulates s. 554 (donation *mortis causa*) stating that with respect to gifts that become effective on the death of the donor, the provisions regarding testamentary gifts shall apply *mutatis mutandis*, to the extent they are not inconsistent with the nature of gifts that become effective on the death of the donor.

779. Cf. A beneficiary must take on the obligation of the testator when he/she receives the whole estate of the testator since s. 990 states that the beneficiary by a universal succession shall have the same legal status as an heir.

732. What happens if a person responsible for allocating gifts to beneficiaries has transferred the real property by way of a gift to a third party after the will has taken effect? In one case, where a successor's creditor seized the real property that was to be a gift after the will took effect, the Supreme Court declared[780] that a beneficiary could not defeat the third party's (i.e., the creditor's) claim unless he/she had registered it in compliance with the procedure of section 177.[781] In the case of a nominative claim to be gifted by a will as a particular gift, a beneficiary cannot defeat the claim of an obligor unless the assignor (testator) gives a notice to the obligor or the obligor has accepted that claim (cf. Civ. section 467).

B. Universal Gifts by Will

733. The aim of universal gifts by will is to transfer 'the whole estate of a deceased person – i.e., the testator' to a beneficiary (Civ. section 964). Under the scheme of universal gifts by will, a beneficiary holds the same rights and duties as a successor as he/she receives the deceased's rights and duties and is jointly entitled to possess the estate with the other beneficiaries and successors (Civ. section 990).

734. However, there are differences between the legal status of a beneficiary and a successor. On the one hand, they are in the same position with respect to inheritance claims, applications and/or participation relating to the acceptance or renunciation of succession, and applications and/or participation relating to the allocation of the estate. However, where one successor renounces succession, the beneficiary's portion will not be changed in the way that the portions of the other successors will be increased due to the renunciation. In addition, a beneficiary must register gifts of real property in order to defeat a claim by a third party.

C. Acceptance and Renunciation of Gifts by Will

735. In the case of particular gifts by will, a beneficiary may renounce the gift at any time after the testator's death and renunciation takes retrospective effect from the time of death (Civ. section 986). In order to protect a party with a legal interest, the person responsible for allocating the estate or any other interested person may give a peremptory notice to a beneficiary within a reasonable period of time in order to effect a renunciation of the gift. If a beneficiary fails to respond within that period, he/she will be deemed to have accepted the gift (Civ. section 987). Meanwhile, a beneficiary of a universal gift by a will must express his/her intention to

780. SD 6 Mar. 1964 Minshu 18-3-437.

781. Section 177 of the Civil Code stipulates that the acquisition, loss, or any alteration in a real right over an immovable asset cannot be claimed against a third party until it has been registered in accordance with the legal provisions concerning property registration. However, this rule does not apply to a dispute between a beneficiary and a third party to whom a successor has made a void disposition of his property (SD 23 Apr. 1987 Minshu 41-3-474).

accept or renounce the gift within three months of the time it becomes effective since he/she is deemed to be in a similar position to a successor.[782]

736. Neither the withdrawal of an acceptance nor the renunciation of a gift by will shall be accepted if they are set aside on the basis of the grounds for revocation as stipulated in the Civil Code. Where a beneficiary dies without any intention of acceptance or renunciation, the successor of the beneficiary may accept or renounce the gift by will on the basis of his/her legal status unless otherwise stated in the will (Civ. section 988). In the event of the renunciation of a gift by will, a successor (if any) will take the assets that a beneficiary would have received, if the testator has expressed no particular intention for the disposition of the assets.

D. Effects of Gifts by Will

737. If a beneficiary dies before the testator, both universal and particular gifts by will shall not take effect (Civ. section 994(1)). In the case of a gift by will with a condition precedent, the gift will not be effective if a beneficiary has died before the condition is satisfied, unless otherwise expressed in the will. If a gift by will has been made in respect of a right (asset) not belonging to the testator's estate at the time of his/her death, it will still generally take effect (Civ. section 996). A gift will also be effective where a testator has intended the right (asset) to be the subject of the gift by will. In this respect, a person responsible for allocating the estate must acquire the right from a third party and then transfer it to a beneficiary. If it seems that such acquisition is difficult or the procedural cost for the acquisition is expensive, the person responsible for allocating the estate must pay the value to a beneficiary, unless any contrary intention is stated in the will (Civ. section 997).

738. Where a testator intended to make a gift to his mistress, the court pronounced that its validity should be judged by considering whether the main purpose of the gift was to maintain their unfaithful relationship or to provide financial support for her everyday life. It also questioned whether the successors were likely to face financial difficulties in the future as a result of the gift.[783]

E. Onerous Gifts by Will

739. Onerous gifts by will are those where a testator does not freely give an asset to a beneficiary but rather attaches some conditions to the gift (Civ. section 1002) (*see* paragraph 749). For instance, a testator may state in his will that he intends to give all his real property to a beneficiary provided that the beneficiary looks after his surviving wife for the remainder of her lifetime. Onerous gifts by will take effect regardless of any failure by a beneficiary to fulfil the obligation. However, where a beneficiary does not commence performance of his/her obligation, a successor (if

782. Tokyo DD 23 Dec. 1980 Hanji 1000-106.
783. SD 20 Nov. 1986 Minshu 40-7-1167.

any such exist) may give the beneficiary a peremptory notice demanding the completion of his/her duty within a specified period. On the failure of the beneficiary to perform his/her obligation, the successor may apply to the family court for a revocation of the onerous gift by will (Civ. section 1027).

740. A beneficiary is liable to adhere to his/her obligation to the extent of the value of the asset given to him/her (Civ. section 1002(1)). If the value of the gift has been reduced due to either acceptance with the benefit of inventory or litigation relating for instance to claims by a forced heir, a beneficiary will be relieved of such liability in proportion to the reduction in value unless any contrary intention appears in the will (Civ. section 1003). When a beneficiary renounces a gift by will, the person who is to receive the benefit of the gift as a result of the renunciation may take over the status of beneficiary, in the absence of any contrary intention (Civ. section 1002(2)).

§7. Procedure of Administering a Will

741. Administering a will includes the necessary act of bringing the provisions of a will into effect. For instance, in the case of an acknowledgement of paternity by will, submission of the notice of acknowledgement of paternity to the family registration office constitutes an act of administering the will.

I. Process of Probate

742. A successor or any other person, who has discovered or kept the instrument of a will, must submit it to the family court without delay on the acknowledging of the opening of succession by a probation determination (Civ. section 1004(1)). This requirement aims to avoid any alteration or forgery of a will. For the purpose of preserving evidence, the sealed instrument of a will must be opened at the family court in the presence of all successors or their representatives (Civ. section 1004(3)). If they refuse to be present, the family court may open the instrument independently. If a person violates these requirements, he/she may be fined up to JPY 50000 (Civ. section 1005). However, such violations do not cause the will to be void. In the case of a will by holographic document (Civ. section 968), no probation process is required once the will has been made according to the particular form and lodged at a legal affairs bureau (section 1, section 4(2) and section 11 of the Lodging Last Will in Legal Affairs Bureau Act 2018).

II. Appointment and Dismissal of an Executor

743. A testator may in his/her will appoint an executor of the estate or nominate another person to make such an appointment without any delay (Civ. section

1006).[784] Where a testator has not declared an executor in the will or the latter has resigned from office, the family court can appoint an executor on the application of any interested persons (Civ. section 1010). However, neither a person declared incompetent nor a bankrupt person is eligible to be an executor (Civ. section 1009). In order to affect the appointment, an executor must accept the position. After the acceptance, the executor must resume his/her task promptly and notify all heirs of the contents of a will without any delay (section 1007(1) and (2)).

744. Any interested person may apply to the family court for the dismissal of an executor due to failure to administer the estate appropriately or other reasonable grounds (Civ. section 1019). For instance, where an executor failed to administer the estate of a testator properly and gave favourable treatment to a particular successor, the court pronounced that there was 'a reasonable ground' for dismissal.[785] An executor, however, may resign from office on other legitimate grounds.

III. Rights and Duties of an Executor

745. An executor has the rights and duties to perform any act which is necessary for the administration of the testator's estate and by which the aim of a will shall be realized (Civ. section 1012(1)). On the basis of these rights and duties, he/she must make an inventory of the estate, administer it and take any other action required to fulfil this purpose. In addition, an executor can make a third person to execute his/her tasks as an executor on his/her own responsibility unless a contrary intention of the deceased shall appear in the will (Civ. section 1016(1)). If there is an absolute necessity for such execution, the executor shall be liable to heirs only for the appointment or supervision of the third person (Civ. section 1016(2)).

746. Any action taken by an executor within his/her authority shall take effect directly for an heir if he/she shows to be an executor (Civ. section 1015) and mandatory provisions (Civ. sections 654 and 655) apply *mutatis mutandis* when the office of executor terminates (Civ. section 1020). An executor may be eligible to be a party to a dispute over the title of the estate or other legal issues concerning the administration of the estate.[786] In this respect, an executor may bring an action against a third party to prevent him/her from administering the estate.[787] Furthermore, he/she may nominate a beneficiary in certain circumstances if such nomination is deemed to satisfy a will.[788] In the case of a will to specify a particular property for succession where a testator specifies the property to be allocated for a particular heir(s) as a means of distributing his/her estate, an executor can take any action for realizing purposes stipulated in section 899-2(1) (Civ. section 1014(2)). In addition, an executor is eligible to withdraw an amount of money from the

784. A legal person is eligible to be an executor (*see* the Trust Act 2008 s. 3(2) and the Business of Trust Act 2004 s. 2(1)).
785. Tokyo HK 23 Oct. 2007 Kagetsu 60-10-61.
786. An executor is eligible to act as a defendant (Tokyo HD 24 Sep. 2003 Kinyuhomu 1712-77).
787. Tokyo DD 28 May 1976 Hanji 841-60.
788. SD 19 Jan. 1993 Minshu 47-1-1.

deceased's bank account if a particular property specified in a will by section 1014(2) is a bank account, and he/she can close the account if the whole amount of the account is specified as such property (Civ. section 1014(3)).

747. As a successor must not obstruct an executor in the administration of the estate, the former must refrain from transferring an estate's asset to a third party, receiving rent from the estate's property, mortgaging the estate's real property, or disposing of any other rights or property of the estate (Civ. section 1013(1)).

748. Where a successor has disposed of a testator's asset or done any act relating to the estate without the executor's authority, such disposition or act will be void but not defeating a claim by a bona fide third party (Civ. section 1013(2)). However, this rule shall not apply to a creditor to an heir who executes his/her right over the testator's asset (Civ. 1013(3)). This rule also applies to cases where such dispositions or acts are completed before an executor has taken office.[789]

§8. Restrictions

I. The Legitim/Reserve (The Compulsory Portion of Testator's Estate)

749. Under Japanese law, there are no provisions for specifying maintenance of the surviving family and the maintenance of a deceased's family is dealt with as part of the compulsory portion of a testator's estate. Provisions relating to the legitim were completely revised in 2018 and a forced heir can claim only the amount of money in proportion to his/her legitim. Under the old scheme, for instance, a forced heir was eligible to claim to return his/her compulsory portion from the real property gifted to a third party but under the new law, he/she (a person succeeds his/her right) is merely entitled to claim the amount of money equivalent to the value of his/her compulsory portion (Civ. sections 1042(1) and 1046(1)). Section 1042(1) of the Civil Code states that successors, with the exception of siblings of the deceased, shall receive the following sum, known as a compulsory portion of the testator's estate, as a result of being a forced heir: (1) where all the successors are merely lineal ascendants, they will acquire one-third of the deceased's estate, but (2) in other cases, they will obtain half of the estate. A forced heir can claim his/her compulsory portion to a testamentary beneficiary or a beneficiary by gift (Civ. section 1046(1). However, the legitim aims to respect a person's testamentary freedom while also seeking to assure the financial situation of the surviving family and to make a fair allocation of the estate among the successors and beneficiaries.[790]

789. SD 23 Apr. 1987 Minshu 41-3-474.
790. *See* Osaka HD 8 Jun. 1999 Kosaiminshu 52-1-1.

II. Forced Heirs and Their Portion

750. Surviving spouses, lineal descendants and lineal ascendants are entitled to become forced heirs. Their portion of the amount of the value for legitim will be decided as follows (*see* sections 1042, 900 and 901):

- where there is a spouse and the parents of a deceased: a spouse: one-third of the calculated value (=the calculated value ×1/2×2/3), each parent: one-twelfth of the calculated value (=the calculated value ×1/2×1/3×1/2) (section 1042(1));
- where there is a spouse and three children: a spouse: one-fourth of the calculated value (=the calculated value ×1/2×1/2), each child: one-twelfth of the estate (= the calculated value ×1/2×1/2×1/3) (section 1042(2)).

751. In order to evaluate each forced heir's share, the following steps must be taken in order to confirm the value of the basic amount of legitim, and the value of the lost amount of each forced heir shall be calculated. First, the basic value of the property for legitim shall be decided by adding the value of an advancement as an *inter vivos* gift (Civ. section 903(1)) to, and by deducting the total value of all the deceased's debts from the net residuary value of the deceased's estate at the time of succession (section 1043(1)). Second, the value of legitim of each forced heir shall be confirmed by multiplying the basic value of the property for legitim by the ratio stipulated in section 1042 (*see* paragraph 750). Finally, the value of the lost amount of each forced heir shall be confirmed by subtracting the value of all gifts made to a forced heir and the value of succeeded property of the forced heir from the value of legitim of each forced heir, and adding the value of the debts assumed by the forced heir to the value of legitim of each forced heir (section 1046(2)). Then, a forced heir is eligible to claim the value of the lost amount to the donee or beneficiary only up to the value of the gifts (Civ. section 1047(1)).

(1) A: the net residuary value of the deceased's estate at the time of succession (the basic value) (Civ. section 1043);
(2) B: the value of all *inter vivos* gifts made by the deceased within one year before the opening of succession in the case of a non-heir (Civ. section 1044(1));
(3) C: the basic value and the value of the *inter vivos* gifts to an heir within ten years before the opening of succession and the aim of the gifts must be limited for marriage, adoption, or capital for livelihood ('hotchpot') (*see* Civ. sections 1044(3), (2), 903(1), (4) and 1028(3));[791]
(4) D: the basic value and the value of any *inter vivos* gifts, made over one year ago between a testator and a beneficiary (an heir and non-heir), which both acknowledged would harm the interests of a forced heir (Civ. section 1044(1));[792]

791. SD 24 Mar. 1998 Minshu 52-2-433 stated that 'hotchpot' should be included in any calculation unless there are exceptional circumstances which may cause a harsh result for a beneficiary.
792. They do not need to know the details of the harm but merely recognize that their act might financially deprive a forced heir.

(5) E: the total value of all the deceased's debts (Civ. section 1043(1));
(6) F: the value of the debts that the forced heir succeeds himself/herself by section 899 if any (Civ. section 1046(2)(iii));
(7) G: the value of succeeded property of a forced heir if any;
(8) in the case of an onerous gift, the value of the gift shall be calculated by deducting the value of burden from the gift (Civ. section 1045(1)) and any onerous transaction made for inadequate consideration between a testator and another party shall be deemed to be onerous gift only if they have the intention of harming the interests of a forced heir (Civ. section 1045(2));
(9) if the property gifted by a deceased is lost by a conduct of the beneficiary or if the value of the property is fluctuated, the value of the *inter vivos* gift shall be deemed as the value at the time of opening of succession in its original state (Civ. sections 1044(2) and 904 (applied *mutatis mutandis*)):
   (a) the basic value of the property for legitim (X) = A + B/C/D – E (sections 1043, 1044 and 1045);
   (b) the value of legitim of each forced heir (Y) = X × the ratio (*see* section 734) (section 1042);
   (c) the value of the lost amount of each forced heir (Z) = X – B/C/D – G + F (section 1046(2)).

III. A Forced Heir's Right to Reclaim His/Her Portion

752. If a forced heir's fixed portion is infringed upon by any person, he/she can exercise his/her right to demand the latter to return the amount of money equivalent to the value of the portion. Unlike the previous law, a forced heir is merely entitled to claim the amount of money as reclaiming his/her compulsory portion (Civ. section 1042(1) and 1046(1)).

753. As to the order of claims, an *inter vivos* gift follows a gift by will (gifts *causa mortis* are treated as gifts by will) (Civ. section 1047(1)(a)). In one case, an *inter vivos* gift was made to a successor almost twenty years before the opening of succession. The court pronounced that the abatement would be effective if the gift was made with the intention of causing future harm to the forced heirs, the subject of the gift still existed, and it could be returned to the successors.[793] However, as mentioned in paragraph 749, this rule does not apply directly under the revised Civil Code, instead a forced heir can claim the amount of money equivalent to his/her share of the estate (*see* section 1046(1)). Where there are several gifts by will, the gifts are abated, in proportion to their value, in the absence of any contrary intention by the testator (Civ. section 1047(1)(ii)). Meanwhile, where there are *inter vivos* gifts, the latest gift will be the first to be abated, moving back consecutively to the earliest (Civ. section 1047(1)(iii)).

793. Tokyo HD 21 Sep. 1993 Hanji 1473-53. SD 24 Jun. 1998 Minshu 53-5-918 declared that a forced heir is eligible to claim his/her portion against the person even where the latter has obtained ownership of the property on the ground of prescription.

754. Under the previous law, no one will be subject to a forced heir's claim unless the right to reclaim his/her portion of the estate is exercised, since that right is exclusively personal.[794] This rule may be applied to a case in the current legitim scheme.

755. A legitim claim by a forced heir shall be denied in some cases by a court to achieve fairness among the parties. Where one of the forced heirs had looked after the testator for nearly twenty years and would have faced serious difficulties in everyday life if the abatement claimed by the other forced heirs had been allowed to occur (i.e., loss of accommodation), the court declared that it would be an abuse of the latter's rights.[795] This interpretation may be maintained by a court under the revised law.

IV. Effects of Abatement

756. Under the previous law, where a forced heir has exercised the right to his/her portion of the estate, titles to the estate's assets which are to be divided belong to the forced heir. Where gifts by will and *inter vivos* gifts have been made to parties other than successors, a forced heir must bring a civil claim to a district court in order to reclaim the assets.[796] However, where a successor is a beneficiary or a donee of a gift by will or *inter vivos* gift, a forced heir may make an application to the family court demanding the allocation of the estate for the purpose of abatement, unless there are special circumstances prohibiting the forced heir from claiming his/her portion.[797] As mentioned in paragraph 749, a forced heir is only eligible to claim the amount of money equivalent to the value of his/her own legitim following the revision of the law in 2018. In a case where a forced heir succeeds a debt of a deceased person in proportion to his/her share to the estate (Civ. section 899) and a donee or beneficiary makes an action for ceasing the debts on behalf of the forced heir (*see* Civ. section 472-3), the donee or beneficiary can claim to be free from the liabilities towards the forced heir in proportion to the value of the ceased debts. In this situation, the donee or beneficiary shall lose his/her right to reimbursement from the forced heir only in so far as the value of the ceased debts (Civ. section 1047(3)). A court can give a donee or beneficiary extension of the term for the part or whole of the payment stipulated in section 1047(1) on an application by a donee or beneficiary (Civ. section 1047(5)).

757. A forced heir shall submit to a loss caused by lack of financial resources of a beneficiary or donee (Civ. section 1047(4)).

794. Tokyo DD 26 Jun. 1990 Kagetsu 43-5-31. This interpretation can be applied to a case of garnishee proceedings filed by a creditor of a forced heir (*see* Civ. s. 423).
795. Tokyo HD 24 Feb. 1992 Hanji 1418-81.
796. Tokyo HK 27 Nov. 1991 Kagetsu 44-12-89 and Tokyo HK 30 Mar. 1993 Kagetsu 46-3-66.
797. SD 11 Jun. 1998 Minshu 52-4-1034.

V. Termination of the Right to Reclaim a Forced Heir's Portion

758. Unlike renunciation of succession, a forced heir may renounce his/her portion before the opening of succession on approval by the family court (Civ. section 1049(1)).[798] Unlike renunciation of the right to succeed (*see* paragraph 686), if a successor (a forced heir) renounces his/her portion of legitim by approval of the family court, renunciation shall not affect the portion of other successors (Civ. section 1049(2)). The family court may dismiss such an application if it considers that a forced heir has not made the decision freely.[799] The family court may revoke a determination of approval if it deems renunciation to be unreasonable and inappropriate under the existing circumstances.[800]

759. The right to claim the amount of money equivalent to the value of a forced heir's share terminates within one year of the forced heir discovering the *inter vivos* gift or gifts by will to be abated being made or within ten years of the opening of succession (Civ. section 1048). The limitation period starts running when a forced heir acknowledges two facts – that he/she is entitled to a portion of an estate as a forced heir and that that portion has been infringed upon.[801] Under special circumstances, for example, whereby a forced heir reasonably believes that the gift by will is void, failure to bring a claim within the limitation period will not constitute an acknowledgement of the gift.[802]

§9. Interpretation of a Will

760. An ambiguous description in a will often causes difficulties in distributing the testator's estate. For instance, if a testator writes in a will 'Noe (one of four successors) shall take the land at such and such address', it allows various interpretations. If Noe is not an heir, that statement evidently indicates that she will take the land as a beneficiary (gift by a will/ a gift *causa mortis*). If Noe is an heir, there can be three interpretations: first, the statement in the will specifies her portion of the estate (*see* Civ. section 902); second, it specifies the method of allocating the estate (*see* Civ. section 908); and third, it implies a particular gift by will (*see* Civ. section 964). These contrasting interpretations are likely to cause disputes among successors.

761. If the first interpretation is adopted, three other siblings may assert that Noe's share would injure their portion of the estate. Suppose that the net value of the estate is JPY 10 million and the net value of the land is JPY 8 million, each of

798. The Facilitation of Succession of Management of Small and Medium-sized Enterprises Act 2008 provides for certain exceptions to the general rule of compulsory portion of testator's estate, which allow the assets of an enterprise to be administered differently from the ordinary legitim procedure (*see* ss 3–11 of the Act).
799. Wakayama FO 14 Nov. 1985 Kagetsu 38-5-86.
800. Tokyo HK 5 Sep. 1983 Kagetsu 36-8-104.
801. Tokyo HD 28 Apr. 1977 Hanji 855-61.
802. SD 12 Nov. 1982 Minshu 36-11-2193.

the three other successors (as forced heirs) will obtain JPY 1.25 million (one-fourth of JPY 5 million). If Noe takes JPY 8 million, she infringes upon the portion of the others (*see* paragraph 750 for infringement of a forced heir's reserve). If the third interpretation is taken and there is a debt of JPY 4.5 million, Noe will be liable for JPY 3.6 million while the others must pay JPY 0.3 million each because a successor is responsible for the debts arising from succession in proportion to the value of his/her acquired share.

762. In fact, where there is no clear or decisive criterion for the interpretation of a will under current succession law, the court follows a general approach of compelling lawyers to discover the testator's real intention, instead of superficially reading the will. Lawyers must therefore understand the relationship between each provision in the will and confirm its general tenor by taking into account all the circumstances from the time the will was issued.[803] However, ambiguity concerning the interpretation of a will still remains. For instance, where a testator states in a will that he/she wishes to have specified heir(s) 'succeed' his/her estate, three interpretations of such instruction are possible. The Supreme Court has interpreted the wording to 'succeed' one's estate in a will as specifying the method of allocating the estate unless there are special circumstances for interpreting the wording as referring to a particular gift by will.[804] Consequently, an heir can obtain the right over an estate at the time of succession without taking any procedure for acquiring the right. In 2018, section 1014 of the Civil Code was revised based on the rule of the Supreme Court (*see* paragraphs 746 and 699).

803. SD 18 Mar. 1983 Kagetsu 36-3-143.

804. In SD 19 Apr. 1991 Minshu 45-4-477, the Supreme Court declared that a will stating that a testator shall make a specified successor 'to inherit an asset' shall be interpreted to specify the method of allocating the estate (*see* paras 746 and 699).

Chapter 3. Acts *Inter Vivos* Related to the Estate

§1. ESTATE PLANNING

763. Six general provisions relating to gifts are incorporated in the Japanese Civil Code (Civ. sections 549 to 554). However, no special provisions for an *inter vivos* gift between family members are stipulated.[805] Also, since the rate of gift tax is higher than that of inheritance tax,[806] a *causa mortis* gift is not necessarily attractive from a tax perspective.[807] For instance, where a spouse and two children succeed to an estate valued at JPY 100 million through intestacy,[808] JPY 30 million and JPY 18 million belonging to the spouse and the two children (JPY 6 million for each successor) is exempt from tax (section 15 of the Inheritance Tax Act 1950). As a result, JPY 52 million is subject to inheritance tax. The spouse is liable to pay inheritance tax for his/her taxable portion but is entitled to claim different exemption as a spouse is not liable to tax unless the value of his/her share exceeds the tax thresholds stated in section 19-2(2) of the Inheritance Tax Act.[809] Accordingly, in this case, the spouse need not pay any inheritance tax. However, the children whose taxable portion is valued at JPY 13 million are liable to pay inheritance tax as they fall within the 15% tax band; thus, they are required to pay JPY 1.95 million inheritance tax.[810]

764. If a person makes an *inter vivos* gift in respect of assets worth JPY 50 million to his/her spouse, the tax is basically calculated as follows. A spouse is entitled to claim an exemption of JPY 1.1 million (section 21-5 of the Inheritance Tax Act),[811] JPY 48.9 million is taxable. Applying the relevant 50% tax band, the spouse will pay about JPY 24.7 million in gift tax.[812] In such circumstances, few people dare to transfer their assets as *inter vivos* gifts.

805. Section 554 of the Civil Code states that a gift *causa mortis* shall be governed by the provisions relating to gifts by a will.

806. Sections 16 and 21-7 of the Inheritance Tax Act 1950. The assets are usually reduced in value for the purpose of calculating tax.

807. The amount of tax calculated in paras 763 and 764 is rough estimation since other exemption and addition shall apply to an individual case (*see* National Tax Agency, Information for Taxpayers: Information about Inheritance Tax and Gift Tax No. 150001-15004).

808. The value of estate in this example is the amount after deducting debts and other necessary expenses such as funeral fee from the total amount of estate at the time of death of a deceased.

809. As of 2021, the maximum amount of exemption is 160 million yen.

810. Sections 15, 16, 17 and 19-2 of the Inheritance Tax Act 1950. In addition, similar special exemption shall be available to a minor child and a disabled heir. The tax rate band and the amount of exemption stated are applicable as for 1 Apr. 2021.

811. A spouse of marring for more than 20 years may claim spousal exemption (the Inheritance Tax Act s. 21-6(1)).

812. Sections 21-5 and 21-7 of the Inheritance Tax Act 1950. If a spouse gifts his/her matrimonial home and their marriage continues for 20 years and over, he/she is entitled to claim an exemption up to JPY 20 million (s. 21-6).

§2. Tax Avoidance Prior to Death

765. As previously mentioned, few people are likely to utilize *inter vivos* gift as a method by which to dispose of their assets due to the high tax rate and lower exemption thresholds. However, an *inter vivos* gift is useful if a small gift is made repeatedly, thus taking advantage of the exemption and tax rate which is comparatively lower for a smaller gift.

766. For instance, if gifts amount to JPY 1.1 million or less per year, they will be free from taxation. If such a gift is made continuously over a long period of time, the donor can avoid having to pay a considerable amount of tax. A spouse who has been married for more than twenty years is eligible to claim that the matrimonial home, or the amount of money needed to acquire such a house, if valued at less than JPY 20 million, is exempt from tax.[813] This privilege applies only once for one marriage (not cohabitation). In addition, where a gift is made between persons of lineal consanguinity for the purpose of buying a house, a special tax rate will apply if certain conditions are met (although this depends on the individual case, it is generally one-quarter of the normal gift tax rate). Furthermore, in order to protect the agricultural industry, if a farm owner makes a gift to an heir apparent of his farmland, the payment of gift tax is suspended for life (with some exceptions) provided the recipient has previously used the farmland for at least three years, and the payment of inheritance tax is suspended or exempted under some conditions.[814]

§3. Trusts

767. A trust can be created by will – a testamentary trust (section 3(2) of the Trust Act 2006). In order to create a testamentary trust, the following matters should be stated in the instrument: the purpose of the trust, the trust property, the name of the trustee, the period of the trust, and the means of payment. Neither a minor nor a person declared to have limited capacity (Civ. sections 8 and 12) is eligible to be a trustee (the Trust Act 2006 section 7).

768. Trusts will take effect if a settlor is capable of committing a legal act, the purposes of the trust are clearly stated, the property to be held on trust and the identity of the beneficiary who can be either a natural person or a legal person is specified. A settlor can designate a prospective beneficiary who does not exist at the time the trust is created. In addition, a settlor must decide the term of the trust, a trustee, any measures that should be taken for the disposal and/or distribution of the trust property. Trusts will be treated as a gift by will in terms of taxation (section 9-2 of the Succession Tax Act 1950).

813. The Inheritance Tax Act s. 21-6.

814. *See* National Tax Agency, Information for Taxpayers: No. 4434 Cases where inheritance tax for farmland is exempted and No. 4147 where a gift tax for farmland is suspended, as for 1 Apr. 2020.

769. As an example of trusts, some people are concerned about whether or not their issues will hold a memorial service for him/her and take care of his/her tombstone after death. Accordingly, they may create a trust for such purposes by appointing as a beneficiary the temple to which they belong. Under this trust, the temple is obliged to use the trust property for the purpose of holding a regular memorial service for the settlor and to care for his/her tombstone until the trust terminates.

770. Furthermore, trusts may be set up to secure the financial situation of a settlor's family members. For instance, where a person is informed that they will die within a month due to a fatal disease, he/she can create a trust for his/her family members with the intention of securing a certain amount of money that will be regularly paid to them after his/her death. In respect of a minor, he/she may appoint a guardian. If such guardian intends to draw up a financial programme for the family at his/her own discretion, he/she may hold his/her property on trust for them. In addition, this trust may be used to secure the assets of the settlor and to protect beneficiaries where an heir apparent is seriously disabled or prone to wastefulness.

§4. INSURANCE CONTRACTS

771. Where a person other than a successor is appointed as a beneficiary by an assured person, the payment of insurance is not included in the estate of a deceased person. If a successor appointed as a beneficiary of insurance receives a payment from the insurance company on the death of an assured, the amount of payment may be dealt with as an advancement of hotchpot which will devolve upon the estate.

772. In respect of inheritance tax, where an assured person who is paying the premiums has appointed himself/herself as a beneficiary, the payment of insurance will be regarded as part of the estate and as such is taxable. Similarly, where the payment is not regarded as part of the estate because a beneficiary is a successor or another party, it is 'presumed to be a part of the estate' and thus liable to inheritance tax.[815]

773. Since insurance usually functions as a crucial means of securing the day-to-day finance of successors, a special exemption applies where only a successor is appointed as a beneficiary (section 12(1)(v) of the Succession Tax Act 1950). For instance, JPY 5 million is currently the amount of exemption for one successor while the total amount of exemption is divided proportionately among successors according to the ratio of each heir's statutory share. Therefore, if a deceased person has appointed his/her spouse and two children as beneficiaries with the payment of insurance being JPY 25 million, the total amount of exemption is JPY 15 million (5 million for each person). This amount is calculated first by subtracting JPY 15

815. Tax exemption is stipulated in ss 12(1)(v) and 16 of the Succession Tax Act 1950.

million from JPY 25 million and then dividing the remainder of JPY 10 million according to a ratio of 2 for the surviving spouse and 1 for each child (*see* Civ. section 900(1)). Accordingly, the surviving spouse is entitled to hold JPY 5 million exemption and each child is entitled to JPY 2.5 million respectively.

Chapter 4. Acquisition and Administration of the Estate

§1. The Seisin

774. Under current succession law, a successor acquires the whole rights and duties of a deceased person on the opening of the succession (Civ. section 896). Where there are two or more successors, the estate is regarded as being jointly owned by co-successors from the opening of the succession (Civ. section 898). With respect to the nature of ownership of the estate (coparcenary), there are two interpretations among lawyers: (1) that it is an ownership in common and accordingly each successor is eligible to claim disposition of his/her share of the estate at any time after the opening of the succession, and (2) that it is a joint ownership such that each successor is prohibited from realizing his/her share until the complete division of the estate. Since the courts affirm the former interpretation,[816] the provisions on ownership in common (*see* Civ. sections 249ff) apply to the estate of the deceased where there is joint possession. In this respect, the seisin does not apply to the estate of the deceased under the Civil Code. Consequently, after the opening of the succession, the relationships of the parties concerned are interpreted in accordance with the principle of ownership in common.

775. Some claim that a dispute over the succession of possession should be dealt with as a matter of administering the deceased's estate held in joint possession, similar to that of seisin. However, in reality, the matter is usually settled as a limitation of action or possessory action.

§2. What Constitutes the Estate of a Deceased

776. All rights and duties of a deceased person are deemed to be transferred to the successor(s) on the opening of succession except those rights and duties belonging to the deceased which are exclusively personal. Since there is no general rule according to which rights or duties are regarded as personal, they are evaluated individually, taking into consideration their nature, fairness among the successors, the intention of the deceased and all other relevant factors.

777. When a successor has acquired rights from a deceased either by division of the estate or other measures, which exceed his/her intended share, he/she shall defeat a claim by a third party as long as he/she obtains legitimate grounds of defeat including registration of the excess portion (Civ. section 899-2(1)). In the case of a successor whose chose in action exceeds his/her intended share, this rule shall be applied similarly if he/she notifies the debtors of the chose in action either of the contents of the will or of the contents of division of the estate. In this case, the notice by the successor shall be deemed to be done to the debtors by all successors (Civ. section 899-2(2)).

816. SD 31 May 1955 Minshu 9-6-793.

I. The Right of Possession

778. Under current law, it may be construed that a person loses the right of possession if he/she ceases to physically control the property. Accordingly, the deceased person's right of possession terminates on his/her death since he/she can no longer physically control his/her property. However, the courts hold that the deceased person's right of possession should be transferred to the successors similarly to the transfer of other assets of the deceased person.[817]

II. Tenancies

779. Successors are entitled to continue to hold any tenancy previously belonging to the deceased person. Is a cohabitee or a de facto adopted child who has lived with the deceased under the same roof eligible to obtain the tenancy of the deceased person? In other words, if the landlord or the successors of the deceased demand him/her to vacate the property rented under the deceased person's name, is he/she able to continue staying at that property even though he/she is not a legal tenant? In a case where the landlord claimed that the de facto adopted child should leave the house, the Supreme Court expressed the following view: (1) that such a child was entitled to be regarded as a legitimate member of the de facto adopter's family; (2) that, as a legitimate member of the de facto adopting family, he/she had the right to reside at the accommodation; (3) accordingly, he/she could rely on the tenancy of the de facto adopter and thus defeat an eviction claim by a third party; and (4) this rule should apply after the death of the de facto adopter on the ground that the de facto adoptee was entitled to rely on the tenancy transferred from the de facto adopter to his/her successor(s).[818] This rule also applies in the cases of cohabitation.[819]

780. Where there is no successor, this rule does not apply. For the purpose of protecting a cohabitee or a de facto adopted child, section 36 of the Tenancy Act 1991 stipulates:

> (1) if, in any case where the lessee of a building used for residence dies without a legal successor and there is a co-resident who has been in a relationship with the lessee akin to that of a spouse or an adopted parent and child, but where a notification of legal marriage or legal adoption has not been made at that time, such co-resident shall exercise the rights and duties of the lessee. This does not apply, if such co-resident has expressed any contrary intention to the lessor within one month of becoming aware of the lessor's death without a successor.

817. SD 30 Oct. 1969 Minshu 23-10-1881.
818. SD 25 Dec. 1962 Minshu 16-12-2455.
819. SD 28 Apr. 1967 Minshu 21-3-780 (in this case a cohabitee is missing).

(2) Regarding the main clause of the preceding paragraph, the claims and obligations accrued in relation to the lease shall be vested in the person who succeeds the rights and duties of the lessee in accordance with the provisions of such paragraph.

Moreover, if a successor of the deceased, who is not living in the relevant property, demands a cohabitee or a de facto adopted child to leave the property on the basis of his/her succeeded tenancy, the court can dismiss such a claim. If the successor has no urgent need to occupy the property and eviction of the de facto adopted child or cohabitee is likely to cause his/her serious damage, the court will classify the claim as an abuse of right.[820]

III. Damages Resulting from Death

A. Damages for Financial Loss

781. A victim of a wrongful act is entitled to demand compensation from the perpetrator for any necessary expenses resulting from that act such as medical fees and for any future loss caused by that act. Once the victim has stated his/her intention to claim such a right and then dies, a successor may succeed the claim of the now deceased victim. However, one question may arise if the victim is killed instantly; namely, does he/she have time to confirm his/her intention to claim damages? The court holds that the successor(s) of a deceased person who was killed immediately is entitled to demand compensation from the perpetuator for any financial loss suffered by the deceased.[821]

B. Damages for Physical and Emotional Suffering

782. It is the general principle that the right to claim compensation for emotional damage terminates on a person's death since it is a highly personal right. However, as an exception to the rule, the courts have held that a successor can succeed to the right of a deceased person to claim emotional damages if the deceased has clearly expressed his/her intention to claim such compensation from the perpetrator, for example, by shouting 'Oh, shucks!' or stating 'he/she (perpetrator) should be responsible'.[822] The Supreme Court has declared that the right of a deceased person to claim emotional damages should be succeeded by the successor unless special circumstances exist, such as an expression by the latter of his/her intention to surrender that right.[823]

---

820. SD 13 Oct. 1964 Minshu 18-8-1578.
821. STD 16 Feb. 1926 Minshu 5-150.
822. STD 30 May 1927 Shimbun 2702-5 and STD 6 Aug. 1937 Hanketsuzenshu 4-15-10.
823. SD 1 Nov. 1967 Minshu 21-9-2249.

783. Meanwhile, the lower courts are likely to dismiss a claim by a successor that he/she has succeeded to the right of a deceased person to demand compensation for emotional damage. Instead, they may apply section 711 of the Civil Code stipulating the successor's own right to claim compensation for the emotional damage caused by the death of the deceased person.[824]

IV. Life Assurance

784. Where a deceased person is assured and he/she has specified a particular person as a beneficiary in the life assurance contract, payment will be made to that particular person as if it were his/her own asset in the event of death of the assured.[825] In such a case, it is understood that the payment will be regarded as an advance to be brought into the hotchpot pool if special circumstances exist such as the payment resulting in extremely unfair outcomes among the successors (*see* Civ. section 903).[826] Similarly, where a deceased person has not named a third party but has merely stated 'a successor(s)' as a beneficiary in the contract, the payment will be regarded as his/her own asset unless special circumstance exists.[827] In this case, the payment is allocated among the successors according to the individual share eligible to each successor as laid down in section 900.[828] In this respect, the payment will not constitute the estate of a deceased person.[829]

785. Where a third party who is named as a beneficiary by an assured dies *before* the assured, a successor of such third party will receive the payment.[830]

786. Where a deceased person names himself/herself as the assured in a life assurance contract and thereafter dies without appointing a beneficiary, the payment will constitute part of his/her estate unless a special clause is incorporated in the contract, for example, worded to the effect that 'the payment shall be made to a successor of the assured where no one is named as a beneficiary'.

V. A Lump Sum Payment on Account of a Deceased Employee and Benefits for the Family Members of the Deceased

787. A lump sum payment may be made to the family members of an employee as severance pay if the employee dies during his/her office. Such payment is considered as part of the deceased employee's estate according to the rules and regulations governing the payment of severance pay. It is generally accepted by the

824. Akita Branch of Sendai HD 24 Mar. 1982 Hanji 1053-119.
825. STD 13 May 1936 Minshu 15-877.
826. SD 29 Dec. 2004 Minshu 58-7-1979.
827. SD 29 Jun. 1973 Minshu 27-6-737.
828. SD 18 Jul. 1994 Hanji 1511-138.
829. SD 2 Feb. 1965 Minshu 19-1-1.
830. SD 13 Mar. 1992 Minshu 46-3-188. For the case of simultaneous death of an assured and the specified beneficiary, SD 2 Jun. 2009 Hanta 1302-108.

courts that the payment belongs to the successors as their own asset, if the payment is aimed primarily at supporting the daily life of the deceased employee's family members.[831]

788. Benefits for family members of a deceased person usually include special payment made to certain relatives of the deceased person, payment of funeral expenses, an allowance for the family, or periodical payments from a deceased pensioner to his/her surviving family members. These payments are made and allocated according to individual acts, rules and regulations. Such payments may be regarded as *causa mortis* gifts and are brought into the hotchpot pool.

VI. The Guarantee

789. It is generally accepted by the courts that successors succeed to the obligation of a deceased person as a direct consequence of succession. This is not the case, however, for an obligation that is substantially based on the personal relationship between the deceased person and the creditor, for instance, a fidelity guarantee or a revolving guarantee. The courts have held that a guarantee based on highly personal factors does not belong to the estate of the deceased person as long as there is no statement concerning the scope of responsibility and the term of guarantee.[832] On the other hand, a guarantor status in connection with a tenancy guarantee can be transferred to successors since there are generally few difficulties in predicting the contents of such guarantee and the scope of the obligation it confers.[833] As for the status of joint and several obligors (guarantee), the Supreme Court has interpreted that it will be transferred to the successors according to their portion of succession.[834]

VII. Unauthorized Agency

A. Where an Unauthorized Agent Succeeds a Principal

790. The courts have held that an act done by an unauthorized agent should be valid if the agent has succeeded the principal. For instance, where a child sold his/her father's house to a third party as an agent but without the necessary authorization and later refused to ratify the contract on the ground of unauthorized agency

831. SD 27 Nov. 1980 Minshu 34-6-815 and SD 3 Mar. 1987 Kagetsu 33-3-31.
832. STD 10 Sep. 1943 Minshu 22-948 and SD 9 Nov. 1962 Minshu 16-11-2270.
833. STD 30 Jan. 1934 Minshu 13-103.
834. SD 19 Jun. 1959 Minshu 15-10-2601.

after the death of his/her father, the court dismissed the refusal by reason that it contradicted the principle of fairness and equity.[835] In this example, if there was a successor sibling in addition to the child, he/she would have been eligible to refuse ratification of the unauthorized transaction because ratification must be made jointly.[836]

B. Where a Principal Succeeds His/Her Unauthorized Agent

791. The courts hold that a principal may refuse to ratify an act by an unauthorized agent on the basis that such refusal will not offend the fair and equitable principle.[837] Once a principal refuses to ratify the act, such act will not be valid even if the unauthorized agent later succeeds to the principal.[838] Thus, a successor is required to decide whether to refuse to ratify the act committed by the unauthorized agent, or to take responsibility for it by reason that he/she will succeed to the status of the unauthorized agent.[839] Where the principal (the successor) refuses ratification, he/she must either accept responsibility for the actions of the unauthorized agent, or be liable for damages if the other party has acted in good faith.

C. Where a Person Simultaneously Succeeds a Principal and an Unauthorized Agent

792. Where a person succeeds his/her father (a principal) just after he/she has succeeded his/her mother (an unauthorized agent of the father), is he/she entitled to refuse succession of the principal? The Supreme Court has declared in such case that the successor is not eligible to refuse by reason that he/she succeeds all the rights and duties of the deceased person.[840]

VIII. The Right to Residence

793. In order to assure that a surviving spouse can use their matrimonial home after the time of opening of succession, the right to residence of a surviving spouse (right of long-term residence) and the right of short-term residence of a surviving spouse became available under the new law in 2018.

835. SD 18 Jun. 1965 Minshu 19-4-986.
836. SD 21 Jan. 1993 Minshu 47-1-265.
837. SD 20 Apr. 1962 Minshu 16-4-955.
838. SD 17 Jul. 1998 Minshu 52-5-1296.
839. SD 3 Jul. 1973 Minshu 27-7-751.
840. SD 1 Mar. 1988 Hanta 697-195.

A. *The Right to Residence of a Surviving Spouse (The Right of Long-Term Residence)*

794. A surviving spouse can continue to stay and use the house after the opening of succession even if he/she does not succeed the house. In this case, a surviving spouse must use or obtain profits from the house with reasonable care and must obtain consent from the owner of the house for reforming or letting the house (Civ. section 1032(1) and (3)). The right is not transferable (Civ. section 1032(2)). When a surviving spouse violates section 1032(1) and (3), the owner of the house can terminate the right (Civ. section 1032(4)).

795. The right to long-term residence of a surviving spouse means that a surviving spouse can continue to stay in a whole part of the matrimonial house and/or gain profits from the house without any payment, basically until the time of his/her death (Civ. section 1030). The right, for instance, may satisfy two different necessities that, on the one hand, an heir child of a deceased can succeed the house and on the other hand a surviving spouse can stay at the house until the time of his/her end of life. The right shall basically continue to take effect until the time of the spouse's death unless specifically provided agreement and it shall cease only when the house belongs exclusively to the spouse (Civ. section 1028(2)). Once the right has ceased, the spouse must return the house to the owner (Civ. section 1035).

796. According to section 1028(1), a surviving spouse shall obtain the right of long-term residence if he/she resides in the house at the time of opening of succession and fulfils the following condition; the right is given to the spouse as a result of distributing the estate of a deceased or the right is gifted by a will of a deceased. For this purpose, the house must be used without any charge and owned either by a deceased exclusively or by a deceased and a surviving spouse jointly at the time of opening of succession. In this respect, the right to long-term residence shall be treated as advancement stipulated in section 903(Civ. section 1028(3)) (*see* paragraph 751).

797. On an application of distributing the estate, a family court shall decide to allocate the right to long-term residence to a surviving spouse in the process of distributing the estate of a deceased either if all heirs agree on that allocation or if it finds necessity of such allocation prior to any loss for an owner who succeeds the house (Civ. section 1029(1)).

798. A surviving spouse can register the right for the purpose of beating a claim from a third person such as a person purchasing the house from an heir and he/she is eligible to request the owner to register the right (Civ. section 1031).

B. The Right of Short-Term Residence of a Surviving Spouse

799. A surviving spouse shall hold the right of short-term residence at the time of opening of succession if he/she has lived in the house owned by a deceased without any payment (Civ. section 1037). By this right, he/she can claim to a new owner of the house either by succession or gift by will that he/she will continue to stay the house without any payment for a certain period even if he/she does not succeed the house as an heir. However, he/she can use only the exact part of the house that he/she uses at the time of the opening of succession. This rule shall not be applied if the surviving spouse is disqualified as his/her status of heir apparent or disinherited (Civ. section 1037). Meantime, this right shall terminate if a surviving spouse obtains the right of long-term residence by section 1030 (Civ. section 1039).

800. A surviving spouse is entitled to use the house at most for six months from the date of the owner of the house being finally confirmed by the distributing procedure of the estate of a deceased, the date of opening of succession or the date when the owner notifies cease of the right (Civ. section 1037(1) and (3)).

801. An owner of the house must not prevent the surviving spouse from staying at the house by any act such as selling the house to a third person (Civ. section 1037(2)). On the other hand, the surviving spouse must use the house with reasonable care, and he/she will lose the right if he/she fails to do so and the owner notifies him/her of termination of the right (Civ. section 1038). Once the right has ceased, the spouse must return the house to the owner (Civ. section 1040(1)). Unlike the right of long-term residence, this right shall not be regarded as advancement in the process of distributing the estate of a deceased.

IX. Others

A. The Right to Maintenance

802. Under certain conditions, a relative may claim maintenance from his/her other relatives (Civ. section 877). While the right to maintenance cannot be succeeded, since it is construed as being highly personal to the deceased it can be succeeded if the deceased person has already made a maintenance claim against his/her relatives prior to his/her death.[841]

B. Membership of a Golf Club

803. The membership of a golf club may be succeeded in accordance with the regulations of the relevant club. Accordingly, for instance, if it is stipulated that membership terminates on the death of a member, the successors of the deceased

841. Tokyo HD 25 Oct. 1977 Kagetsu 30-5-108 and SD 19 Jul. 1979 Hanta 399-129.

member may not succeed the membership.[842] On the other hand, if no regulations exist concerning the death of a member, the successors of the deceased may succeed the membership.[843]

C. *The Right to Bring an Action Concerning the Status of Family Relationship*

804. Where a spouse dies during the course of legal proceedings against the other spouse, in which he/she disputes the validity of the marriage, such action will terminate upon the death of the former.[844] This rule applies to such cases as an application for the acknowledgement of paternity and validity of adoption.[845]

D. *The Right to Division of Matrimonial Property on Divorce*

805. Where a spouse dies after divorce but a dispute over the division of the matrimonial property has not been settled, his/her successor(s) may succeed the deceased's rights relating to the dispute.[846]

E. *The Funeral Expenses of the Deceased Person*

806. It is generally understood that a successor who is actually and substantially in charge of the funeral must pay funeral expenses at his/her expense.[847] Where all successors surrender succession, the funeral fee shall be taken from the estate of the deceased person.[848] In the case of condolence money, utensils of religious rites, the grave and the remains, those shall not constitute the estate but shall belong to a person (usually one of successors) who is mainly responsible for ancestor worship.

§3. The System of Acquisition

I. The Share of an Heir over the Estate of a Deceased Person

807. Under current succession law, there are two categories of shares to which an heir may be entitled in respect of the estate of a deceased person. The first is the basic share which can be divided into two sub-categories; the statutory share as laid down by the Civil Code (Civ. section 900) and a share specified by a testator. The second is the heir's final share of the estate. Actual division of the estate is made on

842. SD 16 Jun. 1978 Hanji 897-62.
843. SD 25 Mar. 1997 Minshu 51-3-1609.
844. SD 13 Oct. 1989 Hanji 1334-203.
845. Nagoya HD 28 Feb. 1984 Hanta 528-288 for an acknowledgement case and SD 27 Jul. 1976 Minshu 7 30-7-724 for an adoption case.
846. Oita DD 14 Jul. 1987 Hanji 1266-103. In the case of cohabitation, *see* para. 590.
847. Tokyo DD 28 Jan. 1986 Kagetsu 39-8-48.
848. Tokyo DD 12 Jul. 1984 Hanji 1150-205.

the basis of each heir's final share. Since the statutory share of an heir was discussed in the previous chapter (Part IV Chapter 1 §3), the specified share and the final share will be discussed in this section.

A. *The Specified Share of an Heir*

808. A person can specify in his/her will a particular share for an heir and delegate such right to specify to a third person (Civ. section 902(1)).

809. Where the deceased has specified a share for only some successors, the rules governing the statutory share apply in relation to the other unspecified successors (Civ. section 902(2)). In this respect, ambiguity may arise if, for instance, a deceased person identifies two-thirds of the whole estate as the specified share of one of his/her two children. In this instance, is a surviving spouse eligible to claim half of the remainder as her/his statutory share? In such a case, it is construed that the surviving spouse may claim half of the remainder of the estate as his/her own portion while the other child is only able to invoke the right to the reserve against the child with specified share.

B. *The Final Share of an Heir with Advancement*

1. Reduction of Advancement

810. It is often the case that one or more successors have already benefited from an *inter vivos* gift or a testamentary gift. For the purpose of achieving a fair and equitable division of the deceased's estate among the successors, the following steps are taken.[849] First, all heirs must return any advancements given by the deceased back to the estate in order to confirm the hotchpot pool. Second, each heir's individual share is calculated by taking account of his/her gifts and other special benefits. Third, the hotchpot pool must be distributed among the heirs depending on the following rules for calculating an individual share (*see* Civ. section 903(1)):

(1) The net estate (the total value of the estate at the time of opening of succession) + the total value of advancements, such as gifts and other benefits (except testamentary gifts) * = the hotchpot pool.
(2) The hotchpot pool × the ratio of the statutory share (*see* Civ. section 900) or each heir's specified share (section 902) = the value of the share that was intended to be allocated to each heir.

849. Section 903(2) states that an heir shall not be entitled to claim his/her final share of succession when the value of an *inter vivos* gift or a testamentary gift is equal to or exceeds the value of his/her final share as an heir. There are, however, several views on how to evaluate each heir's share when the advancements of some heirs exceed their final share as an heir.

(3) The value of the share that was intended to be allocated to each heir – the value of advancements / each heir's testamentary gift = the final share for each heir.

* In the case of marriage of over twenty years, the matrimonial home gifted by the will of a deceased spouse to a surviving spouse shall not be included as advancement (Civ. section 903(4) and *see* paragraphs 794 and 799).

If an heir made a contribution, the value for calculation shall be estimated by deducting the value of contribution from the value of the net estate. Then, the value of the share of each heir shall be calculated by multiplying the value for calculation by the ratio stipulated in section 900. Finally, the value of the final share for the heir contributor shall be confirmed by adding the value of the share of each heir to the total value of his/her contribution to the estate.

Example. (1) Mr March has left only four daughters (Janette, June who has received JPY 8 million as advancement, Margaret who has JPY 2 million as a testamentary gift, and Elizabeth whose contribution to Mr March's assets is valued at JPY 4 million) and (2) the estate is valued at JPY 60 million at the time of death. The final share of each heir is as follows:

The hotchpot pool	60 million + 8 million – 2 million = 64 million
Janette	64 million × 1/4 = 16 million
June	64 million × 1/4 – 8 million = 8 million
Margaret	64 million × 1/4 – 2 million = 14 million*
Elizabeth	64 million × 1/4 + 4 = 20 million**

*Margaret finally receives the total sum of JPY 16 million (14 million as her share + 2 million as the testamentary gift which was deducted from JPY 60 million from the beginning of the calculation).

**Elizabeth finally takes the total sum of JPY 20 million including JPY 4 million as her contribution.

2. Definition of Advancement

811. A testamentary gift may be an advancement and an *inter vivos* gift will also be regarded as an advancement if it has been made especially for the financial support of the heir (Civ. section 903(1)). In the case of matrimonial home, however, if a deceased spouse whose marital period was over twenty years gave the surviving spouse the matrimonial home as gift or testamentary gift, he/she shall be deemed to express that the gift shall not be included in the estate as advancement (section 903(4)). This rule aims at protecting the interest of residence of a surviving spouse. Financial support may include the payment of a lump sum upon his/her marriage, the establishment of an adoption contract, funding higher education and assisting the founding of a business or special payment for the purchase of a house.[850] Meanwhile, the payment of life insurance, lump sum payment for retirement and payment for deceased family members may not be considered as advancements but their own property. However, where the court considers that such payment would cause unfairness among successors, it would treat it as an advancement on account of the special circumstances.[851]

C. Contribution

812. Previously, an heir, who had devoted himself/herself to the care of a testator or had made a significant contribution in obtaining property for the deceased, was, nevertheless, considered equally to other heirs in the division of the estate. This usually caused substantial and unfair results. Therefore, in order to achieve a fairer division of the estate among the successors, case law provisions which valued special contributions made by particular heirs were included in the Civil Code in 1980 (Civ. section 904-2).

813. According to section 904-2, only an heir is eligible to assert a contribution at the time of division of the estate. As a result, where an heir's spouse has made a large contribution in taking care of his/her bedridden parent-in-law, he/she will not be in a position to claim his/her contribution. Instead, it is often construed, in such a case, that the contribution was made by the heir's spouse in his/her capacity as the heir's assistant.[852] In one case where a wife and children of a successor took care of the successor's deceased father for a long time, a court interpreted such acts of care as unpaid special contribution carried out by assistants of the successor.[853] In 2018, section 1050 was newly enacted to achieve a fair result for such a non-heir relative as 'a relative as special contributor' (*see* paragraph 652).

814. The degree of contribution must be 'special'. This is illustrated in the following cases: where an heir has lived with and cared for the testator for over twenty years;[854] where an heir prematurely left school in order to join the family business and has made a great deal of effort to acquire family assets;[855] where an heir has nursed her mother who suffered from senile dementia for ten years;[856] or where an heir is deemed to have obtained an insufficient salary for his work in a testator's business.[857]

850. Niigata FO 3 Aug. 1967 Kagetsu 20-3-81.
851. *See* SK 29 Oct. 2004 Minshu 58-7-1979 and Osaka FO 26 Sep. 1978 Kagetsu 31-6-33.
852. In the case of a wife of the successor, Toyooka branch of Kobe FO 28 Dec. 1992 Kagetsu 46-7-57. Where an heir *per stirpes* has made a contribution of acquiring property for the deceased, he/she is eligible to claim his/her compensation upon the distribution of the estate among the successors (Tokyo HK 28 Dec. 1989 Kagetsu 42-8-45).
853. Tokyo FO 8 Mar. 2000 Kagetsu 52-8-35.
854. Osaka HK 7 Sep. 1982 Kagetsu 25-6-128.
855. Tokyo HK 29 Mar. 1979 Kagetsu 31-9-21.
856. Morioka FO 11 Apr. 1986 Kagetsu 38-12-71.
857. Osaka HK 19 Sep. 1990 Kagetsu 43-2-144.

815. The heirs are entitled to reach an agreement on a sum which represents the amount each has contributed. If they fail to do so, they may request the family court to specify this amount in the distribution of the estate. It is not possible for the parties to make an application to the family court to determine the contribution in any other form, except for the distribution of the estate. However, the family court is obliged to consider the amount of contribution given to the estate on its division by family court mediation or family court determination.[858]

816. When the court evaluates the amount of contribution, it is not allowed to grant a sum which exceeds the value of the remaining estate after the testamentary gifts made by the deceased are deducted (Civ. section 904-2(3)). Meanwhile, there is no provision on the relationship between contributions and legitim in the Civil Code. In practice, the courts tend to evaluate the total amount of contributions by considering all the circumstances in order to avoid infringing upon the reserved portion.[859]

D. Assignment of Rights of Succession

817. An heir may wholly, although not individually, transfer all his/her rights and duties acquired through succession to an assignee before distribution of the estate (Civ. section 905).[860] On such an assignment, the assignee will be in the same position as the heir. But as the assignment of the rights of succession differs from the abatement of succession and the status of an heir does not terminate on assignment, the heir will still be liable to the deceased's creditors after assignment. One heir may often assign his/her rights and duties to the other heir in order to increase the share of the assignee heir.[861]

818. Where the heirs intend to prevent a third party from entering the process of distributing the estate as an assignee, they may recover the assigned rights and duties from the assignee through the reimbursement of the value of the rights and other expenses (Civ. section 905).

II. Inheritance Claims

A. Main Aim of Inheritance Claims

819. In a case where an ostensible successor has started to occupy either all or part of the estate, a legitimate successor may recover the estate on the ground of

858. Osaka HK 18 Jun. 1984 Kagetsu 37-5-60 and Tokyo HK 7 Feb. 1991 Kagetsu 43-12-58.
859. Tokyo HK 24 Dec. 1991 Hanta 794-215.
860. If an heir has assigned his/her whole share to other party, he/she is not eligible to become a party to litigation on challenging the amount of estate of a deceased person (SD 14 Feb. 2014 Minshu 68-2-113).
861. Takamatsu HK 17 May 1988 Kagetsu 41-6-45.

his/her right of inheritance. For instance, a deceased person may have left two children, one of whom is his/her own child (the legitimate successor) and the other of whom is falsely registered as his/her own child (the ostensible successor). The former child may demand the estate acquired by the latter on the ground that there is no right of succession due to the lack of a legitimate parent-child relationship.

820. The legitimate successor should commence an inheritance claim within five years of discovering that his/her share has been infringed upon: this is the five-year prescription (Civ. section 884). The legitimate successor may file a petition for an inheritance claim to the court, apply for mediation to the family court or send a formal notice to the ostensible successor in order to interrupt the prescription. The right of an inheritance claim terminates twenty years after the opening of succession and this is a strict limitation on possible actions (Civ. section 884). However, the main aim of an inheritance claim is to confirm an ostensible successor's right by giving a five-year limited period and protect the stability of transactions with other persons, rather than to encourage a legitimate successor to claim back his/her share of the estate.

B. Disputes and the Parties

1. Disputes Between a Legitimate Successor and an Ostensible Successor

821. As mentioned earlier, where two children of a deceased – a legitimate successor and an ostensible successor – dispute each other's share of the estate, the legitimate successor may reclaim the estate occupied by the ostensible successor on the ground that the latter lacks the status of a legitimate successor. If the ostensible successor has died, the legitimate successor may demand the estate from the former's successor(s).[862] In such a dispute, the legitimate successor must bring an action within the period of time stated in the above paragraph. However, the limitation period will not apply in the following cases:[863]

(1) an ostensible successor is aware that he/she is not a legitimate successor;
(2) an ostensible successor has no reasonable cause to regard himself/herself as a legitimate successor; or
(3) an ostensible successor has negligently believed that he/she is a legitimate successor.

An ostensible successor is eligible to invoke the above-mentioned limitation period if he/she can satisfy any of the conditions set out in items (1) to (3) above. In this respect, an ostensible successor who is falsely registered as a legitimate child of a deceased is entitled to assert his/her rights against a legitimate child as long as he/she has acted in good faith and without fault.

862. Tokyo HD 19 Nov. 1969 Hanji 579-68.
863. *See* SD 20 Dec. 1978 Minshu 32-9-1674.

2. Disputes Between a Legitimate Successor and a Third Party

822. Where an ostensible successor has transferred the estate to a third party in good faith, what action can a legitimate successor take? Some assert that the legitimate successor should bring an action against the third party through an inheritance claim. But others state that he/she should have recourse to an ordinary action against the third-party claiming ownership (revendication). However, the courts seem to hold the opinion that the limitation period does, indeed, apply to a dispute between a legitimate successor and a third party who has acquired the estate through an ostensible successor in good faith.[864]

3. Disputes among Legitimate Successors

823. If a legitimate successor occupies all or part of the estate without a proper claim, can the other successors force him/her to surrender occupation? Under the current law, the provisions governing inheritance claims suggest that it is possible for legitimate successors to dispute each other's status as genuine successors. However, successors may dispute their respective right to occupy the estate instead of their legal status. In this case, no question concerning the limitation period will arise. If the five-year prescription, as laid down in section 884, applies, the rest of the successors may lose their share of the estate and, as a result, fair distribution of the estate among the successors will become impossible.

824. The Supreme Court held that the prescription applies only to cases where a successor has occupied all or part of the estate in good faith and without fault.[865] In reality, the prescription actually does not apply to most cases due to strict requirements set by the court. As a result, a dispute between legitimate successors is likely to be settled through the distribution of the estate.

III. Distribution of the Estate

825. Successors are generally understood to hold the estate under common ownership (cf. Civ. section 249).[866] Indeed, the court has held that a successor was eligible to transfer his/her share of the estate to a third party during the period of distribution on the ground that the estate was owned by successors in common.[867] However, a final share of a successor in the estate will be confirmed either at the completion of negotiation among successors or by determination of the family court unless a last will exists. Where a dispute arises on the distribution of the estate, the family court must issue a determination ensuring fair distribution of the estate among successors by examining factors such as the type and nature of the estate,

864. SD 5 Dec. 1995 Kagetsu 48-7-54.
865. SD 20 Dec. 1978 Minshu 32-9-1634.
866. SD 31 May 1955 Minshu 9-6-793.
867. SD 22 Feb. 1963 Minshu 17-1-235.

the age, occupation and health of the successors, and their family history (*see* Civ. sections 906 and 907, FAPA section 39). In this respect, a successor is not free to dispose his/her own share or it may bring about a dispute over the share between successors and a third party to whom one of the successors has disposed his/her share.

826. Under the procedure of distributing a deceased's estate, each successor owns a specific part of the property as his/her share of the estate. Upon its completion, succession terminates and each successor owns certain property independently.

A. Measures to Distribute the Estate

827. All successors can agree on the distribution of the whole or part of the estate (Civ. section 907(1)) while the deceased may even state in the will that the successors must refrain from distributing the estate for five years after the opening of succession (Civ. section 908). Failure to accomplish this may lead to a petition filed at the family court for mediation and/or a determination of declaring the distribution of the whole or part of the estate unless such distribution may infringe upon the interests of other successors (Civ. section 907(2)). In addition, the court can refrain from distributing the whole or part of the estate for a certain period (Civ. section 907(3)). Conversely, a testator's will is permitted to specify the means of dividing the estate or the appointment of a third party who is commissioned with this task (Civ. section 908). If a property belonging to the estate was disposed of due to some reason before the time of distribution, it shall be deemed to constitute the estate at the time of distribution on the agreement made by all heirs (Civ. section 906-2(1)). If a property belonging to the estate was disposed of for some reason before the time of distribution, all heirs can regard such property as constituting the estate at the time of distribution by their consent (Civ. section 906-2(1)). If one or more heirs have disposed of the property belonging to the estate, no consent shall be required from those heirs (Civ. section 906-2(2)).

828. There are a number of means of dividing an estate among successors: (1) physically specifying the shares of the estate; (2) distributing the estate by valuing it in monetary terms; or (3) one successor acquiring the whole estate and compensating the others. Although, as a rule, the whole estate should be distributed on completion of the division process, the successors may actually agree to distribute parts of the estate prior to completion of the division process. However, the family court must not act in this manner unless special circumstances exist; for example, prospects of an early dispute settlement are poor or it would still be fair to all successors to distribute a part of the estate among them.[868]

829. The family court may forbid distribution of the estate either wholly or partly for a specified period if it is deemed appropriate (Civ. section 907(3)). Indeed,

868. Osaka FO 14 Aug. 1972 Kagetsu 25-7-55 and Osaka FO 25 Nov. 1976 Kagetsu 29-6-27.

the successors may make an agreement on non-distribution of the estate for a maximum of five years. This period can be renewed on agreement (*see* Civ. section 256).

B. When to Value the Estate

830. The value of the estate can often fluctuate in accordance with economic conditions. In order to ensure fairness to the successors, it may be crucial to decide when to value the estate. However, this may still be difficult to calculate at any specified time. Consequently, the court has declared that valuation should occur as close as possible to the date on which the court determination was issued.[869]

C. Profits and Losses Between the Opening of Succession and the Time of Distribution

831. Fluctuation in the value of the estate usually occurs due to a time lag between the opening of succession and the distribution of the estate. Questions, therefore, arise on how to deal with the following adjustments:

Profits and interest

The profits such as rent of the estate's real property and interest, for example, dividends do not constitute part of the estate.[870] These profits will be distributed in proportion to each successor's share of the estate separately to the distribution of the estate.

Losses

Where a part of the estate has been disposed of or lost, it cannot be distributed. Although this may give rise to a right to claim damages or unjust enrichment, these rights cannot be merged into the estate except in special circumstances. However, some lower courts hold the view that such right to bring claims should constitute part of the estate and, as a result, be distributed among successors.[871]

Administration fee of the estate

The estate's administration and maintenance fees will be paid out of the estate itself (Civ. section 885). Where one of the successors has paid such a fee, is he/she eligible to recover it as a part of the distribution of the estate? In the past, a successor, who took care of a testator and paid the tax imposed on the estate, was able to claim settlement of such expenses separately from the distribution of the estate.[872]

869. Tokyo FO 7 Sep. 1971 Kagetsu 24-9-65.
870. *See* SD 8 Sep. 2005 Minshu 59-7-1931.
871. Osaka FO 4 Nov. 1965 Kagetsu 18-4-104 and Nagano FO 6 Nov. 1992 Kagetsu 46-1-128.
872. Tokyo HK 19 Jun. 1981 Hanta 452-158.

D. Others

832. As for chose in action the court has stated that a chose in action may be distributed in proportion to each successor's share of the estate separately to the distribution of the estate.[873] In this respect, choses in action do not constitute a part of the estate (*see* paragraph 840). Therefore, a successor is eligible to claim his/her portion independently to a third party.[874] However, the Supreme Court has expressed a different view by stating that a chose in action will not be distributed in proportion to each successor's share of the estate separately to the distribution of the estate in the case of a fixed deposit of the deceased person.[875] In the case of a bank deposit, an individual successor was eligible to withdraw a certain amount of money from the deceased's bank account in proportion to his/her share of the estate.[876] A bank's general rule requiring all successors to make a unanimous agreement on such a withdrawal is therefore immaterial.[877] However, in some cases, successors may also apply to the family court for distribution of a bank deposit on the ground that it is regarded as part of the estate.[878] In 2016, the Supreme Court altered the precedent stating that a bank deposit shall constitute the estate for distribution and shall not be allocated to each successor in proportion to his/her share of the estate.[879] In 2018, the section 909-2 is newly enacted by which an heir is eligible to withdraw a certain amount of money from one third of the bank deposit of a deceased person in proportion to his/her share to the estate calculated by the criteria of sections 900 and 901. In this case, the heir shall be deemed to obtain that amount resulted by distributing the part of the estate.

833. As for debts, a court has stated that debts do not constitute a part of the estate by reason that they should be distributed among the successors at the opening of succession in accordance with each successor's share of the estate.[880] A creditor of the deceased's debts is eligible to claim his/her rights against each heir in proportion to a share of each heir calculated by the rule stipulated in sections 900 and 901 even if the deceased has specified the share to a particular heir in his/her will. However, this rule shall not apply if the creditor accepts devolution of the debts to the particular heir in proportion to the share specified by the deceased (Civ. section 902-2 and Civ. section 472(2)).

873. SD 8 Sep. 2005 Minshu 59-7-1931.
874. SD 19 Sep. 1977 Kagetsu 30-2-110.
875. SD 8 Oct. 2010 Kagetsu 63-4-122. This rule similarly applies to a government bond (for an individual person), a particular type of investment trust (SD 25 Feb. 2016 Minshu 68-2-173).
876. Tokyo HD 21 Dec. 1995 Hanta 922-271.
877. Nagoya HD 27 Feb. 1978 Kimho 858-34.
878. Nagoya FO 20 Jul. 1990 Kagetsu 43-1-136.
879. SK 19 Dec. 2016 Minshu 70-8-2121.
880. Sapporo HK 26 Dec. 1966 Kagetsu 19-4-68.

E. Effects of the Distribution of the Estate

834. The distribution of the estate takes effect retrospectively from the opening of succession (Civ. section 909). Accordingly, the successors are deemed to acquire their own share of the estate from the opening of succession.

835. If a child, whose father acknowledged paternity after his death, holds the right to succeed by reason of that acknowledgement, such right will take effect retrospectively from the time of birth. Where distribution of the estate has terminated before the time of the acknowledgement, he/she may only claim the value of his/her share of the estate from the other successors (Civ. section 910). However, such a person is eligible to argue the validity of any disposal of the estate against a third party who has already purchased the estate from the other successor(s) even after the time of the acknowledgement.[881] If distribution has not yet been completed, the child will be included in the distribution process or otherwise it will become void.

836. If a dispute arises due to defects in the distributed estate, the rule of warranty will apply as in an ordinary sale of goods. Under this rule, the successors must make a payment to the person suffering loss in proportion to their individual share of the estate (Civ. section 911). Where a successor does not have the finances to make the payment, the reimbursement must be borne by the claimant and the other successors in proportion to their respective share of the estate unless the claimant is at fault (Civ. section 913). Nevertheless, the provisions of the warranty may be altered, either by agreement of all the successors or by the will of the deceased (Civ. section 914).

§4. Administration of the Estate

I. Common Ownership of the Estate

837. One issue which arises under common ownership is the question of the rights and duties that successors hold between the opening of succession and the completion of the distribution of the estate. In particular, as it may take a long time to settle the estate, it becomes important to clarify the legal status of successors, for the purpose of protecting not only their interest but also those of third parties involved in a transaction with them.

838. The Civil Code merely states that the estate is under 'common ownership' during this period, although it does not clearly define the meaning of this term (Civ. section 898).[882] As a result, two views are held by lawyers: common ownership (Civ. sections 249ff) and joint ownership.

881. SD 23 Mar. 1979 Minshu 33-2-294.

882. Section 898 stipulates that if there are two or more heirs, the inherited property shall belong to those heirs in co-ownership.

839. In the case of a chose in action, the court primarily holds that the principle of common ownership will apply and therefore the chose in action must be distributed among the successors in proportion to their own share of the estate. The nature of co-ownership of the estate is not different from that of common ownership laid down in sections 249 and onwards in the Civil Code.[883] However, the principle of common ownership does not seem to have been rigidly applied in individual cases.

A. Succession of Choses in Action and Debts

840. In general, neither choses in action nor debts constitute the estate on distribution except for a particular type of chose in action (*see* paragraphs 832 and 833). Similar to divisible choses in action, divisible debts are divided among the successors outside the distribution of the estate. Where a testator states in a will a portion for each successor, a successor will assume an obligation in proportion to his/her respective share of the estate.[884] In the case of a joint obligation, the joint obligator's successors have shared liability in respect of the original obligator, in proportion to their share of the estate.[885]

B. Where Successors Dispose of All or Part of the Estate

841. Where all the successors have made an agreement to sell a specified real property belonging to the estate before the division of the estate, each respective successor is entitled to claim his/her share of the payment in proportion to his/her share of the estate.[886] Accordingly, any profits arising from such a disposition will not constitute part of the estate to be distributed.

842. On disposition of real property, the Civil Code generally requires prior registration of ownership to ensure a successful claim against a third party. However, where a successor has sold real property belonging to the estate for a value exceeding his/her share of the estate, the other successors have priority over the purchaser in connection with their respective shares even in the absence of prior registration of their ownership.[887]

843. However, where a successor has acquired real property from the division of the estate, which exceeds his/her intended share, he/she should register the excess portion. Failure to do so may allow a claim for the ownership to be made by a third party in respect of that portion of land (Civ. section 899-2(1)).[888] In the case of a

883. SD 8 Apr. 1954 Minshu 8-4-819 and SD 31 May 1955 Minshu 9-6-793.
884. SD 24 Mar. 2009 Minshu 63-3-427.
885. SD 19 Jun. 1959 Minshu 13-6-757.
886. SD 19 Sep. 1977 Kagetsu 30-2-110.
887. SD 22 Feb. 1963 Minshu 17-1-235.
888. SD 26 Jan. 1971 Minshu 25-1-90.

gift by will, a beneficiary must register his/her ownership of the real property if a claim against a third party is to prove successful.[889]

C. *Where a Successor Has Transferred His/Her Share of Property Belonging to a Particular Estate to a Third Party*

844. Section 909 of the Civil Code stipulates that distribution of the estate shall be effective retrospectively from the opening of succession on the condition that no rights of a third party will thereby be prejudiced. A question arises concerning a third party who has acquired specific property belonging to the estate from a successor before its distribution. Should that person commence at the ordinary court litigation for the division of property held in common ownership or alternatively should he/she file at the family court, a petition for the distribution of the estate? The court has held that he/she should take the former course of action on the basis of section 258 of the Civil Code.[890] A third party's claim to that property will thereby become legitimate and it will cause the property to be separated from the rest of the estate.

D. *Disputes Between Successors and Third Parties*

845. All successors are required to file a joint action regarding disputes with a third party over any of the estate's rights or properties.[891] However, litigation brought by an individual successor will serve as a means of recovering property held by all the successors under common ownership, as long as the primary aim of such action is to preserve the estate. Therefore, an action to cancel the registration of real property taken by an individual successor against a third party will be valid if it is to preserve the estate (*see* Civ. section 252).[892] On the other hand, a purchaser who has acquired real property from a testator must file an action against all the successors to cancel any registration of the property by the successors in their own names.[893] However, where real property sold to a third party by the deceased is still registered in the name of the deceased, the third party can bring a claim to change the register against one of the successors.[894]

889. SD 6 Mar. 1964 Minshu 18-3-437.
890. SD 7 Nov. 1975 Minshu 29-10-1525. s. 258(1) of the Civil Code states that if no agreement can be reached between the co-owners, an application for division may be made to the court.
891. STD 13 Jun. 1916 Minroku 22-1200 for an ordinary property case.
892. SD 10 May 1956 Minshu 10-5-487.
893. SD 12 Mar. 1963 Minshu 17-2-310.
894. SD 15 Dec. 1961 Minshu 15-11-2865.

E. How Will the Estate Be Distributed among the Successors

846. Where successors fail to reach an agreement on the distribution of the estate, they are prohibited from bringing an action to divide any of the property held under common ownership. Instead, they must apply to the family court for the distribution of the estate.[895]

F. Where Litigation Confirming the Boundary of the Estate Is Instituted by the Successors

847. Where a dispute arises among the successors as to whether or not a particular property belongs to the estate and thereby requires distribution, they may make a petition to confirm the estate's property.[896] If affirmed, the property will not be owned in common by the successors but must be distributed. All the successors must join in the procedure as an involved party.[897]

G. Where an Interest to Reside in the Property of a Deceased Is Disputed Among the Successors

848. Although a successor may wish to reside in a property owned by the deceased, the other successors may demand he/she vacate the property on the ground that it constitutes their share of the estate. The court has held, in such a case, that an individual in continuous occupation of the property cannot be forced to vacate merely for the reason that the other successors hold the majority share.[898] It concluded in one case that the successor was entitled to reside in the property due to his/her right to use and benefit from the property, which was based on his/her share of the estate. In such a case, other successors can claim either unjust enrichment or damages against the successor in proportion to their own share to the estate.[899] Meanwhile, a surviving spouse eligible to hold the right to reside for some time under the new provisions stipulated in 2018 (*see* paragraphs 799ff).

II. Administration and Use of the Estate

849. The Civil Code sets out the following measures for the administration of an estate: the administration of an estate by successors during the consideration period before the renunciation of succession (Civ. section 918); the administration of an estate on its separation (Civ. section 943); the administration of an estate where successors are unknown (Civ. section 951) (*see* paragraph 654); and the

895. SD 4 Sep. 1987 Hanji 1251-101.
896. SD 13 Mar. 1986 Minshu 40-2-386.
897. SD 28 Mar. 1989 Kagetsu 41-7-81.
898. SD 19 May 1966 Minshu 20-5-947.
899. SD 7 Apr. 2004 Hanta 1034-96.

administration of an estate by an executor (Civ. section 1012(1)). However, there are no detailed provisions to deal with the administration of an estate between the opening of succession and the time of distribution of the estate. Under such circumstances, the provisions on common ownership beginning in section 249 are generally applied.

850. Successors have rights and duties to use the estate in proportion to their respective shares (Civ. section 249) which, in turn, allow each successor to independently bring an action to preserve the estate (Civ. section 252). Where the administration of the estate must be determined, it will be decided in monetary terms by the group of successors holding the majority of the estate (Civ. section 252). If the successors wish to make any alteration to the property belonging to the estate or a successor intends to dispose any property with a value which exceeds his/her share of the estate, they must obtain the consent of all successors (Civ. section 251). The expense of such administration will either be deducted from the estate (Civ. section 885) or the successors will be liable for its payment in proportion to their respective shares of the estate (Civ. section 253(1)).

III. Separation of the Estate and Property Owned by a Successor

851. The rule of unconditional acceptance of succession generally applies unless a successor accepts with the benefit of inventory or renounces after the opening of succession. The distributed share of the estate including the debts of the deceased will merge with the property owned by a successor. Where a deceased is insolvent but a successor has certain assets, the obligee or the beneficiary of the deceased may benefit from the merger while the obligee of the successor may find difficulty in recovering payment from the successor. Similarly, where a deceased person has left an estate but a successor is insolvent, the obligee of a successor may gain benefits from the merger while the obligee or the beneficiary of the deceased may become more vulnerable. For the purpose of protecting those obligees, provisions to separate the estate and the property of a successor are laid down in the Civil Code.

A. *First Type of Separation*

852. Where the deceased is insolvent, the obligee of a successor may file an application of separation to the family court either during the period when the successor is entitled to assert acceptance with the benefit of inventory or before the merger (*see* Civ. section 950(1)). The family court will issue a determination by considering such factors as the amount of debt, other obligations and property of the deceased and successor, and by examining whether there is any necessity to issue the determination.[900]

900. Tokyo HK 20 Jun. 1984 Kagetsu 37-4-45.

B. Second Type of Separation

853. Where a successor is deemed insolvent, either an obligee or a beneficiary of the deceased is entitled to apply to the family court for separation either within three months of the opening of succession or before the completion of the merger if necessary (Civ. section 941(1) and FAPA section 202).[901]

854. Within five days of the family court's determination for separation, the applicant must give a public notice of more than two months to the other obligees and/or the beneficiaries of the deceased to state that a family court's determination has been issued and invite them to join the procedure (Civ. section 941(2)). The successor may either make the payments to those obligees and/or beneficiaries out of his/her own property or he/she may provide security, up to the amount of the payments, in order to quash the family court determination (Civ. section 949). On the basis of the family court determination, these obligees and/or beneficiaries have priority over obligees of the successor for the payment from the deceased's estate (Civ. section 942).

855. After the application of separation has been made, a successor must administer the estate with the same care as he/she would use in respect of his/her own property (Civ. section 944(1)). Furthermore, a family court may issue a determination of disposition with the aim of securing the proper administration of the estate, which may include the appointment of an administrator if it is deemed necessary (Civ. sections 943 and 944).

901. Shibata Branch of Niigata FO 18 Apr. 1966 Kagetsu 18-11-70.

Selected Bibliography

Terminology on judgment by the courts

A. Structure of the Courts

Supreme Court (Supreme Tribunal under the old court system before 1947)
↑ (appeal)
High courts (Appellate Tribunal under the old court system before 1947) (Special Branch for Intellectual Property at Tokyo High Court)
↑ (appeal)
District courts/Family courts/Summary courts

* High courts: 8 main offices and 6 branches
* District courts: 50 main offices and 203 branches
* Family courts: 50 main offices, 203 branches and 77 sub-branches
* Summary courts: 438 offices

B. Judgments by the Ordinary Courts for Civil Cases

*Decree (*Hanketsu*)

Hanketsu is declared by ordinary court after hearings before a judge(s) under the rules of the ordinary civil proceedings mainly based on the adversarial rules. However, for certain types of family cases such as divorce, decree is made through the special proceedings including the inquisitorial type of approach. A decree is effective when a judge(s) declares his/her judgment based on his/her written decision after the completion of the hearings through the parties' exchange of statements before court.

*Order (*Kettei/Meirei*)

An order is a judgment made by a judge(s) through less strict proceedings and need not be made by means of a court hearing.

C. Judgments Made by a Family Court

Determination (order) (*Shimpan*)

A family court may make a determination for certain types of family disputes through special procedures; for example, the procedure of an inquisitorial nature rather than a rigid adversarial one can be applied and the hearing may proceed in chambers. Unlike a court decree pronounced, the determination of a family court is considered as conclusive between the parties and essentially binding upon a third person.

D. Agreement Achieved by Family Court Mediation (Chotei)

Agreement reached by the parties with the assistance of a family court mediation committee (in-court mediation). At the time of completion of agreement, a family court will issue a document with binding force.

Appendix

Appendix 1 Court Structure for Family Matters

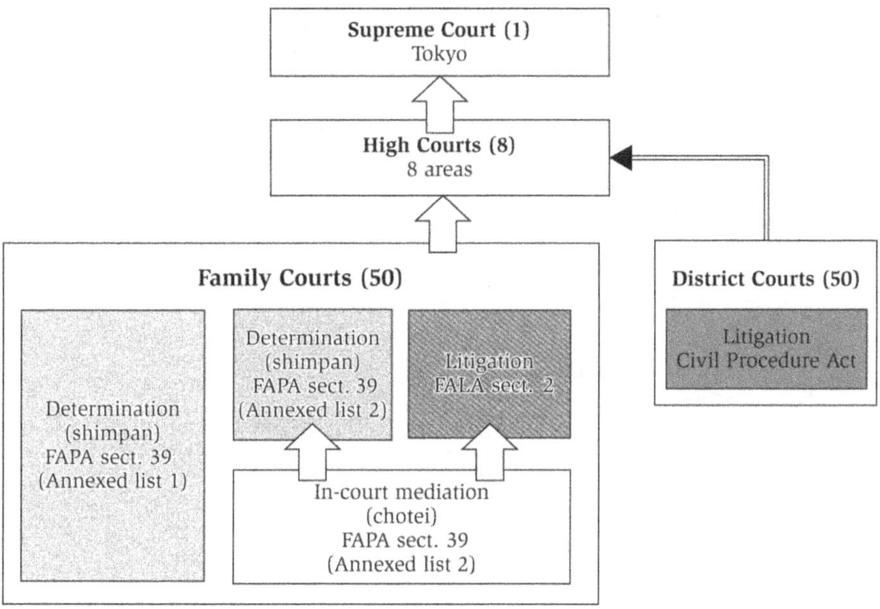

Appendix 2 Family and Relatives

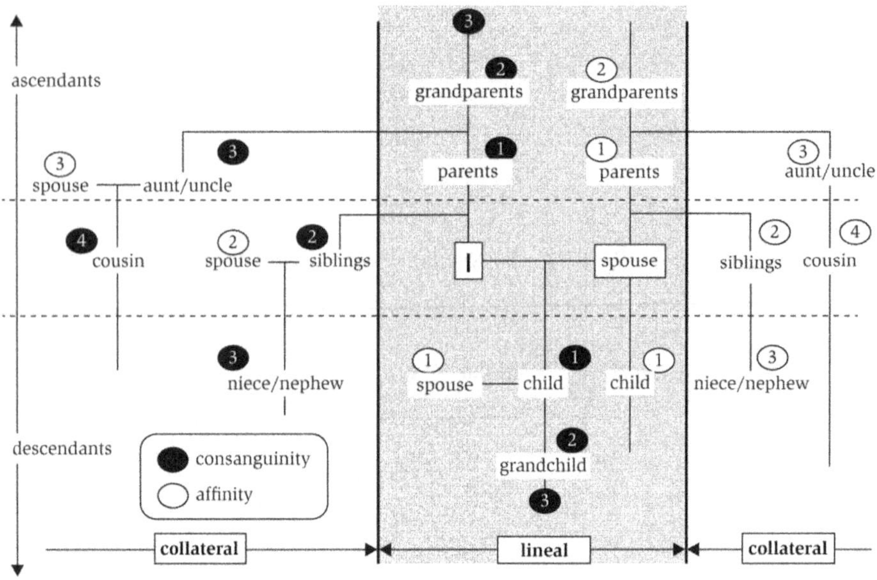

Index

The numbers here refer to paragraph numbers.

Index

www.ingramcontent.com/pod-product-compliance
Lightning Source LLC
LaVergne TN
LVHW011114300926
849160LV00008B/382
* 9 7 8 9 4 0 3 5 4 5 7 0 7 *